The Russian official history of the second war between Emperor Alexander and Napoleon, in 1806 and 1807, using original military and diplomatic documents and the testimonies of witnesses and participants from the war.

First published in 1846, the history considers the reasons for the war undertaken by Emperor Alexander in alliance with Prussia, the disaster that befell Prussia at Jena and Auerstedt, and Alexander's mobilisation when, after the destruction of the Prussians, Napoleon moved to the borders of Russia.

Following Napoleon's crossing to the right bank of the Vistula, the narrative describes the subsequent Russian military operations against Napoleon in both the winter and spring campaigns. The winter campaign culminated with the Battle of Eylau, with consideration to the exhaustion of the fighting armies, frosts, impassable roads, and political factors that stopped the bloodshed in the main theatre of war until May.

The narrative then considers the inactivity of the armies, and exhaustion of all possible resources in anticipation of the spring campaign, before concluding with Napoleon's repulse at Heilsberg, the Russian defeat at Freidland, retreat to the right bank of the Neman and peace at Tilsit.

Born in Russia in 1789, after the death of his father, Alexander Ivanovich Mikhailovsky-Danilevsky used his inheritance to study in Göttingen from 1808-1811, on returning to Russia he became a civil servant.

During the War of 1812, he joined the militia and participated in the Battle of Borodino, after which he served in the Quartermasters Department and was present at many battles from 1813-1814.

From 1815-1820, he was head of the General Staff library but returned to military service until 1832, when he was commissioned to write Russia's official military histories.

He died in 1848 during a cholera epidemic in St Petersburg.

Peter G.A. Phillips is a retired soldier and civil servant who served for 27 years in the British Army Intelligence Corps (in Germany, the Falkland Islands, Northern Ireland, Hong Kong, Bosnia, Iraq and Afghanistan), including working as a Russian, German, and Serbo-Croat linguist, before working for five years as part of a Civil Service team training UK military personnel to serve in diplomatic missions worldwide. He has been translating Russian military histories of the Coalition Wars since December 2019, initially as a hobby, having been encouraged by renowned Napoleonic historian Dr Alexander Mikaberidze following a chance encounter on social media. He now lives in the Philippines with his Filipina wife of 33 years. They have two adult daughters.

# 1806-1807 – Tsar Alexander's Second War with Napoleon

The Russian Official History

Alexander Ivanovich Mikhailovsky-Danilevsky

Translated by Peter G.A. Phillips

Helion & Company

Helion & Company Limited
Unit 8 Amherst Business Centre
Budbrooke Road
Warwick
CV34 5WE
England
Tel. 01926 499619
Email: info@helion.co.uk
Website: www.helion.co.uk
Twitter: @helionbooks
Visit our blog at http://blog.helion.co.uk/

Published by Helion & Company 2023
Designed and typeset by Mach 3 Solutions Ltd (www.mach3solutions.co.uk)
Cover designed by Paul Hewitt, Battlefield Design (www.battlefield-design.co.uk)

Original text published as *Opisanie vtoroj vojny Imperatora Aleksandra s. Napoleon, v. 1806 i 1807 godach* [*History of the second war between Emperor Alexander and Napoleon in 1806 and 1807 written under Supreme command by Lieutenant-General and Member of the Military Council Mikhailovsky-Danilevsky*], St Petersburg, 1846
Translation © Peter Philips 2023
Maps and diagrams by George Anderson © Helion & Company 2023

Cover: A Charge of the Russian Leib Guard on 2 June 1807, Viktor Mazurovsky. (Public Domain)

Every reasonable effort has been made to trace copyright holders and to obtain their permission for the use of copyright material. The author and publisher apologise for any errors or omissions in this work, and would be grateful if notified of any corrections that should be incorporated in future reprints or editions of this book.

ISBN 978-1-804511-93-0

British Library Cataloguing-in-Publication Data.
A catalogue record for this book is available from the British Library.

All rights reserved. No part of this publication may be reproduced, stored in a retrieval system, or transmitted, in any form, or by any means, electronic, mechanical, photocopying, recording or otherwise, without the express written consent of Helion & Company Limited.

For details of other military history titles published by Helion & Company Limited, contact the above address, or visit our website: http://www.helion.co.uk

We always welcome receiving book proposals from prospective authors.

# Contents

| | | |
|---|---|---|
| List of Maps | | vi |
| Translator's Introduction | | vii |
| Author's Introduction | | ix |

| | | |
|---|---|---|
| 1 | Causes of the War | 11 |
| 2 | The Defeat of the Prussians | 20 |
| 3 | Russian Mobilisation | 34 |
| 4 | Russian Forces Cross the Border | 41 |
| 5 | Napoleon's First Encounter With The Russians | 47 |
| 6 | The Army's Manoeuvres Between the Narew and Wkra | 57 |
| 7 | Battle of Pultusk | 63 |
| 8 | The Battle of Golymin | 69 |
| 9 | Military Operations in The Second Half of December [first half of January 1807] | 76 |
| 10 | Bennigsen's Offensive | 82 |
| 11 | Napoleon's Offensive | 89 |
| 12 | The March of The Warring Armies to Preußisch Eylau | 96 |
| 13 | The Battle of Preußisch-Eylau | 107 |
| 14 | Events During The Russian Army's Stay at Königsberg | 119 |
| 15 | Operations Following The Battle of Eylau | 127 |
| 16 | Operations by Essen's Independent Corps | 130 |
| 17 | Emperor Alexander's Visit to The Army | 134 |
| 18 | The Siege And Fall of Danzig | 147 |
| 19 | The Spring Campaign | 154 |
| 20 | The Battle of Heilsberg | 161 |
| 21 | The Road to Friedland | 167 |
| 22 | The Battle of Friedland | 172 |
| 23 | The Conclusion of Hostilities | 179 |
| 24 | The Armistice | 182 |
| 25 | Treaty of Tilsit | 189 |
| 26 | Activities After The Treaty of Tilsit | 203 |
| 27 | Conclusions | 206 |

Appendices

| | | |
|---|---|---|
| 1 | Schedule Of The Number Of Men Needed From Each Governorate To Establish The *Opolchenie*, Divided By *Oblast* | 212 |
| 2 | Order of Battle of Bennigsen's Corps | 213 |
| 3 | Order of Battle of Buxhoeveden's Corps | 214 |
| 4 | Order of Battle of Essen 1st's Corps | 215 |

| | |
|---|---|
| Index | 216 |

# List of Maps

| | |
|---|---|
| Map of Napoleon's War with Prussia in 1806. | 19 |
| Plan of the Battles of Jena and Auerstedt, 2 [14] October 1806. | 23 |
| Map of the Pursuit of the Prussians After the Battle of Jena. | 27 |
| Plan of the Action at Sochocin and Kolozomb, 11 [23] December 1806. | 49 |
| Plan of the Action at Czarnowo, 11 [23] December 1806. | 51 |
| Map of Troop Movements Preceding the Battles of Pultusk and Golymin. | 54 |
| Plan of the Battle of Pultusk, 14 [26] December 1806. | 61 |
| Plan of the Battle of Golymin, 14 [26] December 1806. | 67 |
| Plan of the Action at Mohrungen, 13 [25] January 1807. | 85 |
| Plan of the Jankowo Position and the Action at Bergfriede, 22 January [3 February] 1807. | 91 |
| Map of the Retreat from Jankowo, 23 to 25 January [4 to 6 February] 1807. | 94 |
| Plan of the Action at Hoofe, 25 January [6 February] 1807. | 101 |
| Plan of the Action at Preußisch Eylau, 26 January [7 February] 1807. | 104 |
| First Plan of the Battle of Preußisch Eylau, Morning of 27 January [8 February] 1807. | 108 |
| Second Plan of the Battle of Preußisch Eylau, Evening of 27 January [8 February] 1807. | 113 |
| Plan of Operations at Danzig, May 1807. | 145 |
| Plan of Operations 23 to 28 May [4 to 9 June] 1807. | 152 |
| Plan of the Heilsberg Position and Vanguard Action, 29 May [10 June] 1807. | 159 |
| Plan of the Battle of Heilsberg, 29 May [10 June] 1807. | 163 |
| Map of Operations Between Heilsberg and Friedland. | 165 |
| First Plan of the Battle of Friedland, 2 [14] June, dawn to five p.m. | 170 |
| Second Plan of the Battle of Friedland, 2 [14] June, from six p.m. | 175 |
| Map of the History of the Second War Between Emperor Alexander and Napoleon, in 1806 and 1807. | 211 |

# Translator's Introduction

I chose to translate Alexander Mikhailovsky-Danilevsky's history of the war of 1806-07 after a lifetime of being irritated at how few English language historical works covering campaigns in which Russia was directly involved used any original Russian sources – many relied on memoirs by French, German and British officers in Russian service, others covered the subject only from the British, French, Prussian or Austrian point of view. A welcome few, such as Digby Smith and Christopher Duffy, used German translations of the works of Mikhailovsky-Danilevsky, Milyutin and Bogdanovich. After the collapse of the Soviet Union and easier access for western historians, thankfully, more historians published works in English and I have found the works by Adam Zamoyski, Dominic Lieven and especially the prolific Alexander Mikaberidze to be hugely inspirational, but the nineteenth-century Russian official histories have remained unavailable in English, until now.

So who was Mikhailovsky-Danilevsky, how accurate and reliable is his work and how much of it is reliable history rather than state propaganda?

Mikhailovsky-Danilevsky's military service began in the St Petersburg *opolchenie* in 1812, where his ability and university education led to him being appointed as an aide de camp to the *opolchenie* commander at the time, one General-of-Infantry Mihail Kutuzov. Mikhailovsky-Danilevsky fought on throughout the Patriotic War and subsequent War of the Sixth Coalition and was present at the Congress of Vienna. He began writing in the 1830s and was commissioned by Tsar Nicholas I to write the official military histories of Russia's wars with Revolutionary and Napoleonic France. He started with the Patriotic War of 1812, where his first-hand experience and access to eyewitness accounts from surviving veterans as well as unrestricted access to the military archives and a team of excellent researchers (including Colonel Milyutin, who would become a ground-breaking historian in his own right) would greatly assist him in this endeavour.

His work on the war of 1806-1807 was published in 1846 (somewhat out of sequence; his earlier works covered 1812-1814, the war in Finland in 1808-1809, the war against the Ottomans from 1806-1812 and the Third Coalition War of 1805). A later Imperial Russian military historian, Modest Bogdanovich, describes his fellow military historians as "priests of Truth," and Mikhailovsky-Danilevsky claims a similar dedication to the truth in his works, however, there are points that need to be born in mind regarding his accuracy, precision and reliability. The works were commissioned by the Tsar and were published on condition that the Tsar had editorial control, that he could, and did, censor the manuscripts. Criticism of strategic decision making or of Alexander I's behaviour is, thus, almost entirely absent. There is also no criticism of Alexander I's continued adherence to Tsar Paul's outdated tactical doctrine, based upon a misinterpretation of Frederick the Great's own, and God forbid that any mention be made of Alexander's involvement in the botched coup that resulted in his father's death and his own accession to the throne! There is a theme in all of Mikhailovsky-Danilevsky's histories of Alexander I being elevated into a crusading, almost saintly being in pursuit of his foreign policy objectives and 1806-1807 is no exception. How much of this was down to Nicholas I's direct intervention and how much was self-censorship is difficult to discern. In an ideal world, I would have preferred to have translated Mikhailovsky-Danilevsky's uncensored manuscript (if it were available).

Notwithstanding the assistance of his researchers, Mikhailovsky-Danilevsky's histories are, in general, quite sparse. Bogdanovich was commissioned to re-write the official histories of 1812-1814 and was critical of Mikhailovsky-Danilevsky for omitting so many archival sources that Bogdanovich thought were essential to understanding these conflicts. Mikhailovsky-Danilevsky was also less than meticulous in spotting and correcting errors of fact, for instance in his 1805 work, in the order of battle for Austerlitz, he assigns the 5th Jäger Regiment to General Dokhturov's First Column, when they were in fact part of General Bagration's force on the opposite side of the battlefield. He also had a tendency to repeat errors made by other historians when borrowing from their works; in his history of the war in Finland, when writing about the British General Sir John Moore, he describes his death as occurring at the battle of Ferrol, rather than the battle of Corunna (as every British schoolboy of a certain age knows). Colonel Milyutin took over the drafting of the history of the 1799 campaigns upon Mikhailovsky-Danilevsky's death in 1848 and the level of detail, in comparison, is stunning, Milyutin producing a five-volume masterpiece to cover a single year of campaigning, which has an extensive annex on the sources used, including a candid assessment of their relative value – if only all military histories of this period were so painstaking!

Mikhailovsky-Danilevsky was essentially writing for the approval of the Tsar; he was not driven by the need to score commercial success through book sales, and therefore avoided the pitfall of being put under editorial pressure to sensationalise or draw controversial conclusions in order to produce a page-turner. Having not been present in 1806-1807, he was also not seeking to justify his own actions or embellish his own feats – a common problem with personal memoirs. He was also going to be peer-reviewed in the sense that many of the participants were still alive and could take him to task over errors and omissions.

In conclusion, this history of the war of 1806-1807 is flawed (as is, no doubt, my translation of it), but nonetheless valuable for the detail it provides that is unavailable elsewhere. In no particular order; the story of the command and control disputes between the Russian generals before Bennigsen's appointment as Commander-in-Chief, and clarification of the number of trophies taken by the Russians at Eylau.

In this translation, I have included the Russian tradition of adding an ordinal number after the surnames of Russians who might be confused with a namesake serving at the same time (thus; Lieutenant General Essen 1st is Ivan Nikolaevch Essen, while Lieutenant General Essen 3rd is Pëtr Kirillovich Essen) anything that I have added is shown in squared brackets, including dates using the Gregorian calendar, full names of personalities (wherever I could positively identify them), modern place names etc. Any errors in these additions are entirely my own.

Peter G.A. Phillips
2022

# Author's Introduction

The Emperor was pleased to order me to compose a History of the Second War Between Emperor Alexander and Napoleon, in 1806 and 1807, which concluded the first period of political activity by the Blessed Monarch and which is now being presented to my compatriots. At the beginning of this work, I set out the reasons for the war undertaken in 1806 by Emperor Alexander in alliance with Prussia, the disaster that befell our allies at Jena and Auerstedt, and Alexander's mobilisation when, after the destruction of the Prussians, Napoleon moved to the borders of Russia. This is followed by a description of our military operations against Napoleon, which are divided into two periods, the winter and spring campaigns. The winter campaign began in December 1806, after Napoleon crossed to the right bank of the Vistula, and ended at the end of January 1807, with the Battle of Eylau, when the exhaustion of the fighting armies, frosts, impassable roads and political reasons stopped the bloodshed in the main theatre of war until May. During this inactivity of the armies, Alexander and Napoleon exhausted all possible resources in anticipation of the spring campaign. At the end of May, the fighting flared up. At first, fortune favoured Alexander's forces: His army repelled Napoleon at Heilsberg, but four days later it failed at Friedland, and had to retreat to the right bank of the Neman. Not supported by friendly Powers in the cause undertaken by him for the independence of Europe, Alexander saw no more reason to continue the war: he made a truce with Napoleon and soon afterwards peace in Tilsit.

Such is the essence of the second war between Emperor Alexander and Napoleon. My history is based on original military and diplomatic documents and is backed up with references to official acts. I have always quoted the words of the participants without the slightest change. Trying to use any kind of information that could clarify events, I studied and cross-checked documents with Notes compiled about the war of 1806 and 1807 by some of our generals, including the Commander-in-Chief of the Russian Army at that time, Bennigsen. I have also used the verbal testimonies of the few surviving participants and witnesses of this war, such as Generals Prince Volkonsky, Yermolov, Prince Vorontsov, Baron Jomini, Prince Shakhovsky, Prince Shcherbatov, Prince Chernyshev, Count Pahlen, Roth, Khrapovitsky, Euler, Baron Pahlen, Schubert, Grabbe, Eichen, the two Lashkarevs, and others who honoured me with their insightful conversations and remarks about the time when the stubborn war was raging between the Vistula and the Neman. This war has not yet been described by any Russians [1846]. In our language, there are only disjointed, incomplete passages about it, mostly scattered in periodicals. Foreign works on this subject are not satisfactory. Foreign historians did not know with certainty what was happening in the Russian army. Moreover, they are not official historians, as none of them was called upon to compile a History by their government, did not have access to state archives and therefore could not know the diplomatic activity of that time, the study of which was necessary to understand the events that took place in this theatre of war.

Forty years have passed since Alexander fought against Napoleon for a second time, and false stories about this struggle and then about his alliance with the giant of our century have not passed in their true form from one generation to another. The exploits of the Russian army, in victory and defeat, have not yet been adequately evaluated; the driving reasons for battles and movements have also not been fully disclosed. But the main failing in the histories of the war of 1806 and 1807 is the complete ignorance of the actions of Emperor Alexander. The groundless and mysterious testimonies of writers who did not have original documents at their disposal overshadowed a bright page in the History of Alexander – his second war with Napoleon, and threw an unfavourable shadow over the Peace of Tilsit. To determine the significance of this important epoch in History, it was only necessary to present events truthfully, without evasions or embellishment. To achieve such an aim in the works that I publish now, I tried diligently – and how could it be otherwise in the task entrusted to me by the sacred will of the Monarch?

# 1

# Causes of the War

The state of affairs at the start of 1806. – Emperor Alexander's policy. – Peace talks between Russia and France. – Emperor Alexander's refusal to ratify the treaty. – Report from the Senate. – Napoleon's arbitrariness in European affairs. – Actions of the Berlin Court. – Russian relations with Prussia. – Napoleon's disregard for Prussia. – The demands of the King of Prussia. – Prussian preparations for war. – Prussian relations with Russia. – Emperor Alexander's viewpoint. – His orders to Count Tolstoy. – Napoleon declares war on Prussia.

The first war of Emperor Alexander and his allies against Napoleon in 1805 was marked by Napoleon's victories at Ulm and Austerlitz and had the most unfavourable consequences for the Allied Powers. Emperor Alexander had to temporarily set aside his intention to stop the might of Napoleon by force; Austria lost vast areas to the victor; Prussia concluded a treaty of friendship with him, having taken Hanover from him, while Italy, Holland, Switzerland and every region of German territory from the Rhine to the Inn and the Weser were completely dependent on Napoleon. However, four states had not changed their hostile relations with Napoleon: Russia, Britain, Sweden and the Kingdom of Naples but of these Britain was continuing hostilities only at sea; Russia and Sweden, separated from France by wide swathes of territory, could not face him in direct confrontation and the King of Naples, having been forced to seek refuge in Sicily, had almost no troops. This was the state in which Europe found itself in 1806, at the beginning of which Emperor Alexander's foreign policy objectives were:

'To be in a strong defensive position, having armies ready to go to the aid of neighbours if they are attacked by Napoleon, maintain the closest ties with Britain, and keep Austria and Prussia from being too submissive to Napoleon.'[1]

With the obvious impossibility of preventing a state's enslavement by Napoleon by force of arms, Emperor Alexander believed that restoring peace with him would be the best way to secure the Powers which still enjoyed independence and save those who, hoping for the support of Russia, had sacrificed themselves for the greater good, such as the Kingdom of Naples. It was also thought that having made peace with Russia, Napoleon would cease to violate treaties and the rights of states. Guided

---

1  Supreme instructions to Russian ambassadors; Count Vorontsov in London, dated 25 January [6 February] 1806 and Count Razumovsky in Vienna, dated 12 [24] February 1806.

by these principles, Emperor Alexander set out at the first opportunity to enter into negotiations with Napoleon, but preserving the dignity of Russia and the power of proxy for the foreign Powers. The chance soon presented itself and was initiated by Napoleon. At the start of 1806, the French Consul in St Petersburg, Lesseps – [Barthélemy de Lesseps] Napoleon's governor of Moscow in 1812 – received an order from his Court, to enter into discussions with our Minister of Foreign Affairs about trade matters and touched slightly on Napoleon's readiness to restore amity with Russia. Without rejecting Lesseps' proposal, and not giving it particular importance, in April 1806, Emperor Alexander sent State Counsellor Ubri [Pëtr Yakovlevich Ubri] to Paris under the pretext of taking care of our prisoners who were in France, but in fact to begin peace negotiations. The negotiations did not take long, and on 8 [20] June Ubri signed a peace treaty in Paris. Emperor Alexander found this treaty 'contrary to the honour and duties of Russia in the discourse with our Allies, the security of the State and the general peace of Europe.' The Emperor informed all Courts and Napoleon of his rejection of the treaty, repeating his willingness to resume negotiations but on conditions consistent with the dignity of Russia,[2] and announced these diplomatic actions in a manifesto,[3] the conclusion of which said:

'We are certifying that Our faithful subjects, always motivated by love for the fatherland, always driven by honour and courage, surrounded by great examples of national pride, to join their efforts with ours, how soon the security of Russia, the voice of glory and our commandment will call them to action for the common good. In this firm confidence in the help of God and the zeal of our faithful subjects, we have found it necessary to inform them in advance of our intentions in order to give them new evidence that in all of our enterprises, we are not looking to expand our boundaries and do not seek the vain glories of transient victories but we wish and act in the affirmation of general security, in the protection of Our alliances and in the protection of the dignity of Our Empire.'

The feelings generated in Russia by the manifesto were beyond expression when they read in it that it was a matter of state security. We see a true reflection of these feelings in the following report presented by the Senate at that time:

> The Senate, awed by the wisdom of Your rule and the vigilance of Your care, knows that the world is cruel and unreliable with governments driven solely by a love of power, they are often more dangerous even than a bloody war, and inspired by feelings and devotion to the glory of Your name and Your Empire, dares to solemnly assure Thee, Most Exalted Monarch, that all the estates that You have so much blessed, all the nations, spread across your vast Empire, are ready, at the behest of Your right hand, to sacrifice their property and life itself for our dear homeland. And which of the earthly Kings can expect a little envy and effort from his subjects, if not You, who, from the accession to the throne, a day longed for by Russia, have not stopped pouring blessings on all nations, Thy sceptre is subjugated, and through wise institutions revealing all branches of national welfare, You

---

2   Announcement regarding the treaty concluded by Ubri, dated 14 [26] August 1806.
3   Manifesto of 3 [15] September 1806.

also allow later posterity to enjoy the fruits of Your great deeds and bless the beloved name of Alexander.

The refusal of Emperor Alexander to approve the treaty signed on 8 [20] June, annoyed Napoleon all the more so because he had already proclaimed the conclusion of peace with Russia in a ceremonial meeting of the Senate. So on his orders, the French newspapers began to be filled with caustic articles against Russia and jokes about the vanquished of Austerlitz.

During these events, in the first half of 1806, Napoleon declared his brother [Louis Bonaparte] King of Holland and another [Joseph Bonaparte] King of Naples, his brother-in-law [Joachim Murat] became Grand Duke of Berg, and he gave territories in Italy to his sisters [Maria Anna Elisa and Pauline]. Without forewarning Austria and Prussia, he formed the Confederation of the Rhine [États confédérés du Rhin] under his auspices from Bavaria, Württemberg, Baden, Nassau, Darmstadt and other small principalities of southern Germany, after which the Austrian Monarch [Kaiser Franz I], removing himself from the primacy in German affairs, abdicated the title of Holy Roman Emperor, and took the title 'Kaiser von Österreich' [Emperor of Austria]. Having destroyed the centuries-old structure of the Holy Roman Empire, Napoleon knowing no limit to arbitrary measures for its ruin, levied money from the free cities of Frankfurt, Nuremberg, Hamburg, Lübeck and Bremen, treated the German Princes impertinently, for example, he threatened the Landgrave of Darmstadt [Ludwig X] with dividing his territory between his neighbours if he did not remove his beloved aide de camp from his service, removed territory from the Prince of Orange [Willem Frederik], spouse of the sister of the King of Prussia [Friedrich Wilhelm III], blaming him for the Prince's refusal to join the Confederation of the Rhine or to leave Prussian service. Under various pretexts, Napoleon did not withdraw his troops from German lands, where they were maintained at the expense of his new allies, and where French generals and officials indulged in outbursts of unbridled greed.

The incredibly fast-growing power of Napoleon on the right bank of the Rhine, preoccupied Prussia, until then a silent witness to his actions. To counter the power of Napoleon, the Prussian King intended to form an alliance of the rulers of northern Germany and the Hanseatic cities. Fearing Napoleon, and not trusting Prussia's ill-conceived policies, the rulers of these lands did not show any inclination to answer his call. The Kurfürst von Sachsen [Friedrich Augustus III] and the Herzog von Weimar [Karl August] and Herzog von Dessau [Leopold III] agreed to be members of an alliance, but only on the condition that it must be under the auspices of Emperor Alexander.[4] Equally unsuccessful were the efforts of Prussia to persuade Austria to act in concert with Prussia in the event of war. Only in Emperor Alexander did the King of Prussia see true help. The bilateral relations of these Monarchs – sincere friends before all the incredible turns of their turbulent lives – were as follows: two days after the battle of Austerlitz, Emperor Alexander placed the corps under Bennigsen [Leonty Leontievich Bennigsen or Levin August Gottlieb Theophil von Bennigsen],

---

4   Alopeus' [*Maxim Maximovich Alopeus*] reports, dated 13 [25] and 25 August [6 September].

Count Tolstoy [Pëtr Aleksandrovich Tolstoy] and Essen [Ivan Nikolaevich Essen], located in Silesia, Hanover and Hungary respectively, totalling 75,000 men, at the disposal of the King of Prussia, these brilliant troops had not participated in the Battle of Austerlitz, but were burning to avenge it. Moreover, the Emperor promised to support Prussia with all his might if they declared war on Napoleon or were drawn into a breach with him. The proposal by our Monarch was not accepted, and in December 1805 Prussia concluded peace and an alliance with Napoleon, concealing the contents of the treaty of alliance, however, from the Emperor several times. Our Monarch took no offence at the Prussian secrecy, and gave orders for them to be informed that circumstances did not allow him to wage an offensive war against Napoleon, but Russia and Prussia needed to be allied in order to maintain the independence of northern Europe and Turkey.[5] Convinced by the arguments of Emperor Alexander, and seeing himself abandoned by every Power, the King of Prussia sent an extraordinary embassy to St Petersburg in February 1806 and wanting to give it all possible brilliance, he appointed the Companion of Frederick II, Field Marshal Graf Braunschweig [Karl Wilhelm Ferdinand von Braunschweig-Wolfenbüttel] as Ambassador. He was instructed to clarify the actions taken by the Berlin Court under force of circumstances, to re-establish relations with Russia, confirming their assistance if Napoleon were to turn on Prussia, and finally to ask the Emperor for his assistance in restoring general peace in Europe. Ignoring the recent insincere Prussian actions against him, the Emperor answered Graf Braunschweig with a willingness to help Prussia if they were combatants against Napoleon, advised him not to grant Napoleon incessant indulgence,[6] and ordered Bennigsen, who was waiting at Grodno with 60,000 men, to come under the King of Prussia's command and to go wherever he might be ordered.[7]

Meanwhile, Prussia was exhausted under the burden of a new catastrophe – the war declared on them by Britain for accepting Hanover from Napoleon. The British had detained Prussian ships that were in British ports, blockaded Prussian harbours, and in the shortest time took more than 400 of their ships. In front of the whole world, they showered Prussia with reproaches in parliament, calling them 'Bonaparte's most contemptible servants.' The Swedish King also did not spare Prussia, having declared his determination not to withdraw Swedish troops from the Herzogtum Sachsen-Lauenburg, which was part of Hanover, and issued

---

5     Emperor Alexander's hand-written orders to Prince Chartorysky, dated 22 January [3 February] 1806:
      *Le cabinet de Berlin tarde à nous donner communication des engagements contractés par lui envers la France. Le manque de confiance de la part de la Prusse devait naturellement empêcher que la Russie ne s'avance à faire des propositions pour un objet quelconque, mais elle ne doit pas plus perdre de vue pour cela que son système doit être celui d'une union étroite avec la Prusse. Certainement il ne peut plus être question en se moment de chercher à prendre l'offensive, mais pourquoi ne pas se concerter sur les détails d'une liaison, qui embrassent essentiellement les intérêts des deux états pour prémunir le nord de l'Europe de tout danger, et pour concerver la Porte dans son état actuel, ce qui est un point de la plus haute importance.*

6     Instructions to Alopeus in Berlin, dated 26 February [10 March].

7     Instructions to Bennigsen, dated 23 February [7 March]: '*Je vous autorise à remplir les ordres que le roi de Prusse jugera à propos de vous donner.*'

orders for the blockading of Prussian harbours. The cessation of trade and the decline of industry provoked outrage in Prussia, all the more so as the Prussians' pride suffered, which it had lost from all of Europe, while their fatherland was humbled since, contrary to solemn announcements not to tolerate violations of their neutrality, the Berlin Court had not mobilised against Napoleon when the French passed through Ansbach, and cowed by the Battle of Austerlitz, did not abide by the Potsdam Treaty. The criticism of Prussia made by the British and Swedes and the Austrian curses on them for their inaction the previous year were repeated everywhere. In Berlin, *Leibgarde* officers clearly condemned the Government; at night they sharpened sabres on the steps of the portico of the French embassy; on three occasions in the darkness, the Prime Minister Graf Haugwitz [Christian August Heinrich Kurt Haugwitz], champion of the alliance with Napoleon, had the glass in his windows smashed.

Prussia's predicament delighted Napoleon. He regarded this Power as sacrificial. Considering that after the Prussian alliance with him, they would be helped neither by Russia, nor by Austria, and be left isolated, he began to seek pretexts for starting a war with them, and showed them obvious disrespect. He officially declared that the Prussian Minister of Foreign Affairs Hardenberg [Karl August von Hardenberg] was open to bribery,[8] hindered the formation of a Northern Alliance in every possible way, did not respond to the King's personal letters, and in negotiations with Britain, he had even offered to return Hanover five months before transferring it to Prussia. This neglect of the dignity of the Prussian Monarchy exceeded the patience of the peace-loving Friedrich Wilhelm III. Having received, meanwhile, a reassurance of help from Emperor Alexander, he gave orders to put the army on a war footing at the end of July, and sent General Knobelsdorff [Friedrich Wilhelm Ernst Baron von Knobelsdorff] as ambassador extraordinary to Paris as new representation, since none of the former were respected there. The embassy was not successful. Seeing the futility of negotiations, the King offered Napoleon the following conditions, demanding a satisfactory answer to them without fail within three weeks:

1. French troops were to vacate Germany.
2. Napoleon was not to interfere with the establishment of the Northern Alliance.
3. To move the French behind the Rhine and convene a congress for a general reconciliation of Europe.[9]

Following such a decisive act by Prussia, war with Napoleon was now inevitable. Emperor Alexander believed that Napoleon would not accept the proposals made to him by the Berlin Court and that after their rejection, Prussia would not be able to retract their demands without losing what remained of the confidence of the other powers.[10] Equally convinced of the inevitability of a breach with Napoleon,

---

8   *Monsieur de Hardenberg n'a pas été insensible à la pluie d'or. 34 bulletin.*
9   Count Stackelberg's [Gustav Ottonovich Stackelberg] report, dated 6 [18] September.
10  Minister of Foreign Affairs, Budberg's report to Bennigsen, dated 27 September [9 October] 1806: *Le roi de Prusse s'est avancé dans ses démonstrations envers la France au point, que Sa Majesté ne sauroit plus reculer, à moins de vouloir sacrifier sa dignité et ses véritables intérêts.*

the King of Prussia took the most active measures for mobilisation, asked Emperor Alexander to reconcile him with Britain and end his quarrels with Sweden, and persuaded the neighbouring states to assist him in the impending war. Only Saxony and the Herzog von Weimar entered into an alliance with him; Austria responded with the impossibility of fighting without first putting in order the internal affairs and army after the misfortunes that had befallen them in 1805. Emperor Alexander replied to the King of Prussia that the war declared on him by Britain was most legitimate, however he promised to solicit the reconciliation of Prussia with them and Sweden, and ordered Count Buxhoeveden's [Fëdor Fëdorovich Buxhoeveden] corps to be ready to follow Bennigsen.

Having ensured the support of Emperor Alexander, and not trusting Austria, the Berlin Court wanted our troops, in the event of a shooting war, to secure the left wing of the Prussian army from the direction of Austria, and requested that Bennigsen's corps be sent to Silesia and to threaten Austria with other Russian corps, forcing them to take part in the war, just as our troops had been appointed to persuade Prussia forcibly to commit to an alliance with us the year before. The Prussians equally requested for one Russian corps to be sent to Naples.[11] Expecting that Bennigsen would come to the theatre of war no sooner than two months hence, the Prussians hoped to hold Napoleon alone until then and thereafter, united with us, hoped for certain victory. They were so sure of the possibility of defeating Napoleon that they secretly presented their decisions concerning the fate of the regions that they would undoubtedly wrest from France to our Court. Thus, they wanted to restore the House of Orange in the Netherlands, return Tyrol and Venice to Austria, and expand the territory of the Landgrave of Hesse-Kassel [Wilhelm I]. In Berlin, they feared only that, faced with the formidable military might of Prussia, Napoleon would withdraw behind the Rhine,[12] after which it would be difficult and expensive to wage war in France. It seemed more profitable and cheaper to the Prussians to end the bloody dispute in the middle of Germany.

Emperor Alexander answered the Berlin Court that the aim of the war must be to push the French back over the Rhine, and to occupy the Netherlands so as to completely secure German lands from any subsequent invasion by Napoleon.[13] Our Monarch dismissed the opinions of the Berlin Court regarding Austria. He argued that threatening this Power could lead to war with them, and in any case cause us to waste time. On the contrary, knowing the disrupted Austrian situation, Alexander did not demand their immediate alliance with Russia and Prussia, but expressed his firm hope to the Viennese Court that the Austrians would take advantage of our first victory over Napoleon, then they could rise in arms and, with unified forces, we would restore peace and the balance of power, and also make good the losses inflicted upon them by the Peace of Pressburg [Bratislava].[14] From the response of

---

11   Count Stackelberg's report, dated 22 August [3 September].
12   Count Stackelberg's report, dated 25 August [6 September]: *Ce que le cabinet de Prusse appréhende le plus, c'est la retraite de l'armée françoise audelà du Rhin.*
13   Instructions to Count Stackelberg in Berlin, dated 27 September [8 October].
14   Instructions to the Russian ambassador in Vienna, dated 4 [16 October] 1806.

the Viennese Court it was clear their intention was not to unite with Napoleon and, if our and the Prussians' operations were successful, to declare war on him.[15]

The extreme haste of the Prussians in abandoning their long-time peaceful policy did not give them time to agree with Russia even on the main principles of an operational plan. Arrogant, blinded by the memories of Friedrich's victories, the Prussians were convinced that fate granted them alone the glory of breaking Napoleon's power. All Prussia rejoiced gleefully when they saw the determination of their Government to go to war. In the theatres they sang nationalist hymns. On the streets and squares they congratulated each other on the resurrection of national pride. Thus dazzled, they did not realize that the time was near when all their victorious dreams would crumble in a single day!

As for the Russian troops assigned to help Prussia, Emperor Alexander ordered them to be exclusively under the command of the King, and not any Prussian generals. The will of the King was to be announced to them through Lieutenant-General Count [P.A.] Tolstoy, appointed to the Monarch of Prussia. The Emperor ordered his generals to send reports to the King via Count Tolstoy, who also had orders to observe the Prussian political and military operations, so that no misfortune could befall the Russian troops. The Chamberlain, Count Nesselrode – [Karl Vasilevich Nesselrode] now [1846] State Chancellor – working in the Russian Embassy in Berlin at the time, was appointed to assist him. In order to collect accurate intelligence on the state of French forces, Count Nesselrode was sent from Berlin to their locations in September. At the end of the instructions given to Count Tolstoy, Emperor Alexander wrote:

'In expressing complete authority to My ally, I by no means wish to surrender the welfare and glory of My armies to the arbitrariness of a foreign Power. Strictly observe that the orders they issue to the Russian army must never damage its reputation or glory.'[16]

Napoleon was in Paris when he learned of the Prussian demand for the withdrawal of French troops from German soil. Having gone from being a lieutenant in thirteen years to the ruler of Western Europe by 1806, he rejected the Prussian demands, moved the headquarters of French forces from Paris to Bamberg in Germany and declared war on Prussia, not by a manifesto but through an army order, under the following terms:

> The Prussians demand our return beyond the Rhine. This is madness! May they discover that it is a thousand times easier to destroy our great capital,

---

15   The Minister of Foreign Affairs, Baron Budberg's report to General Bennigsen, dated 27 September [9 October] 1806: *Il paroit positif, que l'Autriche ne se joindra jamais à nos ennemis et qu'elle saisira même la première occasion favorable pour se déclarer ouvertement contre eux.*

16   Supreme rescript to Count Tolstoy, dated 27 September [9 October] 1806: *J'ai bien voulu donner une preuve de confiance à mon allié, mais il ne s'en suit par pour cela que je veuille abandonner le moins du monde à la discrétion d'une Puissance étrangère le bien – être et la gloire de mes armées. Il sera donc particulièrement de votre devoir de veiller avec la plus grande attention à ce que les ordres qui seront transmis par votre canal à M de Bennigsen ne puissent jamais être de nature à exposer mal à propos mes troupes, en un mot, compromettre la dignité et la gloire des armées Russes.*

Paris, than to diminish the honour of a great nation, whose rage is worse than an ocean storm. Did we bear the fickleness of the elements and the heat of Egypt or defeat a Europe united against us just to abandon our allies and return to France like fugitives burdened with guilt, as if the French eagles had flown away, frightened at the appearance of the Prussians? Advance!

CAUSES OF THE WAR 19

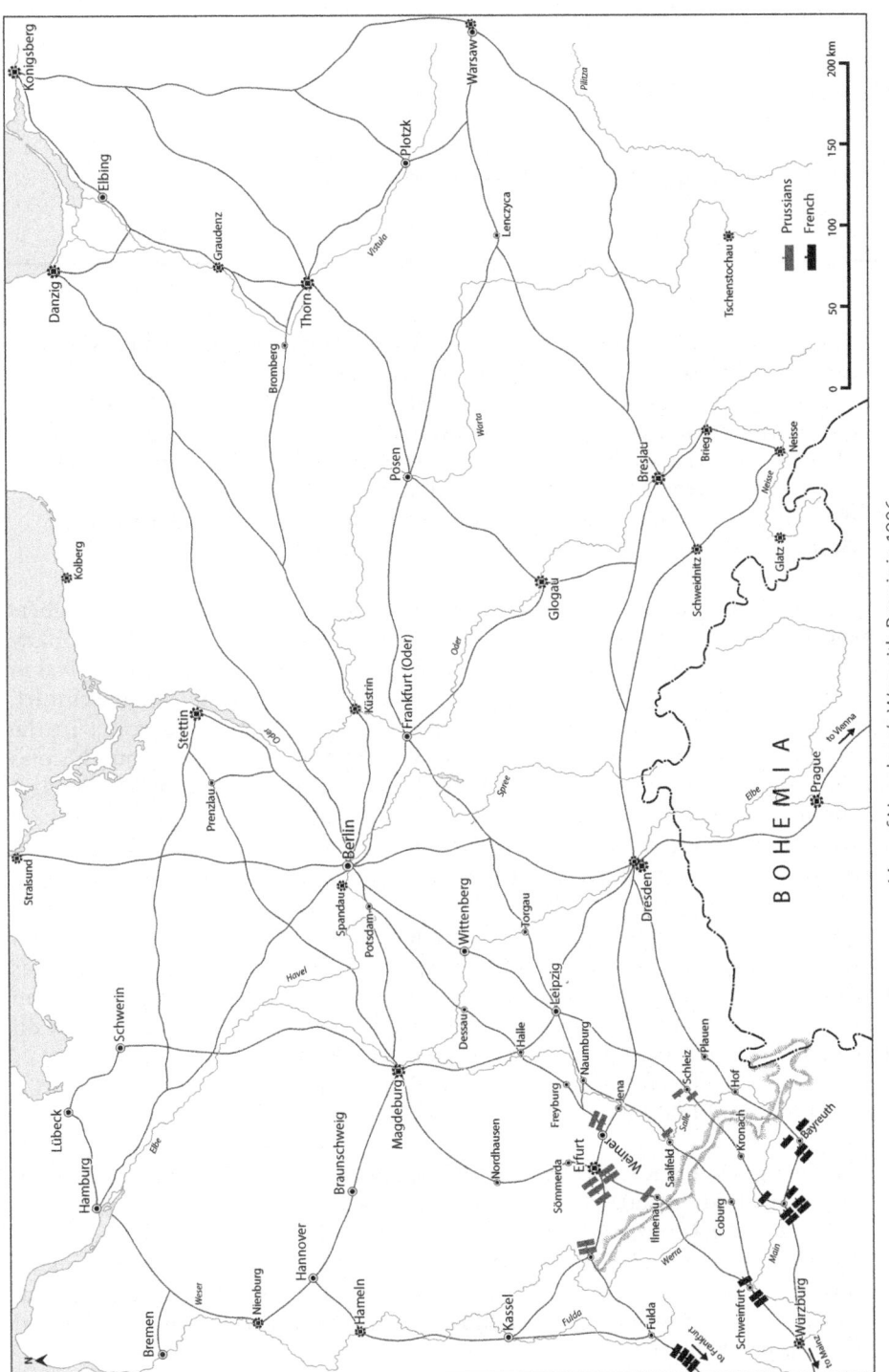

Map of Napoleon's War with Prussia in 1806.

# 2

# The Defeat of the Prussians

The deployment of French forces. – The order of battle of the Prussian army. – Prussian disagreements regarding military operations. – Napoleon's manoeuvre against the left wing of the Prussian army. – The first encounter between the French and Prussians. – The battles of Jena and Auerstedt. – Napoleon's trophies. – The King of Prussia's letter to Emperor Alexander. – Negotiations between the Prussians and Napoleon. – The surrender of the Prussian fortresses. – Polish insurrection. – Napoleon's departure from Berlin to Poznan.

During the negotiations conducted with Prussia, Napoleon increased the numbers of his troops on the right bank of the Rhine, and moved them to central Germany by various means. On 24 September [6 October], on the day of Napoleon's arrival in Bamberg, his army corps were located as follows: on the left wing, at Schweinfurt, Lannes [Jean Lannes] and Augereau [Charles Pierre François Augereau]; in the centre at Bamberg, Bernadotte [Jean-Baptiste Bernadotte] and Davout [Louis Nicolas Davout]; on the right wing at Bayreuth, Soult [Jean-de-Dieu Soult], Ney [Michel Ney] and the Bavarians. In each of the six corps, except the Bavarians, there were three divisions of infantry and one of cavalry. Behind the centre were the *Garde impériale*, under the command of marshals Lefebvre [François Joseph Lefebvre] and Bessières [Jean-Baptiste Bessières] and Murat's *Réserve de cavalerie*: six dragoon and two cuirassier divisions; giving a grand total for the army of some 150,000 men. Marshal Mortier's [Adolphe Édouard Casimir Joseph Mortier] independent corps was marching from Frankfurt, via Fulda, to Kassel. The members of the Confederation of the Rhine hastily assembled their forces, which later joined Napoleon's army on campaign. In France the conscription of 80,000 recruits was announced.

At that time, at the end of September, the Prussians totalling 140,000 men, with 18,000 Saxons and 1,000 Weimarians, were deployed as follows:

1. On the right wing, Rüchel's [Ernst von Rüchel] Corps of 15,000 men at Eisenach;
2. The main body of 60,000 under the personal command of the Herzog von Braunschweig, Commander-in-Chief of all troops, at Erfurt;
3. On the left flank, 50,000 Prussians and Saxons under Prince Hohenlohe [Friedrich Ludwig Fürst zu Hohenlohe-Ingelfingen] at Weimar, having Graf Tauentzien's [Friedrich Heinrich Bogislav Graf Tauentzien von Wittenberg] vanguard at Schleiz;

4. Prince Eugen von Württemberg's [Eugen Friedrich Heinrich Herzog von Württemberg] 15,000 man reserve was on the march from Magdeburg to Halle.

The Prussian King, had Field Marshal Möllendorff [Wichard Joachim Heinrich von Möllendorff] as an advisor and was with the main army. Almost equivalent in numbers, but not in composition, the French and Prussians were separated from each other by the Thüringer Wald. Napoleon led his battle hardened and victorious troops, abundantly supplied with food, ammunition and all the necessities of war. The Prussian army had not participated in military operations for 44 years, since the end of the Seven Years War in 1762, except for the campaign of 1792 in Champagne, a short and inglorious campaign. The seventy-two-year-old Herzog von Braunschweig and the Prussian generals remembered the war only from the debates of their youth. In their arrogance, they and their officers did not follow the advances in the art of war, and lived in the old ages of Friedrich's century, alienated from the changes in warfare brought about by the exploits of Napoleon and Suvorov. The regiments consisted half of foreign soldiers, recruited by force and held with the colours only through excessive discipline. The logistics units of the army had not yet managed to get the training necessary for war; the parks were far from the army, for example: Prince Hohenlohe's park was still on the march from Breslau [Wroclaw] the day after the Battle of Jena, when the corps no longer existed. The army was burdened with baggage carts.[1] Considering espionage in war to be immoral, the Prussians had no spies, whereas Napoleon used this means constantly. They also did not have detailed maps of the theatre of war.[2] There were many diplomats in the headquarters. The Queen was there with her Court. The leading generals: the Herzog von Braunschweig, Prince Hohenlohe and Rüchel, as well as the drafters of operational plans, Scharnhorst [Gerhard Johann David von Scharnhorst], Massenbach [Christian Karl August Ludwig Freiherr von Massenbach], Müffling [Philipp Friedrich Carl Ferdinand Freiherr von Müffling genannt Weiß] and Phull [Karl Ludwig August Friedrich von Phull] (who later transferred into the Russian service) had differing opinions about forthcoming operations. One council of war followed another, ending in nothing; ministers were present in the councils in addition to the military. At first, it was decided to wage an offensive war, but they cancelled this intention, not agreeing where to go or to which flank. Subsequently the Prussians imagined that Napoleon dare not attack them and had concentrated his army behind the Thüringer Wald in a strong position, where he intended to await an attack. Following up on this erroneous thought, they wanted to send strong detachments

---

1     *Geschichte der Feldzüge Napoleons gegen Preußen und Rußland*, Tome I, p 185. One eyewitness wrote: '*Einige Tage vor der Schlacht von Jena sah ich einige preußische Regimenter, welche allein mehr Bagage nachschleppten, als ich zwei Tage darauf bei dem ganzen Corps von Bernadotte und der Reiterei Mürats erblickte.*'

2     Massenbach, *historische Denkwürdigkeiten*. Tome I, p 63. As a witness, Quartermaster-General Massenbach wrote: '*Zum Unglück hatte der Herzog von Braunschweig eine alte Landkarte vor sich liegen, auf welcher der fränkische Saale und die Braunach nach einem so großen Maßstabe gezeichnet waren, daß man jene für den La Plata, und diese für den Missisipistrom halten konnte.*'

to monitor the French, but the council of war had not yet decided who was to lead or where to send the detachments when the time for dispersal came. The council members hurried to disperse, making a final decision on relieving the sentries. Before the dispersal ended, while issuing passwords, they received a report on Napoleon's movements from the left wing of the Prussian army. They did not believe the report, returned to their meeting and sent 10,000 men with the Herzog von Weimar, who knew the local area, through the Thüringer Wald. That same day, the Herzog set out from Erfurt for Ilmenau, where he was to collect intelligence on the French. Meanwhile, there was a shortage of rations due to indiscriminate distribution and poor quality of the bread. The indecision of the commanders was reflected in their troops. The recent enthusiasm had given way to regret that they were going to war, and gave rise to a desire to get out of this predicament without drawing swords. But it was too late! Napoleon was going to cut the Prussian army off from the Elbe and Berlin.

The corps under Soult, Ney and the Bavarians were marching from Bayreuth to Hof and Plauen; Bernadotte, Davout, Murat and the *Garde* from Bamberg to Kronach and Saalburg; Lannes and Augereau from Schweinfurt to Coburg and Saalfeld. Facing the bulk of Napoleon's advancing forces stood Graf Tauentzien with an 8,000 man vanguard on the right bank of the Saale. One of its detachments was at Saalfeld, another at Saalburg and the main body at Schleiz. On 29 September [11 October], the right hand column of Napoleon's army crossed the Saale at Hof, almost without a shot, finding only Prussian patrols on the way and turned on the left wing of the Prussian vanguard at Saalburg. Here the French centre crossed the river, at the forefront of which was Napoleon, wishing to get acquainted with his new enemy. He smashed the Prussians at Saalburg, while Lannes struck them at Saalfeld. The guns and colours of Tauentzien's detachment went to the French. The most serious loss for the Prussian army was the death of the cousin of the Prussian King, Prince Louis-Ferdinand [Louis Ferdinand von Preußen], who was killed in the action against Lannes: the entire army respected him, and had placed their hopes in him. The Prussians fled to Jena in disorder. Moving the army across the Saale, Napoleon turned the heads of the columns to the left, towards Jena, sending Bernadotte and Davout towards Naumburg and a detachment to occupy Leipzig.

Having received a second report about Napoleon's march to the Saale, the Prussians believed that he was making a diversionary manoeuvre there, with the intention of drawing their attention towards the Saale in order to attack them on the right flank, on the route from Eisenach. The defeat of Tauentzien partially disabused the Prussians of this error and they moved all their forces to the left: Prince Hohenlohe marched from Weimar to Jena, the main army moved from Erfurt to Weimar and Rüchel's corps went from Eisenach to Erfurt. As soon as the army started moving, the Prussians learned about the French occupation of Leipzig and Naumburg, where there were large depots and the army's transport. Napoleon took it all. The King of Prussia's headquarters was thrown into turmoil similar to that seen the previous year in Ulm, when Napoleon appeared across the Austrian lines of communication. The King and Herzog von Braunschweig decided to beat Napoleon to the banks of the Elbe and issued orders:

THE DEFEAT OF THE PRUSSIANS  23

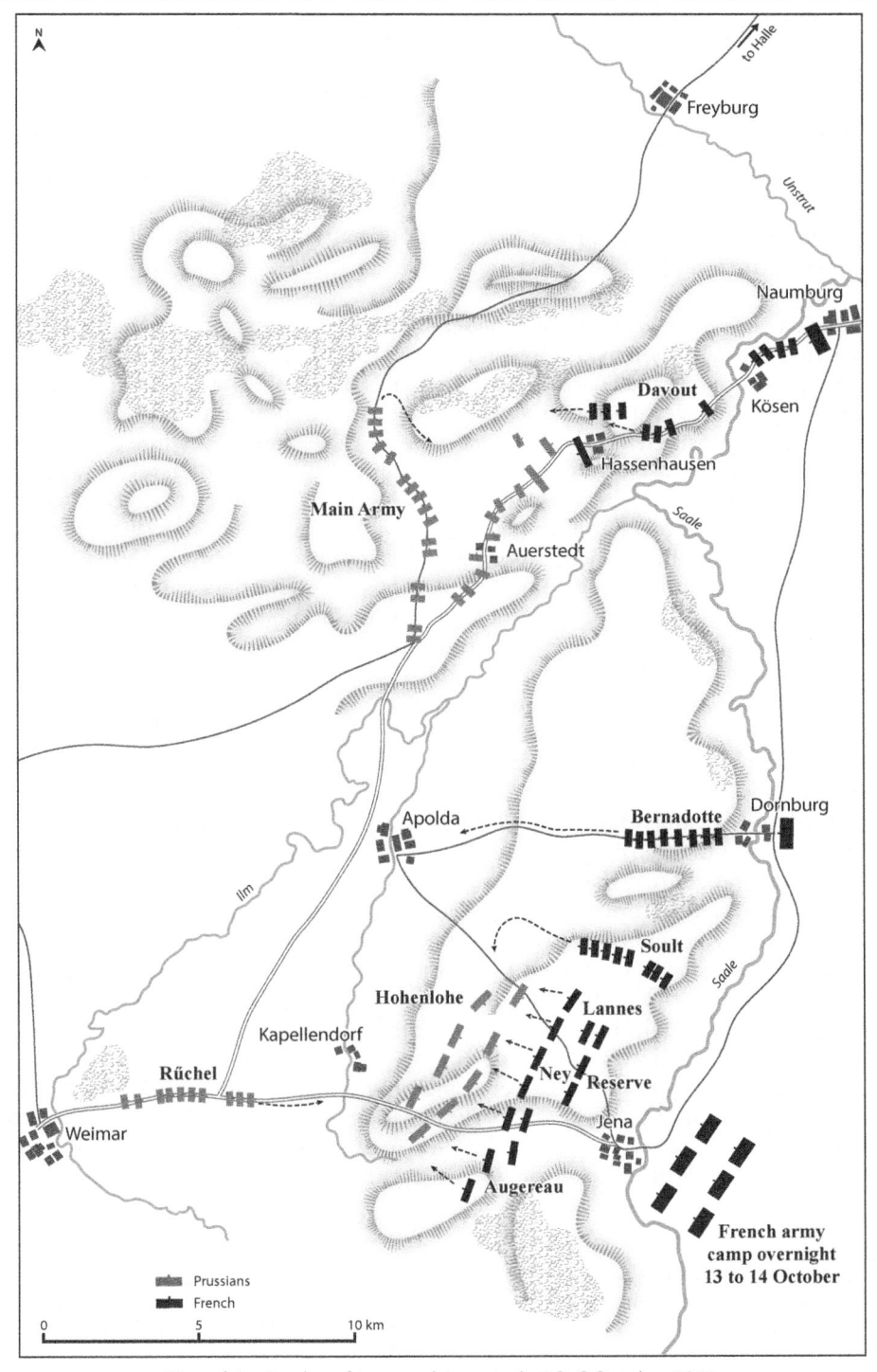

Plan of the Battles of Jena and Auerstedt, 2 [14] October 1806.

1. the main army was to move that same day, 1 [13] October from Weimar, via Freyburg and Halle, towards Wittenberg, linking up with Prince Eugen von Württemberg's reserves on the way;
2. On 2 [14] October, Rüchel's corps was to follow the main army from Weimar;
3. Prince Hohenlohe was to form the rearguard and, on 3 [15] October, was to follow behind Rüchel, but to remain at Jena until then, observing the crossings over the Saale;
4. The Herzog von Weimar was to fall back from the Thüringer Wald and link up with Prince Hohenlohe.

On the day when this decision was made, 1 [13] October, not yet knowing about the departure of the Prussians, Napoleon believed that they were all behind Jena with their left wing at Apolda, and set out to attack them. He concentrated the corps under Augereau, Ney, Lannes and Soult, the *Garde* and Murat on the right bank of the Saale opposite Jena. These troops were to attack frontally, while Bernadotte, crossing the Saale at Dornburg, would envelope the Prussian left wing, whereas Davout would move behind them from Naumburg via Auerstedt. During the evening of 1 [13] October and throughout the night, Napoleon moved his army over the Saale at Jena. The following morning, in the midst of an impenetrable fog, he attacked Prince Hohenlohe's vanguard, in whose headquarters calmness reigned. He and his generals, assuming Napoleon was at Naumburg, remained convinced that there could not be many French troops opposing them.[3] The Prince was more concerned about another issue: as the first shots were fired on the front line, the commanders of the Saxon troops in his corps came to him with the announcement of their intention to leave him and set out for Saxony if they did not receive any bread, since they had not received any rations for several days. While the Prince was busy with measures to supply the Saxons, an artillery bombardment erupted, and he set off for the camp of his corps, located in front of Kapellendorf. The bombardment increased in intensity the closer he got to the camp; individual soldiers from his defeated vanguard were fleeing but it was impossible to make out the movements of the enemy through the fog. Obliged by his orders to hold on until the next day, until Rüchel had departed Weimar for the main army, the Prince set off to attack the French and ordered his troops to stand to arms. Soon, by 9 o'clock in the morning, the fog lifted and the Prussians saw the huge enemy force before them. Prince Hohenlohe began to deploy his troops into battle formation and sent a request for Rüchel to hurry to his aid.

In the meantime, the French were emerging from the Jena defile. As the fog cleared, Napoleon, observing the Prussian positions, placed Augereau's corps on the left wing, Lannes on the right, Ney in the centre, followed by the *Garde* and *Réserve de cavalerie*, and ordered the entire force to attack the Prussians

---

3   Massenbach, *Denkwürdigkeiten. Tome I, p 144*. The Prince's Quartermaster-General reported: 'Allgemein war die Meinung, und ich gestehe, daß es auch meine Meinung war: der Feind werde uns heute nicht mit Macht angreifen, Napoleon habe den größten Theil seiner Armee nach Naumburg und Kösen dirigirt, und werde den König verhindern wollen über die Unstrut zu gehen.'

frontally while Soult was enveloping their left flank. The unequal struggle lasted about three hours. The Prussians fought valiantly. Prince Hohenlohe committed all of his reserves and repeated his request to Rüchel to hurry up and arrive. At midday he observed Soult's corps moving behind his left wing and began to pull back from his positions. The French chased after the Prussians and after several minutes our allies turned their backs. They encountered Rüchel not far from the battlefield. Amid the confusion of those fleeing, Rüchel began to deploy his corps but fell severely wounded. His army, already mentally defeated, seeing the flight of their comrades, was gripped by Napoleon from various directions and after a short resistance was overwhelmed. Being all mixed up, both broken corps fled in different directions. Prince Hohenlohe tried his best to rally them at Weimar and had started to assemble the regiments when musketry was heard: ignoring their commander's shouts, the Prussians fled again.

Napoleon's armed forces triumphed that day and at Auerstedt. Having spent the night of 1 to 2 [13 to 14] October here, the King of Prussia and the Herzog von Braunschweig set off for Freyburg with the main army early in the morning of the 2 [14 October], racing for the Elbe. There were five divisions in this army: Graf Schmettau's [Friedrich Wilhelm Karl Graf von Schmettau], the Prince of Orange's, Wartensleben's [Leopold Alexander von Wartensleben], Kunheim's [Johann Ernst von Kunheim] and Arnim's [Alexander Wilhelm von Arnim], in total, excepting the Herzog von Weimar's detachment in the Thüringer Wald, some 50,000 men. In order to secure the march to Freyburg, where the army was supposed to cross the Unstrut, they sent Graf Schmettau's division to the right, to occupy the heights opposite the Kösen defile. In the dense fog and mountainous terrain near Auerstedt, the movements by the Prussians were very slow. On the way to Kösen, at Hassenhausen, Count Schmettau encountered Gudin's [César Charles Étienne Gudin] division, pushed forward from Naumburg the previous day by Marshal Davout in order to seize the Kösen defile. Hoping that Napoleon would be at Leipzig with the army on the march to the Elbe, the King and the Herzog von Braunschweig did not believe that the enemy encountered by Count Schmettau could be too numerous, and ordered him to attack the French with Blücher's cavalry [Gebhard Leberecht von Blücher]: Gudin repulsed the attack. During the battle, Davout led Friant's [Louis Friant] division to Hassenhausen with the cavalry and placed them on Gudin's right wing. The third division of his corps, Morand's [Charles Antoine Louis Alexis Morand], having spent the night at Naumburg, was hurrying to the action. Seeing the enemy numbers increasing, the Herzog von Braunschweig ordered Graf Wartensleben's division to support Schmettau's and, when they arrived, positioned them on the right wing. He then sent up the Prince of Orange's division and they formed the reserve. Having thus assembled three divisions, the Herzog decided to defeat the enemy which was blocking the divisions of his army from the Unstrut with a powerful blow. He advanced a hundred paces and, noticing a slight disruption in the ranks, stopped and began to dress them. A French bullet shot through both his eyes and he fell to the ground unconscious. At the same time, both divisional commanders, Graf Schmettau and Graf Wartensleben, and two brigade generals were wounded. The removal of the main commanders from the battlefield stopped the Prussians' offensive manoeuvre The King transferred command of the army to the 80-year-old Field marshal Möllendorff and sent the Prince of Orange's division into combat, while Davout sent Morand's. Soon after going into action, Möllendorff and the Prince of Orange were wounded. Graf Kalckreuth [Friedrich Adolf von Kalckreuth] took command of the troops. At the same time, the King was informed of French movements from Dornburg towards Apolda: this was Bernadotte's corps, sent by Napoleon to outflank the Prussian army, when, as mentioned above, he believed the Prussian left wing to be at Apolda. The King, learning about Bernadotte's advance, which threatened to cut the main Prussian army off from Prince Hohenlohe and Rüchel and about whose defeat he had no knowledge, ordered a retreat to Weimar, hoping to link up with these generals there. Davout pursued quickly but the Prussians withdrew in good order. On the march to Apolda, the King saw Bernadotte's corps across his route and diverted to Buttelstedt. Here the mobs of fugitives from Prince Hohenlohe's and Rüchel's force signalled to him the events of Jena. Seeing the impossibility of getting to Weimar, the King decided to direct the troops via Sömmerda and Nordhausen to Magdeburg. He sent aides de camp and orderlies everywhere to get those defeated at Jena to go to Nordhausen. In the midst of the King's hustle and bustle, the order did not reach the troops with the wounded Field Marshal Möllendorff and they took refuge in Erfurt. Darkness was falling. The woeful impressions of a hard day, the exhaustion of the men, the night march along narrow lanes and hunger exhausted the Prussian army. Thousands of fugitives, transport and artillery, crowding on narrow country roads, halted the march at every step, and the triumphant enemy pursued from various directions. The cumulative effects of this situation finally drove the Prussians to panic and broke the bonds of discipline. A large number of soldiers and officers discarded their weapons and scattered in different directions, thinking of their personal salvation. By the morning of the 3 [15] October, the King of Prussia found himself almost without an army, but he was as calm in the midst of calamity as he had been fearless in the preceding battle.[4]

On that disastrous morning, the King received a letter from Napoleon written the day before the Battle of Jena, but not delivered to him in a timely manner. The deliverer, Napoleon's *Adjutant d'aile* [Equerry], Montesquiou [Raymond Aymeric Philippe Joseph de Montesquiou-Fezensac], due to a misunderstanding with the Prussian patrols he met, at first was not accepted as a *parlementaire* by them and then, when they ascertained otherwise, he was detained for a long time in Prince Hohenlohe's headquarters and therefore did not have time to be presented to the King before the battle. Napoleon wrote to the King about the futility of shedding blood and his desire for reconciliation, but he wrote in haughty terms that made reconciliation impossible while the Prussian army was still intact. But as the letter was received after the defeat of his troops, he was in a hurry to reply to Napoleon with an offer to conclude a truce. Napoleon refused, stating 'that he must first reap the fruits of victory.' The fruits were innumerable. Already one day after the battles of Jena and Auerstedt, 60 Prussian colours, more than 200 guns, 25,000 prisoners of war and a final unexpected trophy – the keys to Erfurt, had fallen into Napoleon's

---

4   Massenbach, *historische Denkwürdigkeiten. Tome II p 12*: 'Ich bewunderte die Fassung, in welcher ich den König traf. Er sprach mit großer Ruhe über das große Unglück.'

THE DEFEAT OF THE PRUSSIANS   27

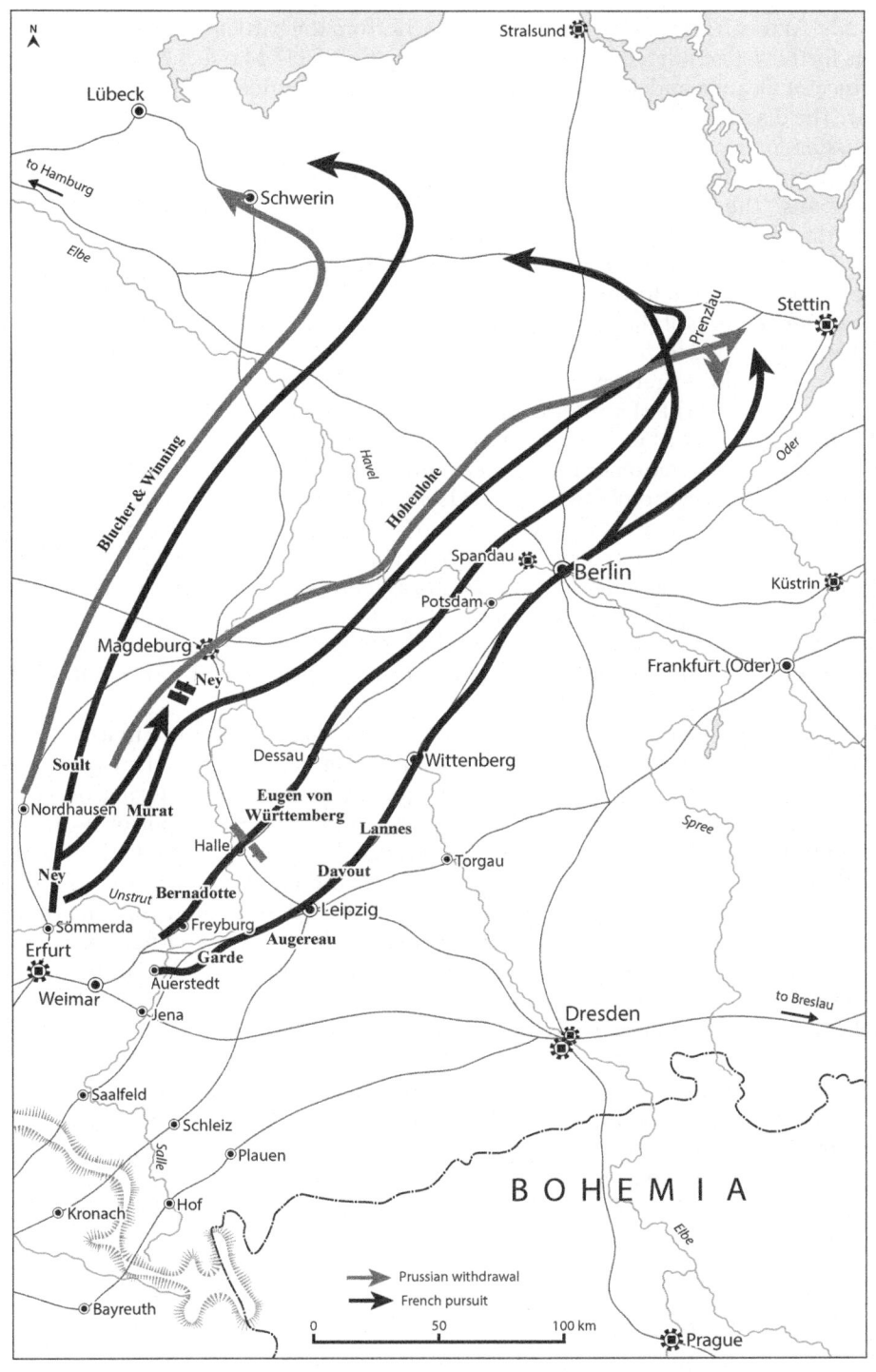

Map of the Pursuit of the Prussians After the Battle of Jena.

hands. At the first request of Marshal Ney, sent from the battlefield of Jena to Erfurt, this fortress surrendered without a shot, and with it Field Marshal Möllendorff, the Prince of Orange and 14,000 men, including 6,000 wounded became prisoners of war. The disgraceful surrender of Erfurt was a foreshadowing of the shame of other Prussian fortresses.

The night after the battle, Napoleon detached Murat and Soult to pursue the Prussians. The next day, while Erfurt was surrendering, he ordered Ney to join him then he, with the corps under Lannes, Davout, Bernadotte, Augereau and the *Garde*, took the shortest route to Berlin, via Dessau and Wittenberg. He released the Saxon prisoners to their homes and invited the Kurfürst von Sachsen to join the Confederation of the Rhine. There was no refusal from Dresden. Napoleon sent a demand to the Herzog von Weimar, hurrying to re-join the Prussians from the Thüringer Wald, to return to Weimar immediately, threatening to confiscate his territory in the event of a refusal. Surrendering command of his troops to General Winning [Christian Ludwig von Winning], the Herzog returned to Weimar and joined the Confederation of the Rhine, along with the other Saxon dukes. Marshal Mortier, marching from Mainz towards Fulda together with a corps of 15,000 Dutchmen, was tasked with the capture of Kassel and to announce to the Kurfürst von Hesse-Kassel that his eternal dislike of France prevented Napoleon from leaving the forces of Kassel behind him, extending to as many as 20,000 men, and forcing the necessity upon Napoleon of demanding their disarmament. Seeing the numerous enemy before him the Kurfürst realised that any resistance to Napoleon was futile, carried out his demands and left Kassel for Holstein. These were the first fruits of the victories of Jena and Auerstedt.

Other events were occurring in the camp of the defeated. On the first day after the defeat, the Prussian King assigned overall command of the army to Prince Hohenlohe and ordered him to retreat as quickly as possible, restoring order on the way, Marquis Lucchesini [Girolamo Lucchesini] was sent to Napoleon as he was going from Magdeburg to Berlin, to begin peace talks. All those who had influence on the decisions of the Prussian King at the time, did not expect any success from further resistance to Napoleon, and all, without exception, were in agreement that peace should be concluded, no matter how harsh the conditions.[5] After spending a very short time in Magdeburg and Berlin, the King hastened to Küstrin [Kostrzyn] in order to adopt defensive measures along the right bank of the Oder, should peace not come about. Having arrived in Küstrin, he wrote to Emperor Alexander:

> Of all this brave and numerous army, there remains to me, at this hour, only a little debris, so scattered, that I myself am unable to appreciate quite the greatness of my loss. It is huge. The French must have entered my capital yesterday, and what crowns my present terrible situation, is the physical impossibility of where I am to present an effective resistance to them and I

---

5 Schladen, *Preußen in den Jahren 1806 und 1807*. p 20: 'Alle Personen, welche in diesem Augenblicke auf den Entschluß des Königs Einfluß haben können, versprechen sich sehr wenig vom Erfolge eines Widerstandes, und alle, ohne Ausnahme, sind geneigt dem Könige zu rathen, sich allen, selbst den härtesten Bedingungen Frankreichs zu unterwerfen.'

find myself reduced to waiting for whatever my generals might have rallied from the remainder of my destroyed army and to lead them to the Oder. If in the bitterness of the affliction under which I write this letter to Your Imperial Majesty, there is something which consoles me, it is the intimate persuasion, that in any case I can count on your assistance. Never more than at this moment have I recognised the full value of the sentiments which Your Imperial Majesty has been kind enough to dedicate to me.[6]

In conclusion, the King informed Emperor Alexander of his sending of peace offers to Napoleon and asked our Monarch not to impede the conclusion of peace and, if peace turned out to be unachievable, begged him to intervene on Prussia's behalf with all his might. Having settled in Küstrin, the King went to Graudenz [Grudziądz] on 14 [26] October, from where he sent Colonel Phull to St Petersburg, to inform Emperor Alexander of the details of the lost battles and to find out what measures of assistance Prussia might expect from Russia.

Meanwhile, the crowds of hungry and half weaponless of the army, pursued and squeezed by the French, were losing men, guns and carts with every step, Prince Hohenlohe hurried towards Magdeburg, hoping to find food there and to rally the army at least a little. His hopes were not realised. The commandant of Magdeburg claimed he only had enough bread for the garrison. The inability to stay at Magdeburg, where the French were quickly proceeding on the heels of the Prussians, forced the Prince to push on to Stettin [Szczecin]. Then, leaving Ney to blockade Magdeburg, Napoleon sent Murat across the path of Prince Hohenlohe, ordering Soult to cut the route of the Prussians who had not yet reached Magdeburg and dealing with those who had turned down the lower reaches of the Elbe, where they were intending to cross to the right bank. These troops consisted of Blücher's detachment and the 10,000 men formerly under the command of the Herzog von Weimar, as well as various men who had joined them on the way who had become separated from their regiments. Napoleon himself was marching swiftly on Dessau and Wittenberg. On the march to the Elbe, Bernadotte encountered Prince Eugen von Württemberg's 15,000 man reserve corps at Halle and routed them, after which, the Prince retreated over the Elbe so quickly that he failed to burn the bridges over it. From Dessau Napoleon detached Bernadotte to the left, ordering him to operate in concert with Murat and Soult against Prince Hohenlohe.

---

6 'De toute cette brave et nombreuse armée, il ne me reste plus, à l'heure qu'il est, que de foibles débris, tellement épars, que moi-même je suis hors d'état d'apprécier au juste la grandeur de ma perte. Elle est immense. Les Saxons se sout séparés de mes troupes. Le François doivent être entrés hier dans ma capitale, et ce qui met le comble à tout ce que ma situation présente d'affreux, c'est l'impossibilité physique où je suis de leur opposer une résistance efficace et me trouve réduit à attendre ce que mes généraux auront rallié du reste de mon armée détruite pour les conduire vers l'Oder. Si dans l'amertume de l'affliction avec laquelle j'écris cette lettre à Votre Majesté Impériale, il est quelque chose qui me console, c'est la persuasion intime, que dans tous les cas je pourrai compterr sur son assistance. Jamais plus que dans ce moment je n'ai reconnu tout le prix des sentimens que Votre Majesté Impériale a bien voulu me vouer. J'ai la conviction qu'ils sont à l'épreuve de tous les évènemens, que je pourrai toujours compter avec certitude sur un parfait retour de l'attachement inviolable et sincère envers Votre Majesté.'

As Napoleon was approaching Wittenberg, Marquis Lucchesini met him with a proposal for the conclusion of peace. Napoleon agreed to a reconciliation on condition that Prussia cede all territories between the Elbe and the Rhine, pay reparations of 100,000,000 Francs and promise not to interfere in matters in Germany. Lucchesini did not sign the conditions, finding them too severe and returned to the King for further instructions, while Napoleon entered Berlin on 13 [25] October, from where Marshal Lannes was sent to cut the retreating Prussians off from the Oder. Napoleon received news of victories daily. Spandau, Stettin and Küstrin were surrendered to him without resistance. Surrounded on all sides, the Commander-in-Chief of Prussian forces, Prince Hohenlohe, surrendered at Prenzlau, after which Murat, Soult, Bernadotte and then Lannes, who had been chasing him, turned north after Blücher and Winning, defeating and capturing both of them at Lübeck. With the exception of a very small number of survivors, none of the Prussian army got over the Oder.

In the midst of Napoleon's triumph, Marquis Lucchesini visited him again, accompanied by the King's Adjutant-General, Zastrow [Friedrich Wilhelm Christian von Zastrow], with the King's consent to cede his territories beyond the Elbe to Napoleon, and to pay the 100,000,000. The conditions dictated by Napoleon on the banks of the Elbe, however, were no longer sufficient for him in Berlin, following the fall of several fortresses and the capture of the remnants of the Prussian army, no matter how earnestly the King begged him to make peace, as can be seen in his letters to Napoleon. He stated in one of his letters, *inter alia*:

> I have the greatest wish that Your Majesty be welcomed and entertained in my palace in a manner which is agreeable to you and, to that end, it is with eagerness that I have taken all the measures which the circumstances allow me. I hope I have succeeded![7]

What was happening to Alexander's allies? In 1805, one had begged Napoleon to spare Vienna, a year later, another was wishing him a pleasant stay in Berlin. How different were Alexander's dealings with Napoleon in the towers of the Kremlin.

Wanting to get the most favourable conditions from Prussia, Napoleon refused peace, offering a truce to the King of Prussia. It was signed by Marquis Lucchesini and General Zastrow, under conditions that Prussian troops were cleared from all Prussian territory on the left bank of the Vistula onto the right bank; to hand over to Napoleon until a reconciliation, the fortresses of Danzig [Gdańsk], Kolberg [Kołobrzeg], Graudenz and Thorn [Toruń], as well as Glogau [Głogów], Hameln and Nienburg, about whose unresisting surrender Napoleon did not yet know; not to let any foreign troops into Prussia, and the Russians, if they had already entered its territory, were to return to Russia; upon the fulfilment of these conditions by the Prussian King, peace negotiations could begin, but if peace could not be concluded, hostilities would reopen in accordance with a preliminary announcement of ten

---

7 *'J'ai le plus vif désir que V M soit accueillie et traitée dans mon palais d'une manière qui lui soit agréable et c'est avec empressement que j'ai pris à cet effet toutes les mesures qui les circonstances me permettoient. Puissé-je avoir réussi!'*

days' notice. The King of Prussia did not approve the truce, which would have betrayed almost the entire state to the whim of Napoleon. Moreover, the King did not know whether Emperor Alexander would agree to withdraw his troops from Prussia. If our Monarch refused, Prussia could become a theatre of war, contrary to the King's wishes.

Losing hope of reconciliation with a vanquished Prussia, Napoleon began to prepare for war with Emperor Alexander. These matters occupied him for more than a month and a half in Berlin and Poznan. Unusually, he was assisted beyond all expectations in his preparations by the fear that had prevailed over the Prussians. Convinced of the futility of standing against Napoleon, the commandants of the fortresses surrendered without resistance as soon as the French appeared. No pen can depict the cowardice of the commandants of the Prussian fortresses. Magdeburg, legendary stronghold of the Prussian monarchy with its 800 guns, submitted after just a few cannon shots against it and not so much as a single man from the garrison was wounded. When the French approached Stettin, the commander of this fortress sent a request to the King asking what to do if the French were to demand his surrender.[8] The commandant of Berlin left the city without the knowledge of the King, having passed command of the city to his son-in-law, and did not even order the evacuation of weapons from its arsenals. The commandant of Küstrin, seeing a French infantry brigade passing by the fortress, ordered for the commander to be asked: 'Does he want to capture Küstrin?' The French general took the offer to be an insulting joke, and continued his march, but on receiving a second invitation, he sent a request for the fortress to verify what was happening there. The messenger discovered a general willingness to surrender, and the French brigade, in front of which the 4,000 man garrison humiliatingly laid down their weapons, occupied Küstrin. Within six weeks, eight fortresses had surrendered shamefully:

| 3 [15] October | Erfurt | 14,000 men. |
| 13 [25] October | Spandau | 1,200 men. |
| 17 [29] October | Stettin | 5,000 men. |
| 19 [31] October | Küstrin | 4,000 men. |
| 20 October [1 November] | Magdeburg | 24,000 men. |
| 7 [19] November | Hameln | 5,000 men. |
| 13 [25] November | Nienburg | 3,000 men. |
| 20 November [2 December] | Glogau | 2,000 men. |
| | Total: | 58,200 men. |

It's easy to imagine what kind of turn the further course of the war could have taken if the Prussian garrisons, of nearly 60,000 men, had fulfilled their sworn and honourable duty, what a huge number of troops Napoleon would then have had to use for

---

8  Schladen, *Preußen in den Jahren 1806 und 1807*, p 24. Formerly in the Prussian King's service, Baron Schladen, describing this event, adds: '*Diese Frage von einem Festungsbefehlshaber in Kriegszeiten gemacht, schien uns allen nicht nur lächerlich, sondern erbärmlich.*'

the blockade or siege of these fortresses, and how great an obstacle to his operations a stubborn defence could have made. On the contrary, a large number of lower ranks who were in the garrisons, willingly entered Napoleon's service. Moreover, he got bread stocks prepared in the fortresses, munitions equipment, shells, pontoons, field and siege artillery. The near simultaneous fall of the Prussian fortresses completed the shock and awe of the Germans before Napoleon. They became unquestioning executors of his will. Using his influence in Germany, Napoleon sent out recruiters, and such was the humiliation of the German people that even sovereign Princes were among the recruiters, namely: from the houses of Isenburg and Hohenzollern-Sigmaringen. Thousands from the defeated Prussian army flocked to Napoleon's eagles, and his recruiters formed five regiments from the troops dismissed by Kassel. Napoleon sent the whole of this numerous rabble to Italy and France and he ordered the veteran regiments from there to come to the army. After the defeat of the Prussian Monarchy, not showing any limit to their obedience to Napoleon, the Kings of Bavaria, Württemberg and other members of the Confederation of the Rhine were in a hurry to send troops to him. The conscription announced in France was incredibly fast. Inflamed by the victories of their fellow countrymen, young men pushed in front of each other to volunteer for service, even those below the legal age.

During October and November, Napoleon used Mortier's corps and the Dutch to occupy Hanover, Braunschweig and the Hanseatic cities. Herzog von Oldenburg [Peter Friedrich Ludwig von Oldenburg] and Herzog Mecklenburg [Friedrich Franz Mecklenburg], he declared deprived of their territories because of their loyalty to Russia. All these rich and fertile lands were burdened with heavy taxes and Prussia, moreover, with a tribute of 150,000,000 Francs. Napoleon confiscated British goods everywhere and sold them for his benefit. In addition to Austria, Silesia and parts of Pomerania, all areas of Germany from the Oder to the Rhine worshipped the victor and were his tributaries. Having thus established himself in Germany and having established administrations in the areas occupied by him, Napoleon extended his vision to the former Poland and issued a loud appeal to them, similar to the ones he published in Vilna [Vilnius] when he occupied it in June 1812. Maintaining by force the promises made to the Poles, he moved Davout's corps to Poznan. The entire Polish population from the Oder to the Vistula rebelled against the Prussian government: rushing to Napoleon's eagles, expelling Prussian officials and stealing the state's money. The 500 man Prussian garrison in Tschenstochau [Częstochowa] surrendered to a squadron of hussars sent by Marshall Davout to reconnoitre this fortress.

Having given the army a rest, showering it with awards, strengthening and equipping it with everything necessary, Napoleon began to move his troops beyond the Oder. New corps, made up of Württembergers and Bavarians, under the command of Napoleon's brother, Jérôme, and Vandamme [Dominique Joseph René Vandamme], entered Silesia, where the Prussians had five fortresses: Breslau, Brieg [Brzeg], Neisse [Nysa], Schweidnitz [Świdnica] and Glatz [Kłodzko]. Napoleon ordered Marshal Mortier to guard the army's rear area between the Oder and the Rhine and Marshal Kellermann [François Étienne Christophe Kellermann] to form a reserve army at Mainz. These were the last major orders from Napoleon in Berlin. Having sent 345 Prussian colours, as well as the sash, sword and Order of the Black Eagle from the tomb of Friedrich II, to Paris, he departed from Berlin on 13 [25] November for Poznan, greeted enthusiastically by the Poles. He assigned the fortress of Lenczyca [Łęczyca], from where the inhabitants had driven out the small Prussian garrison, to be the main storage depot for rations, ammunition and munitions equipment. Having finished his preparations, Napoleon moved to the Vistula, and announced the start of a war with Russia by army orders, reviving the courage of the troops with repeated reminders of Austerlitz.

# 3

# Russian Mobilisation

Emperor Alexander's policy aims. – Expansion of the Russian armed forces. – Emperor Alexander's orders upon receiving the news of the Prussian defeat. – Bennigsen's orders. – Strengthening of forces on the western border. – The temporary internal opolchenie. – Restrictions on the French living in Russia. – Recall to service of retired lower ranks. – Declaration by the Synod. – Emperor Alexander's relations with Britain and Austria. – Emperor Alexander's letter to Erzherzog Karl.

Having outlined the circumstances preceding the second war between Emperor Alexander and Napoleon, we now describe Russian mobilisation.

Upon Emperor Alexander's return from Austerlitz to St Petersburg in December 1805, one of his main concerns was to bring the Russian armed forces up to a formidable defensive standard, in order to be ready to go to the aid of neighbouring States, should they be attacked by Napoleon. Under his personal chairmanship, Emperor Alexander established a Military Council, whose members were: field marshals Prince Saltykov [Nikolai Ivanovich Saltykov] and Kamensky [Mikhail Fedotovich Kamensky], generals Kutuzov [Mikhail Illarionovich Golenishchev-Kutuzov], Vyazmitinov [Sergey Kuzmich Vyazmitinov], Lacy [Boris Petrovich Lacy], Sukhtelen [Pëtr Kornilovich Sukhtelen] and Count Tolstoy, and Minister of the Navy, Chichagov [Pavel Vasilievich Chichagov], while the Governor of affairs was the Head of the Military Field Chancellery, Count Lieven [Khristofor Andreevich Lieven]. The duties of the Council were:

1. Draft operational plans for the event of an outbreak of war with any powers from which, for political reasons, it could have been expected;
2. Indicate the resources and orders for bringing the plans into action in the most successful way;
3. The assignment of the numbers of troops, which should be added to counter the malicious intentions of the enemies of the State and to reinforce military operations in the event of war;
4. The search for methods for the most efficient generation of new forces, and the resources for their earliest possible formation, as well as everything that concerns this subject.

The first measure in fulfilling these decisions was the compilation of 13 divisions from the inspections, into which the troops had been divided until then. Only the Caucasian and Siberian inspections remained in their earlier form. The divisions included cavalry, infantry, artillery and Cossacks, and were numbered from 1st to 13th. Soon afterwards another was formed, 14th Division. All these troops, divided into four formations, were located as follows:

First, which included the Lifeguard, in St Petersburg and Finland;
Second, five divisions on the Prussian border;
Third, three divisions on the Austrian border;
Fourth, five divisions on the Dniester.

Thereafter new regiments were formed: the Grodno Hussars, Lubny Hussars; Finland Dragoons, Mittau Dragoons, Nezhin Dragoons, Yamburg Dragoons, Serpukhov Dragoons, Arzamas Dragoons, Tiraspol Dragoons, Dorpat Dragoons; Brest Musketeers, Kremenchug Musketeers, Minsk Musketeers, Neyshlot Musketeers, Yakutsk Musketeers, Okhotsk Musketeers, Kamchatka Musketeers, Mingrela Musketeers, Wilmanstrand Musketeers, Libau Musketeers, Pernov Musketeers; 24th Jägers, 25th Jägers, 26th Jägers, 27th Jägers, 28th Jägers, 29th Jägers, 30th Jägers, 31st Jägers and 32nd Jägers. The cadres of the new regiments were formed by extracting veteran platoons, companies, squadrons and battalions, as well as six musketeer battalions, two of jägers, and five squadrons of dragoons sent from Siberia. A second battalion was added to the Lifeguard Jäger Battalion, and combined they became the Lifeguard Jäger Regiment. Following the order to form new regiments, four more divisions were added to the existing 14; the 15th, 16th, 17th and 18th. Of these, 15th Division was formed from regiments that had been stationed on the Ionian islands; Rtishchev's [Nikolai Fedorovich Rtishchev] 16th Division was formed in Smolensk, and was assigned to the Dniester Army; Prince Lobanov-Rostovsky's [Dmitry Ivanovich Lobanov-Rostovsky] 17th Division was formed in Moscow and Prince Gorchakov 2nd's [Andrei Ivanovich Gorchakov] 18th Division in Kaluga. Having been brought up to the proper establishment, both these last divisions were to go to the western border. The foundations were laid for the formation of the Noble Regiment by inviting nobles, no younger than 16 years old, to join the cadet corps for a short time to teach them service regulations, after which they were assigned to the army as ensigns or cornets. Inadequate nobles were dismissed to travel to St Petersburg. Students, nobles and those of no class who completed a course of science at university could be accepted into military service on condition that they serve three months as private soldiers, and three as sub-ensigns, after which they could be promoted to officers, even though there were no vacancies in their regiment. Officers were added to the jäger regiments, increasing the numbers in each by 12 ensigns. Remounts of war horses for the cavalry and artillery was entrusted to a specially appointed general under the title 'Chief Commissioner for Military Remounts.' Eight Battery and six horse artillery companies, and two pontoon companies were formed. The previous subordination of artillery into regiments and battalions was abandoned, the Lifeguard Artillery Battalion was disbanded. All the artillery, consisting of ten foot regiments, two horse battalions and a pontoon regiment, were re-subordinated into seventeen brigades, divided into companies and assigned to the divisions, the brigades taking on the number of their parent division. Each division had a pioneer company assigned to it. The production of weapons from the Tula and Systerbäck [Sestroretsk] factories was increased. Private individuals were allowed to make and put weapons in the treasury. A new weapons factory was ordered to be built on the banks of the Sama river, and the manufacture of firearms and bladed weapons in some mining plants. It was ordered that during time of war those retired non-commissioned officers and soldiers not dismissed on retirement from field regiments and voluntarily offering their service, replenish provincial companies and standing commandos. In the event of movement of troops located on the western border, mobile magazines were established, for which 5,382 wagons, 6,192 pairs of oxen and 3,588 drovers from the governorates of Poltava, Chernigov, Kharkov, Yekaterinoslav [Dnipro] and Kiev were assembled. In Vilna, Nezvizh and Brest, eight park divisions were established in the parks, divided into two halves: the first was to follow the army, and the second later, at the request of the Commander-in-Chief. Finally, magazines were laid up in the following places, with orders to keep these stocks always in hand:

| *Chetvert* [1.54 litres or 2.7 pints] | Flour | Grain | Oats |
| --- | --- | --- | --- |
| In Ponevezha [Panevėžys], Birsen [Biržai] and Bauska. | 21,000 | 2,000 | 18,500 |
| In Vilna. | 31,000 | 3,000 | 52,000 |
| In Minsk, Kobryn and Pinsk. | 31,000 | 3,000 | 58,000 |
| Total: | 83,000 | 8,000 | 128,500 |

In early September, as the Prussian army was assembling on the banks of the Saale, a conscription of four men per 500 souls was announced, with permission to take recruits half a *vershok* [2.3 cm or 1 inch] below the minimum height i.e. 2 *arshins* and 3½ *vershoks* [1.58 m or 5' 2"]. Finally, Mikhelson's [Ivan Ivanovich Mikhelson] Dniester Army was formed, consisting of five divisions; the eight divisions assembled on the western border were divided into two operational corps, Bennigsen's and Count Buxhoeveden's, and the foundations were laid for a reserve army assigned to Rimsky-Korsakov [Alexander Mikhailovich Rimsky-Korsakov]. The Neva Musketeer Regiment, 21 Garrison battalions, six Cossack regiments, 13 replacement squadrons and the last of the conscripts were assigned to it. To speed up the delivery of conscripts to the reserve army, 25 peasant carts were provided for every 100 men. The conscripts alternated between walking and riding on carts, making marches of at least 35 and not more than 50 *versts* [37 to 52 km or 23 to 33 miles].

At the first news of Napoleon's declaration of war on Prussia, Emperor Alexander ordered Bennigsen, who was located between Grodno and Jurburg [Jurbarkas], to move via Warsaw to Silesia, and to be at the complete disposal of the King of Prussia.[1] As Bennigsen was preparing to depart, Prussian commissars arrived warning that

---

1 Supreme orders to Bennigsen, dated 6 [18] October.

the rations for the Russian troops were not yet ready, and we must not enter Prussia before 17 [29] October.[2] While Bennigsen was sorting out the ration arrangements with the commissars, he received news from the Russian envoy in Dresden about the Prussian defeat, and received orders from Emperor Alexander soon afterwards: 'because of the uncertainty over what decisions the King of Prussia might make following this disaster to his army, do not cross the Vistula, but deploy your corps along the right bank between Warsaw and Thorn, and operate as you see fit.'[3] The Emperor wrote to him 'The distance I am from you, deprives me of the means to give you guidance, but I trust your insight, your military talent and your diligence in my service.'[4]

Thus the form of operations had changed. Instead of a war on the Elbe and combined operations with the Prussian army, the theatre of war was suddenly transferred to this side of the Vistula, from an offensive posture we switched to the defensive, instead of intending to drive Napoleon beyond the Rhine it became necessary to think about protecting the borders of Russia. Without the slightest hesitation, Emperor Alexander declared war on Napoleon on 18 [30] November. Stating in a manifesto that; 'the sword, drawn with honour to defend the allies of Russia, in all fairness should look to the defence of its own security for the homeland.' Following the announcement two months earlier for four conscripts per 500 souls, an additional man was ordered, accepting men above 2 *arshins* and 3 *vershoks* [1.55m or 5' 1¼"] and not older than 36. Officers on leave were ordered to report to their units, excluding those dismissed on sick leave. Mikhelson, assigned to occupy Bessarabia, Moldavia and Wallachia with five divisions, was ordered to detach two divisions to Brest, entrusting them to Essen 1st's, and Count Buxhoeveden was ordered to speed up the assembly of a corps between Grodno and Brest and then to cross the border.

Anticipating Napoleon invading Russia, Emperor Alexander turned to emergency measures. In a manifesto dated 30 November [12 December] 1806, he ordered the establishment of a militia of 'temporary internal *opolchenie*' of 612,000 soldiers, taken from 31 Governorates, which would be divided across seven *Oblasts* [regions].[5] Governorates not listed were required to supply cash, bread, weapons and munitions. It was pledged that the *opolchenie* would be disbanded once the need had passed, returning the soldiers to their former status. Having a shortage of firearms, they armed only a fifth of the *opolchenie* with muskets, while the remaining soldiers were given pikes or spears. For this reason, the *opolchenie* were deployed in 4 or 5 ranks; only the front rank having firearms. Old muskets found all over the empire were repaired and issued to the *opolchenie*; representatives were sent to London and Vienna to buy 160,000 muskets. The *opolchenie* commanders for each *Oblast* were recommended by the Commander-in-Chief, and were selected by the Emperor, vested with the power to arrest and bring to trial the disobedient and violators of the

---

2    Bennigsen's report, dated 13 [25] October.
3    Supreme orders to Bennigsen, dated 27 October [8 November].
4    The Emperor's hand-written rescript to Bennigsen, dated 30 October [11 November]: '*La distance où je suis, m'ote tout moyen de vous donner des instructions, mais je me fie à vos lumières, à vos talens militaires et à votre zèle pour mon service.*'
5    See Appendix 1.

oath of loyalty. The orders of the Commander-in-Chief had the authority of Supreme Orders; his judgements were executed immediately, even if they involved capital punishment. The Governorate, 1,000 man, 500 man and 50 man commanders were selected from the nobility. The bourgeoisie, *odnodvortsy* [landed gentry], state and privately owned serfs, no older than 50 and no younger than 17 years, could join the *opolchenie*. Landlords were obliged to put forward their soldiers within two weeks of the publication of the manifesto, giving each three Roubles, provisions for three months and supplied with weapons, if possible. Regular troops were assigned to train the *opolchenie*. Generals and officers had special uniforms. The soldiers wore their own clothes, whatever they wore before entering the service; heads and beards were not shaved. Eighteen of the Governorates where *opolchenie* were formed were each assigned to deliver one battalion of marksmen of 600 men, giving a total of 10,800. These battalions were equipped with muskets, and sent to the army. Each marksman battalion was assigned either a 1,000 man or a 500 man commander, while sixteen 100 man commanders with previous military service were assigned.

All classes in the State were called upon for donations of money, bread, munitions equipment and, most of all, weapons. The offerings were great, but not as huge as during the Patriotic War. The Moscow Nobility was marked by the greatest competition. As a reward, Emperor Alexander ordered a special chapter to be compiled in the book of nobility for the Moscow Governorate, and entered into it the names of the commanders of the local army selected by the nobility, as well as the names of donors from Moscow. To manage the affairs of the *opolchenie* and the distribution of donations, a Committee was established, in which Field Marshal Count Saltykov and the Minister of War, Vyazmitinov, Minister of Foreign Affairs, Baron Budberg [Andrey Yakovlevich Budberg], Minister of Internal Affairs, Count Kochubey [Victor Pavlovich Kochubey] and Privy Councillor Novosiltsev [Nikolai Nikolaevich Novosiltsev] met. In order to prevent the vacillations that could occur during wartime, a Committee was formed with the Minister of Justice and two Senators 'for the consideration of crimes tending to breach the general peace.' All native French persons living in Russia, as well as those who became Napoleon's subjects due to the annexation of lands to France, were ordered to be deported unless they had become subjects of Russia. Those who wanted to stay in Russia had to take an oath within eight days in a commission specially established for that purpose. French non-commissioned prisoners of war were assigned to be sent to the Vyatka and Perm Governorates, while officers would be sent to Simbirsk. Compassionate in advance for the fate of prisoners of war, the Emperor appointed an allowance for captive generals of 3 Roubles per day, colonels and lieutenant-colonels 1 Rouble 50 Kopecks, majors 1 Rouble, subalterns 50 Kopecks, non-commissioned officers 7 Kopecks and soldiers 5 Kopecks.

Retired lower ranks were called up for temporary service. Those of them who served for three years were promised a medal for wearing in a buttonhole on a red ribbon with the inscription: '*за усердие к службе*' [for diligent service]. Those serving beyond three years received an increase in pay, and longer than four years, in addition to the medal, non-commissioned officer rank, if this had not already been reached. Completing six years, he received a medal for wearing in his buttonhole, on a blue ribbon, with the inscription: '*Въ честь заслуженному воину*' [in honour of a meritorious warrior], non-commissioned officer rank and full soldier's salary as a pension on retirement for life. Lists were compiled of all retired men, and divided them by ability into four categories: some were assigned to the army, others to the *opolchenie*, a third group to the Governorate's standing commandos, the decrepit were left in their homes. Those who did not heed the call voluntarily were compelled to join the service. The infantry withdrew [officers'] spontoons. In all regiments, except for the Lifeguard and hussars, queues were cut off. To reward the lower ranks, the insignia of the Military Order was established.

The synod ordered the clergy 'to convince parishioners that our Orthodox Church, threatened by the invasion of the enemy, calls on her faithful children to the temporary *opolchenie* and that it's not in search of futile glory that they put weapons in their hands, but the security of the borders of the State and the personal well-being of all.' The synod called the clergy to arm themselves with the power of the word of God, not to run like mercenaries, to have care for the salvation of the faithful, not to join in the anti-Christian undertakings and expressions of Napoleon, to exemplify, exhort and excite the courage to defeat the enemy and fulfil the oath in the souls of all.

Protecting the State with the armed forces and the voice of the Faith, Emperor Alexander persuaded Britain to take part in the war, making landings in German soil, by distributing money for an uprising against Napoleon in Germany, and wished for the mediation of Great Britain for a loan, which was supposed to be arranged in London for Russia. Later we will see that none of these three wishes of Emperor Alexander's was satisfied by the British Government. After the misfortunes of Prussia and the inaction of the Austrians, believing it impossible for landings to restore the situation on continental Europe, the British sent their ground forces on operations in Egypt and South America.

Before the start of the war between Napoleon and Prussia, Emperor Alexander approved the armed neutrality of Austria, but after the disaster of Jena he wrote to Kaiser Franz that the situation had changed completely, stating 'For the sake of Europe do not allow Austria to remain a mere spectator of the war, and requires your assistance; this is an auspicious moment to restore equilibrium between the Powers, to reimburse Austrian losses by moving troops behind Napoleon.'[6] This was not limited to Alexander. Knowing how much influence on the affairs of Austria their hero Erzherzog Karl [Archduke Charles] had at the time, he wrote to him:

'Sir, my brother and cousin! The importance of the present circumstances has determined me to join with your august brother in our efforts to stop the total ruin of the world, threatened in a frightening manner of dissolution and slavery. Considering the necessity of the enterprise and the difficulties which are inseparable from it, my thoughts fell upon Your Royal Highness, and I counted your intervention and employment of your great talents as amongst the most effective means to obtain victory. Encouraged by successes as brilliant as those that Your Royal Highness has often won over the same enemy, I am convinced that the obstacles will only animate your great courage, and that you would see, in the career that opens before you, only the opportunity to acquire a kind of glory that will never have been surpassed by no

---

6   Letter from the Minister of Foreign Affairs to Field Marshal Count Kamensky, dated 10 [22] November.

other example in history. The nature of this letter prevents me from entering into reasoning which will become the object of examination and deliberation for your august brother, but I wanted your Royal Highness to receive from me a statement of the price that I put on his opinion in such a serious matter and to your talents if, as I hope, you were to deploy them for the common defence.'[7].

Colonel Pozzo di Borgo [Karl Osipovich Pozzo di Borgo], who later became famous as a diplomat, was sent with the letters from Emperor Alexander to the Austrian Monarch and Erzherzog Karl. He also took an operational plan for combined operations by the Austrian and Russian Armies to Vienna, and confirmatory assurance of the inevitable ruination of Austria if they did not take part in the war and should Napoleon be successful against us.[8] The evidence for these arguments and the benefits should Austria put troops across Napoleon's lines of communication, at a time when the theatre of war was shifting to the banks of the Vistula, could not reverse the neutrality of the Viennese Court. Thus, the whole burden of war fell upon Russia alone, all the more difficult because Emperor Alexander had to split his forces, because a breach with the Porte followed, and the war between Russia and Persia was ongoing.

---

[7] 'Monsieur mon frère et cousin! L'importance des circonstances actuelles m'a determiné à votre auguste frère de réunir nos efforts pour arrêter la ruine totale du monde, menacé d'une manière effrayante de dissolution et d'esclavage. En considévant la nécessité de l'entreprise et les difficultés qui en sont inséparables, mes idées se sont portées sur Votre Altesse Royale, et j'ai compté au nombre des moyens les plus efficaces pour obtenir la victoire, l'intervention et l'emploi de ses grands talents. Encouragé par des succès aussi brillants que ceux que Votre Altesse Royale a souvent remportés sur les mêmes ennemis, je suis persuadé que les obstacles ne feront qu'animer son grand courage, et qu'elle ne verrait, dans la carrière qui s'ouvriroit devant elle, que l'occasion d'acquérir un genre de gloire qui n'aura jamais été surpassé par aucun autre exemple de l'histoire. La nature de cette lettre m'empêche d'entrer das des raisonnements qui devendront objet d'examen et de délibération pour votre auguste frère, mais j'ai voulu que Votre Altesse Royale reçut de ma part un témoignage du prix que je mets à son opinion dans une affaire aussi grave et à ses talents si, comme je l'espère, elle devait les déployer pour la défense commune. Je suis avec les sentiments de la plus haute estime et de l'amitié la plus sincère. Alexandre.'

[8] Supreme orders for Colonel Pozzo di Borgo, dated 8 [20] December.

# 4

# Russian Forces Cross the Border

> Bennigsen departs abroad. – The Order of Battle of his corps. – His correspondence with the King of Prussia. – The deployment of Russian troops at Pultusk. – The French approach the Vistula and the fall of Warsaw. – The Russians abandon the banks of the Vistula. – Bennigsen's retreat to Ostrolenka. – His return to Pultusk. – The arrival of Count Buxhoeveden's and Essen's corps in the theatre of war. – Emperor Alexander's problems choosing a Commander-in-Chief. – The appointment to this post of Field Marshal Count Kamensky. – Empress Catherine II's opinion of him. – Count Kamensky's departure from St Petersburg, and his arrival with the army.

While Napoleon reaped the fruits of his victories over the Prussians, on 22 October [3 November] Bennigsen crossed the border at Grodno and had deployed around Ostrolenka [Ostrołęka] by 1 [13] November. His corps consisted of: Count Osterman's 2nd Division [Alexander Ivanovich Osterman-Tolstoy], Sacken's 3rd Division [Fabian Wilhelmovich Osten-Sacken], Prince Golitsyn's 4th Division [Dmitry Vladimirovich Golitsyn] and Sedmoratsky's 6th Division [Alexander Karlovich Sedmoratsky], in all some 70,000 men including service support troops, and 276 guns.[1] These troops did not participate in the battle of Austerlitz, having been in Hanover or Silesia at the time, and were in excellent condition, delighted at having a chance to measure themselves against the victors of Jena. The Prussian King subordinated the only surviving remnant of his army, L'Estocq's [Anton Wilhelm von L'Estocq] 14,000 man corps, which was on the right bank of the Vistula, to Bennigsen, and recommended that Bennigsen move from Ostrolenka to protect Old Prussia. Bennigsen replied that in doing so, he would give an enemy column the opportunity to march on Warsaw and threaten the Russian frontier, from where he had no right to strip the troops. Therefore, Bennigsen asked the King for permission to remain at Pultusk, having his vanguard on the Vistula, while monitoring the development of Napoleon's operations and awaiting the arrival of fresh troops from Russia. The King endorsed Bennigsen's suggestion and allowed him to act at his discretion.[2] Bennigsen departed from Ostrolenka to Pultusk, ordering Sedmoratsky

---

1  See Appendix 2.
2  Bennigsen's letter to Rimsky-Korsakov, dated 16 [28] November: *'Le roi de Prusse m'a donné plein pouvoir de faire ce que je veux.'*

to occupy Praga with 6th Division; Barclay de Tolly [Mikhail Bogdanovich Barclay de Tolly] to remain in Plotsk [Płock] with his detachment; L'Estocq to hold on to Thorn with the Prussian forces; for all three of these Generals to remain in communication with each other through posts located along the banks of the Vistula. Moreover, Sedmoratsky was ordered to send patrols to his left, to the Austrian border, at that time about 15 *versts* [16 km or 10 miles] from Warsaw and L'Estocq to the right, to the lower reaches of the Vistula. Colonel Yurkovsky's [Anastasiy Antonovich Yurkovsky] detachment of a battalion of Alexandria Hussars, two *Sotnia* of Cossacks, two squadrons of Prussian cuirassiers and two horse artillery pieces, were sent over the Vistula, to Blonie. The Prussians fortified Danzig, Pillau [Baltiysk], Graudenz and Thorn and stationed a weak garrison in Warsaw.

The King of Prussia visited Pultusk soon after Bennigsen's arrival. Welcoming our generals, he told them that having severed all diplomatic ties with Napoleon, he would entrust the fate of Prussia to Emperor Alexander; repeated to Bennigsen the declaration of his full freedom of action and left for Königsberg [Kaliningrad] to extract all remaining resources from his Monarchy in order to continue the war.[3] These resources were even more pitiful than those of Austria after the defeat at Ulm. The whole area from the Vistula to the Neman was in turmoil. Shocked by the outcome of the Battle of Jena, the inhabitants of Old Prussia waited anxiously for the French, the Poles subjugated by Prussia rejoiced at the thought of the imminent restoration of Poland. With such unrest, Bennigsen's orders for food and hospitals were met with strong resistance. The local authorities in the areas inhabited by indigenous Prussians had lost confidence, while in the Polish regions administered by Prussia, they invented pretexts to avoid carrying out Bennigsen's orders. The commandant of Warsaw refused to supply rations to Sedmoratsky's division in Praga. Bennigsen proposed that he confiscate bread stores located in various places on the left bank of the Vistula. The commandant replied the he was unable to comply with this measure without royal permission. The King was far away, and while waiting for his answer, the warehouses were taken by the French. Finding themselves garrisoned by the Russians, the inhabitants of Lutsk hid bread from Barclay de Tolly. Our generals and regimental commanders began to content themselves with the soldiers, buying bread, meat and wine with their own and *artel* [Mess] funds. This solution was soon exhausted, and the soldiers began to procure food by force; the inhabitants fled, taking with them their last crumbs.

Thus early [mid] November passed and meanwhile the French army, totalling 150,000 men, approached the Vistula along three routes: Bernadotte, Ney and Bessières cavalry corps marched on Thorn; Soult and Augereau on Plotsk; Davout, Lannes and the *Garde* on Warsaw. Each of the three formations was followed by Murat's *Réserve de cavalerie*. On 14 [26] November, the first shots in this stubborn six-month war rang out with an attack by the French vanguard on Yurkovsky, at Blonie. In accordance with the orders given to him, Yurkovsky refused the unequal battle and made a fighting withdrawal over to the right bank of the Vistula at Praga. The Prussian garrison in Warsaw followed him and burned the bridge over the Vistula. The French occupied Warsaw, to the frantic cheers of the people.

---

3   Count Tolstoy's report to the Tsar, dated 17 [29] November.

Two days later, Sedmoratsky, who was in Praga, received an agent report about a French plan to cross the Vistula upstream of Praga, into [Austrian] Galicia. This same intelligence was secretly confirmed by an Austrian Colonel, Graf Neipperg [Adam Albert von Neipperg], who commanded a regiment on the Galician frontier. Sedmoratsky believed the report, which later turned out to be false and left Praga based on an order 'to retreat should particularly large numbers of the enemy begin to cross upstream of Warsaw.' The French took advantage of his precipitate haste and immediately occupied Praga,[4] beginning to fortify it and to build a bridge over the Vistula. On 20 November [2 December], on discovering this, Bennigsen pulled back from Pultusk to Ostrolenka, ordering Barclay de Tolly to go there from Plock, while L'Estocq was to move from Thorn to Strasburg [Brodnica] to defend Old Prussia. To accusations that Bennigsen failed to defend the banks of the Vistula, he replied:

> The course of this river from the Austrian border to Graudenz is 350 *versts* [367 km or 232 miles]. To hold the enemy across such a large space, it would be necessary to extend my entire force. The French army, more than twice as strong as mine, has the support of the entire population on its side and has already captured the crossings at Warsaw. Back in 1805, at the opening of the war with Austria, Napoleon did not respect the neutrality of Prussia, entered Ansbach and Bayreuth and surrounded the Austrians at Ulm. Consequently, it could be assumed that Napoleon, disrespecting the rights of nations, would envelope my left wing through Galicia if I had stayed on the banks of the Vistula.[5]

Having received this report of Bennigsen's assessment, Emperor Alexander equally permitted him to disregard Austrian neutrality should Napoleon cross their territory.

The French did not follow Bennigsen to Ostrolenka, but completed their crossing of the Vistula: Bernadotte, Ney and Bessières at Thorn and Soult and Augereau at Plotsk. Lannes, Murat and the *Garde* remained at Warsaw. Only Davout departed from Praga towards the Narew, beginning to build a bridge upstream of Modlin [Nowy Dwór Mazowiecki]. Seeing that besides Davout, none of the other Marshals were moving forward, Bennigsen returned from Ostrolenka to Pultusk four days later, on 24 November [6 December] and positioned his main force there, posting Barclay de Tolly's vanguard at Kolozomb [Kołozab] and Sochocin on the Wkra, Count Osterman at Czarnowo and Baggovut [Karl Fedorovich Baggovut] at Zegrze, while L'Estocq was ordered to retake Thorn. On the march, L'Estocq discovered that there were three French corps at Thorn and returned to Strasburg, avoiding getting entangled with overwhelming numbers of the enemy.

Shortly after these movements, on 4 [16] December, Count Buxhoeveden arrived in Ostrolenka, having orders from Emperor Alexander to form Bennigsen's reserve

---

4 Bennigsen's letter to the Minister of Foreign Affairs, Budberg, dated 2 [14] December: '*La faute de Sedmoratzky est très grave.*'
5 From Bennigsen's hand written notes.

and to plan operations with him.[6] Count Buxhoeveden's corps consisted of four divisions; Tuchkov 1st's [Nikolay Alekseevich Tuchkov] 5th Division, Dokhturov's [Dmitry Sergeevich Dokhturov] 7th Division, Essen 3rd's [Peter Kirillovich Essen] 8th Division and Anrep's [Roman Karlovich Anrep] 14th Division; 55,000 all ranks including service support troops, with 216 guns.[7] Count Buxhoeveden's slow arrival in the theatre of war was due to the fact that his corps consisted for the most part of regiments defeated at Austerlitz and they had not yet been reorganised; the infantry needed muskets and ammunition, the cavalry needed bladed weapons and the artillery needed horses.[8]

Bennigsen and Count Buxhoeveden were independent of each other, which is why, to maintain unity between them on operations, Emperor Alexander sent Lieutenant-General Count Tolstoy to the army, invested with his complete authority, with orders secure agreement on the opinions of the corps commanders and report frankly on everything to the Tsar being, so to speak, the eyes and ears of the Monarch in the army. There was enmity between the corps commanders. Count Buxhoeveden considered himself offended and complained that Bennigsen, his junior in rank, was entrusted with more troops than him, that these troops were in the best condition, that he was left in reserve, special trust being placed in Bennigsen, a foreigner and his subordinate in previous wars.

Around the same time, [I.N.] Essen 1st's corps began to approach Brest from the banks of the Dniester, consisting of two divisions; Prince Volkonsky's [Dmitry Mikhailovich Volkonsky] 9th Division and Meller-Zakomelsky's [Peter Ivanovich Meller-Zakomelsky] 10th Division, a little over 37,000 men including service support troops, with 132 guns.[9] Thus, the three individual corps assembled in the theatre of war included:

| Corps | Officers | Men | Service Support | Total | Guns |
| --- | --- | --- | --- | --- | --- |
| Bennigsen's | 2,120 | 62,255 | 3,268 | 67,643 | 276 |
| Count Buxhoeveden's | 1,600 | 49,374 | 4,036 | 55,010 | 216 |
| Essen 1st's | 1,043 | 33,585 | 2,624 | 37,249 | 132 |
| Total: | 4,763 | 145,214 | 9,925 | 159,902 | 624 |

This shows the number of troops according to the rolls, but the rolls were compiled incorrectly at that time, and there were fewer troops in reality, as can be seen from Field Marshal Count Kamensky's report to the Emperor. He wrote to the Monarch: 'in Count Buxhoeveden's *corps d'armée* instead of the 55,000 men reported to me on the returns, there were only 40,000.'[10] The main thing missing was a leader who was able to direct the army with one thought, one will. It was extremely difficult for

---

6   Buxhoeveden's report to the Tsar, dated 5 [17] January 1807.
7   See Appendix 3.
8   Count Tolstoy's report to the Tsar, dated 17th [29th] November.
9   See Appendix 4.
10  Report dated 26 November [8 December].

Emperor Alexander to choose an adversary worthy of Napoleon, marching triumphantly towards the borders of Russia.[11] Calling his most senior generals by name, he said: 'Here they all are and I do not see one in which the requisite qualities are found.[12] Kutuzov was not among the named generals. The disgrace of Austerlitz lay upon him. In the war described here, the sole participation by Kutuzov, who was Military Governor of Kiev in 1806, was that he was once sent from Kiev to Nesvizh and Brest to form the reserve parks. Meanwhile, the opinion of Russia, especially in rich and luxurious Moscow, recognized Field Marshal Count Kamensky as a worthy rival to Napoleon. Everyone knew of his excellent operations in the Turkish wars of Empress Catherine, but no one knew the Great Monarch's opinion of him, discovered on the following occasion. Before his death, Prince Potemkin [Grigory Alexandrovich Potemkin] groomed General Kakhovsky [Mikhail Vasilievich Kakhovsky] to lead his army against the Turks. Being senior in rank to Kakhovsky, Count Kamensky did not want to obey him and convened a meeting of the generals to resolve the issue: who should lead the army? Upon learning of this, the Empress wrote in her own hand to the Secretary of State Popov [Vasily Stepanovich Popov]: 'I felt in my heart that there would be no good from Kamensky in the army, when upon the departure of the Prince from Tsarskoye Selo, I was begged to have him dismissed. A meeting of subordinate generals for the sake of judging to whom command should go, proves the collector's rather recklessness and after this act it is hardly possible to give my authority to him.'

In 1806, the general voice in favour of Count Kamensky, then a 69-year-old senior, was almost unanimous as in the 1812 preference for Kutuzov. Emperor Alexander, relying on the opinions of the entire State,[13] appointed Count Kamensky Commander-in-Chief of the independent corps under Count Buxhoeveden, Bennigsen and Essen 1st, commanding them to form the army to be known as the 'Abroad', and honoured Field Marshal Count Kamensky with the following script:

> I entrust you with the glory of the Russian armed forces, the security of the Empire and the peace of My subjects. You have my unlimited authority to act and therefore I consider it unnecessary to issue you here with any kind of instructions. Deploy the troops and operate in all events at your

---

11  Emperor Alexander wrote to Count Tolstoy personally: *'L'embarras dans lequel je me trouve est difficile à décrire. Quel est donc chez nous cet homme jouissant de la confiance générale, qui réunit les talents militaires à une sévérité indispensable dans le commandement? Quant à moi, je ne le connais pas.'*

12  The same letter to Count Tolstoy: *'Les voila tous, et je n'en vois pas un, dans lequel les qualités requises soyent réunies.'*

13  The Minister of Foreign Affairs, Baron Budberg wrote, by Supreme Command, to the Commander-in-Chief in Moscow Tutolmin [Timofey Ivanovich Tutolmin], dated 8th [20th] January: 'In appointing Count Kamensky as the main commander against the French, the Sovereign Emperor based this choice on the general opinion that placed his hope in the skills and experience of this general.'
Baron Budberg then wrote to the Russian Ambassador in London, Count Vorontsov: *'Sa Majesté, en confiant au comte Kamenski le commmandement de l'armée, s'étoit déterminée à ce choix par égard pour l'opinion publique qui s'étoit avantageusement prononcé sur les talents et l'expérience de ce général.'*

discretion. I'm sure that all your plans will result in the defeat of the enemy, to the glory of the fatherland and the greater good.

The Emperor set Count Kamensky just three circumstances to keep in mind:

1. If successful, to pursue the enemy as far as possible without endangering himself.
2. Do not fall for proposals for a truce or peace with Napoleon, as stated in the rescript 'for whom nothing whatsoever is sacred.'
3. To have several positions that you could rely on in case of a reverse.[14]

On 10 [22] November, Count Kamensky left St Petersburg and was greeted enthusiastically along the way. A few days later he felt ill, took a month on the journey and reported to the Emperor from Vilna:

> I have almost lost the last of my vision; I can't find a single town on the map and am forced to use the eyes of my colleagues. I have pain in my eyes and head; I am unable to ride for any length of time; allow me, if possible, a mentor, a faithful friend, a son of the fatherland, in order to give him command and live with him with the army. Truly I feel incapable of commanding such an extensive force.

Approaching Pultusk, Count Kamensky, imitating Suvorov, sat in a cart and arrived at the headquarters in it. The troops rejoiced when they saw the venerable commander. With him were the Duty General, Count Tolstoy, Quartermaster-General Steinheil [Thaddeus Fedorovich (Fabian Gotthard) Steingel] and on the diplomatic side the Chamberlains, Count Nesselrode and Ribopierre – [Alexander Ivanovich Ribopierre] now [1846] Upper-Chamberlain. Having not led an army until this point, having never faced military commanders other than the ignorant Turks, unfamiliar with European warfare, Count Kamensky soon felt the full burden of the assignment entrusted to him exceeding his strength. Two days later, upon his arrival in Pultusk, having looked into the situation, he informed the Emperor:

> I am too old for the army; I can't see anything; I am almost unable to ride, but not from laziness, like others; I can't find places on the maps at all and I don't know the ground. I dare to submit for consideration the smallest part of the correspondence, consisting of six papers with which I have had to deal in one day, which I can't bear for any length of time, which is why I dare to ask for relief for myself. I sign, I do not know what.[15]

---

14  Rescript to Count Kamensky, dated 10 [22] November.
15  Report to the Tsar, dated 10 [22] December.

5

# Napoleon's First Encounter With The Russians

The locations of the belligerent armies. – Napoleon's offensive. – Field Marshal Count Kamensky's dispositions. – Actions at Kolozomb and Sochocin. – Battle of Czarnowo.

Having taken command of the army, Count Kamensky left it in the locations already occupied: Bennigsen in Pultusk, Count Buxhoeveden in Ostrolenka, Essen 1st in Brest and L'Estocq in Strasburg. The vanguards remained under Count Osterman in Czarnowo and Barclay de Tolly in Sochocin and Kolozomb and Baggovut in Zegrze. The French corps were positioned with Bernadotte, Ney and Bessières in Thorn; Soult and Augereau in Plotsk; Lannes, the *Garde* and most of the *Réserve de cavalerie* around Warsaw; Davout near Modlin and Czarnowo.

On 7 [19] December, the day that Count Kamensky arrived in Pultusk, Napoleon arrived in Warsaw. The ringing of bells and cannon salutes greeted their imagined restorer of Poland. Two days later, on 9 [21] December, he began a general movement:

1. The left wing of Bernadotte's and Ney's infantry corps and Bessières' cavalry was to depart from Thorn towards Strasburg, tasked with keeping L'Estocq separated from the Russian army and then to operate behind our right flank and rear.
2. The centre of Soult's and Augereau's infantry corps together with most of the *Réserve de cavalerie* was to move from Plotsk towards Sochocin and Kolozomb.
3. The right wing, led by Napoleon and consisting of Lannes' infantry corps, the *Garde* and Murat's *Réserve de cavalerie* was to leave Warsaw on the right bank of the Vistula towards Czarnowo, where Davout's corps was waiting.

The movements made by Napoleon's right and left flanks were not yet known when Barclay de Tolly reported the French march from Plock to Plonsk. On the evening of the 9 [21] December, Barclay de Tolly sent a second report, more detailed than the first, saying that from prisoners taken by his patrols, he had learned about the movement of Marshals Soult and Augereau towards him, pushing in his outposts on the right bank of the Wkra. Count Kamensky intended to drive Soult and Augereau back behind the Vistula, and ordered:

1. Bennigsen's Corps to go from Pultusk to Kolozomb and Sochocin, cross the Wkra there and attack the enemy.

2. Count Buxhoeveden to split his corps into two parts:
   a. Tuchkov's 5th Division and Dokhturov's 7th Division to go from Ostrolenka via Makow and Golymin, then over the Wkra to link up with Bennigsen's right wing;
   b. Essen 3rd's 8th Division and Anrep's 14th Division were to leave Ostrolenka and go down the left bank of the Narew towards Popowo in order to protect the left wing of the army and the space between the Bug and the Narew.
3. Essen 1st was to leave Brest and move to establish communications with Anrep and Essen 3rd.

The movements ordered by the Field Marshal began on 10 [22] December, on the eve of the day appointed by Napoleon to advance in two places, near Sochocin and Czarnowo. On the evening of the 10 [22 December], close to the French, the Cossacks of Barclay's detachment crossed from the right bank of the Wkra to the left, while Soult's and Augereau's leading troops were closing in. Barclay de Tolly dismantled the bridges over the Wkra on the bank of which, opposite Kolozomb, he had built a redoubt in advance. His detachment consisted of the Tenginsk Musketeer Regiment, 1st Jägers and 3rd Jägers, Yefremov's [Ivan Yefremovich Yefremov] Cossack Regiment, five squadrons of Izyum Hussars and Prince Iashvili's [Levan Mikhailovich Iashvili] Horse Artillery Company.

Barclay de Tolly placed the 3rd Jäger Regiment, of which he was Colonel-in-Chief and two squadrons of the Izyum Hussars (Lashkarev [Alexander Sergeevich Lashkarev], now [1846] a Lieutenant-General) and Gluskov, opposite Kolozomb; five *versts* [5.2 km or 3⅓ miles] to their right at Sochocin were Davydovsky's [Yakov Yakovlevich Davydovsky] 1st Jäger Regiment and three squadrons of Izyum Hussars (Major Potapov [Peter Ivanovich Potapov]); Yershov's [Pëtr Ivanovich Yershov] Tenginsk Muskteteers were in the woods between Kolozomb, where Barclay had his command post, and Sochocin where Davydovsky had his. Some of the 1st Jägers were in the hollows and behind hillocks while the others were behind gabions and a stockade. Our troops were deployed by the evening of 10 [22] December, as Soult and Augereau, eagerly assisted by the Poles, prepared rafts and approached the Wkra.

At dawn on 11 [23] December, the French began to cross on rafts, punting against the river bed with poles. We opened fire and the French turned back. Having laid out their dead and wounded on the far bank and replenished the rafts with fresh men, they came forward again. The second enemy attempt was also beaten off. Augereau sent the rafts forward a third time, meanwhile, he was sending other troops to the right in order to envelope Barclay de Tolly's left flank. These troops managed to land on our bank and, establishing themselves upon it, quickly laid a bridge across the Wkra. Some of the French cavalry also crossed to our side at this place. Barclay de Tolly ordered the Izyum Hussars under Lieutenant Gluskov to attack their squadrons. The attack was brilliant: the enemy were crushed. But their success was unable to completely stop the French. More and more of them crossed to our bank. Under cannon and musket fire and seeing an attack from the flank developing against him, Barclay de Tolly ordered 3rd Jägers to pull back having sent the same order to Yershov and Davydovsky and to remove the guns from the redoubt. The French rushed the redoubt and captured six guns – their first trophies from us

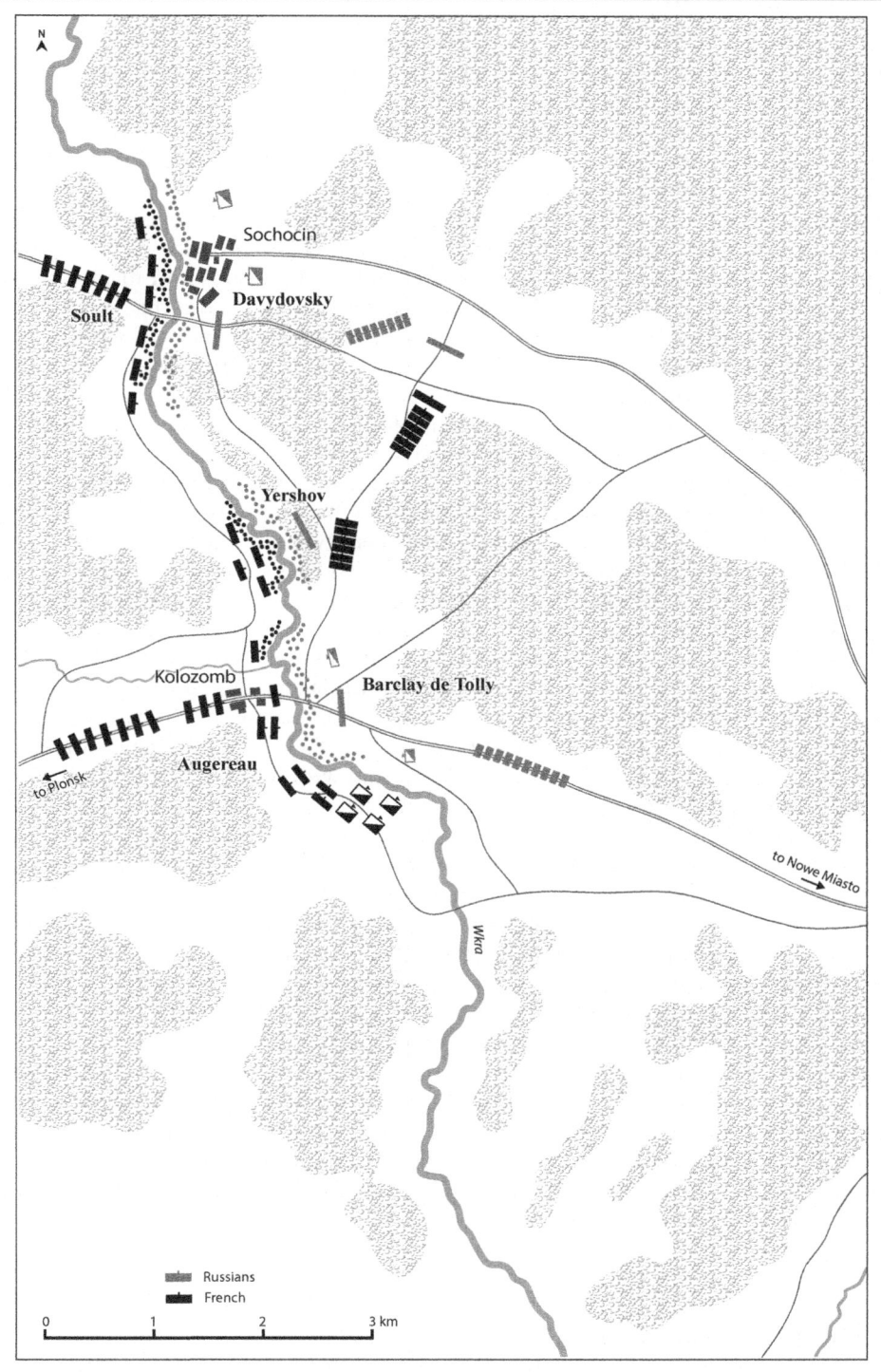

Plan of the Action at Sochocin and Kolozomb, 11 [23] December 1806.

on this campaign. The commander of these guns, Captain [N.N.] Lbov, in despair at the loss of his guns, lost his mind. Such was the spirit of the Russian officers in the war we are describing! The French rushed at 3rd Jägers with loud screams along the road to Nowe Miasto; the other enemy detachment moved to the left through the woods where the Tenginsk Musketeers were waiting. For a long time this regiment had prevented the enemy from landing on our bank and, having received the order to fall back, had been unable to link up with 3rd Jägers and moved through the woods towards Sochocin with the intention of joining Davydovsky. Firing rapidly, the men of the Tenginsk Musketeers emerged from the woods and formed up at its edge. They believed that they had effectively crushed them and that it would be easy to continue their withdrawal to Davydovsky's men. The French swiftly emerged from the woods towards the Tenginsk Musketeers. Lowering their muskets and with the band playing and drums beating the men of Tenginsk advanced and, in the full sense of the word, crashed into the French column and pushed them back into the woods. There are witnesses to this feat still living [in 1846].

We turn now to Davydovsky's men. His detachment, coming under attack at dawn as was Barclay de Tolly's, fought off all French attempts to cross, inflicting heavy casualties on them. It is unlikely that there was any other regiment in the Russian army more skilled at marksmanship than 1st Jägers. Before the war, working deep in the Karelian forests, Davydovsky trained his soldiers to hunt according to special principles drawn up for this skill and brought the men to such perfection in shooting that every jäger scored as many enemy kills as there were cartridges in his pouch. Amusing himself with the success of his jägers, Davydovsky was lightly wounded in the leg and began to write a report for Barclay de Tolly, resting the paper on a drummer's back. A bullet grazed across Davydovsky's temple and blood streamed down his face. He pressed on the wound with his glove and continued to write. A minute later the drummer was shot and fell dead. Davydovsky immediately dropped to one knee and finished his report, assuring Barclay de Tolly that he would hold the crossing. The order was soon brought to him to pull back immediately. He commented; 'Is that so, otherwise I would not have allowed the French onto our bank.' Linking up with the Tenginsk Musketeers, Davydovsky fell back to Nowe Miasto and rejoined Barclay de Tolly there. Such was the Russian defence of the Wkra crossings, Barclay de Tolly reported; 'during which, a few battalions held of the rapid assault of an entire enemy corps for a considerable time.'[1] The following deeds from this action were preserved for posterity: Lieutenant-Colonel Pershin [Peter Ivanovich Pershin] of 3rd Jägers, wounded in the side by a bullet, did not leave his battalion and, supported by two jägers, calmly led his men until he received the order to pull back. Pershin was awarded the Cross of St George. During the attack by a squadron of the Izyum Hussars, its commander, Lieutenant Gluskov rode forward and, on seeing a French colonel, who was also ahead of his cavalry, he hastily fired a single shot at him and brought him down.[2]

---

1  Barclay de Tolly's report to the Tsar, dated 15 [27] December 1806.
2  This deed is even mentioned in one of Napoleon's bulletins; only there it was mistakenly reported that it was not an officer, but a Russian Ulan that cut down the colonel.

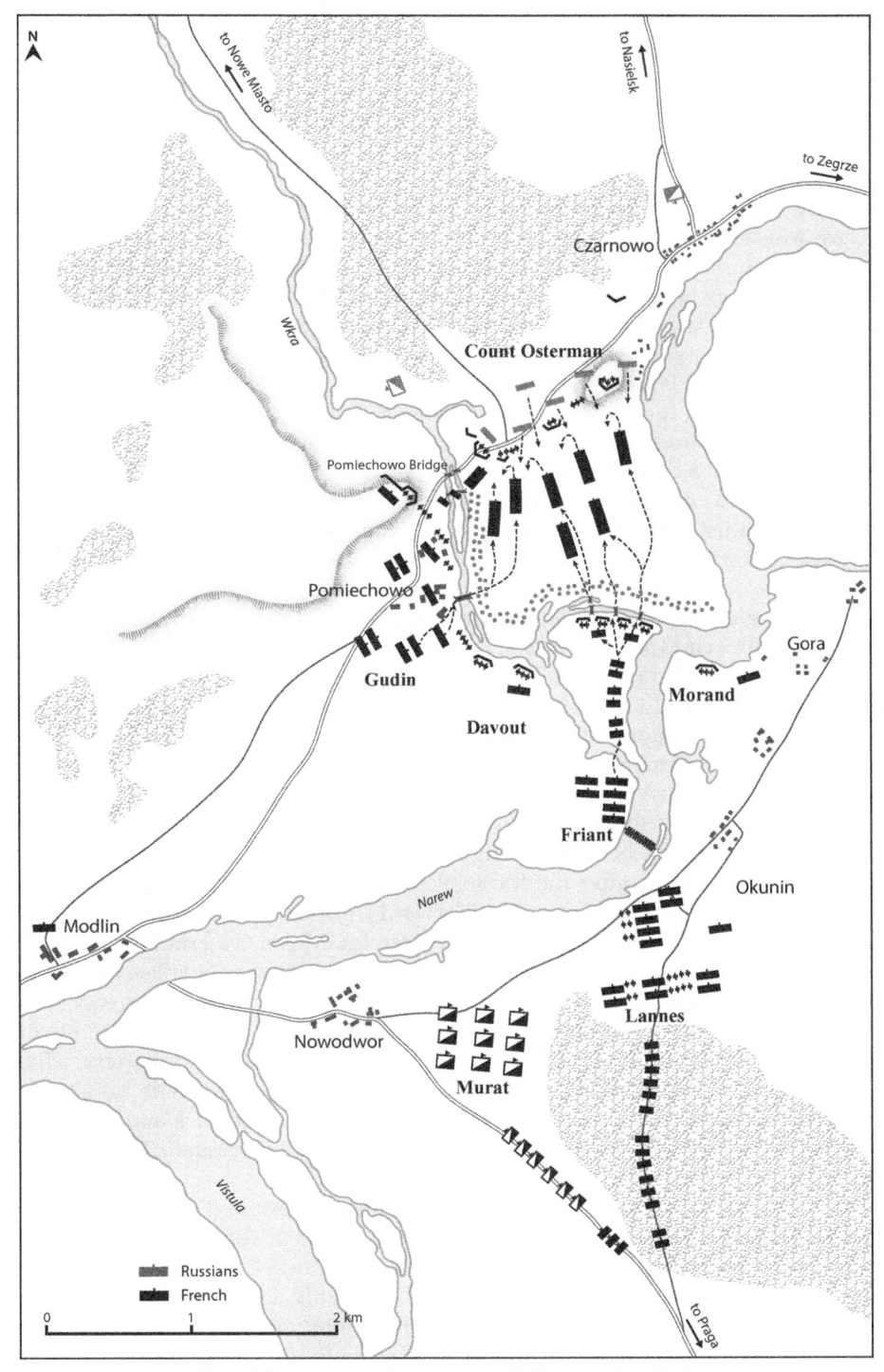

NAPOLEON'S FIRST ENCOUNTER WITH THE RUSSIANS    51

Plan of the Action at Czarnowo, 11 [23] December 1806.

Let us move on to another action that took place on this same day, 11 [23] December, with Count Osterman's detachment.

When, on 7 [19] December, Count Osterman took command of the vanguard at Czarnowo, Marshal Davout had already occupied Modlin, having laid one bridge over the Wkra and another over the Narew at Okunin, and established himself on the island lying close to the right bank of the Narew. Count Osterman's detachment consisted of seven battalions from the Pavlov Grenadiers, St Petersburg Grenadiers, Rostov Musketeers, 4th Jägers and 20th Jägers, two squadrons each from the Alexandria Hussars and Izyum Hussars, one Cossack regiment, a Battery Artillery Company and six horse artillery guns. Since it was impossible for this weak detachment to remove Davout's corps from the right bank of the Narew, Count Osterman placed a battery opposite the Pomiechowo bridge and took up a strong position in front of Czarnowo. Four days later, on 11 [23] December, Napoleon joined Davout with Lannes' corps, the *Garde* and the *Réserve de cavalerie*. Having surveyed Count Osterman's positions from the bell tower of the village of Gora, he said that having rewarded Davout's corps for the victory at Auerstedt by allowing them to be first French troops to enter Berlin in triumph, he gave them now a brilliant reward – the first to go against the Russians in his sight! Napoleon ordered Morand's division to attack Count Osterman's left flank; Gudin's division to strike their right flank; Friant's division, Lannes' corps, the *Garde* and Murat formed the reserve. Napoleon ordered a night attack, ordering the cannon to open fire an hour after they see a beacon in Pomiechowo.

Already that morning, having noticed the enemy concentration opposite him and their movements, Count Osterman guessed that the sudden ignition of a fire in the village was a signal for some sort of operation being plotted by the French. He prepared for action, not realising that he was about to be honoured as the first Russian general to face Napoleon in his second war with Alexander. As if to greet the great commander formally, Count Osterman's detachment were in full dress uniform, since they had been expecting Field Marshal Kamensky to visit Czarnowo that morning. An hour after the fire in Pomiechowo, the French cannon opened fire. While it was still dark, they moved forward from the island and from the right bank of the Wkra, using bridges, boats and ferries. Major-General Lambert [Karl Osipovich de Lambert] with six companies of Frolov's [Grigory Nikolaevich Frolov] 4th Jägers and Bistrom's [Karl Ivanovich Bistrom] 20th Jägers held the enemy at bay but Count Osterman soon ordered them to fall back, saving the jägers from the fire of numerous enemies. The French advanced in column towards our battery, which was forward of our main position, opposite Pomiechowo. Greeted with canister fire and thereafter bayonet charged by the jägers, they were pushed back and pursued to the banks of the river. Thus was Napoleon's first attempt disrupted. The battle fell silent.

After half an hour, gathering strength, Napoleon resumed the attack on all Russian batteries. The French closed upon them again but could not stand the fire and turned back, pursued by a battalion of Rostov Musketeers. Expecting a third attack and wanting more freedom for their movements, Count Osterman ordered four horse guns to be placed in the Pomiechowo battery in exchange for the heavy guns already there, which he ordered to be dragged to his main positions. As soon as the artillery manoeuvre was complete, the enemy charged at Count Osterman for a third time and was again ejected from the main positions but at the Pomiechowo crossing the four horse guns and their escort were forced to fall back. Count Osterman sent a battalion of St Petersburg Grenadiers there under Major Moshinsky [Denis Denisovich Moshinsky], known among other things for a memorable event during his command, in honour of his Colonel-in-Chief, His Majesty the King of Prussia Friedrich Wilhelm III, the St Petersburg Grenadiers alone carried out all the guard duties in Berlin in 1815. Moshinsky restored the action opposite Pomiechowo in our favour. Meanwhile, cannon and musket fire was rolling throughout the line. In the dark of a December night it was impossible to assess the enemy's numbers but the attacks persisted to shouts of: '*Vive l'Empereur!*' And finally, statements by prisoners of war confirmed to Count Osterman that he was facing Napoleon. Concluding that this large number of troops were supposed to be with Napoleon, Count Osterman ordered the withdrawal to Czarnowo. First, he sent back the heavy artillery, under escort from a battalion of Pavlov Grenadiers and replaced them with light foot and horse artillery forward of the position. The Russian troops had not yet had time to move from their positions before the French attacked them again and were, again, unsuccessful. Following the repulse of this fourth attack, everything fell silent. Count Osterman, withdrew behind Czarnowo without enemy interference, leaving a battalion of jägers and six horse guns in front of this village. In less than an hour and a half, Napoleon moved forward for a fifth time. Count Osterman ordered the jägers and artillery in front of Czarnowo to fall back to the positions where our detachment was located. The French chased after them and attacked our position ferociously. Count Osterman repulsed them with cannon and musket fire; the generals themselves led the columns in bayonet charges; the Izyum Hussars and Alexandria Hussars hacked at the French. After a desperate defence the Russians held firm and Napoleon ended the fighting. The French fell back to Czarnowo and merely fired round shot and incendiaries.

Soon it would be getting light. Considering that in the morning light Napoleon, having seen the tiny size of our detachment, would be able to destroy them, Count Osterman gave the order to retreat at four o'clock in the morning. Not being pursued by the enemy, he went to Nasielsk, ordering Baggovut's detachment, which was not under his command, to hurry from Zegrze to Pultusk and to hold the bridge over the Narew there at all costs. This unauthorized order – evidence of military anticipation by Count Osterman – had, as we shall see below, the most beneficial consequences. Our casualties at Czarnowo were four officers and 315 other ranks, killed, our wounded included Major-Generals Count Lambert, Prince Shakhovsky and Mitsky [Ivan Grigorievich Mitsky], 34 field officers and subalterns and some 500 lower ranks. Count Osterman concluded his report on the battle of Czarnowo with the same expressions as his report on the battle of Kulm ends: 'There is no other way to recommend those who have distinguished themselves this night than to submit a list of all those who were there in person.'[3]

---

3   Count Osterman's report to Bennigsen, dated 15 [27] December from Pultusk.

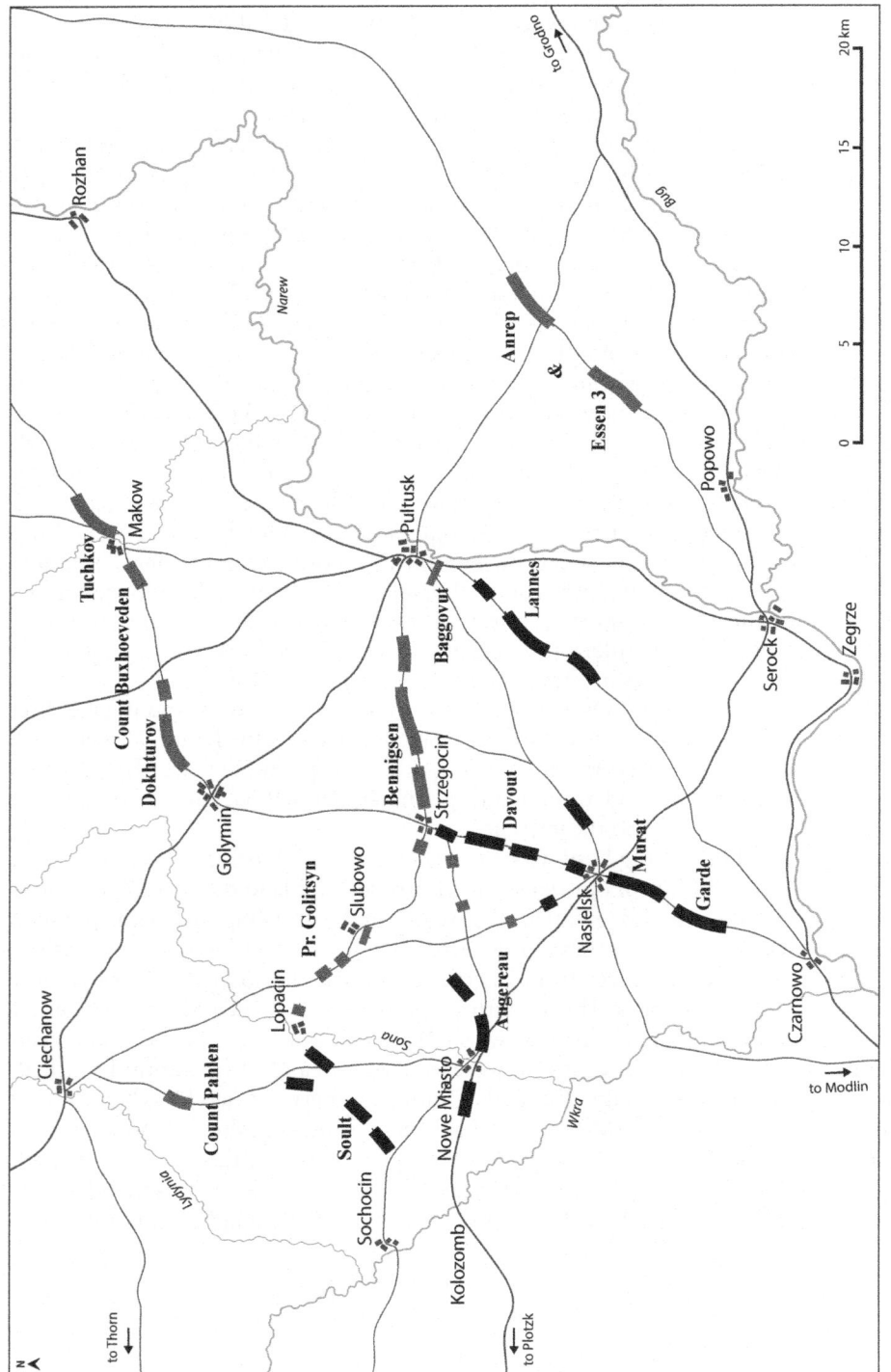

## 54   1806-1807 – TSAR ALEXANDER'S SECOND WAR WITH NAPOLEON

*Map of Troop Movements Preceding the Battles of Pultusk and Golymin.*

One foreign witness to the bloodshed wrote: 'The Russian troops looked with awe and confidence at their commander, who was fearless in the greatest danger. Both the commander and the troops, though justifying their country's wildest hopes, were ashamed at having to leave the battlefield to the enemy and were reluctant to withdraw.'[4] The French wrote: 'Count Osterman manoeuvred very militarily and his troops showed great valour and firmness.'[5] The battle of Czarnowo was the dawn of Count Osterman's glory and here, as in all the battles where he participated, he was like a slab of granite against which the waves of an angry sea break in vain. He named his generals, Count Lambert and Prince Shakhovsky, as his main assistants, memorials in Russian Military History. Shakhovsky had the bones in his hand crushed at Czarnowo, from which he could no longer participate in the war of 1806 and 1807. About his Chief-Quartermaster Berg – [Burkhard Maksimovich Berg] he died as Commandant of Vyborg – Count Osterman wrote to Bennigsen: 'All the awards that you can deliver to Berg, I ask as a special favour for me.'[6] Emperor Alexander granted the Order of St George 3rd class to Count Lambert, and 4th class to; Major-General Mazovsky [Nikolai Nikolaevich Mazovsky] and Major Palibin [Ivan Nikiforovich Palibin] of the Pavlov Grenadiers, Colonel Zhivkovich [Ilya Petrovich Zhivkovich] of the 20th Jägers, Major Moshinsky of the St Petersburg Grenadiers, Major Depkin [Gustav Karlovich Depkin] of the Rostov Musketeers and the artillery field officers; Merlin [Pavel Ivanovich Merlin], Osipov [Stepan Leontyevich Osipov] and Kudryavtsev [Vasily Filippovich Kudryavtsev].

Count Osterman's courageous defence had important consequences. Having held the French at the crossings for more than ten hours, he deprived them of the opportunity of forestalling Bennigsen at Pultusk and cutting him off from the Narew crossing. The battle at Czarnowo was all the more glorious for the Russians because it was sustained by seven battalions against Napoleon and the very troops that had defeated the Prussian army two months before at Auerstedt and at a time when Napoleon's marvellous successes against the Prussians had inflamed the French with extraordinary courage.

At 10 o'clock in the morning on 12 [24] December, Count Osterman arrived at Nasielsk and positioned his weary detachment on the high ground beyond this town. At noon the Field Marshal arrived in Nasielsk and gave orders for Count Osterman, if the enemy attacked strongly, to go to Strzegocin, Bennigsen's assembly area for the corps that day. On the return journey, the Field Marshal was nearly captured by French patrols. At one o'clock that afternoon the enemy approached Nasielsk and directed a column to outflank Count Osterman in preparation for an assault. The batteries on both sides thundered. Soon after, learning about the large number of Frenchmen who were approaching Nasielsk and about Napoleon's arrival with

---

4    Plotho, *Tagebuch während des Krieges 1806 und 1807*, p. 25: *Die Russischen Truppen blickten mit Ehrfurcht und Vertrauen auf ihren in den größten Gefahren unerschrockenen Anführer. Beide, der Führer und die Truppen, obgleich sie die kühnsten Hoffnungen ihres Vaterlandes gerechtfertigt, waren dennoch beschämt, daß sie das Schlachtfeld dem Feinde überlassen mußten, und ungern erfolgte die nothwendige Rückzug.*

5    Dumas, *Précis des évènemens militaires, Tome XVII*, p. 145: *Le Comte Ostermann manoeuvra très militairement, et ses troupes montrèrent beaucoup de valeur et de fermeté.*

6    Count Osterman's report to Bennigsen, dated 15 [27] December from Pultusk.

the vanguard, Count Osterman pulled back in perfect order. Eyewitnesses likened his retreat to a manoeuvre on a training area.[7] A few hours later, they arrived safely in Strzegocin. Giving thanks to the troops, Count Osterman reminded them how gloriously they had celebrated the birthday of Emperor Alexander.

---

7   Plotho, *Tagebuch während des Krieges 1806 und 1807*, p. 26: *Nur der Kanonendonner erinnerte mich, daß ich auf keinem Exerzierplatz war.*

# 6

# The Army's Manoeuvres Between the Narew and Wkra

**Russian troop movements. – Napoleon's plan of operations. – The Russian withdrawal to Pultusk. – Napoleon's quandary – Count Kamensky's orders to his divisional commanders. – Count Kamensky resigns his command of the army. – His report to Emperor Alexander.**

On 11 [23] December, while the French were seizing crossings over the Wkra and Narew, the Russian army, fulfilling Count Kamensky's initial idea of attacking Soult and Augereau, was moving in three formations: Bennigsen's corps was marching from Pultusk to Sochocin; two of Count Buxhoeveden's divisions, Tuchkov's and Dokhturov's, followed from Ostrolenka, also towards the banks of the Wkra, while the other two divisions of this corps, Essen 3rd's and Anrep's, left Ostrolenka for Popowo. Having learned the details of the battles fought by Barclay de Tolly and Count Osterman, Count Kamensky ordered Bennigsen and Count Buxhoeveden to discontinue the march towards the Wkra and to return: Bennigsen to Strzegocin and to concentrate his corps there; Count Buxhoeveden was to place Dokhturov's division in Golymin and Tuchkov's in Makow; Anrep's and Essen's divisions were to hold Popowo between the Narew and Wkra. The Russian army found itself in these positions on 12 [24] December.

On that day, transferring the army across the Wkra and Narew, Napoleon drew up a plan of action guaranteeing him a victory as decisive as at Ulm and Jena. He intended to cut the Russian army off from the crossings over the Narew at Pultusk with his right wing, while his left enveloped their right wing and rear. In order to achieve this, he ordered:

1. Lannes' corps, reinforced by one infantry division from Davout's corps and one of dragoons taken from the reserve, to take possession of Pultusk and build a bridgehead there.
2. Soult and Augereau from Sochocin, Davout, the *Garde* and the *Réserve de cavalerie* from Nasielsk, were to march on Golymin, Makow and Rozhan [Różan], pushing back any Russian troops they might encounter and blocking our line of retreat to Ostrolenka.
3. Bernadotte, Ney and Bessières were to continue their previously ordered advance from Thorn to Strasburg and, pushing L'Estocq northwards into Old Prussia, turn right via Mlawa to the rear of the Russian army.

Thus, on 12 [24] December, the Russian and French armies were in full motion, but the movements were slow. A storm was raging; raindrops and snowflakes darkened the sky. The roads turned into bottomless swamps.

As midnight approached on 12 [24] December, some of Bennigsen's corps arrived in Strzegocin and informed Count Kamensky of the appearance of the French at Pultusk: this was the vanguard of Lannes' corps. Trying to beat the Russians to Pultusk, Napoleon ordered Lannes to hurry as quickly as possible in order to lay the foundations for the success of Napoleon's plan: to intercept the Russian crossings over the Narew at Pultusk. Lannes raced forward but was unable to complete the mission assigned to him.[1] Napoleon's intention here was disrupted by the man who was also later destined to destroy his plans at Kulm – Count Osterman. We saw that, departing from Czarnowo, Count Osterman instinctively ordered Baggovut to go from Zegrze to Pultusk. When Lannes' vanguard arrived there, this town was already occupied by Baggovut and repelled the enemy after a bitter fight. Divining Napoleon's true intentions from the appearance of the French at Pultusk, at midnight Count Kamensky ordered Bennigsen immediately to rush from Strzegocin to Pultusk. Our men had just left Strzegocin when Davout's corps, marching from Nasielsk, occupied it blocking Bennigsen's rearmost troops from the road to Pultusk, returning from the banks of the Wkra and had not yet managed to reach Strzegocin. The following had been cut off by the French: Military Order Cuirassiers, Malorussia Cuirassiers, Pskov Dragoons, Pavlograd Hussars, Sumy Hussars, Taurida Grenadiers, Dnieper Musketeers, Kostroma Musketeers, 21st Jägers and two Cossack regiments. The unit commanders of this force found alternate routes and, two days later, arrived in Golymin. During this retreat to Pultusk and Golymin, many carts and more than fifty guns were abandoned in the mud.

On 13 [25] December, as the main part of Bennigsen's corps was approaching Pultusk, Count Kamensky ordered the troops to be put in position, deciding to give battle to allow the army time to concentrate and drag their carts and artillery out of the mud. At the same time he wrote to Count Buxhoeveden:

> Tomorrow we hope to have the enemy as our guests. It would be good if your divisions (Tuchkov's and Dokhturov's) could come to this location, even without their heavy guns. I ordered Dokhturov to bring all his regiments closer, to stay hidden and only appear once the real fighting has started.[2]

To Anrep's and Essen's divisions, which were at Popowo, the Field Marshal ordered:

> pull back from Popowo and occupy the woods downstream or directly opposite the Pultusk bridges, so that any enemy that appears at Pultusk cannot stealthily lay a bridge and cannot get behind us.[3]

---

1   Dumas. *Précis de évènemens militaires. Tome XVII*, p. 153: *Le Maréchal Lannes fit le même jour plus de dix lieues, malgré les difficultés des chemins qu'un dégel subit rendoit impraticables. L'ardeur du général en chef se communiquant aux soldats, resqu'aucun ne resta en arrierè.*
2   Order No 31 to Count Buxhoeveden, dated 13th [25th] December.
3   Order No 32 to Essen, dated 13 [25] December.

Thus, almost the entire army would have been concentrated near Pultusk. Before dusk, the Field Marshal drove into the position greeted joyfully by the regiments, giving him a sense of unlimited authority. Nobody imagined that their greetings were the last parting farewell for the commander and that the troops were seeing him for the last time!

On that same day, 13 [25] December, as Lannes' corps was nearing Pultusk and all the other French corps were on the march to Golymin, Napoleon suddenly stopped, perplexed, in Nasielsk with the *Garde* and *Réserve de cavalerie*. Which way? Confused by our retreat, in which the cut off Russian regiments wandered on various roads and appeared as it seemed to the French, first on one route, then on another. Without understanding the reasons for their appearance on many roads and believing the incoherence of our actions to be the result of some manoeuvre, the French generals stopped and requested orders from Napoleon's headquarters. As with Kutuzov, the spies Napoleon sent and then questioned himself, confirmed these reports from the vanguard generals about some sort of complicated movements made by the Russians. Looking into the future, Napoleon could not immediately guess what we were up to and did not move from Nasielsk with the reserves. Assessing, however, the reports from his generals and the statements from prisoners and informants, he finally became convinced of the current situation and continued towards Golymin. Delaying him for several hours in Nasielsk was very beneficial to us, because Napoleon's *Garde* and *Réserve de cavalerie* could not make it to the battle that took place the following day at Golymin.

Anticipating an imminent encounter with the enemy, Count Kamensky sent the following orders to the divisional commanders, in case any of them was attacked:

1. All divisions are to form up by brigade; each brigade is to be in three lines, so that for each infantry regiment the 1st battalion forms the first line, the 2nd forms the second and the 3nd the third.
2. Battalions are to form column of divisions [a frontage of two companies] and the battalions behind are to be at least 70 *sazhen* [150 metres of 160 yards] behind one another, so that if they become disordered, they cannot disrupt those behind.
3. Brigades shall be separated from each other by a hundred *sazhen* [210 metres of 230 yards] or so or 50 so that it is possible to move the artillery freely and so that the entire regiment can deploy into line.
4. One squadron of cavalry will be assigned to each brigade.

Having issued these orders, Count Kamensky wrote to the divisional commanders – and here again his actual words were:

> If our fate is unfortunate, the retreat of the entire army will be on the Russian border, no longer on Grodno and, as I don't know the roads in Prussia, the generals and brigade commanders themselves should check on the shortest route to our border, to Vilna or further downstream on the Neman; firewood is everywhere, and fodder and carts should be taken and

brought to the seniors so that there is no delay for anything and, having crossed the border after any such misfortune.

Subsequently, having become the senior in the army a short time later and, informing the Emperor of receiving this order, Count Buxhoeveden added that the Field Marshal also ordered him to abandon the heavy artillery on the road if it impedes the movement of troops to the borders of Russia and to keep in mind only the salvation of the men. The orders given by the Field Marshal to individual generals that each should follow the road which he considers to be the most convenient, indisputably testifies to his mental confusion.

On the night of 13 to 14 [25 to 26] December, in the midst of a raging storm, when the piercing wind was scattering the bivouacs of the Russians and the French, Field Marshal Kamensky was exhausted. Since his arrival in the army, knowing no-one in it, trusting no-one, he concerned himself with the most trivial orders, personally sent couriers, wrote march routes himself, and entered copies of his orders into the war diary, he travelled from one division to another, giving orders to regiments encountered on the way, bypassing their immediate superiors. The burden of care and responsibility, aggravated by frequent outbursts of anger, crushed the old man, deprived him of sleep and confidence in himself. Amidst the struggle with the elements, he battled with himself. Finally, he sent for Bennigsen and, when he arrived – it was three o'clock in the morning – gave him the following written orders:

> I am injured, I cannot ride and simultaneously command the army. You and your *corps d'armée* have been brought by defeat to Pultusk; here it is open, and without firewood and without fodder, therefore it is necessary to help and, since it was referred to by Count Buxhoeveden himself yesterday, a retreat to our borders must be considered, which is to be done today. Take both divisions of Count Buxhoeveden's *corps d'armée*, Essen's and Anrep's with you, which will cover your retreat. You are to come under the command of Count Buxhoeveden upon receipt of this; he is located two *meilen* [20 km or 12½ miles] from here, in Makow.

Giving these orders to Bennigsen, Count Kamensky said that he did not want to lose his former glory and washed his hands of the army. His relative, Count Osterman, was trying all ways to convince him to postpone his intention and said that in leaving the army without a Supreme Commander, the Field Marshal was violating his sacred duty; indicating to him the reproaches of Russia in the judgement of posterity. Bennigsen and Count Tolstoy made representations in a similar vein, although not as heatedly as Count Osterman. It was all in vain! A road *chaise* stood at the entrance, and Count Kamensky drove to Ostrolenka, from where he informed the Emperor:

> I developed a saddle sore from all my journeys which, in addition to my previous dressings, completely prevents me from riding and commanding such an extensive army, therefore, I placed this command on the General who is next in seniority to me, Count Buxhoeveden, having sent to him all

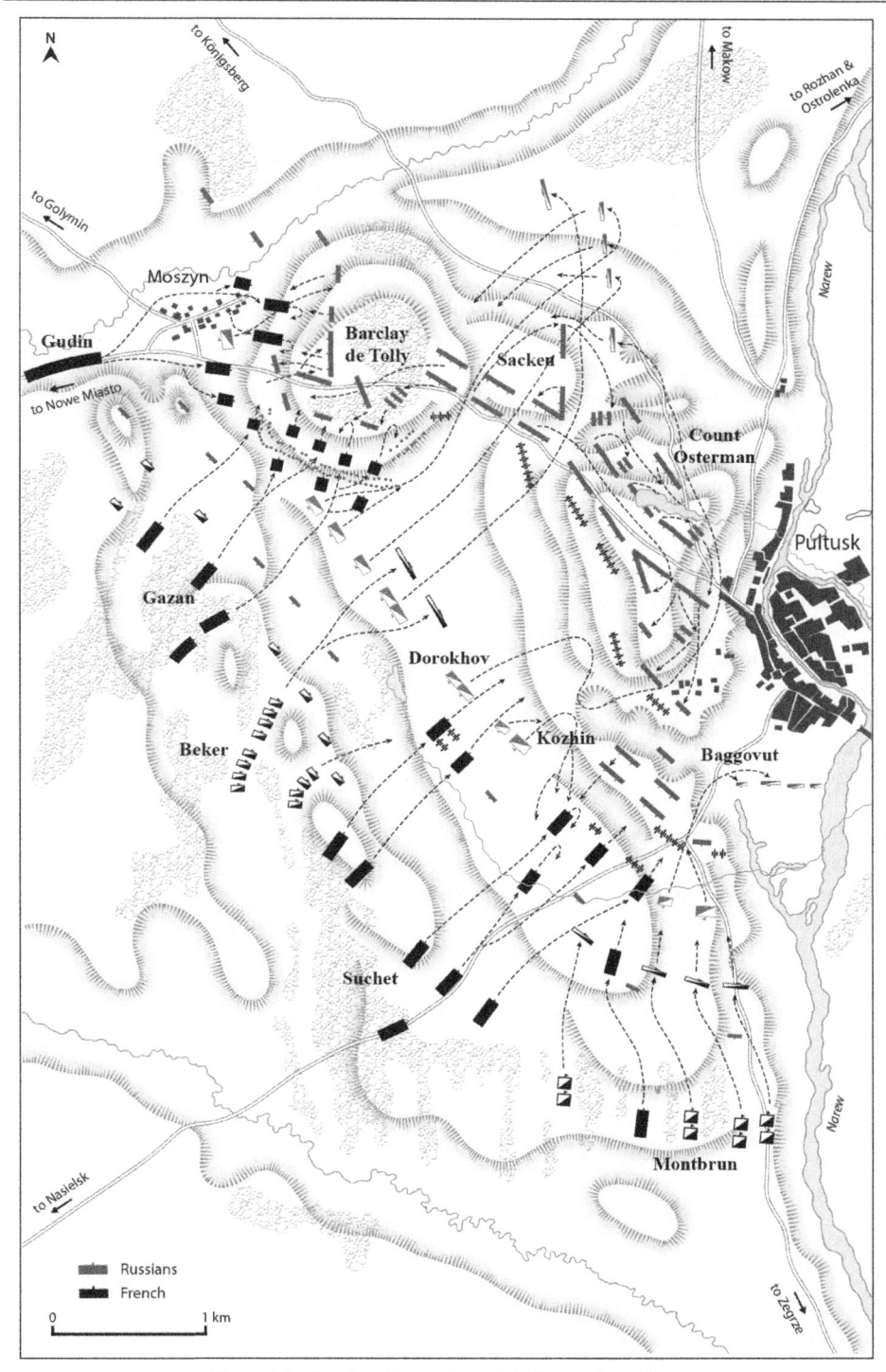

# THE ARMY'S MANOEUVRES BETWEEN THE NAREW AND WKRA 61

Plan of the Battle of Pultusk, 14 [26] December 1806.

duties and everything concerned with it, advising him, if there is no bread, to retire further into the interior of Prussia, because there was just one day of bread left *and other regiments had nothing, as the divisional commanders Osterman and Sedmoratsky reported*,[4] but the men have eaten everything; while I am recovering myself, I will stay in the hospital in Ostrolenka, which is included in the most faithful, reporting that if the army is going to remain in the current bivouacs for another fifteen days, then in the spring not a single healthy man will remain. Moreover, with an open heart, before my Sovereign, I confess that, during my current short stay with the army, I have not been myself: having no resolve, no patience for such work or time and, most of all, none of my old eyesight and, without that, had to rely on other men's reports, which were not always true. Count Buxhoeveden, I boldly hope will accomplish everything, as I did; not the slightest disorder was noted in his *corps d'armée*. Can a man of my rare age endure the current bivouacs? Dismiss the old man to the manor, who remains so derelict that he could not fulfil the great and glorious fate for which he was selected. I shall await your merciful permission here at the hospital, so as not to play the clerical role, and not the commander's role in the army. My dismissal from the army will not produce the slightest indication that the blind man has departed from the army; there are thousands of men like me in Russia.[5]

That ended the seven-day command of Count Kamensky. After spending a few days in Ostrolenka and then in Lumbsee [Łomża], he went to Grodno and was about to return to the army, but at the very hour of departure he was brought the decree for his dismissal from the appointment of Commander-in-Chief, with orders to reside in Grodno. Count Kamensky replied to the Emperor:

It is all the same to me where I reside, if deprived of your esteem. I cherish that alone. That alone could draw me from the solitude to which I have long been condemned by both age and illness, but it will return to me, in that I hope for you yourself, for God, and for that I most surely dare to assure you.[6]

Having received permission to return to his estate, the Field Marshal did not live long and died at the hands of a murderer [24 August, 1809].

---

4   Italics added to indicate words written in the Field Marshal's own handwriting.
5   Report dated 18 [30] December from Ostrolenka.
6   Report dated 31 December [12 January, 1807].

# 7

# Battle of Pultusk

---

**Bennigsen's decision to give battle. – The deployment of Russian forces at Pultusk. – The opening of the battle of Pultusk. – The operations of Baggovut and Count Osterman on our left wing. – Barclay de Tolly's and Sacken's battle on the right wing. – The resumption of the French attacks. – Bennigsen's counter-offensive. – The French withdrawal. – The night following the battle of Pultusk. – Bennigsen's retreat. – Observations on the battle of Pultusk. Awards.**

Early in the morning of 14 [26] December, having spent the night with Count Kamensky, Bennigsen remained in Pultusk, with orders to fall back on Russia. Contrary to his orders, he decided to wait for the enemy in the positions occupied the day before, in accordance with the previously accepted intention, to give the regiments and baggage lagging behind the army time to assemble and then, if necessary, move back together. Bennigsen also hoped that Anrep's and Essen's divisions would have time to arrive at Pultusk from Popowo, not knowing that during the night the Field Marshal, cancelling the orders given to them to go to Pultusk, had ordered the divisions to withdraw from Popowo directly to Ostrolenka and to join Bennigsen there.[1]

Bennigsen's approximately 40,000 man corps formed the left wing resting on Pultusk. The infantry were formed into three lines. In the first, from right to left were the Lithuania Musketeers, Koporsk Musketeers, Murom Musketeers, St Petersburg Grenadiers, Yelets Musketeers, Rostov Musketeers and Pavlov Grenadiers; in the second were the Chernigov Musketeers, Polotsk Musketeers, Navazhinsk Musketeers, Tobolsk Musketeers, Volhynia Musketeers and Nizov Musketeers; in reserve were the Tula Musketeers and two battalions of the Reval Musketeers. Count Osterman commanded the left wing and Sacken the right. Forward of Pultusk, protecting the town, was Baggovut's detachment of the Staroskol Musketeers, Vilna Musketeers and 4th Jägers, one battalion of Reval Musketeers, the Tatar Horse, two squadrons of Kiev Dragoons and the Cossacks. Barclay de Tolly's detachment, of the Tenginsk Musketeers, 1st Jägers, 3rd Jägers and 20th Jägers and five squadrons of Poland Ulans, was located in front of the extreme right wing, in the scrub and bushes. The cavalry regiments, screened by the Cossacks, were a *verst* [1,050m or ⅔

---

1   From Bennigsen's handwritten Notes.

mile] away in front of the battle lines and stood as follows, starting from the right: the Kiev Dragoons, Kargopol Dragoons, Yekaterinoslav Cuirassiers, Alexandria Hussars, Izyum Hussars and His Majesty's Leib-Cuirassiers.

At 10 o'clock in the morning, French *chasseurs à cheval* appeared in front of the Cossacks. Having orders to fall back, the Cossacks withdrew, exchanging fire with the enemy. An hour later, Marshal Lannes arrived with two infantry divisions, Suchet's [Louis-Gabriel Suchet] and Gazan's [Honoré Théodore Maxime Gazan], Montbrun's [Louis Pierre de Montbrun] light cavalry and Beker's [Nicolas Léonard Beker] dragoons. Gudin's division from Davout's corps was marching along the Nowe Miasto road towards our right wing and appeared on the battlefield later. Having finished deploying, Lannes moved forwards. Bennigsen ordered the cavalry to pull back behind the infantry lines. Marching closer, the French opened an artillery bombardment against our centre and simultaneously attacked Baggovut and Barclay de Tolly. Thus, from the outset the fighting became general.

The French attack on Baggovut was savage and they pressed him. Bennigsen sent Major-General Kozhin [Sergei Alekseevich Kozhin] to reinforce him with His Majesty's Leib-Cuirassiers and two squadrons of Kargopol Dragoons transferred to the left wing under Major Stal [Karl Gustavovich Stal], Count Osterman followed them up with the Izyum Hussars, Pavlov Grenadiers and Murom Musketeers. Before their arrival, Baggovut, holding the French with the Staroskol Musketeers and a battalion of 4th Jägers, charged the nearest enemy column with bayonets fixed. Then Kozhin crashed into their flank with His Majesty's Leib-Cuirassiers and two squadrons of the Kargopol Dragoons. According to Kozhin's report, the 3 to 4,000 man column was crushed, losing 300 men taken prisoner.[2] Major-General Dorokhov [Ivan Semënovich Dorokhov], moving in front of Count Osterman with the Izyum Hussars and having seen Kozhin's charge, raced to join with him, but arrived at a time when the cuirassiers had already accomplished their feat. This failure did not shake Lannes. He resumed the attack. Noting that the Izyum Hussars had a battery close behind them, Dorokhov directed it at one enemy column and, approaching the guns he quickly turned to the left, opening up scope for the battery to go into action. Soon Count Osterman arrived with the infantry and not only stopped the enemy but threw them back to the site that Baggovut had occupied at the beginning of the battle and held it for the rest of the day.

Lannes then attacked Barclay de Tolly again. Bennigsen reported; 'Despite the courage and fearlessness of this general, he was forced to give way to a savage and rapid attack.' The French even captured one of our batteries. The Tenginsk Musketeers standing behind it, joined by 1st Jägers and 3rd Jägers scattered in the scrub, instantly recaptured the cannon captured by the enemy. Yershov, the Colonel-in-Chief of the Tenginsk Musketeers, wounded during this action by a bullet through the arm, did not leave the battlefield until nightfall. Sacken reinforced Barclay de Tolly, personally bringing the Chernigov Musketeers and Lithuania Musketeers standing at the extremity of the first two lines of the right wing to his aid. Having taken command of Barclay de Tolly's detachment, Sacken, after bloody resistance,

---

2   Kozhin's report to Bennigsen, dated 16 [28] December.

drove the French out of the scrub. Marshal Lannes stopped the attacks on our right wing and continued the battle with a cannon bombardment here, waiting for Gudin's division, marching from Nowe Miasto. Soon Gudin appeared and burst into the village of Moszyn, outflanking Sacken on the right while Lannes attacked him frontally, ordering Suchet to renew the attack on Count Osterman. Upon learning of Gudin's arrival on the battlefield, Bennigsen went to the place under threat and forestalling the French outflanking our right wing, ordered Sacken and Barclay de Tolly to change front, wheeling the right flank back and supported them with artillery. The French bravely marched forward, showered with canister. Fending off the attack from the front, Bennigsen ordered Barclay de Tolly to charge with the bayonet at Gudin's left wing. The order was brilliantly executed and Major-General Prince Dolgorukov 5th's [Vasily Yurievich Dolgorukov] Chernigov Musketeers were especially distinguished. Five squadrons of Lieutenant-Colonel Zhigulin's [Nikolai Semënovich Zhigulin] Poland Ulans completed the defeat of the column crushed by Barclay de Tolly. Lannes halted his forces, having received a report from Suchet about the impossibility of beating the Russians, who were in front of him at Pultusk.

Assured by reports from Count Osterman about his left wing, that he would not yield a single step to the enemy, Bennigsen decided to go on the offensive. He ordered Count Osterman, reinforced by the Tula Musketeers and two Reval Musketeer battalions, who were in reserve, to attack the French. As soon as Count Osterman started, Bennigsen also went ahead with the troops of the right wing, taking with him another 20 squadrons. The simultaneous offensive of the flanks and the skilful operation of the artillery, especially the battery directed by *Flügel-Adjutant* Stavitsky – [Maxim Fëdorovich Stavitsky] later a Senator – decided the battle. Lannes persisted in a desperate defence, lasting several hours into the darkness of the December evening and finally, having realized that it was impossible to fulfil the mission entrusted to him by Napoleon, began to withdraw at seven o'clock in the evening. During Count Osterman's evening attack, Knorring's [Karl Bogdanovich Knorring] Tatar Horse Regiment hacked into the enemy several times and Somov's [Andrey Andreevich Somov] Tula Musketeers charged with the bayonet. Darkness and a blizzard prevented Bennigsen from pursuing the enemy and he decided to spend the night on the battlefield. Count Lambert stood in front of the army with his detachment, guarding its safety. With the battering and howling wind, the efforts of our troops to light camp fires were in vain. Subjected to hardships of all kinds, the Russians rejoiced and in mutual congratulations reflected on the French spending a long sleepless night. Our casualties were as high as 3,500 men. French historians show that Lannes' forces suffered some 2,200 casualties, but these statements do not deserve trust, since they are unofficial. We captured some 700 French.[3] Generals Suchet, Claparede [Michel Marie Claparède], Vedel [Dominique Honoré Antoine Marie, comte de Vedel] and Bonnard were wounded, as was Marshal Lannes himself, but lightly. A Russian bullet hit him as he was rallying one disordered column during Bennigsen's last attack, carried out under a cloud of heavy hail falling at that time. The clash of the fighting, the orders of the commanders, the

---

3   Bennigsen's report to the Tsar, dated 27 December [7 January 1807] from Lomsee.

moaning and cries of the wounded were not heard in the fierce massacre drowned out by the tempest.

At midnight, having received intelligence of the arrival of the French at Golymin, on his right wing, Bennigsen decided to withdraw from Pultusk and set off for Ostrolenka via Rozhan at dawn on 15 [27] December, taking the wounded with him. Unaware of the reasons behind the retreat, the Russian troops sadly left the battlefield, having hoped all night to be allowed to complete the enemy's defeat the next morning as a reward for their struggles. Count Lambert remained in Pultusk until noon on the 15 [27 December] and went to observe the enemy but saw nobody for a distance of ten *versts* [10.5 km or 6⅔ miles]. The whole area was covered with wounded and exhausted Frenchmen lying in the mud and carts and cannon abandoned by Lannes. There was no way to drag them out of the mud.[4] These guns, as well as those abandoned by our army during the retreat from the Wkra, remained in the mud until spring. Whereupon the Russian guns were sent to Warsaw by Napoleon and notoriously put on display as trophies. Of course, they amounted to legitimate booty for the French, but they were not captured in battle but recovered from the morass and were not Napoleon's trophies, just as it would be a lie to call a warship of any hostile Power thrown by a storm onto the Russian coast a trophy.

Napoleon proclaimed Lannes' repulse at Pultusk as a complete victory on his part. This lie is still repeated even by the best French historians, Jomini, Dumas [Guillaume-Mathieu Dumas] and Bignon [Louis Pierre Édouard, Baron Bignon]. Victory indisputably belongs to Bennigsen, although he must admit that he exaggerated it, reporting that Napoleon, who was then at Golymin, was commanding against him, having two marshals, Davout and Lannes, under his command. Having given battle contrary to Field Marshal Kamensky's orders and not knowing Count Buxhoeveden's intention, under whose command he was ordered to be subordinate, Bennigsen was under great responsibility, especially if he had been defeated. But as Catherine the Great said; 'victors are not put on trial.' And so it was with Bennigsen. Emperor Alexander rewarded him with the Order of St George 2nd class and 5,000 *Chervonets* [a 3.47g gold coin] and, soon thereafter, as we will see below, the highest military honour – the command of the Russian army against Napoleon. The recipients of the Order of St George 3rd class for the battle of Pultusk were: Lieutenant-General Count Osterman, major-generals Baggovut, Barclay de Tolly and Kozhin, and Colonel Davydovsky. Having not recovered from the wounds received by him at Sochocin, Davydovsky did not leave his 1st Jäger Regiment. At Pultusk he was hit in the chest by a bullet. Mortally wounded, he was dragged away under fire and lay in the snow until the end of the battle. In the evening, his officers carried him in their arms to Pultusk, from where he was driven in Count Osterman's carriage to Grodno where he soon died. Returning from France in 1814, officers of the 1st Jäger Regiment erected a monument above the remains of the valiant Davydovsky, which was later graced with a visit by Emperor Alexander. The Cross of St George 4th class was awarded for Pultusk to: field officers; 4th Jäger Regiment, Frolov, Poland Horse, Zhigulin, Tatar Horse, Knorring, 3rd Jägers, Kniper [Willim Karlovich Kniper],

---

4   According to the words of Captain Count Vorontsov of the Lifeguard Preobrazhensky Regiment now Prince and Viceroy of the Caucasus, who served under Count Lambert.

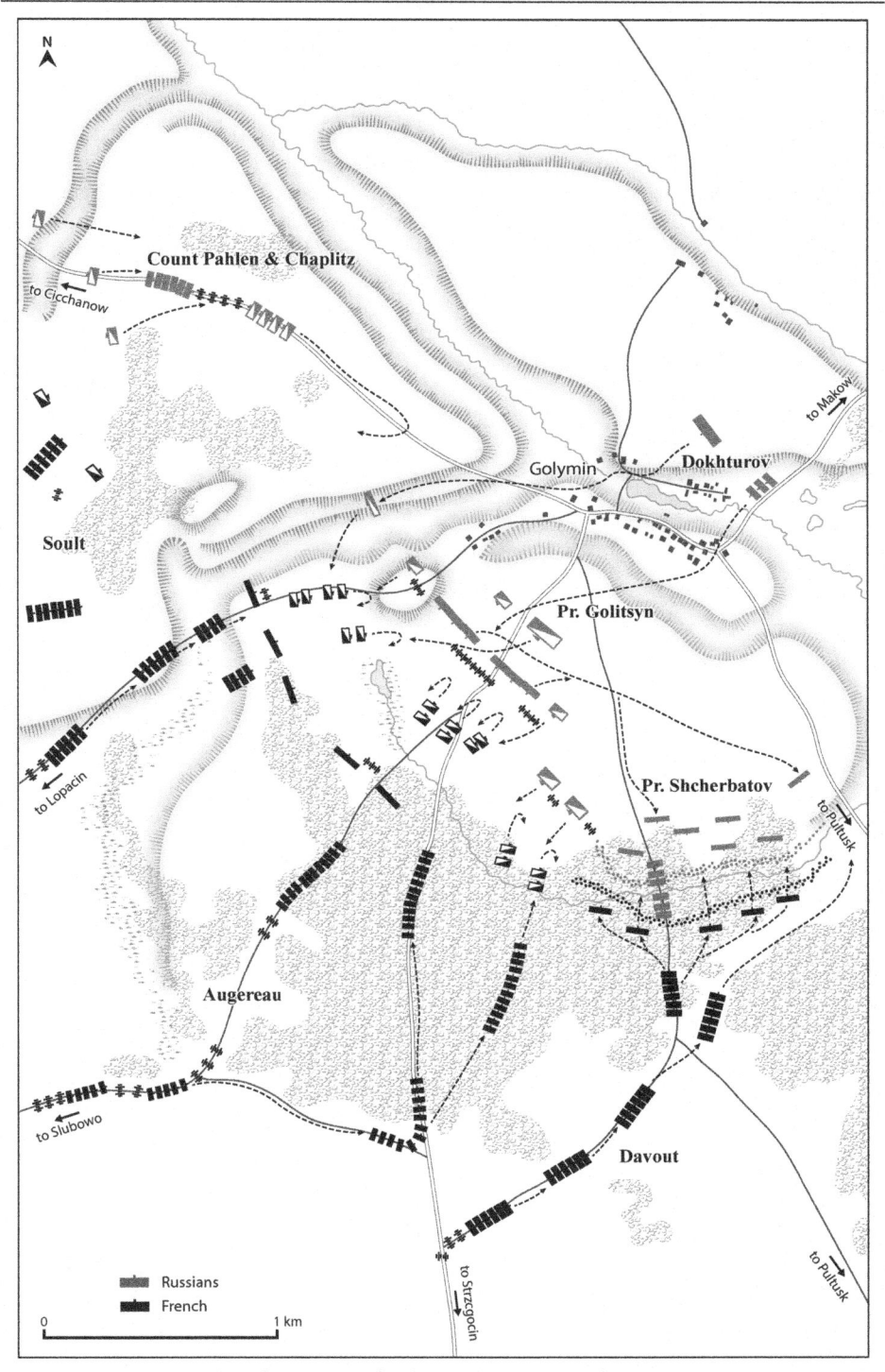

Plan of the Battle of Golymin, 14 [26] December 1806.

*Flügel-Adjutant* Stavitsky, unit Quartermaster Frederici ([Yermolai Karlovich Frederici] now [1846] Commandant of Pavlovsk), artilleryman Vasiliev [Alexander Mikhailevich Vasiliev] and Kargopol Dragoons, Stal (now a Senator). Among those presented for excellence in this battle, we find a major general, until then unknown in the ranks of the Russian army, and later loudly praised for his exploits amongst the numerous host of commanders in Alexander's century – Prince Eugen von Württemberg [Friedrich Eugene Karl Paul Ludwig von Württemberg]: his military career began at Pultusk. From the time of the Battle of Pultusk, the name Bennigsen has become and still remains renowned in Russia.

# 8

# The Battle of Golymin

**Count Buxhoeveden's advance from Makow to Pultusk. – His return to Makow. – Count Buxhoeveden's justification for not taking part in the battle at Pultusk. – Prince Golitsyn's advance towards Slubowo. – His junction with the regiments cut off by the enemy. – Prince Golitsyn's march to Golymin. – Battle of Golymin. – Count Pahlen's and Chaplitz's actions. – The reasons for the French failures at Pultusk and Golymin. – Remarks on these battles. – Austrian policy. – Emperor Alexander's orders to the Russian Ambassador in Vienna. – French revelations. – Emperor Alexander's countermeasures.**

Count Buxhoeveden, carrying out Field Marshal Kamensky's orders, issued to him on 13 [25] December, the day before the battle of Pultusk, set off on the morning of 14 [26] for Pultusk with Tuchkov's division from Makow, ordering Dokhturov, who was in Golymin, to follow the same route via Makow. After five *versts* [5.25 km or 3⅓ miles] through terrible mud, he saw a Yelisavetgrad Hussar riding at the side of the road from Pultusk and summoned his duty officer Major Fedorov [Alexander Ilyich Fedorov] to ask where he was going. The Hussar answered that he had been sent with documents for Count Buxhoeveden and asked where he might find him. Having been brought to the Count, the hussar handed him an envelope containing the Field Marshal's orders:

> Return to Makow, and stay there until Bennigsen passes through Ostrolenka and then go, with Dokhturov's and Tuchkov's divisions through Prussia to the Russian border and take over command of the army, in addition to Essen's independent corps.

Such important orders had not even been sent from the headquarters with a quick officer but entrusted to a simple, illiterate hussar! After reading the message, Count Buxhoeveden ordered Tuchkov's division to stop and pile muskets while he rode up a rise to where there was some dry ground and invited the generals who were with him to a conference. This lasted about an hour, after which Count Buxhoeveden returned to Makow with Tuchkov's division.[1] On the march, he heard cannon fire

---

1 There are still witnesses to this event: Baron Pahlen [Pëtr Petrovich Pahlen], at the time Tuchkov's aide de camp, now General-of-Cavalry and Member of the State Council and

from the left and right side – the rumble of the raging battles at Pultusk and Golymin. Count Buxhoeveden decided not to leave Makow until the matter was resolved and news could be brought to him from Bennigsen in Pultusk and from Dokhturov in Golymin and from his two divisions, Anrep's and Essen's, who were on the left bank of the Narew and had received orders directly from the Field Marshal. Thus, remaining the senior general in the army, he did not know and could not know what was happening to it and had at his disposal only one division.

Soon after Count Buxhoeveden's arrival in Makow, Bennigsen's Duty General, Count Tolstoy visited him from Pultusk, informed him of the Field Marshal's departure and requested that Count Buxhoeveden go to Pultusk and participate in the battle. Count Buxhoeveden answered that although it was only 15 *versts* [15.75 km or 10 miles] from Makow to Pultusk he would not be able to arrive there, along barely passable roads, before dusk, would appear there after the battle and still didn't know the reasons for the cannonade heard from Golymin and therefore decided to remain in Makow. Subsequently, Count Buxhoeveden was criticised for why he had not moved to join Bennigsen. In justification, he reported to the Emperor:

> I hurried towards Pultusk but the Field Marshal turned me back halfway. I could not know what the reason for this prescription was and even if I knew, as was revealed to me afterwards, that the reasons were insignificant, I could not disobey these orders, knowing how to obey my superiors strictly, as it was my primary duty in military service, although I really should not have been told to return to Makow, since I would have arrived at the beginning of the battle to strike the enemy in the left flank and, of course, would have decisively defeated him. In my life there have been many cases of attacking an enemy when I did not stop after having been commanded, when I was a subordinate.[2]

Leaving Count Buxhoeveden at Makow, while Bennigsen was fighting at Pultusk, let us turn to what was happening at Golymin.

During his offensive from Pultusk to the Wkra, Count Kamensky sent the commander of 4th Division, Prince Golitsyn, towards Slubowo with the Kostroma Musketeer Regiment, the Military Order Cuirassiers and Pskov Dragoons and 18 heavy guns, ordering him to send the Kostroma Musketeers and heavy artillery from there to Lopacin to Sacken's 3rd Division and, with the Military Order Cuirassiers and Pskov Dragoons, to form a reserve for Bennigsen, who was going to Nowe Miasto. Upon arrival in Slubowo, Prince Golitsyn went to Nowe Miasto, where the Field Marshal's headquarters was located, but nobody was there except the wounded, since everyone had already gone to Strzegocin. Returning to Slubowo, Prince Golitsyn sent men out to search for the headquarters and to request orders. He was ordered to go to Strzegocin. Night fell as he was about to set off and the Field Marshal came to him, ordering him to remain in Slubowo, to observe the

---

independent artillery Major-General Papkov [Pëtr Afanasyevich Papkov], former St Petersburg Police Chief.
2 Count Buxhoeveden's report, dated 22 December [3 January 1807].

enemy with patrols and to send to Bennigsen for further orders. That night and during the morning of 13 [25] December, regiments separated from their divisions came to Slubowo: the Dnieper Musketeers, Tauride Grenadiers and the Malorussia Cuirassiers and two squadrons of the Sumy Hussars. They had been on their way to Strzegocin. Prince Golitsyn stopped them, having learned that Strzegocin was already occupied by the French. Soon he was informed that the enemy had also been seen along the road from Lopacin. Finding himself in the midst of the French, the Prince, with all his lost detachments, turned towards Golymin, where he hoped to link up with Dokhturov. After four *versts* [4.2 km or 2⅔ miles], he was halted by his heavy artillery. It had got so stuck that for ten hours during the hours of darkness, more than half of the guns could not be saved. Seeing the futility of their efforts, Prince Golitsyn ordered the bogged in guns to be spiked; to harness their horses to the other guns and to distribute the ammunition amongst the cavalry. Continuing the movement and manhandling guns out with every step, Prince Golitsyn notified Dokhturov of his march, adding that the French were passing him on both sides. Dokhturov received this news shortly after he was ordered by the Field Marshal to go to Pultusk via Makow, where he had already sent his entire division. Only the Moscow Dragoons and Moscow Musketeers had not yet departed. He wanted to wait with them in Golymin for Prince Golitsyn, to help him if necessary and to retreat with him. Arriving at Golymin at eight o'clock on the morning of 14 [26] December, the day of the Battle of Pultusk, Prince Golitsyn had to stop due to the complete exhaustion of his men and horses.

During the action described here, Augereau, Davout, and Soult were on the march to Golymin, from where Napoleon had ordered them to turn via Makow behind the right wing and rear of our army. The mud hindered the enemy manoeuvre Augereau was the first to approach Golymin but not with his entire corps: his rearmost troops were mired in the morass. Prince Golitsyn ordered his detachment to stand to arms, in front of Golymin and sent Major-General Prince Shcherbatov – [Alexey Grigorievich Shcherbatov] now the Moscow Military Governor-General – with the Kostroma Musketeers and four guns to occupy the woods in front of his left wing. To the right, in a clearing, were three squadrons of Pskov Dragoons and the Military Order Cuirassiers. Prince Golitsyn's front line was made up of the Tauride Grenadiers and the Dnieper Musketeers and those squadrons of the Military Order Cuirassiers and Pskov Dragoons not assigned to Prince Shcherbatov's detachment; the Malorussia Cuirassiers, two squadrons of Sumy Hussars and the regiments from Dokhturov's division, the Moscow Dragoons and Moscow Musketeers, were in reserve.

Prince Shcherbatov marched into the woods. In the Kostroma Musketeers there was not a single officer nor soldier who had been in combat before. Running into French skirmishers, the regiment fled.[3] With a Colour in his hand, Prince Shcherbatov rushed forward and the regiment followed behind him. Prince Shcherbatov ordered the colours to be placed in the battalion intervals and the soldiers immediately rallied to them. That order was so quickly restored, proved

---

3   From Prince Shcherbatov's autobiographical notes.

that the confusion came from inexperience. Ashamed of their instant panic, the Kostroma Musketeers fought for the rest of the day like lions. Continuing the battle in the woods, the French also extended to their left nearby and when they entered the clearing, were showered with accurate fire from our batteries. French cavalry attacked the batteries, but was overthrown by the Military Order Cuirassiers and Pskov Dragoons. Augereau ordered the first infantry division to make amends for the cavalry's failure and to take out the Russian guns that impeded his movements, without fail. But, according to Augereau's own words 'Russian canister and an impassable swamp forced the division to fall back.'[4] Meanwhile, the rearmost troops of his corps and Davout's leading columns approached Marshal Augereau. Pressed from different directions, Prince Golitsyn reinforced the left wing under Prince Shcherbatov with a battalion each from the Tauride Grenadiers and Dnieper Musketeers. Watching the battle unfold, Dokhturov sent the Moscow Musketeer Regiment in their place and noticing an accumulation of French opposite our right wing, supported it with the Moscow Dragoons. They arrived there just as the right wing was attacked by French cavalry but without success, after which the Moscow Dragoons and Malorussia Cuirassiers went on the attack.

Prince Golitsyn and Dokhturov held on stubbornly, with the aim of waiting for nightfall to retreat. Their numbers were incomparably smaller than the enemy but surpassed them in the amount of artillery. Between 2 and 3 o'clock in the afternoon, reinforcements came to them about which they had not at all considered – Count Pahlen's [Pavel Petrovich Pahlen] and Chaplitz's [Yefim Ignatievich Chaplitz] detachments, cut off on the march by the French. The first of these was accompanied by Laptev's [Vasily Danilovich Laptev] 21st Jäger Regiment, eight squadrons of Sumy Hussars and Pirogov's Horse Artillery Company. During the general retreat from the Wkra, Count Pahlen had received no orders. Located on the extreme right wing and seeing that everyone was leaving, he also pulled back, heading for Pultusk but encountered the French at Lopacin in overwhelming numbers and was attacked by them. Here Count Pahlen came under fire for the first time – the most distinguished in the Russian army in all the wars of Emperors Alexander [I] and Nicholas [I]. He repelled the attack but, seeing the impossibility of breaking through the powerful enemy to Pultusk, turned towards Ciechanów, so closely pursued that he had to abandon three damaged guns. As he was crossing a narrow causeway, the French rushed on his rearguard, consisting of three squadrons of Sumy Hussars, under the command of Major Potapov – [Alexey Nikolaevich Potapov] now [1846] General-of-Cavalry – and overwhelmed him after courageous resistance, moreover, Potapov suffered three sabre wounds to the face and one to the shoulder. The reward for his courage and bloodshed was the St George Cross. Having arrived in Ciechanów, Count Pahlen met Major-General Chaplitz there, with the Pavlograd Hussar Regiment and with Colonel Yermolov's Horse Artillery Company – [Alexey Petrovich Yermolov] now [1846] General-of-Artillery. Chaplitz had been sent on a reconnaissance by Count Buxhoeveden and, having been cut off by the French, slipped away from them. Linking up in Ciechanów, Chaplitz and Count Pahlen marched to Golymin,

---

4    Marshal Augereau's report to Napoleon.

where both joined Prince Golitsyn and Dokhturov.[5] The unexpected arrival of these troops, immediately thrust into action, gave our generals the resources to stay on the battlefield for the remainder of the short December day. At dusk they began to fall back. At that time, the head of Soult's corps appeared on our right flank and Napoleon arrived on the scene, ordering a relentless pursuit of the Russians. The French broke into Golymin behind us, where in the darkness they hacked at the Russians, fighting with bayonets and musket butts. The next day, Prince Golitsyn and Dokhturov joined Count Buxhoeveden in Makow, having lost up to 1,000 men at Golymin and having endured a most persistent battle:[6] otherwise they would have fallen victim to a horde of enemy. Exhausted by long marches, drenched, the army fought amongst blizzards, which at times prevented identifying objects in the immediate vicinity. Emperor Alexander awarded the Order of St George 3rd class to Prince Golitsyn, and 4th class to Count Pahlen, Prince Shcherbatov and Lieutenant-Colonel Raden [Fëdor Fëdorovich Raden] of the Military Order Cuirassier Regiment.

Thus, the Russians marked the most memorable day of the whole campaign on 14 [26] December by wrecking the plans for which Napoleon had manoeuvred his army at Pultusk and Golymin. The reasons for the failure of his operations were the courage of the Russian troops and, as mentioned above, our superiority in artillery. French guns could not keep pace with their infantry and cavalry through the mud and the batteries that were in action could not be conveniently transported from one place to another. The roads deteriorated to such an extent that even the mules, laden with Napoleon's maps, food and linen, drowned in the mud. The battles of Pultusk and Golymin, as well as Count Osterman's action at Czarnowo and Barclay de Tolly's on the Wkra had a strong influence on the morale of the fighting troops. The fabulous successes gained by Napoleon over the Austrians and Prussians in the space of one year convinced the French army of Napoleon's invincibility but the first four clashes with the Russians in 1806 shook their self-confidence and gave birth in the minds of the French an idea, hitherto alien to them, questioning the likelihood of defeating them. On the other hand, the Russian generals, due to Field Marshal Kamensky's uniquely complicated orders, giving battle without permission, prevented Napoleon from triumphing and Alexander's troops celebrated the restoration of their glory, which had faded for a moment at Austerlitz. Napoleon falsely declared Golymin his victory, as he had at Pultusk, again indicating the cannon taken by him. The truth was soon announced throughout Europe.

The European states closely followed events in the theatre of war and especially the Viennese Court, at the time divided in outlook on the way ahead. Kaiser Franz and Prime Minister Graf von Stadion [Johann Philipp Karl Joseph Graf von Stadion] wanted, but were afraid of, a breach with Napoleon. Erzherzog Karl, elevated to the rank of generalissimo, was a champion of peace and by the will of Kaiser Franz, supreme commander of the entire armed forces. Fearing that war would bring new disasters to Austria, he did not dare to assume responsibility for the lot of the state. The noblest families in Vienna wanted peace,[7] preferring the integrity of their

---

5   Count Pahlen's report to Count Buxhoeveden, dated 20 December [1 January, 1807], No 748.
6   Prince Golitsyn's report to Bennigsen, dated 24 December [5 January, 1807].
7   Count Razumovsky's report, dated 3 [15] January.

estates, which could, as in the previous year, be ruined by war, to the honour of the state and freedom of Europe. Defenders of a third option advised not to violate the peace, according to a calculation that Napoleon, having exhausted his strength in a bloody struggle with Russia, would then leave them alone for a while. Trying in every possible way to justify their inaction to Emperor Alexander, the Austrians said that the war that was raging between Russia and the Porte kept their army busy, forcing them to place a significant corps on the Turkish border, to protect Hungary from any surprise invasion. Moreover, they did not hide their concern about Russia's future intentions towards the Porte, despite the assurances of our Court, that we did not seek conquest but had merely decided to force the Sultan not to violate our treaties. Not wanting, however, to show complete indifference to the war between Emperor Alexander and Napoleon, which would be incompatible with the status of a great Power, such as Austria, General Saint [sic] Vincent [Karl Freiherr von Vincent] was sent from Vienna to offer the mediation of Kaiser Franz to Napoleon in his reconciliation with Russia. Saint-Vincent was also ordered to report in detail on military incidents, so that Austria could coordinate its actions on the successes of one or the other belligerent, in a word, it acted exactly as Prussia had in the previous year, 1805, in the war of Emperors Alexander and Franz against Napoleon.

Despite such disagreement, however, one common feeling prevailed in Vienna – a sincere desire for the success of our Monarch, and the intention to turn against Napoleon should the Russian army win a decisive victory. For two months, our ambassador in Vienna, Count Razumovsky [Andrei Kirillovich Razumovsky] and Colonel Pozzo di Borgo, tried fruitlessly to persuade the Austrians to take up arms. But when they learned in Vienna about Napoleon's failure at the opening of the campaign, about the brutal rebuff he met, the negotiations took a different turn. Pozzo di Borgo reported:

> After the battle of Pultusk, Austria was animated by a new energy. Their ministry has become more amenable and, although they have not yet declared themselves, we have no less hope that Austria will perhaps abandon the deep lethargy in which it was plunged. Another brilliant victory and we can flatter ourselves that the court of Vienna will join their efforts with ours.[8]

In ordering Count Razumovsky to use this change of opinion in Vienna to our advantage and to persuade Austria to our side, Emperor Alexander wrote to him:

> Could it be that a Court as enlightened as Vienna's did not want to see all the benefits that await them in the current state of affairs? Do they not see that having missed a decisive moment now, which, perhaps, will not recur

---

8   *Après la bataille de Poultousk l'Autriche fut animée d'une nouvelle force. Son ministère devient plus coulant, et quoiqu'il ne se soit point encore déclaré, il ne nous reste pas moins l'espoir que l'Autriche quittera peut être la profonde léthargie dans laquelle elle est plongée. Encore une victoire éclatante et nous pouvons nous flatter que la cour de Vienne réunira ses efforts aux notres.*

for a long time, they are laying in a serious cause for regret for themselves, but later? How can they not calculate all the accidents of fate for Austria if Bonaparte, forced to retreat behind the Vistula, halts on the Oder and takes possession of the last Prussian fortresses in Silesia? Then the concentrated position of the French army, strengthened by inexhaustible resources, as are found on German soil, will threaten Austria directly. Their existence will be sacrificed to the whim of the insatiable conquest of the enemy, with whom they are in a fragile, insincere peace.

For his part, Napoleon did not miss any opportunity to keep Austria inactive. He achieved his goal all the more easily by skilfully directing general opinion in Europe through newspapers and magazines printed in the countries he controlled from the Vistula to Lisbon and from Hamburg to Naples. Distorting the truth incredibly with regard to his enterprises and military operations, he strictly forbade them from printing anything unfavourable about him. His threats were received with trepidation: the death of the Nürnberg bookseller Palm [Johann Philipp Palm], who was shot on Napoleon's orders for publishing a book contrary to his interests, was still fresh in everyone's memory. The descriptions of Napoleon's success over the Russians, which were constantly published, were in the hands of all, they gave the French embassies at different Courts the opportunity to successfully defend Napoleon's actions and scare them with fictitious victories. On the contrary, the Russian embassies were deprived of this weapon by their great distance from St Petersburg. When they did receive news of military operations from there it was late, they remained ignorant of events for a long time and sometimes did not know what to believe. Eliminating this inconvenience, Emperor Alexander ordered Bennigsen, meanwhile appointed Commander-in-Chief, and the independent corps commander, Essen, to be in frequent correspondence with envoys, especially with Count Razumovsky, giving them a way to refute the lies spread by Napoleon's bulletins, magazines and embassies.[9] Starting to receive reports from Bennigsen and Essen, Count Razumovsky asked the Austrian Ministry to place them in Viennese newspapers. This was refused, under the pretext that only articles already published in foreign newspapers could be reprinted in Vienna. The St Petersburg gazette, then published twice a week, reached Vienna rarely and late, therefore, they republished news from Napoleon's magazines and bulletins. Righting this wrong as well, Emperor Alexander allowed the publication of a newspaper with the true depiction of military and political events and ordered the Russian envoys to attach their reports and information deserving of publicity to special articles. Here we see new evidence of the efforts by Emperor Alexander not to neglect any means in his struggle against Napoleon.

---

9   Instructions to Count Razumovsky, dated 20 January [1 February].

# 9

# Military Operations in The Second Half of December [first half of January 1807]

Bennigsen's withdrawal from Pultusk to Ostrolenka. – Count Buxhoeveden's withdrawal. – Essen's and Anrep's manoeuvres – The general movement of the Russian army to Nowogrod. – Indiscipline on the march. – Bennigsen's carelessness – Field Marshal Count Kamensky's orders. – Count Buxhoeveden's complaints against him. – General Knorring's arrival in the army. – The Council of War at Nowogrod. – Napoleon's operations. – Bennigsen's appointment as Commander-in-Chief of the army. – Bennigsen's disagreement with Count Buxhoeveden. – Operations by Essen's independent corps and L'Estocq.

On the day after the battle of Pultusk, 15 [27] December, Bennigsen marched via Rozhan to Ostrolenka. Here he crossed the Narew on 17 [29] and burned the bridge, although he knew that Count Buxhoeveden with just half of his corps was in Makow, on the right bank of the Narew. Bennigsen avoided any junction or even for a meeting with Count Buxhoeveden by all possible means, until it was decided who should be Commander-in-Chief. For example, on the march from Pultusk to Ostrolenka, he was about 15 versts [15.75 km or 10 miles] from Makow but did not go to Count Buxhoeveden, despite the obvious need to agree on mutual operations with him.

On the day that Bennigsen departed from Pultusk, Count Buxhoeveden was at Makow with Tuchkov's 5th Division, waiting for Dokhturov's 7th Division to come from Golymin. Upon the arrival of Dokhturov, Count Buxhoeveden went with him and Tuchkov to Nowa Wies but because of the burning of the bridge in Ostrolenka he could not cross the Narew and link up with Bennigsen. As for the other two divisions belonging to Count Buxhoeveden's corps, Essen's 8th Division and Anrep's 14th Division, they were on the left bank of the Narew, at Popowo and on 13 [25] December, on the eve of the battle of Pultusk, they received Count Kamensky's orders to support Bennigsen and go to Pultusk. Then, when he left the army, the Field Marshal, without informing either Bennigsen or Count Buxhoeveden, sent orders to Essen and Anrep to hurry to the Russian border, to abandon their artillery if it delayed the march and to think only of saving the men. Essen and Anrep set out on the march in accordance with these orders. On the march, they received orders from Count Buxhoeveden to link up with him on the right bank of the

Narew, across the bridge at Ostrolenka. While they were marching towards this town, Bennigsen had already burned the bridge, after which Essen and Anrep joined him and Count Buxhoeveden remained with two divisions on the right bank of the Narew, with the impossibility of joining either Bennigsen or the other two divisions of his corps, because he had no materials to build a bridge over the Narew, choked with floating ice. Repeating to Bennigsen about the need for joint operations, Count Buxhoeveden invited him to link up at Nowogrod. Agreeing to the proposal, Bennigsen went to Nowogrod along the left bank of the Narew and Count Buxhoeveden marched there along the right. His rearguard consisted of Count Pahlen's detachment, who did not have chance after the Golymin battle to rejoin Bennigsen's corps to which he belonged.

The withdrawal from Pultusk to Nowogrod occurred in the midst of thaws and night frosts. There were no rations. The soldiers found food for themselves wherever they could. The famine created an unprecedented evil in the Russian army – marauding. Thousands of looters scattered in all directions, plundering villages and posting houses, which hindered communications with Russia. Not having chance to take prisoners of war in any of the earlier actions, the French caught a lot of our vagrants. The indiscipline in Bennigsen's corps was especially widespread. Brave to the point of heroism, Bennigsen did not care about military command and control. Garrison duties were neglected in his headquarters. Sentries were rarely posted at the houses occupied by him. In Rozhan, marauders broke into Bennigsen's rooms three times, even into his office and instead of a strict punishment, he would calmly call: 'Drive out the fiends!' But there was often no one to drive them out. Bennigsen's aides de camp and orderlies came to him whenever they wanted; at times he remained in his quarters completely alone. At that time the General Staff did not exist in the army; there were no terms of reference defined for each official post and Bennigsen assigned the drafting and distribution of orders to the first person he met. As a result there could be no continuity of business or accountability; in all parts of the administration there was an inexpressible confusion, and many precious documents concerning this second war between Emperor Alexander and Napoleon were misfiled.

Count Kamensky made this unfortunate state of affairs even worse. Having abandoned his command, he hung about for some time in the army's rear area, without notifying Count Buxhoeveden and Bennigsen of his actions which were often contrary to what was ordered by them. They complained to the Tsar. Count Buxhoeveden reported:

> Having entrusted me with the army, the Field Marshal drafts orders, which, with his remoteness from local information and with ours and the enemy's movements unknown, disrupt the good order. I order vehicles to go to the army, and he sends them in a different direction. I need the 25th Jäger Regiment and the Finland Dragoons here, and I told them to come to the army but the Field Marshal, I don't know why, sent them to Russia; having come to the army he turns back to Russia; he is especially involved in the construction of a hospital and carts in Lumbsee and he orders me to either retreat to Russia, go to Prussia and protect Königsberg, beat Napoleon, or

settle down in dispersed cantonments. For these reasons, I dare to ask for Supreme Orders, or to expedite my removal from the supreme commander, or to forbid him, so as not to impede me in my decisions.[1]

The misunderstandings between Count Buxhoeveden and Bennigsen did not give hope for the restoration of good order. Bennigsen did not consider himself obligated to fulfil the will of the Field Marshal, who had ordered him to come under Count Buxhoeveden's command before his departure from the army. As an independent corps commander, Bennigsen believed that such subordination required a Supreme decree. At the same time, General Knorring [Bogdan Fëdorovich Knorring] came to the army, who would later, in 1809, become Commander-in-Chief in Finland. As Napoleon approached our borders, Knorring was summoned out of retirement and accepted into the service, under the condition that he would not serve under the command of anyone junior in rank and sent to the Army Abroad as an assistant to Count Kamensky. He met the Field Marshal near Tykocin, talked with him for an hour and a half on the road during a blizzard and fruitlessly urged him to return to the army. As a consequence of their meeting, Knorring caught a cold. Having lain in bed for several days, he joined the army during Count Buxhoeveden's dissent with Bennigsen. He was senior to both of them, would not recognise their authority and saw them as incapable of commanding an army.[2] This was not something that happened in Napoleon's camp. The unity of thought and will of the great commander was blindly performed by his Marshals. Fortunately, the severity of winter stopped Napoleon's operations: otherwise, the consequences of our lack of authority could have done us the greatest harm.

On 19 [31] December, Count Buxhoeveden arrived in Nowogrod with Tuchkov's and Dokhturov's divisions and began building a pontoon bridge over the Narew but it would not hold. A day later, a bridge of barges was built. Having ordered his corps to cross over to the right bank of the Narew, Bennigsen went to Nowogrod, where a Council of War was convened, which was attended by Knorring, Count Buxhoeveden, Bennigsen, Count Tolstoy, Steinheil and the divisional commanders Tuchkov and Prince Golitsyn. They unanimously proposed:

1. To transfer the entire army to the right bank of the Narew and go to Johannisburg [Pisz], so as not to let the enemy cross our borders through northern Prussia, deprive the French of food in this area and stop Napoleon's offensive operations there.
2. Essen 1st's independent corps will move from Brest and stand between Zambrow and Wysokie Mazowieckie.
3. If it becomes necessary to retreat, then the army and Essen are to go to the Russian border via Knyszyn to Sokolka.

---

1   Count Buxhoeveden's report, dated 28 December [9 January 1807].
2   Knorring's letter to the Minister of Foreign Affairs, Budberg, dated 31 December [12 January 1807]: *Il m'est impossible de voir dans les généraux en chef des hommes que les circonstances reclament.*

As soon as the council ended and Bennigsen returned to the left bank of Narew, the bridge was broken by ice, over which only part of 8th Division had managed to cross. After this unpleasant incident, they marched to Tykocin: Bennigsen on the left bank of the Narew and Count Buxhoeveden on the right. On 28 December [9 January 1807] they arrived in Tykocin, where there was a strong bridge and the army was united. The magazines located in this town were a real joy to the starving troops.

The French quietly followed Count Buxhoeveden and Bennigsen from Pultusk and Golymin, meeting the same obstacles as us on the way. Their artillery and wagons were bogged down in the mud, which Napoleon then referred to as the fifth element. The French made short marches, stopping before dusk. At that time, Napoleon had not yet neglected the health of the troops, as in his later wars with Emperor Alexander, and took care to supply the men with everything they needed in a fatherly manner. Content with the Russian retreat and the occupation of the Polish regions belonging to Prussia, Napoleon stopped his advance on 18 [30] December and left for Warsaw, stationing the army in cantonments. Lannes' corps stood between the Narew and the Bug, Davout around Pultusk, Soult at Makow, Augereau at Wyszogród on the banks of the Vistula, the *Garde* in Warsaw, Ney at Mlava, Bernadotte around Elbing [Elbląg]. The troops of the Confederation of the Rhine and the Poles recruited by Napoleon were assembling at Thorn; they were assigned to besiege Danzig and Graudenz.

Bennigsen and Count Buxhoeveden remained at Tykocin for two days in order to give the army a much needed rest and, on 30 December [11 January], carrying out the requirements of the Council of War, which had taken place in Nowogrod, they moved to Johannisburg. On the march the signed decrees were received ordering Bennigsen to take over the command of the Army Abroad and for Count Buxhoeveden to be the Military Governor of Riga. Emperor Alexander, having received a report on the departure of Field Marshal Kamensky from the army, appointed Count Buxhoeveden as Commander-in-Chief, but the decree already signed by the Monarch was not sent before a report of the Battle of Pultusk arrived in St Petersburg. After this, the appointment of Count Buxhoeveden was cancelled and Bennigsen received the following Supreme Rescript:[3]

> It is with particular pleasure that I express my gratitude to you for the battle of Pultusk. The advanced skills that you have demonstrated on this day give you a new right to act on My authority and there is no greater proof than entrusting you with the supreme command over the army, including Essen's corps. I have no doubt that you will justify My decision and bring about new feats to testify My appreciation to you.

Emperor Alexander also subordinated Rimsky-Korsakov's reserve army, forming at Grodno and Vilna, to Bennigsen despite the fact that he was junior in rank to Korsakov. In entrusting Bennigsen with the command of His forces, Emperor

---

3   The decree on the appointment of Count Buxhoeveden was kept in the Office of the Minister of War.

Alexander ordered him to use the strictest measures to halt the disorder in the army, especially marauding, and granted him the right to execute capital punishment. He vested this same authority in the Duty General Count Tolstoy and allowed him to shoot vagrants and violators, at his discretion, without mercy, without asking Bennigsen's permission.[4] Wishing to stamp out this evil with all his power, the Emperor intended to give the right to the death penalty even to divisional commanders.[5]

During the 1 [13] January 1807, arriving in Biala, Bennigsen took on the rights of the Commander-in-Chief and announced this in an order to the army. Count Buxhoeveden went to Riga, writing a letter to the Tsar justifying his actions. He accused Bennigsen in strong language, especially because, having received an order from Count Kamensky that he was under his command, he was told nothing; had presented his reports to the Emperor without his knowledge; unnecessarily accelerated the march during the retreat from Pultusk; crossed the Narew and burned the bridge in Ostrolenka, exposing Count Buxhoeveden with two divisions as a sacrifice to the French; avoided combined operations with him, which disrupted his planning and, finally, allowed all kinds of indiscipline in the army, even the robbing of locals. Count Buxhoeveden's complaints remained uninvestigated. Complaining at his removal from the army and believing that it was based off an unjust report by Bennigsen, Count Buxhoeveden challenged him to a duel, naming Memel [Klaipėda] as the battlefield.[6] Bennigsen replied that he was answerable to the Government for his actions, not to private individuals.[7]

Having described events in the main theatre of war, we will now depict the operations of Essen 1st's and L'Estocq's independent corps. On his way from St Petersburg to the army, on 5 [17] December, Field Marshal Kamensky ordered Essen to go from Brest to Wyszków on the Bug and to establish communications with Count Buxhoeveden, then on the 10 [22 December], he ordered him to return to Brest, keeping the troops as concentrated as possible so as to be secure from any direction. On 15 [27] December, the Field Marshal notified Essen that, having entrusted the army to Count Buxhoeveden, he left Essen's corps independent, not subordinated to Count Buxhoeveden. Four days later, on the 19 [31 December], the Field Marshal, although he had already handed over command of the army, ordered Essen to send one division to Bennigsen, who also demanded it from Essen. On the day he received these orders, Essen also received orders from Count Buxhoeveden to depart from Brest with his corps for Wysokie Mazowieckie. The courier carrying this order was intercepted by the Field Marshal, who ordered Essen, via the same courier, not to carry out the movement commanded by Count Buxhoeveden. Reporting to the Emperor about these contradictory orders that had rendered him

---

[4] The Tsar's handwritten letter to Count Tolstoy, dated 3 [15] January, 1807: *Je vous prescris d'user de mon nom pour des actes d'autorité partout où vous le jugerez nécessaire, sans craindre jamais d'être désavoué. Faites fusiller tout de suite, sur la place, sans la moindre compassion, et sans attendre la permission du général en chef.*

[5] The Tsar's hand-written letter to Count Tolstoy, dated 3 [15] January, 1807.

[6] Count Buxhoeveden's challenge to Bennigsen, dated 11 [23] March.

[7] Bennigsen's reply to Count Buxhoeveden, dated 9 [21] April.

ineffective throughout the whole of December, Essen intended to remain in Brest until the question was decided whom to obey, Count Kamensky, Bennigsen or Count Buxhoeveden. Moreover, he considered his stay at Brest necessary in order to protect the borders of Russia, if Napoleon were to violate the neutrality of Galicia and turn towards our borders.[8] In early [mid] January 1807, Essen's bewilderment was resolved by the assertion of unity of command in the army and Bennigsen's orders with the objective of defending the area between Grodno and Brest.[9]

Finally, with regard to L'Estocq, he was in Strasburg at the beginning of Napoleon's offensive operations, with orders not to lose communications with the Russian army and to defend Old Prussia, especially Königsberg. On 11 [23] December, the day the French crossed the Wkra and Narew, L'Estocq sent a 6,000 man detachment to Bieżuń, with orders to remain between his corps and our army. The detachment was encountered by Bessières, who was marching ahead of Ney and Bernadotte and defeated with the loss of five guns, after which L'Estocq made his way from Strasburg to Soldau [Działdowo] to rejoin his defeated detachment and be closer to the Russians. Having cut him off from the Narew, Napoleon ordered the aforementioned French Marshals to observe L'Estocq with some of their troops while the remainder established communications with the main French army via Mlawa. This was the situation when Napoleon stopped any further offensive operations and dispersed the troops into winter quarters. L'Estocq moved behind Neidenburg [Nidzica], holding the road to Königsberg and maintaining communications with Bennigsen via Johannisburg.

L'Estocq's failure, the departure from the army of Field Marshal Count Kamensky, the disagreement between Count Buxhoeveden and Bennigsen and, finally, the retreat of our army from Pultusk and Makow filled the Prussian Court, located in Königsberg, with fear. The court servants, the treasury, precious objects and the most important state archives were sent from Königsberg to Memel. The Prussian King sent Major Klüx [Joseph Friedrich Karl von Klüx] to convince Count Buxhoeveden and Bennigsen not to abandon Prussia, promising to take every possible care of the food supply for their troops. Captain Schoeler – [Reinhold Otto Friedrich August von Schoeler] later the Prussian Envoy to our Court – was ordered to hurry to St Petersburg and to beg Emperor Alexander to order the Russian troops to remain in Prussia. A few days later, the King, with his family and ministers, went from Königsberg to Memel and, soon after arriving in this city, lying on the extreme edge of East Prussia, he was comforted to receive a notification from Emperor Alexander that Russian troops would protect him to the bitter end.

---

8  Essen's report to the Tsar, dated 22 December 1806 [2 January, 1807].
9  Essen's reports to the Tsar, dated 5 and 6 [17 and 18] January, 1807.

# 10

# Bennigsen's Offensive

**Bennigsen's orders for an offensive. – His objectives. – The start of operations. – Disagreement with the King of Prussia on a truce. – Bennigsen's intention to smash Bernadotte or Ney. – Action at Liebstadt. – The battle of Mohrungen. – Count Pahlen's attack at Mohrungen. – The army's new schedule. – The end of Bennigsen's offensive.**

In the first days of 1807 [mid January], a new phase began for the Russian troops with the start of Bennigsen's command. Switching to the offensive, Bennigsen had behind him:

1. Sedmoratsky with most of the 6th Division, ordered to remain in Gonionds by him, protecting the army's rear and to come under Essen's command and in communications with him – 8,000 men.
2. In Biala, for Sedmoratsky's communications with the main army – 1,100 men.
3. The Tatar Ulan Regiment were assigned to maintain order in the convoys following the army from Grodno and Białystok – 650 men.
4. In Tykocin, in the magazines – 360 men.
   Total in these detachments – 10,110 men.

The purpose of Bennigsen's offensive was to prevent Napoleon from occupying Königsberg or Pillau, the possession of which would enable him to block our overland communications with Danzig and dominate the coast of the Baltic Sea from this fortress to Königsberg. The preservation of Königsberg was also important because the Prussians were stocking up warehouses of bread and military supplies there and the fall of this city, the second capital of Prussia, would, in the general opinion, deprive the Monarchy of the last of its diminished forces.

Beginning to carry out his operational plan, Bennigsen entrusted the right wing to Tuchkov, the left to Count Osterman, the centre to Dokhturov, the reserve to Somov and Count Kamensky – [Nikolai Mikhailovich Kamensky] later the conqueror of Finland. He ordered Essen 1st's independent corps to depart from Brest to Brańsk and defend Russia's borders from Brest to Grodno. On 4 [16] January, the army advanced from Biala between the lakes, amidst the snow and cloaks. The first march was to Arys [Orzysz], the second to Rhine [Ryn]. Three vanguards, one under Markov [Evgeny Ivanovich Markov], another under Barclay de Tolly, and the third under Baggovut, marched on the left, around the lakes, securing the army's march.

Of the French marshals, Ney was the first to receive intelligence on the movement of the Russian advanced troops, as he had moved his corps forward from their winter quarters unilaterally and without Napoleon's orders, and General Colbert's [Auguste François-Marie de Colbert-Chabanais] vanguard had even occupied Guttstadt [Dobre Miasto]. Hearing about the appearance of Cossacks from various directions, Ney ordered Colbert to offer a meeting with General L'Estocq, who was waiting near Königsberg and to the Governor-General of Königsberg, Rüchel. The offer was taken. Speaking of the need to rest the troops in the harsh winter, Colbert proposed a truce, with the condition not to start hostilities without giving four days' notice. The King of Prussia gave orders to reply to the French that he would not enter into any negotiations without the knowledge of Emperor Alexander and wrote to Bennigsen:

> The truce is disgusting to me: stopping your movements, it will give rise to false talk. I wish to eliminate any act that runs counter to the views of Emperor Alexander. The French proposal proves that, not accustomed to operating in the winter, they only want to buy time and assure us that we have nothing to fear for Königsberg and they have no hostile intentions against it. I would be better pleased to obtain my salvation from the brave army of Emperor Alexander, rather than relying on the ambiguous and unreliable promises of our enemies. The decisive moment approaches: of course you shall seize it.

Bennigsen continued the offensive and on 9 [21] January reached Bischofstein [Bisztynek]. The Cossacks from our vanguards began to seize French patrols and foragers, already being close to the winter quarters occupied by the enemy. Bennigsen found out from prisoners that Bernadotte's corps was in Elbing and Ney's corps was 70 *versts* [73.5 km or 46½ miles] from there, between Guttstadt and Allenstein [Olsztyn] and that both corps were a fairly long distance from Napoleon's main force. This intelligence inspired Bennigsen to cut them off from one another, to get between them and then smash either Bernadotte or Ney. Having sent strong detachments to unsettle Ney's vanguard and Guttstadt, Bennigsen went from Bischofstein towards Heilsberg, from where he intended to move on Liebstadt [Miłakowo]. Concerned about the appearance of Russian detachments from various directions, Ney hastily abandoned his winter quarters and concentrated his scattered corps to his rear, near Hohenstein [Olsztynek], where he wanted to await Bennigsen's future intentions and orders from Napoleon. He wrote to Marshal Berthier [Louis-Alexandre Berthier]; 'I don't think the Russians have sufficient strength to attack me. At the moment, I see they have a lot of cavalry, not enough infantry and I don't notice artillery at all.' These words from Ney, taken from a report intercepted by the Cossacks, prove that on 10 [22] January he still did not know about Bennigsen's general advance.

On 11 [23] January, Bennigsen arrived in Heilsberg and moved to Wormditt [Orneta] the next day. In the evening, Markov halted five *versts* [5.25 km or 3⅓ miles] short of Liebstadt with his vanguard. Soon afterwards, having heard that Liebstadt was held by a weak French detachment, from locals who came to him from this town, Markov decided to seize it that same night. For this attack, he assigned two battalions, one from 5th Jägers and the other from the Pskov Musketeer Regiment, ordering the regimental commanders, Gogel [Fëdor Grigorievich Gogel] and Lashkarev [Pavel Sergeevich Lashkarev], who was famous for his brilliant courage (now deprived of his sight after an incredible wound to the head, which he received while defending the Shevardino redoubt) to go with them. They approached Liebstadt in the darkness and learned from a townsman who came to them that there were many more Frenchmen in the town than Markov had supposed. Without hesitation, Gogel and Lashkarev ordered an attack and quickly penetrated the outposts. Caught off-guard and half asleep, the enemy defended themselves in the houses and streets, as Napoleon's soldiers, at that time, would not think of surrender without a bloody battle. The French were overrun and fled the town, having lost 16 officers and 270 privates as prisoners of war and many killed.[1] Our casualties were 27 men. The prisoners admitted to Markov that they belonged to Bernadotte's vanguard, consisting of the division under General Pacthod [Michel-Marie Pacthod] (taken by Emperor Alexander at Fère-Champenoise) and that Bernadotte was on the way to Mohrungen [Morąg]. Without understanding the significance of this statement, at dawn on 13 [25] January, Markov continued to move via Liebstadt towards Mohrungen. Lieutenant-General Anrep followed half a days' march behind him, with several regiments of cavalry; the army marched that day from Wormditt to Liebstadt.

Bernadotte received the intelligence of a large-scale advance made by the Russian army, while in Elbing. Reporting to Napoleon in Warsaw, the experienced warrior realized the need to move closer to the locations of the French army and, not anticipating orders, he immediately left Elbing, intending to establish communications with Ney. Following forced marches, Bernadotte reached Mohrungen with most of his corps as Markov was approaching the village of Georgenthal [Jurki], where the French pickets were located. The Cossacks seized them; only one hussar escaped and managed to warn Bernadotte about the closeness of the Russians. Wishing to give the rearmost troops and all the baggage of his corps time to assemble at Mohrungen, Bernadotte turned towards Markov, having also ordered Dupont's [Pierre Antoine Dupont] Division, hurrying up from Elbing, not to go to Mohrungen but to turn Markov's right flank. For his part, Markov, having heard from the seized picket that Bernadotte was in Mohrungen, concluded that, being a Marshal, there would be a lot of troops with him, which is why, having passed Georgenthal, he stopped on the high ground and deployed his detachment into battle order. The Pskov Musketeer Regiment was on the right wing; and the 25th Jägers on the left; the Yekaterinoslav Grenadiers were in the second line; two battalions of 5th Jägers were deployed as skirmishers forward of the position, with their third battalion forming the reserve; the Yelisavetgrad Hussars were the vanguard. Protecting himself from being

---

1   Dumas, *Précis des évènemens militaires*. Tome XVII, p. 311: *Nos courageux soldats s'opiniatrèrent à se défendre; ils surent paesque tous pris ou tués; cent dragons furent entièrement détruits.*
   *55e Bulletin de la Grande armée*. Napoleon himself mentions this failure in passing, saying: *Une colonne russe s'est portée sur Liebstadt, et a enlevé une demie compagnie de voltigeurs.*

BENNIGSEN'S OFFENSIVE 85

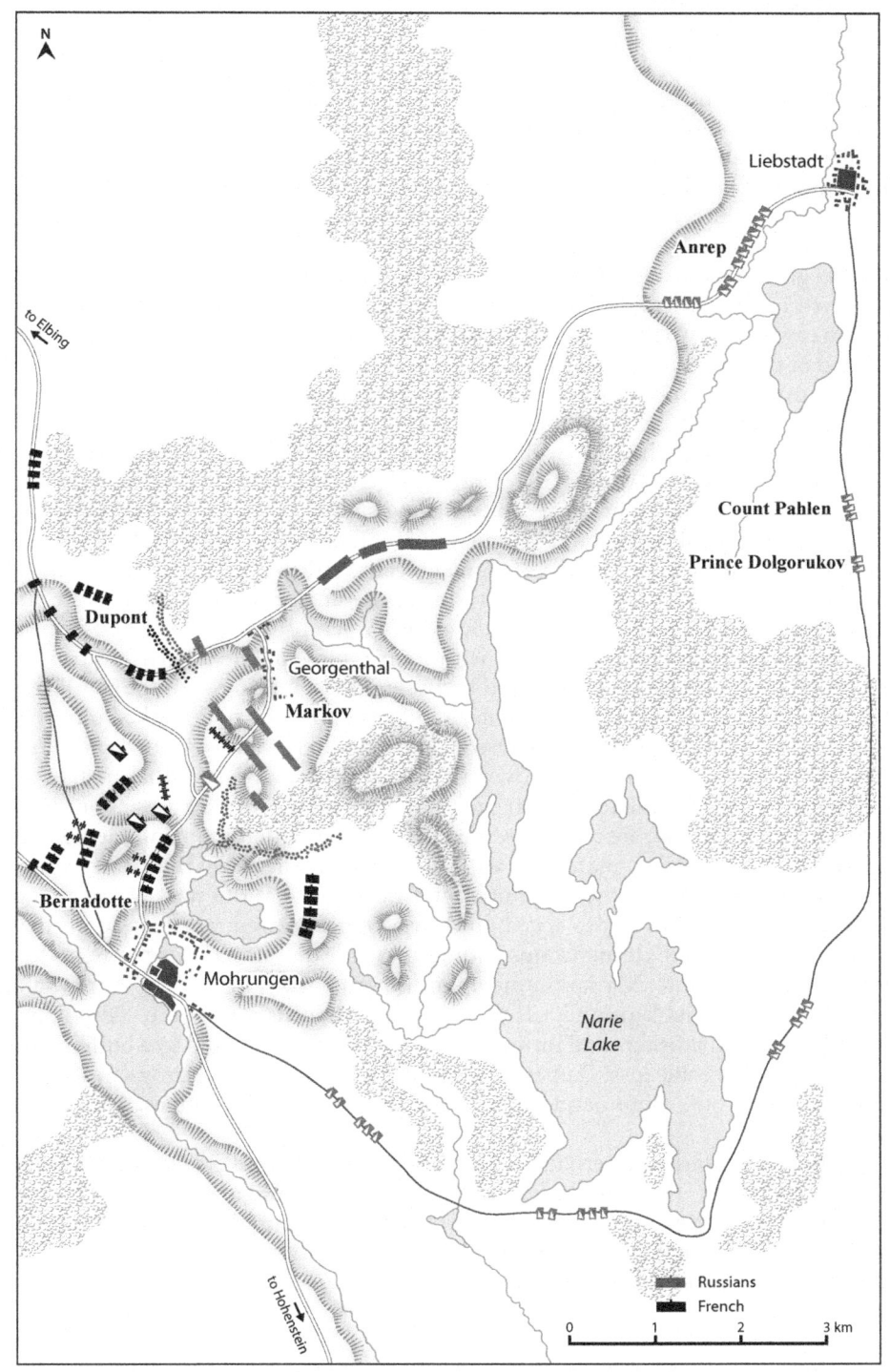

Plan of the Action at Mohrungen, 13 [25] January 1807.

outflanked, Markov sent two battalions of 7th Jägers along the road to the right of Georgenthal, which he occupied with another battalion from this regiment. Cossack patrols rode out in various directions.

As soon as the deployment was complete, at 1 o'clock in the afternoon, French cavalry attacked the Yelisavetgrad Hussar Regiment and was repulsed. Running back, they stopped by their horse artillery, which had just come into action. The fire of the French battery forced our hussars to fall back. Wanting to make amends for their initial failure, the French cavalry rushed after our hussars. Gogel with the 5th Jäger Regiment and Colonel Yermolov with his horse artillery company, passing the Yelisavetgrad men themselves, stopped the Frenchmen with cannon and small arms fire, after which they fell back to the position and stood on its left wing. This marked the end of the vanguard action.

Approaching our positions, Bernadotte unmasked his batteries. In order to deliver a general attack, he had waited for Dupont to get into our rear and sent a column to envelope Markov on the left. Soon Dupont appeared along the Elbing Road and attacked the two battalions of 7th Jägers that were there. This regiment, consisting for the most part of recruits, having suffered heavy losses at Austerlitz, fell back. The third battalion, holding Georgenthal, came running to their aid. Seeing the need to keep his line of retreat clear, Markov reinforced the 7th Jäger Regiment with two battalions of Yekaterinoslav Grenadiers, where there were still up to a hundred grenadiers who were Suvorov's veterans from Turkey and Poland: they were known as the *'Potëmkinsky'* within the regiment. The terrifying survivors of Catherine's marvellous century and their comrades, uniting with the 7th Jägers, temporarily halted Dupont. Meanwhile, another column had outflanked our position from the left. Having manoeuvred his troops into Markov's rear and flank, Bernadotte moved forward. Markov realised his mistake too late, that he had left a village forming a defile to his rear and, it being obvious that he was about to be surrounded by superior forces, he ordered the retreat. At that moment, Lieutenant-General Anrep arrived, marching with the cavalry ahead of the army, whom Markov had informed of the encounter with Bernadotte at the start of the action. Having ordered the cavalry to speed up their advance, Anrep raced ahead of them and arrived with the fighting troops with just an aide de camp as they were pulling back into Georgenthal. Markov came up to him and asked for orders. Anrep said; 'Wait, let me take a look around.'[2] Those were the last words of our hero. He galloped forward to the skirmishers and immediately fell mortally wounded by a bullet in the head. An irreplaceable loss! Emperor Alexander and the Russian army saw Anrep's potential to become Commander-in-Chief and respected the Noblest qualities of the soul in him.

It was already dark but Bernadotte pursued Markov doggedly, who was hindered on the retreat by the long street in Georgenthal crowded with the defeated Yekaterinoslav Grenadiers and 7th Jägers, pressed from the side by Dupont's marksmen, when suddenly a bombardment was heard to the rear of Bernadotte and after that horsemen arrived, reporting a Russian attack on Mohrungen. Bernadotte

---

2  According to a witness who was with Markov, the commander of the Pskov Regiment and now a Major-General, Lashkarev.

ordered a stop to the general assault on Markov, left a detachment to monitor him and, in the evening darkness, amazed by the unexpectedness of the report, led the troops back himself. The circumstances of the situation were as follows: the commander of the cavalry of the left flank of the army, Prince Golitsyn, having come to the high ground by Liebstadt, sent forward three squadrons of Prince Dolgorukov's [Mikhail Petrovich Dolgorukov] Courland Dragoon Regiment and, behind him, Count Pahlen [Pavel Petrovich Pahlen] with six squadrons of Sumy Hussars for a reconnaissance. Although they were marching about a *verst* and a half [1.6 km or 1 mile] from the field where Bernadotte was attacking Markov, they could not hear the cannon fire: the howling wind drowned out the cannonade. At dusk, rounding the Narie lake, they discovered that only French convoys were in Mohrungen and very few troops. Count Pahlen launched an attack on the town. He left part of the detachment in reserve and he went ahead and galloped into Mohrungen with the rest. The Frenchmen who were here with the baggage were not expecting an attack at all, being in the rear of their corps. During our incursion into the town, an inexpressible panic occurred. The armed men and escorts wanted to defend themselves; but they were trampled, stabbed and cut; the French rushed in all directions and hid.

Leaving Prince Dolgorukov with the Courland Dragoons to round up the fleeing French and drag away the carts, Count Pahlen made for the outposts on the Liebstadt road with the Sumy Hussars, advancing a short way and sent the *Leib* squadron to scout ahead. Soon, in complete darkness, Count Pahlen heard the movement of Bernadotte's corps coming towards him, hastily returning to Mohrungen, he retreated with Prince Dolgorukov, taking with him 10 officers and 350 lower ranks as prisoners of war. Most of them escaped into the woods at night and only 4 officers and 160 soldiers were held. Also released at Mohrungen were up to a hundred Russians and Prussians, who had been captured by the French. The *Leib* squadron of the Sumy Hussars sent on a reconnaissance in the darkness, went too far, was surrounded, but broke out through the enemy and, at night, rejoined the detachment, losing their commander, Baron Kreutz — [Kipriyan Antonovich Kreutz] now [1846] a Count and General-of-Cavalry. After a heroic defence, he was cut down and remained in the hands of the French. Returning to Mohrungen, Bernadotte found the streets littered with tattered documents and all kinds of debris. The town was deserted. The Russians and French – everyone had disappeared. Bernadotte himself had only the one uniform that he had been wearing during the battle. Our men took away his entire convoy. Bennigsen later returned all Bernadotte's personal belongings.

The day after the action at Mohrungen, the 14 [26] January, Bennigsen arrived in Liebstadt with the army and drafted a new order of battle of four corps: L'Estocq's I Corps on the right wing, consisting of Prussians and including the Vyborg Musketeer Regiment and a regiment of Cossacks, Tuchkov's II Corps, Prince Golitsyn's III Corps and Sacken's IV Corps. He assigned the vanguard to Prince Bagration [Peter Ivanovich Bagration], who had arrived that day from St Petersburg. On 15 [27] January, Bennigsen departed from Liebstadt for Mohrungen, intending to attack Bernadotte. One corps marched directly on Mohrungen, and two more bypassed the city to the right and left. But Bernadotte was no longer in Mohrungen: he had retreated to Osterode [Ostróda], along the road to the fortress of Thorn, having received orders from Napoleon, informed in the meantime of Bennigsen's operations, to have the defence of Thorn as the sole objective of his operations.[3]

For his part, Bennigsen, realising that the offensive, which had lasted two weeks, could no longer be a secret to Napoleon, moved slower, waiting for the reaction of his opponent and ordered L'Estocq to lift the French blockade of Graudenz. This order was executed successfully. When L'Estocq appeared, the troops from Darmstadt, who were blockading Graudenz, retreated, after which Bennigsen ordered L'Estocq to hold at Freystadt [Kisielice] and the other corps to come in line with him: Tuchkov at Osterode, Prince Golitsyn at Allenstein, Sacken at Sensburg [Mrągowo], Prince Bagration at Löbau [Lubawa] with the vanguard, where Bernadotte was located. *Flügel-Adjutant* Prince Dolgorukov's detachment held Passenheim [Pasym], after a short resistance from the enemy and formed the vanguard of the left wing of the army. Starting to receive positive intelligence about the French moving out of their winter quarters, Bennigsen ordered the corps commanders to be in frequent communication with each other, to help each other in case of need and to send patrols out in various directions to reconnoitre enemy movements. These were the positions of the Russian army on 20 January [1 February], sixteen days after the start of the offensive from Biala.

---

3 Napoleon's orders to Bernadotte: *Couvrez la place de Thorn par tous les moyens en votre pouvoir. Subordonnez tous vos mouvemens à cet unique objet.*

# 11

# Napoleon's Offensive

> Napoleon's doubts about the Russian army's advance. – Napoleon's orders for the offensive. – The advance of the French army. – The events that upset Napoleon's plans. – Prince Bagration's retreat. – Concentration of the Russian army at Jonkowo. – Napoleon's preparations for battle. – Action at Bergfriede. – Bennigsen's retreat. – Prince Bagration.

Having received the initial intelligence of a march by Russian troops across Old Prussia, Napoleon believed that not all of the Russian army was involved in this advance. He thought that this march, which was first reported to him by Marshal Ney, was being carried out by a corps sent to cover Königsberg. Napoleon did not pay much attention to Ney's report, because, as we saw, he did not know himself about Bennigsen's intentions. Nonetheless, Napoleon ordered the Marshals to double their precautions and repeated to them the instructions given before for actions on a sudden attack on their winter quarters. Once Napoleon had confirmed through subsequent reports that Bennigsen was advancing with the entire army, he decided to envelope Bennigsen's left wing, cut our army off from Russia and push it into the Vistula. To execute this decision, he ordered: Ney and Augereau to concentrate their corps between Mlawa and Neidenburg; Soult, Davout, Murat's *Réserve de cavalerie* and the *Garde* to assemble at Willenberg [Wielbark]; Bernadotte, guarding the left wing at Löbau, was to leave a cavalry regiment in the camp at night to maintain the bivouac fires and, marching under cover of the dark of night, move the corps to the right of Löbau towards Neidenburg, to join up with Ney and Augereau. Dividing the army thus into three formations, Napoleon assigned Allenstein as the rendezvous for all the corps, except for Davout's corps, which was intended to operate on the far right wing of the French army.

Preparing for the offensive, Napoleon simultaneously secured his rear and flanks. He ordered General Savary [Anne Jean Marie René Savary] commanding Lannes' corps, due to the illness of the Marshal, to hold between Brok and Ostrolenka, to monitor Essen and prevent him from either linking up with Bennigsen or marching on Warsaw. Despite it being winter, Napoleon ordered: Savary to swiftly continue the fortifications begun in Pultusk and Serock; Engineer General Chassel was to strengthen the Praga defences and build temporary fortifications around Warsaw; Marshal Lefebvre, who was waiting in Thorn with the German troops and newly recruited Poles, with whom he had been assigned to depart for the siege of Danzig, was ordered not to go there but to remain in Thorn and improve the fortifications of this city. Raising strongholds against Alexander's troops on the Vistula, Bug and Narew, a great distance from Paris, Napoleon could only wonder seven years later that he would bitterly but irrevocably regret not fortifying Paris against Alexander!

On 15 [27] January, Napoleon's orders were issued and his *Garde* set out from Warsaw for Willenberg, where Napoleon arrived on the 19 [31 January]. The next day he moved forward, all the more confident of the success of his operation, as he was unaware that Bennigsen had called off his offensive and he still believed that Bennigsen was continuing to move towards the Vistula, moving away from the borders of Russia and making it easier for Napoleon to get behind him. Unexpected events would disrupt the plans of the great commander. A patrol of the Yelisavetgrad Hussars seized and brought a French officer to Prince Bagration who had been sent by the Chief of the General Staff of Napoleon's Army, Marshal Berthier, to Bernadotte with the plan of operations. The hussars caught the courier so quickly that he did not have time to destroy the documents brought by him from headquarters for Bernadotte. After reading the dispatches, Prince Bagration sent them and the captive to Bennigsen and believed that, perhaps wanting to deceive us about their intentions, the French had deliberately delivered us their operational plan, having plans contrary to the orders set forth in the instructions from Marshal Berthier. However, just in case, Prince Bagration ordered his detachment to be ready to retreat. Less than two hours later, Cossacks seized another French courier, with a duplicate of Bernadotte's earlier orders. Whereupon, no longer doubting the authenticity of the documents or Napoleon's plans and comprehending the disastrous consequences of him remaining any longer in Löbau, Prince Bagration did not wait for Bennigsen's orders and pulled back to be closer to the army.[1] Wanting to disguise his retreat from Bernadotte, Prince Bagration ordered – sometime later –

1. Increase the number of fires and make the men move between the bivouac fires in order to show the enemy the appearance of some kind of preparations being made in our camp;
2. The commander of his vanguard, Yurkovsky, was to attack the French outposts the next morning, attempting to convince the French of the resumption of our (temporarily halted) offensive.

After several diversionary actions, Yurkovsky was to return to Prince Bagration by forced marches. This ruse of war was successful. Having not received the orders intercepted by the Elizavetgrad men and Cossacks, Bernadotte did not know Napoleon's will and concluded, according to the activity he had noticed in Bagration's camp in the evening and the manoeuvres made by Yurkovsky in the morning, that the Russians were actually moving forward again. According to Napoleon's orders to: 'defend Thorn at all costs,' Bernadotte withdrew from Löbau, moving closer to Thorn but disconnecting from the French army.

---

1  According to Prince Bagration's Senior Quartermaster, Eichen – [Fedor Yakovlevich Eichen] now a Lieutenant-General and member of the Audit-General, and Prince Bagration's Adjutant, Ofrosimov – [Konstantin Pavlovich Ofrosimov?] now Major General, retired.

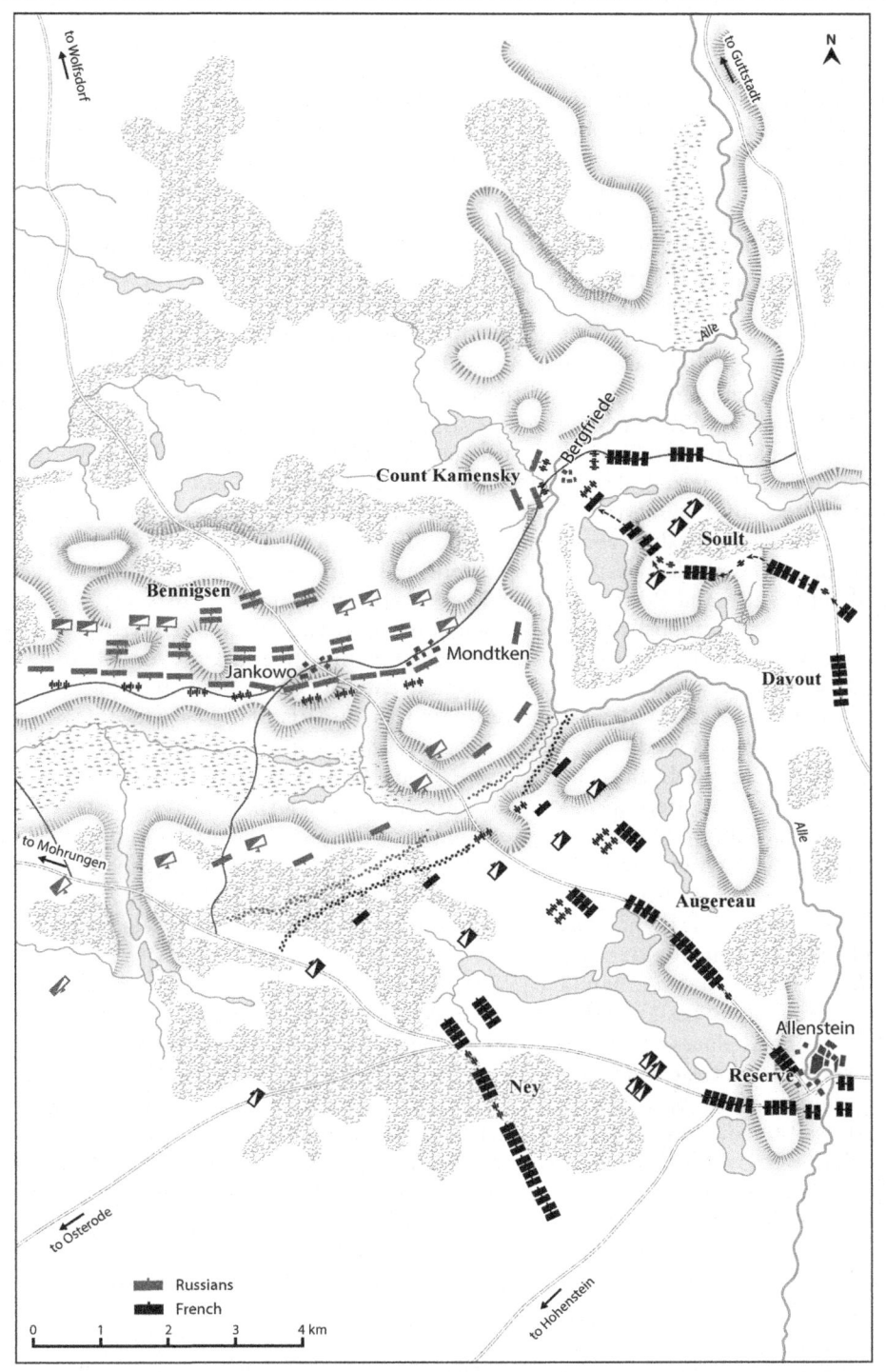

Plan of the Jankowo Position and the Action at Bergfriede, 22 January [3 February] 1807.

Having received Napoleon's operational plan from Prince Bagration, on 20 January [1 February] Bennigsen ordered all corps to immediately and quickly assemble at Jonkowo and moreover, to Prince Golitsyn upon leaving Allenstein, to leave Barclay de Tolly there so that he could serve as a support for Prince Dolgorukov when he withdraws from Passenheim. The next day, the French ejected Prince Dolgorukov from Passenheim and marched on Allenstein. The beginning of the achievement of Napoleon's plan could clearly be seen from this advance, Bennigsen ordered Barclay de Tolly to slow down the French advance as much as possible, giving the Russian army time to assemble at Jonkowo, to where they were rushing by forced marches. As the divisions arrived at Jonkowo, Bennigsen put them into positions where, at dawn on 22 January [3 February], all our troops were concentrated, except for L'Estocq's corps. Jonkowo was occupied by the centre, the left wing rested on the village of Mondtken [Mątki] and the right wing adjoined the dense scrub. Count [N.M.] Kamensky's detachment, consisting of the Arkhangelogorod Musketeers, Uglits Musketeers and Tenginsk Musketeers was deployed behind the left wing, at Bergfriede [Barkweda]. At the same time, Prince Bagration and Barclay de Tolly joined the army, having tried to delay the French vanguard for two days. His casualties from these two days were 126 killed and wounded. Loving to do justice to his troops, Barclay de Tolly especially praised the Izyum Hussar Regiment, 3rd Jägers and 20th Jägers and Prince Iashvili's Horse Artillery Company. He wrote; 'Worthy of praise, such composure and presence of mind by the commanders. Attacked by an enemy four times their strength, they faced them with courage everywhere.'[2]

Great was Napoleon's surprise when he eventually discovered that the Russian army, which he thought was on the march to the Vistula, was concentrated at Jonkowo and was ready for battle. He observed them and ordered an attack as follows: Ney's corps in the centre, Augereau on the right wing, the *Garde* and Murat in reserve. Bernadotte, expected at any moment, was to form the left wing, however, Bernadotte did not appear, having not received the orders sent to him by Marshal Berthier and having gone further from the army on the road to Thorn. As usual, wanting to win a decisive victory, Napoleon ordered Soult and, after him, Davout, to follow the river Alle [Łyna] downstream, take control of the crossing near Bergfriede and strike into the Russian rear.

Much of the day of 22 January [3 February] passed in preparation for the battle. While the corps designated to attack Bennigsen from the front were moving to their assigned places according to battle orders and a firefight was happening in the forward screen, the cavalry marching at the head of Soult's corps, at three o'clock in the afternoon was approaching Bergfriede, where a battalion of the Uglits Musketeers were stationed, from Count Kamensky's detachment. The French attempted to charge into Bergfriede but were repulsed by small arms fire and went around Bergfriede, intending to cut off our battalion, which had a causeway and a bridge, 80 *sazhen* [168 m or 187 yards] long in its rear. Canister from the cannon placed on the bridge scattered the enemy and the battalion, for the loss of six men, crossed to the left bank of the Alle. Soon, Soult's columns began to appear on the far bank

---

2   Barclay de Tolly's reports to Bennigsen, dated 30 January [11 February] 1807, Nos 102 and 103.

and his batteries thundered. The French cannon fire did little harm to Kamensky's detachment, which stood on a reverse slope; round shot could not ricochet in the deep snow. After some time, one French column moved forward. Coming under Russian artillery fire, they calmly and quickly passed over the bridge and charged at our guns lining the banks. Count Kamensky charged with the bayonet and overthrew the leading French platoons. They fled but were stopped by the troops sent by Soult to support them. Shying away from the crossing, the French turned into one huge immobile crowd: those behind were pushing forwards while those at the front were falling back, fighting off the Russians. On the bridge and on the causeway they fought with bayonets and musket butts. Finally, the French fled, blocking the crossing with their corpses. In the heat of the pursuit, Captain Andreev's [Yakov Andreevich Andreev] grenadier company from the Uglits Musketeers, was carried along with the enemy to the right bank of the River Alle but, met by a hail of bullets in Bergfriede, they were forced back with heavy losses.[3]

Bennigsen reinforced Count Kamensky with fresh troops, ordering him to hold out until nightfall, at all costs and received a report from L'Estocq, who wrote about the impossibility of getting to Jonkowo. Concerned about finding himself in the midst of the French columns, L'Estocq went from Freystadt to Saalfeld [Zalewo] and Wormditt, where he hoped to link up with the Russian army. Before dusk, Soult again launched a column across the Bergfriede bridge. Stepping over the bodies of the dead and wounded, the French crossed with the same courage and charged in a frenzy to our bank. Count Kamensky again drove them off with the bayonet after a most fierce resistance. Darkness fell; the French did not renew their attack and the crossing was left to us. Napoleon announced the opposite in his bulletin, adding that the French had captured four guns from us.[4] This lie is still repeated by foreign writers. Having presented an accurate depiction of the Bergfriede action, it must be said that since then Count Kamensky's great renown began and the eyes of the Russian army turned respectfully towards him.

Napoleon did not assist Soult by attacking Bennigsen frontally. He merely increased the skirmishers opposite our position and fired a cannon bombardment. Due to the exhaustion of the men, fatigued by long marches over the previous days, Augereau's and Ney's corps, followed by the reserves, slowly pushing through the bushes and snow-covered fields and ditches, got into position just before dusk. Napoleon postponed the attack until the next day and Bennigsen, waiting for the night, withdrew from the Jonkowo position and marched in three columns to Wolfsdorf [Wilczkowo], hurrying to get on the Königsberg road before the French and, in the meantime, link up with L'Estocq on the way. Deep snow, narrow roads and the forest made the night march difficult: infantry and cavalry got mixed up with carts and artillery; guns and carts skidded into the trees; gunners and drivers were forced to cut down trees, sinking waist deep in the snow. The protection for

---

3   The French fully appreciated the extraordinary courage of this company. When captured by us in May, the French General Roguet found out that Captain Andreev was in the same town as him, convalescing from the wounds received in Bergfriede, he hurried to visit him with expressions of sincere respect.
4   *56ème bulletin de la Grande armée.*

# 94  1806-1807 – TSAR ALEXANDER'S SECOND WAR WITH NAPOLEON

Map of the Retreat from Jankowo, 23 to 25 January [4 to 6 February] 1807.

this slow movement was assigned to Prince Bagration, appointed commander of the rearguard. Bagration's nights were short: three, at most four hours sleep per day. Everyone sent to him with orders or reports, as well as those returning from patrol, had to wake him. In wartime Bagration loved to entertain extravagantly but only for others and not for himself, leading a most moderate life. He remained dressed day and night. His clothes then consisted of a frock coat, with the star of St George, a sword presented to him by Suvorov in Italy, a gray cap on his head and a whip in his hand. In the winter campaign he did not maintain this form: putting on warmer clothes.

# 12

# The March of The Warring Armies to Preußisch Eylau

Napoleon's orders. – Prince Bagration's orders. – Baggovut's operations. – Prince Bagration's rearguard action. – Barclay de Tolly's retreat. – The action at Hoofe. – Napoleon's orders for the pursuit of the Russian army. – The rearguard action at Preußisch Eylau. – Comments on the winter campaign.

At dawn on 23 January [4 February], the day appointed by Napoleon for battle, he learned that the Russian army had retreated from Jonkowo. Seeing his plans upset again, Napoleon did not depart from his concept by which the campaign could be given a different turn: to cut off Bennigsen's route to Russia, and ordered Soult and Davout to go to Guttstadt and Heilsberg, enveloping the Russian army from the right; Ney turned to the left, towards Liebstadt, on the junction of L'Estocq's route to Bennigsen; Augereau, the *Garde* and Murat's reserve cavalry were to follow the Russian army closely, while Bernadotte was to quickly join Napoleon by forced marches to make up for the time lost as a result of his failure to receive the orders intercepted by the Russians. On 23 January [4 February], the movements prescribed by Napoleon began.

Remaining the commander of the rearguard, Prince Bagration divided it into three detachments, ordering each to cover the march of one of the three columns in which the army was moving. The detachments were each commanded by a Major-General: the central under Markov, the right under Baggovut and the left under Barclay de Tolly. We shall start with Baggovut's operations. In this detachment were the Sofia Musketeers, Belozersk Musketeers and Staroskol Musketeers, 4th Jägers and Alexandria Hussars, Sudakov's Artillery Company and Cossacks. Having marched a few *versts* from Jonkowo on the road to Waltersmühl [Konradowo], Baggovut stopped because the column he was covering was not far from him. The French approached Baggovut's position, and prepared to attack him. Count Lambert overran the leading French with the Alexandria Hussars. Having completed his deployment, the enemy vanguard commander moved his troops towards our centre and flanks. While Sukin [Alexander Yakovlevich Sukin], with the Sofia Musketeers, and Gordeev [Athanasius Demidovich Gordeev?], with the Belozersk Musketeers, held the enemy on the flanks, the Alexandria Hussars and Cossacks made several successful attacks. Having repulsed the enemy, Baggovut ordered the retreat, first to the cavalry, as the route led through a forest and then the infantry. Emerging from the woods, Count Lambert noticed a French column trying to cut us off. Count Lambert rushed to engage them with the Alexandria Regiment, ordering the Staroskol Musketeers to hurry after the hussars. The French column did not wait for the hussars and retreated. Meanwhile, the Belozersk Musketeers and 4th Jägers from Baggovut's rearguard, emerged from the forest. French cavalry surrounded them in the open. A witness to the battle, Prince Bagration reported to Bennigsen: 'Without confusion, laying down fierce fire, the Belozersk and 4th Jägers' bullets repulsed the cavalry attacks and, charging several times with the bayonet, cleared their path'. Their success was helped by two squadrons of Alexandria Hussars sent to the rescue of the rear guard under Major Lukyanovich – [Andrey Fëdorovich Lukyanovich] later Governor of Simbirsk. Having received reinforcements in the shape of His Majesty's Cuirassiers, Military Order Cuirassiers, Malorussia Cuirassiers, Pskov Dragoons and 7th Jägers, Baggovut halted, placed the cavalry on his flanks and the infantry in three lines, 120 paces from one another. Seeing the strengthening of the Russian rearguard, the French stopped their attack, waiting for their rearmost troops; the battle was limited to cannon fire and musketry between the skirmishers. Having won more time, Baggovut moved back by bounds by regiment, having cavalry at the rear because the terrain was open. The French cavalry followed us, manoeuvring but did not attack. Approaching the gorge near the village of Waltersmühl, Baggovut stopped and ordered the 4th Jägers to occupy the village and Colonel Gordeev, crossing the ravine to hold the high ground with some of the infantry and position batteries there. Upon completion of this order, Baggovut signalled the cavalry to fall back. Once they had passed through Waltersmühl, the rest of the infantry followed. The French moved forward and suffered heavy casualties from the battery on the high ground. They continued the pursuit until nightfall but getting weaker by the hour. At three o'clock in the morning of 24 January [5 February], Baggovut arrived in the village of Warlack [Worławki] and there he joined up with Markov, whom the French had not strongly pursued.

At dawn on 24 January [5 February], as Bennigsen was on the march with the army from Wolfsdorf towards Landsberg [Górowo], encountering the same local obstacles on the route as on the previous day, Prince Bagration took Baggovut's and Markov's detachments two *versts* [2.1 km or 1⅓ miles] back from Barclay, behind Wolfsdorf. Yurkovsky's Yelisavetgrad Hussars were positioned in front of the village with Malakhov's and Sysoev's [Vasily Alekseevich Sysoev] Cossack regiments and two horse artillery pieces, while the village was held by Frolov's 4th Jägers. At 7 o'clock in the morning, the leading French troops came into view. The Yelisavetgrad Hussars and the Cossacks outflanked them. Soon after, having noticed the buildup of significant enemy forces against him, Prince Bagration ordered Yurkovsky, the Cossacks and Frolov to fall back on the position. Passing the cavalry through Wolfsdorf and stopping the pursuit of the enemy cavalry with small arms fire, Frolov left the village with the 4th Jägers on Prince Bagration's right flank. Yurkovsky deployed on the left flank.

Entering Wolfsdorf, Murat, who was commander of the French vanguard that day, sent two strong columns, enveloping Prince Bagration's right wing, into the woods occupied by Gogel's 5th Jägers and Vuich's [Nikolai Vasilievich Vuich] 25th Jägers. Bitter fighting ensued. The French tried to take possession of the woods but failed. All attacks were repelled all the more successfully because the terrain did not allow the enemy to successfully use artillery, while our guns did them great harm. The French, however, did not hesitate and finally one of their columns moved boldly into the woods. Vuich and the 25th Jägers drove them off with the bayonet, following which, Count Lambert and the Alexandria Hussars and Andreyanov's Cossack Regiment cut into the column. A similar successful attack was happening at this time on our left wing, where the French had sent cavalry on a flanking manoeuvre One of Emperor Alexander's favourites, Prince [M.P.] Dolgorukov — who was later killed at Idenzalmi [Iisalmi] — charged into them with the Courland Dragoons and turned them back. Repelled on the flanks, Murat limited himself to a cannonade while waiting for fresh troops. As this action continued, Prince Bagration was informed that many private vehicles and peasant carts were crowding behind his rearguard and permission was sought to disperse them into the fields to clear the way for the army. Prince Bagration replied; 'The fields are covered with snow and the carts will be lost. Why are we the rearguard? So as not to gift the enemy so much as one wagon or one wheel.'[1] Having held fast for more than three hours, Prince Bagration ordered the retreat, sending the cavalry first, because they had to cross a deep water filled ditch over which there was only one bridge. The infantry marched behind the cavalry. Markov formed the rearguard. The French moved forwards but Markov crossed the ditch without loss, after which Prince Bagration retreated slowly and in in good order, stopping from time to time. A distinctive feature of this manoeuvre made in his presence was the calm silence. Whilst moving swiftly, Bagration did not rush anybody. The majestic composure of our hero flowed into the troops he led, giving him unlimited power and authority.

Pressing behind Prince Bagration, the French sent columns to outflank him, trying to cut him off and trap him in the villages of Arnsdorf [Lubomino] and Open [Opin]. These efforts failed! Prince Bagration pre-empted and dispersed the enemy everywhere, with one brilliant attack being made by the Yelisavetgrad Hussars and the Courland Dragoons along with Yermolov's Horse Artillery Company. Passing the village of Open and heading into a large forest, Prince Bagration covered his retreat with all his Jäger regiments, assigning the Yekaterinoslav Grenadiers and Pskov Musketeers as their support. A deadly fire raged in the forest, graphically illuminating the gloomy night. The battle fell silent an hour before midnight, as Prince Bagration passed through the forest and settled down at Kaschaunen [Kaszuny], having covered 28 *versts* [29.4 km or 18⅔ miles] during the day. Before dawn on 25 January [6 February], the French resumed the pursuit but only with light troops. Prince Bagration arrived in Frauendorf [Babiak], fighting all the way, where he met Barclay de Tolly's detachment and ordered him to form the rearguard, having received Bennigsen's orders to continue with Baggovut and Markov on the march to Landsberg, the army's rendezvous area for that day. Prince Bagration could brag of his troops, particularly the Jägers. Here are his own words from a report to Bennigsen: 'It is in the nature of the service of Jägers that there is danger at every step, incredible feats, the deprivation of all comforts, even of accommodation for

---

1   According to the witnesses, Lieutenant-General Eichen and Major-General Lashkarev.

themselves throughout a whole campaign, the security of the army was bought by the blood of the Jägers, they have a right to be favoured; it is my most sacred duty to request from you the rewards that they merit.'

Having described the actions of Baggovut's and Markov's detachments, we will depict what was happening to Barclay de Tolly's detachment, which, as said earlier, was ordered by Prince Bagration to form the rearguard of the army's left column.

In Barclay de Tolly's detachment were the Izyum Hussars and Olviopol Hussars, a battalion of the Poland Horse, the Kostroma Musketeers, 1st Jägers, 3rd Jägers and 20th Jägers, two Cossack regiments and Prince Iashvili's Horse Artillery Company. At 3 o'clock in the morning of 23 January [4 February], Barclay de Tolly was attacked by cavalry. The Olviopol Hussars, Izyum Hussars and Cossacks supported by the horse artillery, withstood the attack and several times went into the hack themselves. Their success was helped by the 3rd Jägers and some of the 20th Jägers, occupying the scrub on our right wing, accurately shooting into the French cavalry from there. Enemy infantry repeatedly attacked the scrub but fell back, repulsed by the Jägers. Only once did the French manage to get the better of us but not for long. The Russians broke the French and held their ground with Colonel Bistrom and the 20th Jägers particularly distinguishing themselves. Alarmed by their imminent defeat, Barclay galloped to the Jägers, Bistrom vowed loudly to drive the French out of the scrub and kept his word. This was the beginning of Bistrom's reverberating fame, who died as an assistant to Grand Duke Mikhail Pavlovich in command of the Lifeguard Corps.

Holding his position until 10 o'clock in the morning, Barclay de Tolly ordered the Hussars and Cossacks to fall back by bounds to the high ground held by the infantry and artillery. Several brave Frenchmen climbed the slopes with the last sections of our cavalry and paid for their courage with their lives. As the infantry retreated, the French pressure increased. The artillery of Prince Iashvili prevented them from triumphing. Only the 3rd Jägers, who were in the castle, were surrounded by cavalry. Barclay de Tolly sent Lieutenant-Colonel Zhigulin's battalion of the Poland Horse and Ilovaysky 9th's [Grigory Dmitrievich Ilovaysky] Cossack Regiment to the rescue. They drove off the French cavalry and freed the Jägers. Barclay de Tolly wrote in his report; 'Then I continued the retreat, not in a rush and in the best order but under the strongest enemy fire, who occupied all the high ground that I had left with numerous artillery.' Halfway through the retreat, Barclay met five infantry battalions and several squadrons sent for his support. Strengthened by them and having entered the forests and defiles, he screened his march with the 1st Jägers 3rd Jägers and 20th Jägers and that night he halted a considerable distance from the army. As he reported; 'I cannot praise enough with what bravery, courage and composure the troops of my detachment made every movement ordered of them, in sight of a numerous enemy, with order and without haste. I am sure that the enemy, who had all the means to break up my detachment, was only kept from further attempts through this laudable order.' For our part, in this action 261 men were killed or wounded; 146 horses were lost.[2]

---

2    Barclay de Tolly's report to Bennigsen, dated 5 [17] February 1807, No 104.

The next day, 24 January [5 February], Prince Bagration ordered Barclay to retreat no further than Frauendorf and then wait for his arrival. During the first half of the march, the French did little to harass Barclay de Tolly, preparing to intercept his route near Launau [Łaniewo], where they had sent a force by night. Barclay de Tolly learned of this enemy manoeuvre on the march from patrols sent in various directions and by forcing the march he forestalled them in Launau. Not having chance to get in the way of our detachment, the French tried to cut off Barclay de Tolly's rearguard, which consisted of four squadrons of Olviopol Hussars, a battalion of Jägers, Ilovaisky 9th's Cossack Regiment and two horse artillery pieces. The rearguard drove off the French. Then they turned after our troops, 'but at every suitable location they found cavalry or infantry pushed forward with artillery, in full readiness to receive them.'[3] Nightfall brought an end to the action. Barclay was located near Frauendorf where the next morning, the 25 [6 February], Prince Bagration arrived and, as mentioned above, continuing the march to Landsberg to join the army, ordered Barclay to form the rearguard.

At 5 o'clock in the morning of 25 January [6 February], Barclay de Tolly set off from Frauendorf on the road to Landsberg. The beginning of the march was quiet. Short of Hoofe [Dwórzno], Barclay de Tolly received Bennigsen's orders to hold on until the army had taken up positions at Landsberg and placed the army behind the river; a battalion of the 20th Jägers held the village of Sienken [Żołędnik], forward of which were two squadrons of Izyum Hussars and Lieutenant Sukhozanet's – [Ivan Onufrievich Sukhozanet] now [1846] General-of-Artillery – two horse artillery pieces. At 3 o'clock in the afternoon, Barclay de Tolly was informed of the approach of the French and of Napoleon's presence with the vanguard. Dorokhov went forward with two squadrons of Hussars to strengthen the advanced detachment and took command of it. Soon under attack, he held on as long as he could but then retreated in the face of overwhelming numbers. Sukhozanet's two guns were already being bombarded by the French batteries with round shot, so that after half an hour only four gunners remained alive; all the others, including the horses, were either killed or wounded. The prisoners captured by Dorokhov confirmed the reports of Napoleon's presence with this force. The present generation cannot have a clue about the impact on his opponents that the news of Napoleon's appearance on the battlefield made! But Barclay de Tolly remained unshaken. It was said of his composure that if the universe lamented and threatened to crush the earth under its pressure, he would gaze without a shudder at the destruction of the world. He reported 'In any other case, I would have retreated in advance since, with such an imbalance of power, to lose my entire detachment would be useless, however, from the officers whom I sent to the headquarters, I learned that most of the army had not yet been assembled at Landsberg, were on the march and no positions were occupied. For these reasons, I considered it a duty better to sacrifice myself with my entire detachment to such a strong enemy rather than to retreat, drawing the enemy behind me and thereby putting the entire army in peril'. From these officers, Barclay de Tolly received assurances from Bennigsen that he would soon send help.

---

3   A direct quote from Barclay de Tolly's report to Bennigsen.

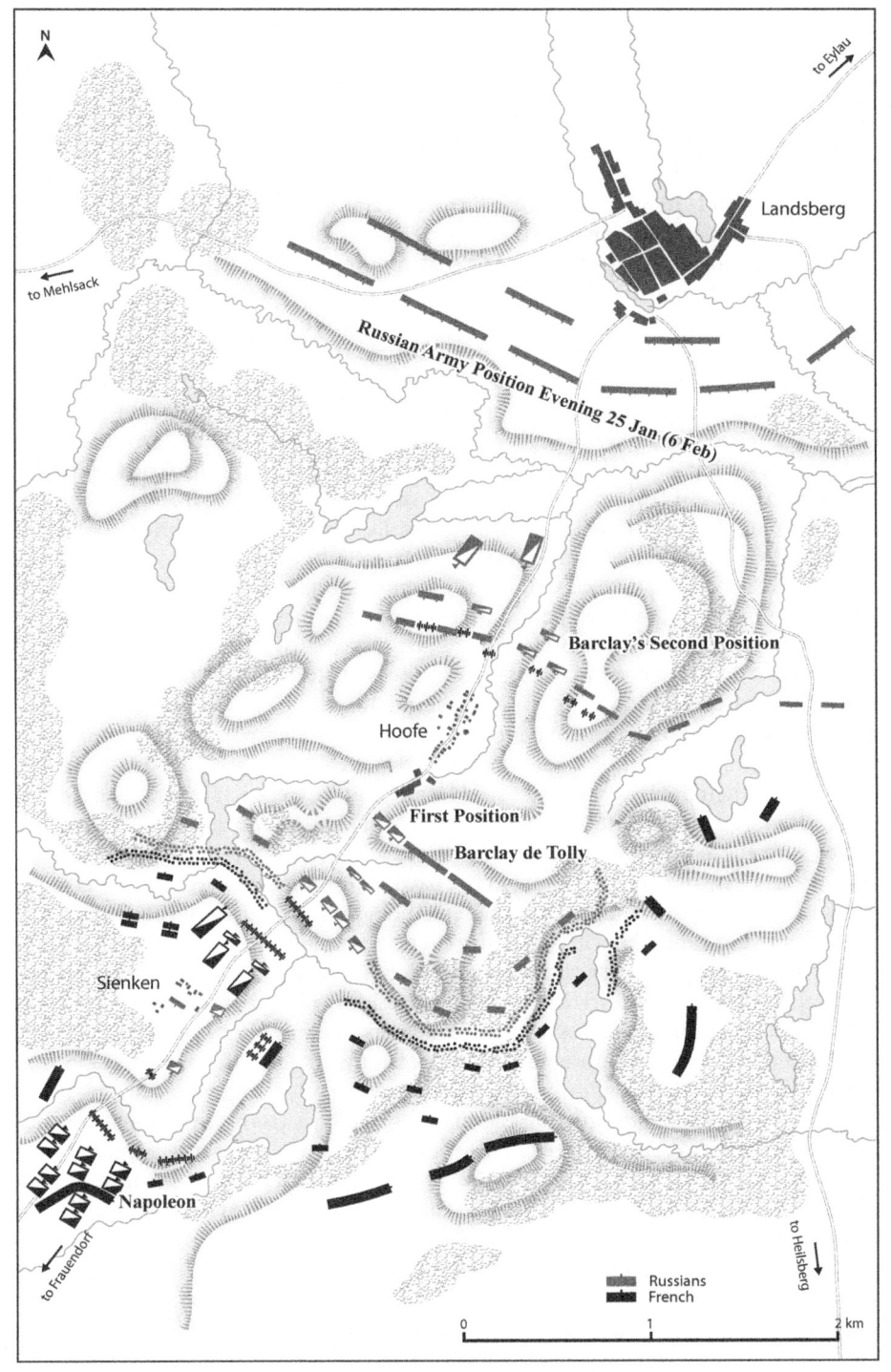

THE MARCH OF THE WARRING ARMIES TO PREUßISCH EYLAU 101

Plan of the Action at Hoofe, 25 January [6 February] 1807.

Abandoned for the time being to the will of his own forces, less than five thousand men, Barclay de Tolly placed the Izyum Hussars and horse artillery at the bridge over which the enemy had to pass; forming the second line were the Olviopol Hussars, 20th Jägers and Kostroma Musketeers; the 1st Jägers occupied a wooded hill on the right wing, while the 3rd Jägers were deployed on the left, in woods that French skirmishers had already reached. Protecting himself from being outflanked around this wood, Barclay de Tolly reinforced the 3rd Jägers with the 20th Jägers and, having made these dispositions, he waited for Napoleon. The French soon approached the bridge and attempted to cross it; they were held back by canister fire. Napoleon arrived and the fire of his batteries forced our artillery to pull back; his *Chasseurs à Cheval* quickly crossed the bridge. Dorokhov attacked with the Izyum Hussars and Cossacks and drove the enemy from the bridge. The successful attack emboldened the Olviopol Hussars. Without orders they rushed forward, past the bridge but were driven off by the French facing the Izyum Hussars and dispersed. Having managed to deploy his Horse Artillery Company, Prince Iashvili held up the French cavalry galloping behind the hussars, whereupon Dorokhov wanted to attack them, but fell from his horse having suffered contusions from a round shot and had to leave the battlefield. Moving away, he ordered the senior field officer in the Izyum Hussars to take command and to remember his enduring instructions, that is: 'before a battle, take care of the regiment as you would your bride and when the fighting flares up, do not spare either men nor horses.' With doubled strength, the French rushed forward, attacked the Hussars, drove them back and struck Prince Shcherbatov's Kostroma Musketeers. He withstood three attacks, driving the enemy away with battalion volleys. After each repulse, the Kostroma Musketeers fell back on command and by drum beat and as soon as the French cavalry approached them, momentarily turning to the front, they met them with volley fire. Raging to make up for their failure, the Izyum Hussars and Olviopol Hussars attacked the French dragoons driven off by the Kostroma Musketeers and scattered them. They did not stop there but attacked the cuirassiers who had come up in support of the dragoons. Having not yet taken part in the battle, the cuirassiers were at full strength and crushed our hussars, tired from repeated charges. Pursued by the French, they rushed back and together with the cuirassiers, a whole cloud of horsemen crashed into the Kostroma Musketeers. Barclay de Tolly reported; 'I had the misfortune to see the almost complete destruction of this matchless regiment.' It was here that the French took the guns of the Kostroma Musketeers and its colours, except for one. At that moment as a French cuirassier tried to grab this colour, it was pulled from the hands of the Sub-Ensign by *Junker* Tomilovsky, who was riding past with the Izyum Hussars. During these actions, Napoleon had placed his troops in a semicircle near our detachment and moved in from all sides. Unable to hold on any longer, Barclay de Tolly hurried through Hoofe, deciding to fight for the village to the last.

Meanwhile, fighting on our right wing, the 1st Jägers were cut off from the detachment and began to fall back, several times repulsing the cavalry surrounding it and finally, scattered by the French, escaped into the woods. The 3rd Jägers and 20th Jägers that were on the left wing, also under heavy attack, fell back in good order. Concentrating his forces and holding the enemy in Hoofe, Barclay de Tolly arrived in his second position, where he met Major-General Prince [V.Y.] Dolgorukov 5th, sent to him with five infantry battalions. Hastily deploying the detachment, Barclay de Tolly ordered Prince Dolgorukov to stay in his current position and went to the left into the scrub with the 3rd Jägers and 20th Jägers himself where the French were moving, intending to cut him off from Landsberg. While he was holding the enemy there, Napoleon attacked and began to wear down Prince Dolgorukov. At that time, His Majesty's Cuirassiers and the Military Order Cuirassiers came from Landsberg to the battlefield; it began to get dark and Napoleon stopped the attacks. The reasons for him not destroying our detachment were the onset of evening darkness and deep snow, which hindered the rapid French manoeuvres.

Our casualties at Hoofe are unknown. The day after this action, Barclay was wounded and did not have time to collect the data on the losses of men, guns and colours and, three days later, the Battle of Eylau took place. It dwarfed the previous rearguard actions with its enormity. Barclay de Tolly concluded his report on the action at Hoofe with the following words;

> It remains for me and my comrades, who have bravely fought through this action to hold our position and through this the army was protected from an immediate attack by the entire enemy force: such was our aim and our whole purpose and, if this succeeded, then all the sacrifice will have been rewarded. I leave it to your discretion – whether this was accomplished by us, or not? While I hope that justice will not have forsaken us.[4]

Having beaten Barclay de Tolly, Napoleon settled down for the night in Hoofe, in sight of the Russian army assembled at Landsberg. The stubborn three-day resistance of the Russian rearguards led him to the conclusion that, perhaps, Bennigsen would give battle at Landsberg. Therefore, Napoleon ordered Soult's and Davout's corps, detached to the right and Marshal Ney, sent to the left in pursuit of L'Estocq, to hurry and try to get to Landsberg: the first two onto Bennigsen's left wing and Ney on his right; Napoleon himself wanted to attack him from the front with Augereau's corps, the *Garde* and Murat's *Réserve de cavalerie*. Bernadotte was reminded of his orders to speed up his march to rejoin the army. As Napoleon was issuing his orders on the night of 25 to 26 January [6 to 7 February], Bennigsen sent his heavy artillery ahead and marched from Landsberg to Preußisch-Eylau, where he hoped to link up with L'Estocq and wanted to defend Königsberg. Having learned of Bennigsen's departure, Napoleon, in cancelling the orders issued a few hours previously, still ordered Ney to cut across L'Estocq's route to the Russian army, Davout to envelope our left wing, and for Soult to join the army. Moreover, Napoleon forbade Ney and Davout from crossing the high ground at Preußisch-Eylau and ordered them to be ready at any moment to participate in a battle, which he considered close, in the hope that Bennigsen would not give up Königsberg without a fight.

On setting out from Landsberg, Bennigsen ordered Prince Bagration to follow with the rearguard as quietly as possible, giving the army and heavy equipment time to get through Eylau. On the morning of 26 January [7 February], Napoleon moved out of

---

4   Barclay de Tolly's report to Bennigsen, dated 9 [21] February, 1807, No 105, from Memel.

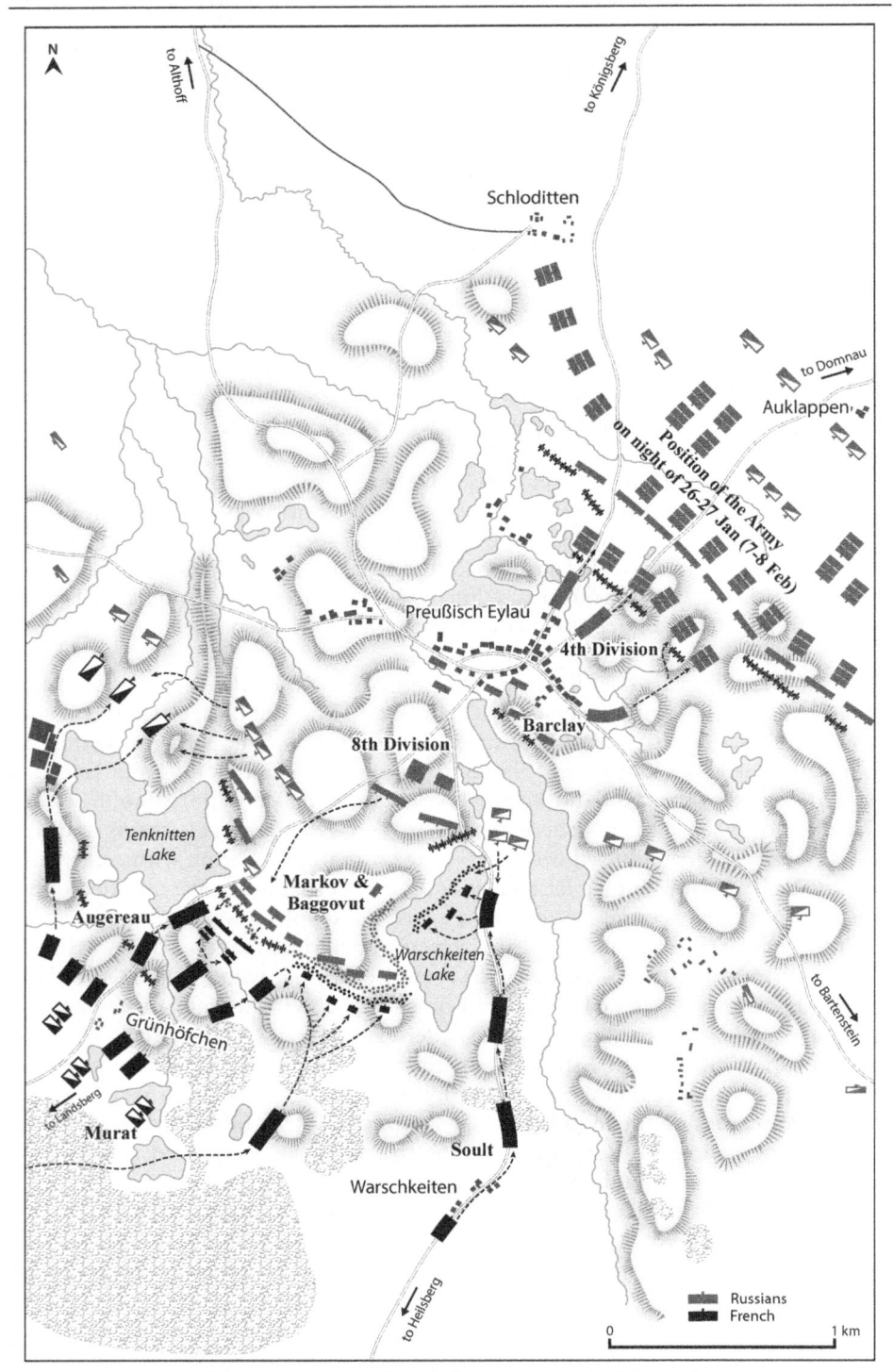

Plan of the Action at Preußisch Eylau, 26 January [7 February] 1807.

Hoofe and at eight o'clock his vanguard, under the command of Murat, was already going into action against Prince Bagration, who was waiting behind Landsberg. Prince Bagration secured his flanks on the forests and held on for more than an hour. Then he began to fall back and stopped a *verst* [1,050m or ⅔ mile] behind the village of Grünhöfchen [Grądzik], in an advantageous position chosen earlier that morning by officers sent for this purpose. Markov's and Baggovut's detachments were deployed between the frozen ponds at Tenknitten [Shirokoye] and Warschkeiten [Warszkajty]; behind them was 8th Division sent by Bennigsen to Prince Bagration and several cavalry regiments; Barclay de Tolly's detachment was placed forward of Eylau with orders to support the rearguard as Prince Bagration passed through Eylau. Deducing Prince Bagration's intention to give battle from the deployment of the Russian troops, Murat halted, waiting for the main body of his vanguard to move closer.

After 1 o'clock in the afternoon, Murat moved three columns onto the heights occupied by Markov and Baggovut. The fire of Yermolov's Horse Artillery Company and the marksmen of the Pskov Musketeers did not stop the enemy. The leading column marched in good order with shouldered arms. Prince Bagration ordered the Sofia Musketeers and Pskov Musketeers, having the St Petersburg Dragoons in support, to stop the enemy attack and, without shooting, to defeat them with the bayonet. The regiments wordlessly approached the French. A few minutes later, the equally brave forces crashed into one another. The French were pushed back. The second French column rushed to the aid of their comrades but in a fast manoeuvre, were attacked on the left flank by Dekhterev's [Nikolay Vasilyevich Dekhterev] St Petersburg Dragoons, were overrun and lost a colour. The third column hastened to help out the first two and was stopped, showered with canister fire. Murat rallied the French repulsed from Grünhöfchen and opened a cannon bombardment.

Half an hour later, when some of Augereau's corps and the head of Soult's corps arrived level with Murat, the French attacked again: Murat from the centre, Augereau on our right from Tenknitten and Soult from Warschkeiten. In all three locations the attack was repulsed: in the centre by the Pskov Musketeers, Sofia Musketeers, Moscow Grenadiers and 24th Jägers. On the right wing His Majesty's *Leib*-Cuirassiers, Yelisavetgrad Hussars, Kargopol Dragoons and Ingermanland Dragoons hacked into the French cavalry which was leading Augereau's columns and drove them off. The enemy sent against our left flank was halted by the batteries of 8th Division. The French sent marksmen against the batteries but the Izyum Hussars scattered them.

Following Murat's unsuccessful attacks, Napoleon arrived on the battlefield and personally deploying for the attack, attacked Prince Bagration's centre and enveloped his flanks. Not having the strength to resist the overwhelming enemy, Prince Bagration ordered the retreat and hurriedly passed through Eylau. The French followed behind him. Located in the gardens and at the exits of the town, Barclay de Tolly met the enemy with cannon and musket fire. Stopped for a moment, the French broke into the town where blood poured in streams. The enemy attacked fiercely and met with fierce resistance. The artillery of both sides fired in the streets at a distance of several *sazhens* [a *sazhen* equals 2.1 m or 7'] from one another. The town of Eylau was filled with more and more French. Prince Bagration and Barclay de Tolly could not hold them and fell back step by step. By the end of the fighting Barclay de

Tolly had been wounded by a bullet in the arm, fracturing the bone. This wound laid the foundation for his astonishingly rapid promotion. Going to St Petersburg to recover, Barclay de Tolly was honoured with visits from Emperor Alexander and had lengthy conversations with Him about military operations and the state of the army. During these conversations, Barclay won the complete trust of the Monarch: going from Major-General at Eylau, two years later he was General-of-Infantry and Commander-in-Chief in Finland, after three years War Minister and five years later the leader of one of the armies appointed to repel Napoleon's invasion of Russia.

On leaving Eylau, Prince Bagration met Bennigsen with 4th Division and received orders from him to drive the French out of the town. Dismounting from his horse, Prince Bagration stood at the head of the division and led them to Eylau. They silently followed the hero. At the outposts Prince Bagration called for a cheer, repeated a thousand times and in three columns, like flaming lava, the troops flooded, stabbing and slaughtering the French in the streets and in the houses. Nightfall ended the fighting. The town was left to us. Having left a senior general, Somov, with orders, Prince Bagration went to Auklappen [Maloye Ozernoye] manor, Bennigsen's headquarters. The taking of the town by force produced the natural consequence of a successful attack – disorder amongst the troops. It was necessary to round up and rally them. Somov ordered the assembly to be beaten without specifying a location for it. The drums thundered on the side of the town farthest from the enemy, at the ends of the streets leading to the positions of our army. Everyone rushed to the gathering point, leaving the gates of Eylau, the square and the streets without protection. The enemy took advantage of this and entered the town evacuated by the Russians.[5] Securing himself from a night attack, Bennigsen positioned 4th Division between the army and the town and Napoleon, having occupied Eylau, set Legrand's [Claude Juste Alexandre Louis Legrand] division ahead of it for the same purpose. During this deployment, the French colour captured by the St Petersburg Dragoons was carried along the ranks of our army. Since 1812, we have become accustomed to looking casually at Napoleon's eagles, brought to Kutuzov by the dozen but in 1807, the conqueror's eagle, torn from the hands of the French, was considered a great trophy among us. Soon bonfires flamed in both armies on the snowy plains cut by black bands of troops.

The rearguard actions, which began on 23 January [4 February] at Jonkowo, were concluded. Of course, in none of the wars conducted thus far had they operated in winter with such vehemence as in the era we are describing. The Russians and French overcame frosts, deep snow, impassibility. Only the darkness of the January nights put an end to the bloodshed. At the end of the fighting, the soldiers threw themselves on the frozen ground for a short rest and fell comatose in a dead sleep. When, at the flickering of dawn, it was necessary to rise from the overnight stay, it was difficult to wake those sleeping. In the ranks, they looked as if they were stupefied and the weakest, moving a short distance from the bivouac site, lay down on the snow and fell asleep again. Nature came into its own, prevailed over the strength of the brave but did not exhaust the courage of the French and Russians, ready to fight to the last drop of blood.

---

5    There is still a witness to this incident [1846] – General Alexei Petrovich Yermolov.

13

# The Battle of Preußisch-Eylau

> The aim of the battle. – Deployment of the Russian army. – French deployment. – The troop strengths. – The morning before the battle. – Napoleon's orders. – The battle begins. – The defeat of Augereau's corps. – The cavalry charge. – Davout's arrival on the battlefield. – The fighting at Serpalen and Sausgarten. – French successes against our left wing. – Count Kutaisov's movement. – The repulse of the French. – L'Estocq's arrival on the battlefield. – Success on our left wing. – Bennigsen's intention to attack. – Action at Schmoditten. – Location of forces after the battle. – Casualties. – Trophies. – Comments on the Battle of Eylau. – Awards.

The terrible night that followed, from 26 to 27 January [7 to 8 February], found Napoleon and Bennigsen in preparation for the battle. Bennigsen's objectives were to unite with L'Estocq and defend Königsberg; Napoleon's objective was to rout the Russians if they gave battle.

The Russian army rested its right wing on Schloditten [Zagorodnoe] and the left extended almost to Sausgarten [Bolshoye Ozornoye]. The village of Serpallen [now the border crossing between Poland and Kaliningrad], in front of Sausgarten, was held by Baggovut's detachment. The Königsberg road ran behind the right wing of the army, while the road to Russia via Domnau [Domnovo] and Wehlau [Znamensk] lay behind the centre. Four divisions, going from right to left, 5th Division, 8th Division, 3rd Division and 2nd Division, with Markov's detachment in the middle, were deployed in two lines, the first in line, the second in column. A strong battery was positioned to their front. The reserve was in two locations: Count Kamensky's 14th Division was behind the left wing while Dokhturov was behind the centre with the 7th Division and 4th Division, which had spent the night ahead of the army and at dawn was taken back into the reserve. Prince Bagration, the most junior of the Lieutenant-Generals, did not have his own command but served under Dokhturov. The cavalry was positioned on the flanks and in the centre of the army. The Cossacks, who came under the command of *Ataman* Platov [Matvey Ivanovich Platov], who had reached the army the day before, were located in various places along the battle line. Tuchkov commanded the right wing, Count Osterman the left and Sacken the centre. Rezvy [Dmitry Petrovich Rezvy] was the artillery commander but on the day of the battle he directly commanded only the artillery on the left wing, delegating that on the right wing to Count Kutaisov [Alexander Ivanovich Kutaisov] and the

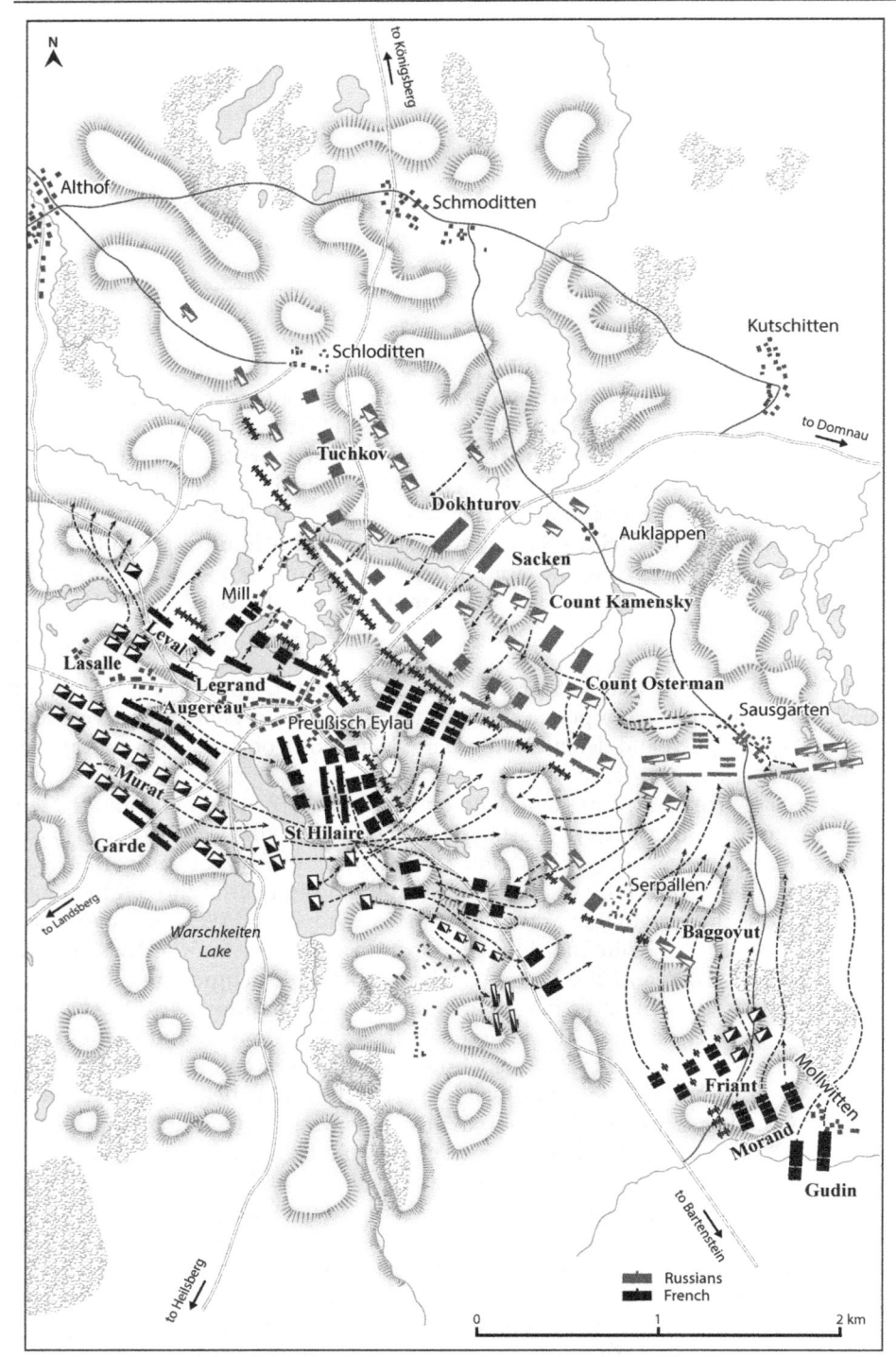

First Plan of the Battle of Preußisch Eylau, Morning of 27 January [8 February] 1807.

centre to Löwenstern [Karl Fedorovich Löwenstern]. L'Estocq, separated from the Russian army by Ney, was sent instructions at night to do his best to catch up with the fighting and upon arriving on the battlefield, join the right wing of the army at Schmoditten [Ryabinovka].

On the night of the 26 to 27 [7 to 8 February], the French army was deployed as follows: Soult's corps in the front line, having Legrand's division in front of Eylau, Leval's [Jean François Leval] division on the left wing with Lasalle's [Antoine-Charles-Louis, comte de Lasalle] light cavalry behind him; Saint-Hilaire's [Louis-Vincent-Joseph Le Blond, comte de Saint-Hilaire] division on the right. In the second line, to the left of the town, Augereau's corps, either side and behind him was all the cavalry and the *Garde*. Napoleon hoped to fix Bennigsen frontally with these troops and, moreover, he ordered Marshal Davout, detached to cut Bennigsen's communications with Russia during the French advance from Jonkowo, to hurry through Mollwitten [Molwity] to Serpallen and Sausgarten, into the left wing and rear of the Russian army, while Marshal Ney, preventing L'Estocq from joining Bennigsen with his rearguard, was to get behind the rear of our right wing, via Althof [Orekhovo] and Schmoditten, cutting off our communications with Königsberg.

The Russian army consisted of 68,000 men. According to the statements by French historians, Napoleon also had up to 70,000 men, but conscientious German historians and witnesses to the Battle of Eylau, claim that his army increased to 90,000.[1] Conscious of the various statements about the subject of the number of troops that were at the beginning of the war we are describing and those who joined him during the campaign, it is necessary to agree with the opinion now accepted in Prussia, that Napoleon had 80,000 men at Eylau.[2]

The Russian army was located on a rolling plain, covered with snow a quarter *arshin* [18 cm or 7" deep]. The frozen ponds on it appeared as flat surfaces convenient for the operations of infantry and cavalry, but, due to the thin ice, dangerous for artillery manoeuvres. The sky was often dark with snow. The temperature was less than four degrees. The Russian army stood to arms at first light. Campfires were still smouldering at the bivouac sites but not a single shot was fired anywhere: there were slight movements in the columns as they came to final order; 4th Division moving back from the vanguard to the reserve. Napoleon, having left the town, surveyed the locations of the Russian troops from a hill. Ensuring that the action was not going to be an encounter with a rearguard but a battle with the entire Russian army, he loudly blamed fate, why, on the decisive day, it deprived him of the assistance of Bernadotte's corps. Aides de camp rushed to Ney and Davout with orders to hurry to their appointed places, in the rear of the Russians. Then, summoning Marshals Soult, Augereau and Murat, Napoleon ordered: Soult to form the left wing with the infantry divisions of Leval and Legrand and Lassalle's cavalry, moving to the left of the Königsberg road; Marshal Augereau was to rest his left flank on Legrand and make up the centre, placing the corps in two lines, Desjardin's [Jacques Desjardin] division in the first, and Heudelet's [Étienne Heudelet de Bierre] in the second;

---

1  Schütz, *Geschichte des Krieges von Preußen und Rußland gegen Frankreich*.
   Plotho, *Tagebuch während des Krieges 1806 und 1807*.
2  *Preußisches Militairisches Wochenblatt, Jahrgang 1842*.

on his right flank was Saint-Hilaire's infantry division from Soult's corps and the dragoons; Murat was to deploy his cavalry as he saw fit. Napoleon personally issued orders to the *Garde* and he explained his intentions to all three marshals: the town of Eylau had the honour of being the axis of operations and to fix the Russian army with diversionary attacks and, once Davout approached, all other troops, except Soult's, were to move forward with the right wing, assisting Marshal Davout to cut us off from Russia and Ney to cut our route to Königsberg.

Just then, as the French army was set in motion to fulfil Napoleon's orders, Bennigsen opened fire from the battery on the right wing: sixty guns roared at the enemy leaving Eylau and and from those that were deployed to the left of the town. Eighty cannon from Soult's corps and twelve from the *Garde* answered with their fire. Under this cannonade the French took up their assigned places. The cannon fire increased as Napoleon's army was deployed, becoming parallel with the Russian but was hotter and with more power to the left of the town than in other places, on our part, because Bennigsen was trying to prevent Legrand's and Leval's divisions from attacking his right flank, and on the part of Napoleon, so that, by causing Bennigsen concern for his right wing, it would facilitate Davout's operations, whose arrival should decide the outcome of the battle. For this purpose, Napoleon ordered Soult to occupy the mill lying in front of our right wing. Tuchkov ordered Major-General Foch [Alexander Borisovich Foch] to push the French out of there with two infantry regiments with the Riga Dragoons and Livland Dragoons. Foch fulfilled the assignment successfully, drove the enemy out of the mill and then attacked them with dragoons. This was the only noteworthy combat on our right wing.

The fire of several hundred guns lasted about three hours but nothing in particular happened during the battle. At ten o'clock, having received a report of the approach of Davout to the battlefield, Napoleon ordered Soult to hold Eylau and the position he occupied at all costs, while Saint-Hilaire was to move to the right and link up with Davout when he arrives at Serpallen, while Marshal Augereau was to move to the right and then make a small turn to the left, maintaining communications with Saint-Hilaire. The cavalry behind Saint-Hilaire and Augereau was to cover their movements, while some of the *Garde* and *Réserve de cavalerie* occupied the space made by Augereau's corps. The troops had just set off when a blizzard rolled in. A piercing wind blew snowflakes right into the faces of the French, blinding them. The sky darkened. Augereau's corps went astray and, at that moment, the weather cleared unexpectedly for us and for them in front of the batteries of the Russian Centre. Seventy guns struck them with canister. The French were dumbfounded. Marshal Augereau and both of his divisional commanders, Desjardins and Heudelet, fell, seriously wounded and were carried back. In the blink of an eye the Moscow Grenadiers, Shlisselburg Musketeers, Vladimir Musketeers and others, whose names have been lost to history, charged with the bayonet. The fighting was unprecedented. More than 20,000 men on both sides stabbed at each other with their triangular blades and cut without mercy. Some of the French rushed forward making for our guns, took possession of them for a moment, then breathed their last under bayonets, butts and rammers. Piles of bodies fell, showered with fresh piles. Finally, Augereau's corps was driven off and pursued by infantry and cavalry, having lost several colours. Their ardour turned to disbelief! During the pursuit, one Russian battalion – from which regiment is unknown – appeared at the cemetery, a hundred paces from Napoleon. A regiment of the French *Vieille Garde* and cavalry scattered it. Saint-Hilaire's division, moving to the right, also lost its way in the blizzard. When it cleared away, they found themselves at Serpallen and, as they were turning back, were attacked by Major-General Kakhovsky [Pëtr Demyanovich Kakhovsky] with the Malorussia Cuirassiers and Poland Horse: they overran the 55e *régiment d'infanterie de ligne*, which had come closer than the others to Serpallen.

After the storm had passed, having seen the state of affairs, Napoleon ordered Murat to rescue Augereau's corps with the *Réserve de cavalerie* and to forestall any forward movement by the Russians, while Bessières was to support Murat with the *cavalerie de la Garde*. Murat immediately sent Klein's [Dominique Louis Antoine Klein] dragoon division to the right to help Saint-Hilaire and led Grouchy's [Emmanuel de Grouchy] dragoon division forward himself, ordering d'Hautpoul's [Jean Joseph Ange d'Hautpoul] cuirassiers to follow him. Having engaged the Russian cavalry chasing Augereau's corps, Murat drove them off but, taken in the flank by our cavalry, the dragoons were forced back. In this attack the Courland Dragoons and Military Order Cuirassiers particularly distinguished themselves, capturing an Eagle. Major Masyukov, commander of this regiment, was killed. D'Hautpoul's cuirassier division coming to the aid of Grouchy, overran and drove the Russian cavalry onto our infantry. Greeted here by musket and cannon fire, the cuirassiers turned back and were pursued by the Russian cavalry. Our success lasted a few minutes. Bessières with the *cavalerie de la Garde* drove them off. In the heat of battle, several squadrons of Napoleon's *Garde* galloped through the first and second lines of our infantry, and reached the reserve. Greeted by small arms fire, they came to their senses and turned back. Yurkovsky with the Yelisavetgrad Hussars, Count O'Rourke [Joseph Kornilovich O'Rourke] with three squadrons of Pavlograd Hussars and Kiselev's Cossack Regiment scattered them in all directions. Some of the French raced into the middle of our infantry lines, on the right flank, rode from there to the rear of Count Kutaisov's artillery and tried to escape through the gaps between the guns. Most of the brave men who penetrated into the middle of the Russian army fell victim to their enthusiasm. In these cavalry attacks, as the snow swirled around the riders like clouds of dust, the commander of the cuirassier division, d'Hautpoul, Napoleon's Adjutant-General Corbineau [Claude Louis Constant Juvenal Spirit Gabriel Corbineau] and the commander of the *Chasseurs à Cheval de la Garde*, Dahlmann [Nicolas Dahlmann], were killed. Only fragments of Augereau's corps remained, for example, in the two battalions of the *14e régiment d'infanterie de ligne*, all the officers were killed or wounded. After the bloodshed that occurred from an unforeseen event – the blizzard, both belligerent armies settled down and rallied. Bennigsen reinforced the battle lines with most of Dokhturov's reserve. Throughout the army only the cannonade thundered.

An hour passed. At about noon, on the crests of the hills opposite our left wing, the Cossacks retreated and the appearance of enemy flankers [cavalry scouts] was noticed; cavalry appeared behind them. Count Osterman ordered two squadrons of Izyum Hussars to monitor the enemy and received a report from them that many infantry were following the cavalry: this was Davout's 25,000 man corps. His arrival on the battlefield was delayed beyond the time Napoleon expected him, having been caught up on the way by the blizzard that had led to the destruction of Augereau's corps. Davout marched from Mollwitten into the gap between Serpallen and Sausgarten; in the lead was Friant's infantry division having a light cavalry division to its right; in the second line marched Morand's infantry division, with Gudin's division following. On seeing Davout's columns, Napoleon ordered Saint-Hilaire's division to eject the Russians from Serpallen and to move in concert with Davout, forming his left wing. Klein's and Milhaud's [Édouard Jean-Baptiste Milhaud] dragoon divisions were to follow Saint-Hilaire, receiving orders to come under Davout's command. Bennigsen, for his part, sent orders to L'Estocq, cancelling the assignment given to him the previous night and to go to the left wing of the army, not the right.

Attacked simultaneously from two sides by Saint-Hilaire and Friant, Baggovut could not hold on in Serpallen, set fire to the village and retreated to Sausgarten. Anticipating the storm that the Russian army would suffer here, Bennigsen strengthened Baggovut with Count Kamensky's 14th Division, which formed the reserve of the left wing. Baggovut and Kamensky deployed either side of Sausgarten, which was held by the Ryazan Musketeers. From Serpallen, Friant and Saint-Hilaire advanced towards Sausgarten; in the second line were Gudin, Morand and the cavalry. During this movement, the enemy came under heavy fire from batteries turned towards them by Count Osterman. Davout attacked Kamensky and Baggovut standing near Sausgarten. The French broke into Sausgarten but were driven out the the Ryazan Musketeers. Bitter fighting ensued around this village, while the divisions under Gudin and Morand attacked our extreme left wing. The Russian and French batteries closed for a canister bombardment. Count Pahlen and Korff [Fëdor Karlovich Korff] attacked Morand with twenty squadrons and forced him back. Klein's dragoon division came to Morand's rescue in time and tipped the balance in favour of the French. Count Osterman ordered Sausgarten to be abandoned and changed front, turning back his left flank, to the end of which Baggovut and Kamensky were attached. The French raced in to occupy Sausgarten, after which Davout formed up in parallel with Count Osterman, smashed him with cannon from the hills and tried to envelope him further and further with his right wing.

Following the movements of Davout and Count Osterman, Napoleon moved Augereau's shattered corps forward and to the right, placing it under the command of Compans [Jean Dominique Compans], with some of the *Réserve de cavalerie*. Dokhturov reinforced the left wing with the last of his reserves but this support was not enough: Count Osterman still had to fall back. The French penetrated as far as Auklappen manor, after which Davout extended his right wing as far as Kutschitten [Znamenskoye]. By that time, the Russian army almost formed a right angle, standing under crossfire from Napoleon's and Davout's batteries. The situation was all the more difficult, since the aides de camp sent to Bennigsen could not find him. Wanting to accelerate L'Estocq's advance, he went to meet him himself, got lost and, for more than an hour, the army was without an overall commander. Heavily battered by the crossfire and seeing the army being outflanked, Sacken told Count Osterman and the commander of the cavalry of our left wing, Count Pahlen [Pëtr

THE BATTLE OF PREUSSISCH-EYLAU   113

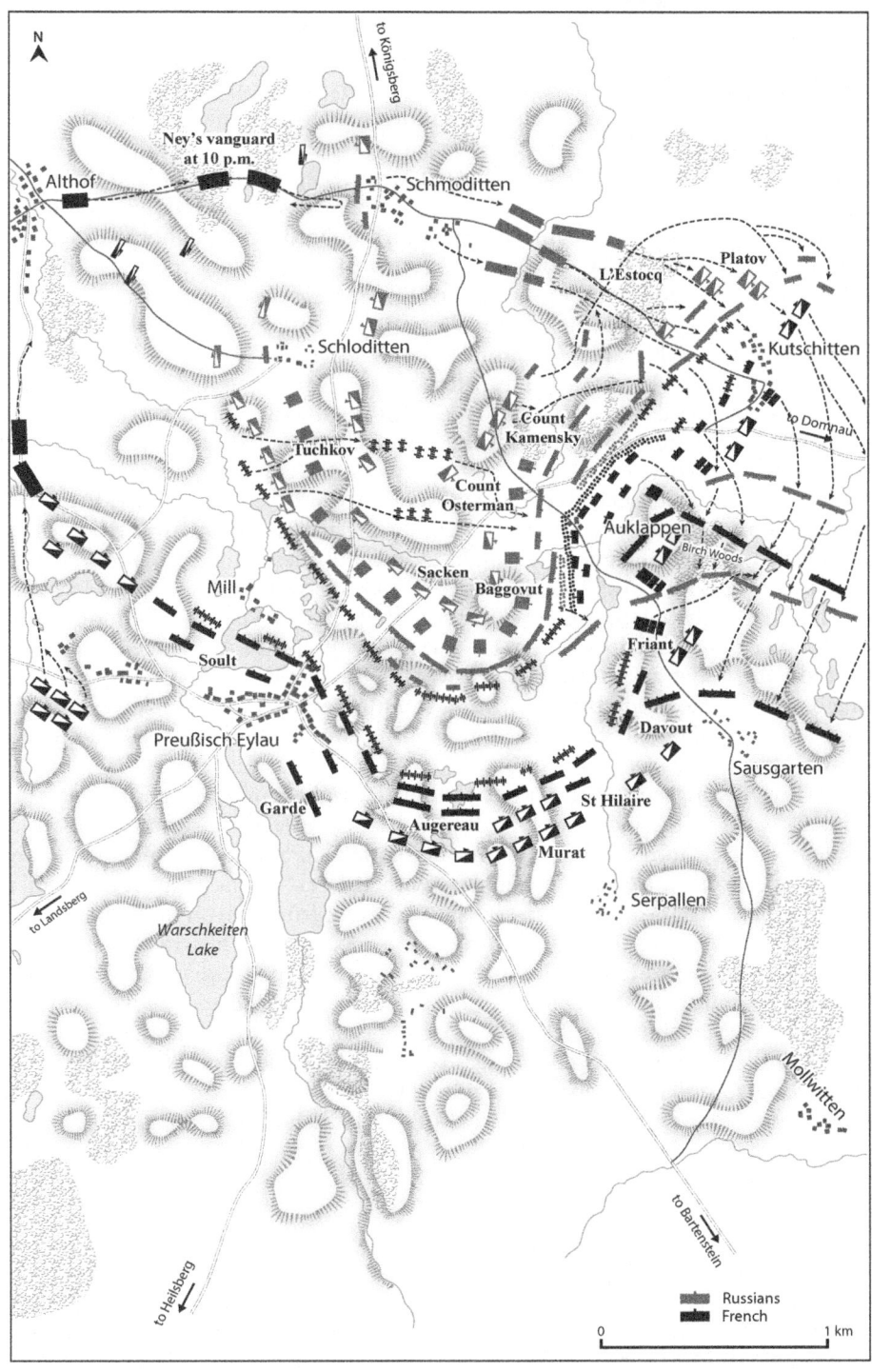

Second Plan of the Battle of Preußisch Eylau, Evening of 27 January [8 February] 1807.

Petrovich Pahlen],³ standing next to him: 'Bennigsen has disappeared; I remain the most senior; in order to preserve the army, it is necessary to retreat.' The proposal, which was borne out of a moment of despair, remained unfulfilled and suddenly the situation unexpectedly turned around for us with the appearance of thirty-six horse-artillery pieces.

The commander of artillery of the left wing [sic], Count Kutaisov, saw that the French were not attacking there, limiting themselves to a relatively rapid fire bombardment. Missing the regularity of such a bombardment and not finding satisfaction for his burning desire to fulfil the vow to which he devoted his life – to glorify the name of Kutaisov – he went, a twenty-three-year-old youth, to the centre. From here he surveyed the battle and having noted the precarious situation of Count Osterman, ordered his aide de camp, Arnoldi — [Ivan Karlovich Arnoldi] now [1846] a Lieutenant-General — to transfer three horse companies, Prince Iashvili's, Yermolov's and Bogdanov's [Nikolai Ivanovich Bogdanov], from the right wing to the left.⁴ The companies rode at full speed to Auklappen at the very moment that the French sensed victory. As soon as the first guns unlimbered, they quickly opened fire with canister and once all thirty-six were lined up their well-aimed fire shook the French. They wavered, began to move backward, dodging from the canister fire and fled from Auklappen, set alight by incendiaries from Yermolov's battery. Kutaisov's bright idea and its successful execution gave time for Count Osterman and Sacken to rally the troops.⁵ The French wobble did not last long. Reinforcing his artillery, Davout pressed forwards. He wanted to recapture Auklappen once more but could not, being smothered by the fire of the Russian batteries. Count Osterman hung on grimly. He needed only a little new reinforcement to beat back Davout, who had over extended his strength in occupying Kutschitten. Reinforcements arrived in the nick of time – it was L'Estocq.

Fulfilling Bennigsen's initial order to join the right wing of the Russian army, L'Estocq set off in the morning for Althof but encountered Ney's vanguard which had been ordered to block his route to the battlefield. Skilfully manoeuvring and sacrificing a brigade to hold the French, with the rest of the troops, 5,584 men, including our Vyborg Musketeers, he slipped away from Ney, marched to Althof and received orders on the way: to hurry to our extreme right wing. Then he was met by Bennigsen and led to Kutschitten by him, arriving there at 5 o'clock in the afternoon. Forming the detachment into battle formation, L'Estocq moved forward. Pillar's [Yegor Maksimovich Pillar] Vyborg Musketeers marched at the head of the detachment. Behind him came Rüchel's regiment to his left and Schöning's [Ernst Emanuel Sigismund von Schöning] regiment to his right; in the second line were the Prussian grenadiers and cavalry. Platov followed L'Estocq with his Cossacks. The

---

3    Now [1846] a member of the State Council.
4    From Lieutenant-General Arnoldi's notes.
5    Two and a half months after the Battle of Eylau, Emperor Alexander visited the army, surveyed the battlefield and then seeing Kutaisov, told him in the presence of other generals – there are still witnesses to the Monarch's words: 'Yesterday I examined the field where you, with such forethought and with such skill, helped us get out of trouble and preserved our honour in this battle. My business will be to never forget your service.'

Vyborg Musketeers charged into Kutschitten with incredible courage and almost completely wiped out the French *51e régiment d'infanterie de ligne* and four companies of the *108e régiment d'infanterie de ligne* and liberated three Russian guns taken by the French during their attack on our left wing.[6] L'Estocq's other troops hurried behind the Vyborg Musketeers into Kutschitten, while Platov and the Prussian lighthorse regiment, known as '*Kameraden*', bypassed the village on the left. All these troops and Platov, chasing on the heels of those who fled from the village, completed their defeat. Having recaptured Kutschitten, L'Estocq lined up his detachment in front of it, facing a birch wood occupied by the French, making several cannon shots at it and then, with bands playing, entered the woods, enveloping it on the left with Rüchel's Regiment, the Cossacks and the *Kameraden*. The Prussians and the Vyborg Musketeers worked as successfully in the woods as in Kutschitten, they stabbed and drove out the French. Outflanked on his right, when he thought that he was outflanking, Davout hurriedly sent Friant's division to the woods from where the French had already rushed out and were attacked by the Moscow Dragoons and Pavlograd Hussars who had arrived in time to help L'Estocq. Davout began to fall back. Count Osterman followed up behind him, putting Count Kamensky and Baggovut in the front line. Taking advantage of the rage of his detachment and the reinforcements that had arrived, L'Estocq prevented Friant from establishing himself and drove him back. Davout rushed to take up an advantageous position on either side of Sausgarten and set up a battery there. Thus Davout's operations, which had required him to deliver the decisive blow to the Russian army, were frustrated.

Seeing Davout's retreat and the increase of our troops, Napoleon doubted Davout's ability to hold at Sausgarten and said to his Chief of General Staff, Berthier: 'the Russians have been reinforced and our ammunition is almost exhausted. Ney is not here, while Bernadotte is far away: it would be best to meet them head on.'[7] To meet them the marshals took to mean to go back, to retreat, but Napoleon would not utter the word 'retreat,' expecting to attack Bennigsen, whether he moved forward or halted. The decisive moment of the battle had arrived and Bennigsen wanted to turn it to his advantage. He ordered Count Osterman to prepare for an attack and Laptev, with three Jäger regiments, would precede him. The Russian columns cheerfully formed up and Laptev moved forward but Bennigsen soon stopped him and cancelled his decision to attack the French, due to the approaching darkness. Shaking of the pursuit and attacks, Davout continued his bombardment. It was continued by both sides into the darkness until 9 o'clock in the evening. All the surrounding villages were in flames. The reflected light of the fires illuminated the weary troops. Camp fires were lit and the wounded dragged themselves in a jumble towards them. The battle fell silent.

Bennigsen went to meet Tuchkov. Finding that the right flank of our army was infinitely less affected than the other troops and being assured by prisoners of war of the dejection in the enemy army, Bennigsen set out with his right wing to launch

---

6   Dumas, *Précis des évènemens militaires. Tome XVIII*, p. 33: *Le 51-ème régiment de ligne et quatre compagnies du 108-ème qui défendoient Kouchitten, furent enveloppés, taillés en pièces, et leurs débris purent à peine regagner la tête du bois, d'où ils avoient débouché.*
7   According to General Jomini, who was standing next to Napoleon.

the attack that had been cancelled on the left. He ordered Tuchkov to go forward, when suddenly, at ten o'clock shots were heard at Schmoditten, in our rear: it was an attack by part of Ney's corps, pushing the brigade that L'Estocq had left behind ahead of them. Falling back step by step, the detachment arrived in Schmoditten, which was full of our wounded. The escorts tasked with their protection joined the Prussian brigade and a heavy firefight ensued. At the first shots from Ney's corps, one of our officers exclaimed: 'we're surrounded!' – 'So what?' said the soldier standing next to him – 'push through!' Whoever has been to war knows the destructive influence of the words: 'we're surrounded, cut off' and will understand the true value of the response.[8]

Wanting to verify what was happening, Bennigsen sent the Tauride Grenadiers, Voronezh Musketeers and two cavalry regiments to Schmoditten. They drove the French out of the village and learned of Ney's approach to the battlefield from their prisoners of war. This was the circumstance that prompted Bennigsen to postpone the night attack, which, according to the French, could have had detrimental consequences for Napoleon. In 1813, talking to our officers about the Battle of Eylau, Bernadotte said: 'Luck never favoured Napoleon more than at Eylau. An attack by Bennigsen in the evening would have taken at least 150 guns for which the horses had been killed.'[9]

That night after the battle, the French troops remained from Sausgarten to Eylau and to the left of the town. Napoleon sent one light cavalry division to Althof, ordering them to establish communications with Ney. The left wing of the Russian force was located in front of Kutschitten, went along the birch wood, occupying it with infantry at the outer edge and along to the central battery, starting from which the troops still stood in their original positions. The question was: whether to resume the battle in the morning, whether the Russians should retreat to Königsberg or the French to the Vistula, these were the overwhelming thoughts of Napoleon and Bennigsen. There was a noisy meeting in our headquarters. Knorring, Duty General Count Tolstoy and Quartermaster-General Steinheil called for an attack. Bennigsen was of the opposite opinion and, after midnight, ordered a retreat to Königsberg. He wrote; 'Let every experienced soldier judge, was it not better for me to retreat to Königsberg, to refresh the army there, watch over the wounded, repair the artillery, replenish ammunition, occupy and strengthen the position at Königsberg, leaving Napoleon in the snow and uninhabited locations around Eylau, where he had no food and no opportunity to heal the wounded or repair his artillery. After my retreat, Napoleon faced one of two courses of action: to march on Königsberg and attack me in a fortified position or to withdraw. The great commander, who never neglected the opportunity to crush his opponents, chose the latter. Consequently, I was not mistaken in my assessment. Having retreated to Königsberg without loss, I gained the same advantages that I would have gained from another battle.'[10]

---

8   When, in 1815, Count Vorontsov led 12th Division into France, he gave an unwritten order that during a battle should anyone shout out: 'we are surrounded or cut off' they would be summarily executed.
9   According to Grabbe (now a Lieutenant-General), who was in Bernadotte's Northern Army.
10  From Bennigsen's autobiographical notes.

The Russian dead and wounded from Preußisch-Eylau were some 26,000 men; nine generals were wounded but their names are not recorded in Bennigsen's report. The morning following the battle it was believed that our losses were much greater than they really were, without counting many, as they did not know the number of those who were evacuated wounded or had been scattered before the end of the fighting. French historians have stated the losses to Napoleon's army as 18,000 men, but generals and officers who had been present at Eylau have told us that their losses were much more significant. Augereau's corps had suffered to such an extent that it was disbanded and the troops from which it was constituted were assigned to other corps. Our trophies consisted of several colours, the number of which could not be determined, due to the following curious circumstance. In Bennigsen's report on the Battle of Eylau, drafted by *Flügel-Adjutant* Stavitsky, it stated that 12 colours were taken but only five were sent to St Petersburg. In response to Emperor Alexander's question about those missing, Bennigsen answered: 'that at the time of the battle, only verbal reports had been received, that they were not then gathered in one place and some were sold by soldiers in Königsberg at the market, as the soldiers were paid in gold for French Eagles.'[11] The Russians did not lose any guns or colours; the number of prisoners of war, almost the same on both sides, was less than 700 men. Incredibly, Napoleon distorted the Battle of Eylau in his bulletins and gilded his battle with invented trophies: 18 Russian colours and 15,000 prisoners of war.

Both warring parties claimed the victory at Eylau. In the general ten-year struggle between Alexander and Napoleon, their wars from 1805 to 1815 appear to be one continuous war, with short intervals. During this momentous era, it was a life and death struggle for both adversaries. For as long as incorruptible Fate did not favour Alexander in the resolution of this dispute, he would sacrifice his capitals, ready to retire to Siberia, grow a beard and eat dry bread. Napoleon, ejected from the Kremlin to Fontainebleau, humiliated, takes poison! Everyone, Alexander and Napoleon, the Russian troops and those who were hostile to us, had bright days in the war and black days, but great are the eyes of posterity and both powerful adversaries and their armies had no need of fictitious victories or of fake laurels for their immortal crown. For what purpose was the Battle of Eylau given to Napoleon? He wanted to encircle the Russian army with Ney's and Davout's corps and cut it off from Königsberg and Russia but did he achieve the aim? Ney did not arrive in time for battle and Davout's attacks were unsuccessful. Where was the victory? If Napoleon really had won, he would have pursued the retreating enemy and it would have been easy for him to breach and capture Königsberg, a city of great military and political importance at the time. Napoleon was not one of those commanders who, stopping after victory, would fail to seize the fruits of a battle won. But after the Battle of Eylau, he did not gain the slightest substantial advantage, he lost colours without having taken a single one and had to remain in one place for several days. His army, like a raked ship of the line with tangled rigging, drifting, incapable not only of attack but even of movement or fighting: there were only seven rounds of ammunition left per gun.

---

11   Report, dated 24 February [8 March].

The Battle of Eylau was the most bitter and bloody battle of its time and left a deep impression on the French for a long time. Many years later, when the French described any cruel, unsuccessful battle for them, such as Aspern, they always compared it with Eylau, adding that the emotions in France after such a disadvantageous battle were like the emotions produced by the Eylau battle. As a commander, Napoleon was so highly regarded by his contemporaries that the mere fact that he did not win at Eylau would be considered a victory for the Russians; he was considered invincible to such an extent that the failure of an attack was regarded as a defeat. Napoleon's statement by his chosen historiographer, Bignon, reads: 'The indecisive Battle of Eylau had thrown Paris into incredible consternation; the party of opposition to the Empire poorly disguised their glee at his public disaster under feigned pain. There was a noticeable drop in revenue.'[12] Napoleon himself did not hide the consequences of his failure. In 1809, after the battle of Aspern, strolling in the Schönbrunn Gardens with Emperor Alexander's representative, *Rotmistr* [cavalry captain] Chernyshev (now [1846] the Minister of War) and talking to him about the war of 1807, he said: 'I proclaimed myself victorious because you were kind enough to withdraw.'[13] The Battle of Eylau was the first threat to Napoleon's Providence, the first hint to him by Fate about the possibility of defeat.

The Battle of Eylau made a different impression in St Petersburg. The captured French colours were paraded through the streets by the Chevalier Guard to the sound of trumpets. Emperor Alexander awarded Bennigsen the Order of St Andrew the First-Called and granted the Order of St George 3rd class to Lieutenant-Generals Essen 3rd and L'Estocq; Major-Generals Steinheil, Markov, Titov [Vasily Petrovich Titov], Somov, Count Kamensky, Count Pahlen [Pëtr Petrovich Pahlen], Foch, Count Lieven [Ivan Adreevich Lieven], Baron Korff [Fëdor Karlovich Korff], Kakhovsky [Pëtr Demyanovich Kakhovsky], Zapolsky [Andrey Vasilievich Zapolsky], Count Kutaisov, Yurkovsky, Prince Dolgorukov [Mikhail Petrovich Dolgorukov] and Duka [Ilya Mikhailovich Duka] and to Colonel Dekhterev, four more than were granted for the battle of Borodino. The Order of St George 4th class was awarded to 33 field officers and subalterns, two fewer than were awarded for the battle of Borodino. Officers who were presented St George's and Vladimir's Crosses, but did not receive orders, were awarded special golden crosses made to commemorate the Battle of Eylau for wearing with a buttonhole ribbon of St George. Those who were honoured with these crosses had the time limit for the award of the Order of St George reduced by three years.

---

12   Bignon, *Histoire de France. Tome, VI*, p. 147: *L'indécision de la bataille d'Eylau avoit jetté dans Paris une consternation incroyable; le parti ennemi de l'Empire déguisoit mal, sous une feinte douleur, la joie que lui causoit un désastre public. Une baisse sensible s'étoit opérée dans les fonds.*

13   According to Prince Alexander Ivanovich Chernyshev: *Je me suis proclamé vainqueur parceque vous avez bien voulu vous retirer.*

# 14

# Events During The Russian Army's Stay at Königsberg

The retreat of the Russian army from Preußisch-Eylau. – The condition of the French army. – The Russian army's stay at Königsberg. – The poor condition of the Prussian army. – Bennigsen's proclamation. – Napoleon threatens to confiscate Bennigsen's property. – Napoleon's correspondence with the Prussian Court. – Emperor Alexander's thoughts regarding negotiations with Napoleon. – Emperor Alexander's correspondence with Britain and Austria. – Prussia's correspondence with Austria. – Bennigsen's request to resign his command of the army. – Emperor Alexander's orders.

On the night of 27 to 28 January [8 to 9 February], setting off from the Eylau battlefield in two columns, the Russian army continued to march towards Königsberg on the following day. The troops were dirty with bivouac smoke, icy hoarfrost, in bullet riddled shakos and greatcoats. Prince Bagration, commander of the rearguard, seeing no movement from the French, remained on the battlefield until it was completely daylight. The French army was exhausted and even without bread, because, during their rapid advance on Eylau, the ration carts fell behind. There were many enemy looters. The French were convinced that the Russians would attack them at dawn. Only Napoleon was of a contrary opinion: he assured those around him that Bennigsen was unable to resume the battle. The best depiction of the state of the French army at the time could be the following words of an ardent admirer of Napoleon, his Adjutant-General Savary: 'Our huge losses at Eylau did not allow us to take any offensive action the next day. We would have been completely defeated if the Russians had not retreated but had attacked us and even Bernadotte could not have joined the army for another two days.'[1] Giving Bennigsen time to take the army back a fairly long distance, Prince Bagration withdrew from the battlefield at about 9 o'clock in the morning on 28 January [9 February], not pursued by the French and in the evening, after 17 *versts* [17.8 km or 11⅓ miles], he stopped at Mahnsfeld [Polevoye]. Then, the only sighting by his Cossacks were some French *Chasseurs à*

---

1   *Mémoires du duc de Rovigo, Tome III.*

*Cheval*. They constituted Murat's vanguard, sent by Napoleon to observe the Russian army and forbidden from starting any fighting.

On 29 January [10 February], Bennigsen arrived at Königsberg, choked with wounded, transport and stragglers separated from their regiments. The army deployed in front of the city in hastily fortified positions; the rearguard remained on the right bank of the river Frisching [Prokhladnaya]. L'Estocq's corps occupied Allenburg [Druzhba], guarding the space between the Frisching and the Alle. Napoleon remained around Eylau with his army, wanting to stay on the battlefield to show the world the undoubted evidence of the victory won by him. He put the army in order, giving everything he could to the troops and ordered the delivery of ammunition to Eylau, the consumption of which had been unprecedented in the battle. The warring armies remained in these positions for nine days, exhausted by a winter campaign and many days of bloodshed.

The pause at Königsberg was beneficial to the Russian army. The Prussian local authorities supplied us with what they could: carpenters, locksmiths, tailors, shoes, food, doctors. The most honoured of Königsberg's citizens, the Prince of Holstein-Beck, Graf Don, Graf Schlieffen and Governor General Rüchel made up a Society of Aid for our wounded. The Prussian King sent his personal physician Görke, while Louis XVIII sent his own doctor, Distelle, who lived in Mitau [Jelgava]. The Unfortunate Monarch of France, the Duke of Angoulême and his wife, who drank the entire cup of human calamities, congratulated Bennigsen on the Battle of Eylau. Louis XVIII expressed his regret to Bennigsen that he could not take part in the war, to share his labours and, perhaps, his glory and sent him a proclamation asking him to distribute it to the French army.[2] In the proclamation, the King exhorted the French to leave Napoleon's colours and return to their legitimate Monarch. Our Court did not find it appropriate, for the time being, to fulfil Louis' wishes and the proclamation was not issued. The King of Prussia gave Bennigsen 200 Louis to distribute to the wounded, regretting that the unfortunate circumstances did not allow him to grant everything to the brave Russian soldiers that their hearts desired.[3] Indeed, the Prussian Monarchy was in the worst condition. Every region, from the Vistula to the Weser, was occupied and mercilessly ravaged by the French. Only East Prussia still followed the King but a devastating war was raging there and there wasn't even enough space to build up reserves of 12,000 men, under the command of Princes Wilhelm and Heinrich. Therefore, the King asked Emperor Alexander for permission to send them to Russia, to Kovno [Kaunas] or Jurburg, so that they could complete their education there.[4] While remaining with the Court in Memel, the King could not find a corner of his territories where it would be safe to keep the rest of his treasury and valuable possessions. At his request, the treasury, pearls, diamonds, gold and silver objects were sent via a Prussian convoy to Russia,

---

2 Louis XVIII's letter to Bennigsen, dated 3 [15] February: *J'éprouve un regret profond de n'être que spectateur de cette grande lutte, de ne pas partager vos travaux, peut être votre gloire.*
3 Bennigsen's report, dated 15 [27] February.
4 Request from the Prussian Minister Zastrow to the Russian Envoy at the Prussian Court, dated 30 December [11 January, 1807].

where they were kept for the duration of the war.[5] The best horses from state studs were also transferred to Russia. In his misfortune, the King was supported only by his confidence in the intercession of Emperor Alexander and in the courage of the Russian army.

Even Napoleon was shocked by the resolve of Alexander's troops. Being assured from all the actions and battles that had occurred since the opening of the campaign that it was difficult to break the Russians and to win cheap victories, as in his previous campaigns and, unable to foresee the time of his return to Paris, where his presence was needed, Napoleon wanted to end the war and offered Bennigsen a truce. Bennigsen not only did not accept the offer, but, at the behest of Emperor Alexander, issued a veiled appeal to the German nations, which they tried to spread across German soil by every possible means, especially through Britain.[6] Highlighting Napoleon's dangerous military situation, drawn to the right bank of the Vistula in winter, Bennigsen invited the Germans to mobilise themselves against the French. Germany's awakening hour had not yet begun and our arguments for it to join in rebellion were not successful; they served only as an excuse for the next laughable incident. Napoleon, learning about the existence of the appeal, ordered the public bodies in Hanover, where Bennigsen's estates were, to appeal to him through the newspapers to leave the Russian service and immediately return to Hanover or risk losing his hereditary estates. This appeal was an unprecedented example in History: the commander of an army invites his opponent to surrender command of his troops and go to a country occupied by the enemies of the Monarch, who has entrusted him with the honour of his armed forces!

Having received Bennigsen's refusal to conclude a truce, Napoleon asked him to allow Adjutant-General Bertrand [Henri-Gatien Bertrand] to travel freely to the King of Prussia. Bennigsen fulfilled Napoleon's request and sent Bertrand to Memel. Having no doubt that Bertrand was entrusted with the task of initiating peace negotiations, Bennigsen wrote to the King asking His Majesty not to heed Napoleon's peace proposals, giving the letter to the Prussian Major Klüx, who had been sent to escort the French. Bennigsen stated to the Prussian King; 'Napoleon's desire for peace comes from the frustration of the French army. I dare to assure Your Majesty that victory over them is inevitable should I receive reinforcements.' Bertrand informed the King of Napoleon's desire to conclude a separate peace with Prussia and by signing it, convene a congress for the general reconciliation of all Powers. Napoleon wrote to the King; 'But congresses deliberate slowly, which is why it would be more beneficial for Your Majesty to bring your state out of its present disastrous situation by concluding a separate peace favourable to it.'[7]

---

5   Request from Adjutant-General Count Lieven to the War Ministry, dated 14 [26] December.
6   Request by the Minister of Foreign Affairs to the Russian Ambassador in London: *Afin d'augmenter autant que possible les embarras de l'ennemi, nous avons rédigé une proclamation, adressée par le Général Bennigsen aux peuples de la Germanie, afin de ranimer leur courage, et pour les engager à concourir efficacement à la délivrance de leur pays du joug étranger.*
7   To his envoy in Vienna, Graf Finckenstein [Karl Friedrich Albrecht Finck von Finckenstein], who informed Count Razumovsky: *Bonaparte m'insinue comme un parti plus simple, plus expéditif et plus conforme à mes intérêts de faire avec lui une paix séparée, par laquelle je devrais, selon lui, retirer de grands intérêts.*

The Prussian King was displeased that Bennigsen had given Bertrand free passage to Memel without his permission. Nonetheless, he granted Bertrand a private audience lasting no more than five minutes, took Napoleon's letter and directed Bertrand to his Foreign Minister, Zastrow, who had not long before taken the place of Graf Haugwitz, for further explanation. Together with some individuals who had some influence on matters, Zastrow advised the King of Prussia to enter into negotiations with Napoleon but the King rejected his recommendation.[8] He gave orders that Bertrand should be told that a separate peace was out of the question. After releasing Bertrand, the King sent Captain Scheller to St Petersburg – later the Prussian Envoy to Russia – ordering him to notify the Tsar of Napoleon's proposals and inform him of the decision by our Monarch. Emperor Alexander replied to the King;[9]

> I do not oppose the opening of negotiations with Napoleon but they should be open to Russia, Britain and Prussia, held on neutral ground, for example, in Galicia, and Napoleon must first declare his conditions for the establishment of a general peace.

Napoleon responded to the letter written on this subject by the King of Prussia with readiness to convene a congress but did not state his conditions, which is why the King of Prussia refused to enter into negotiations, on the advice of Emperor Alexander, who saw in Napoleon's actions not a desire for peace but a need to gain time to get out of the predicament he was in.[10]

Trying by every possible means to support the Prussian King, Emperor Alexander insisted that Prussia should receive considerable financial assistance from London, which the King of Prussia had vainly requested from the British. The benefits to Britain itself convinced its sovereign to support Prussia. He wrote to his ambassador in London;

> What will become of Great Britain, if all the other Powers have succumbed, for want of having been rescued in time by them? England, so keenly interested that the outcome of this war be favourable to us and that at last we manage to take away from Bonaparte the means of pursuing his endless plans for invasions and despoilment, would be unjustifiable, if they were to persist in the inactivity in which they remain at the moment when it should

---

8   Baron Krüdener's [Pavel Alekseevich Krüdener] report to the Minister of Foreign Affairs, Baron Budberg, dated 2 [14] February.
9   The King of Prussia's instructions to his ambassador to Vienna, Graf Finckenstein: *C'est à l'Empereur Alexandre, mon fidèle allié, que je m'en suis remis à apprécier les intentions et les offres de Napoléon, en lui déclarant, qu'il ne saurait être question d'une paix séparée, et que je ne répondrai au dernier, qu'au retour du courrier que j'ai expédié à l'Empereur Alexandre.*
10  Supreme instructions to Count Vorontsov, in London, dated 6 [18] March and to Count Razumovsky, in Vienna, dated 9 [21] March: *L'Empereur Alexandre ne voyant rien dans les expressions de Bonaparte qui dénote autre chose, que le besoin de gagner du tems et de sortir d'une position critique, n'a pas cru pouvoir changer le langage que Sa Majesté Impériale a tenu jusqu'à présent, et en communiquant Ses observations au roi de Prusse sur cette nouvelle tentative, Elle lui a témoigné la même fermeté à s'y refuser qu'aux précédentes.*

be the time for them to redouble their efforts to act in concert with us. Do they not in some way make themselves guilty of the same faults for which they once reproached Prussia and of which Austria has been guilty to this day?[11]

Not content with insisting on aid for the King of Prussia, Emperor Alexander pointed out to the British Ministers the need for a landing in Holland or northern Germany. He stated;

> Russia will always have enough strength to defend its own borders but it will not have enough to wage an offensive war in the long run. Bonaparte, by reinforcing all the conscripts he brings from within France, as well as numerous contingents from the Confederation of the Rhine, will soon have a formidable new army to bear against the Russian army, reinforced in its turn by regiments which on all sides are in movement to join them, we will be able to be face fairly but will not be able to wrest from the usurper the conquests he has made and give him the ability to defend successfully that very advantageous position.[12]

Having recounted all the benefits that might come from a British landing in the rear of Napoleon, Emperor Alexander finally said that if the British want to help us with the army, then let them scatter guineas in German soil, Switzerland and Holland, where, close to despair, a general grumbling could be found against Napoleon. Emperor Alexander pointed to Hesse-Kassel in particular to the British, where 8,000 men from Kassel's armed forces, disbanded by Napoleon, armed themselves against the French, captured Marburg and the fortress of Ziegenhain [Schwalmstadt]. The emperor ordered his ambassador to London to persuade the British Ministers to spread the uprising by landing in northern Germany and, if they found it impossible because of the winter weather, then convince them to send

---

11 Supreme instructions to the Russian ambassador in London, Count Vorontsov, dated 6 [18] March 1807: *Que deviendra enfin la Grande Bretagne, si toutes les autres Puissances aurout succombées, faute d'avoir été secourues à temps par elle? L'Angleterre si vivement intéressée à ce que l'issue de cette guerre nous soit favorable, et qu'enfin on parvienne à oter à Bonaparte les moyens de poursuivre ses projets illimités d'envahissemens et de spoliation, seroit injustifiable, si elle persistoit dans l'inactivité dans laquelle elle reste au moment où il seroit instant qu'elle redoublat d'efforts pour agir de concert avec nous. Ne se rend elle pas en quelque sorte coupable des même fautes, qu'elle reprochoit autrefois à la Prusse, et dont jusqu'à ce jour l'Autriche se rend coupable?*

12 Supreme instructions to Count Vorontsov, in London, dated 6 [18] March: *La Russie aura toujours assez de force pour défendre ses propres frontieres, mais elle n'en aura pas suffisamment pour faire à la longue une guerre offensive, Bonaparte, en se renforçant de tous les conscrits qu'il fait venir de l'intérieur de la France, ainsi que de nombreux conting ens de la ligue du Rhin, aura sous peu une nouvelle armée formidable à porter contre l'armée russe, et quioque celle ci, renforcée à son tour par les régimens qui de tous côtés sont en mouvement pour la rejoindre sera peut être en état d'y fair face, elle ne sera pas moins dans l'impossibilité d'arracher à l'usurpateur les conquêtes qu'il a faites, et que des positions très avantageuses lui donnent la faculté des défendre avec succés.*

weapons and money to Hesse-Kassel. Equally, Emperor Alexander drew the attention of the British Ministry to Calabria, where the inhabitants had waged a partisan war against the French occupying the Neapolitan Kingdom, while the British troops stationed in Sicily were idle spectators of the fierce struggle by the Calabrians for the throne of their rightful Monarch. Emperor Alexander wrote to Count Vorontsov [Semën Romanovich Vorontsov]; 'Persuade the British to abandon this incomprehensible inaction, instruct them of the disastrous consequences which might come from this for Britain itself.'[13]

Emperor Alexander ordered Count Razumovsky to notify the Viennese Court of his rejection of Napoleon's offer to the Prussian King and to persuade Austria again into an alliance with us, to remind them of the example of Prussia, who suffered for their neutrality in 1805, to keep in mind the courage shown by the Russian army, to declare that the fortunes of the struggle are on our side but, that if we are defeated, Europe will be sacrificed to Napoleon absolutely and that the only way to prevent such a general disaster is for the Austrians to immediately move to the rear of Napoleon. Count Razumovsky had to inform the Austrians that, having missed the current action, they assume responsibility for the outcome, why they didn't take advantage of a favourable set of circumstances when the probability of success was evidently on their side. The usual response of the Viennese Court to such representations by our ambassador was that if Austria declared war on Napoleon, he would shift the theatre of operations from the banks of the Vistula and Narew to the bowels of Austria, crush them and that a success by Russian forces should precede their accession.[14] Such was the state of our relations with Vienna up until the end of February. The news of the Battle of Eylau, in which nations saw the dawn of the liberation of Europe from the hated yoke, energised the Viennese Court and prevailed over their hesitation. Even opponents of a war believed that the time had come to draw swords but, being cautious, at first they wanted to know the consequences of the fighting. Bennigsen's retreat to Königsberg and Napoleon's occupation of the battlefield, from where he sent out portentous-sounding proclamations about his imaginary victory, cooled the desire for war in Vienna. Erzherzog Karl considered the Battle of Eylau to be a great step towards a brighter future but not quite decisive enough to prompt Austria into taking part in the war. Not seeing the commonly expected fruits of victory from our side, the Austrians decided to continue to wait on our success.[15]

The efforts of the Prussian King to induce Austria to go to war against Napoleon were equally unsuccessful. Wanting to prove his unlimited sincerity in relation to Austria, the King finally proposed to Kaiser Franz, to hand over to Austrian troops the small number of Silesian fortresses remaining under Prussian control, from that moment until a general settlement. The offer was rejected.[16] So much respect for

---

13  Supreme instructions to Count Vorontsov in London, dated 14 [26] March.
14  Count Razumovsky's report, dated 25 January [6 February]: *En dernier résultat, je crois pouvoir affirmer, que rien ne déterminera la cour de Vienne à changer de système qu'une suite de succés de nos armées.*
15  Freiherr von Schladen, *Preußen in den Jahren 1806 und 1807*, p. 109.
16  Report from the Russian Ambassador, Baron Krüdener, to the Prussian Court in Memel, dated 23 February [7 March]: *Les représentations du comte de Finkenstein, ministre de Prusse*

Prussia was lost in Vienna then that the equerry of the King of Prussia, Graf Götzen [Friedrich Wilhelm von Götzen der Jüngere], sent with an offer, was not even received by the Austrian Ministry.[17] The only concession granted by the Austrian Government to Prussia was permission for the Prussians to purchase weapons in Austria. An irrelevant concession! Prussia had almost no troops.

Both the burden of war and the complexities of diplomatic negotiations lay with Emperor Alexander, since his ally, Prussia, had lost its voice in Europe. The breadth of thought and activity of our Monarch was vast! And when all his thoughts were turned to finding means inside and outside of Russia to defeat Napoleon, he suddenly received from the person to whom he had entrusted the army a petition to release him from the appointment of Commander-in-Chief. On the third day after the Battle of Eylau, Bennigsen sent *Flügel-Adjutant* Benkendorff [Alexander Khristoforovich Benkendorff] to St Petersburg with a request to be released from his command, expressing his readiness to remain with the troops and serve under whichever commander.[18] Following Benkendorff, Bennigsen sent Prince Bagration to St Petersburg to present to Emperor Alexander the current situation of the army, since this had been falsely represented in private letters written from the theatre of war to St Petersburg. There were various reasons, prompting Bennigsen to ask for release from the appointment of Commander-in-Chief. He began to feel the grip of disease, which, as we will see in the description of the spring campaign, subsequently completely compromised his health. Other painful circumstances combined with his physical ailment. The kindness and gentleness of Bennigsen's temper gave rise to unfavourable talk in the army about his actions. Since the opening of the campaign, giving Napoleon a fierce rebuff, not yielding a foot of ground to the French without the most stubborn defence, everyone regretted that gladly shed blood and the trials of heroic courage had one constant consequence – retreat. The self-confidence of Russian power required offensive action and the failure to fulfil this general desire was blamed on Bennigsen's lack of enterprise. Rumours weakened his authority but he did not know how to counter the boastful talk of his critics or stop the disorder spreading from hour to hour in the logistics management of the army. Bennigsen's disagreements with General Knorring, who had been sent to the main army as an advisor, once reached such an extent that both grabbed their sword hilts, deciding to settle the argument with a duel. A witness to the quarrel, Quartermaster-General Steinheil, managed to reconcile them.

After listening to Benkendorff and Prince Bagration, Emperor Alexander expressed a desire for Bennigsen to remain Commander-in-Chief, recalled Knorring from the army and sent there one of his favourites, Novosiltsev, with orders to establish agreement between the generals and to inspire greater firmness from Bennigsen. Then the Emperor ordered Tsarevich Konstantin Pavlovich to go from St Petersburg

---

    *à Vienne, faites dans des audiences demandées à l'Empereur François, à l'archiduc Charles et au comte de Stadion, ont été infructueuses.*
17  Baron Krüdener's report, dated 23 February [7 March]: *Le comte de Goetzen, aide de camp du roi de Prusse, destiné à proposer à l'Autriche d'occupper les forteresses de la Silésie, qui étoient encore au pouvoir du roi de Prusse, n'a pas même été reçu.*
18  From Count Benkendorff's autobiographical notes.

to Jurburg with 1st division, which included the Lifeguard; Rimsky-Korsakov was to send as many troops as possible from the reserves to Bennigsen; Princes Lobanov-Rostovsky and Gorchakov [2nd] were to hurry to depart for the Neman from Moscow and Kaluga with 17th Division and 18th Division, while the *opolchenie* commanders were to send musket battalions to the army quickly. Utilizing all the resources of his State to continue the war, Emperor Alexander hoped that by the time the reinforcements assigned by him to the army arrived, the war would take a better turn, that Britain and Austria finally comprehend the weight of the arguments communicated to them, abandon inaction and move into Napoleon's rear. Neither in London nor in Vienna did the words of Alexander find an echo!

15

# Operations Following The Battle of Eylau

**Napoleon's retreat to the Passarge. – Bennigsen's move from Königsberg to Landsberg. – The Deployment of the French army. – Napoleon's situation. – Bennigsen's advance from Landsberg to Heilsberg. – The order of battle of the Russian army. – The appointments of Platov and Prince Shcherbatov. – Reasons for the inaction of the main armies. – Platov's operations.**

Having paused for nine days on the battlefield of Eylau, Napoleon retreated on 5 [17] February, through Landsberg, Mehlsack [Pieniężno] and Wormditt, to the left bank of the Passarge [Pasłęka]. Following the departure of Prince Bagration for St Petersburg, Platov took over command of the vanguard and followed the French. The entire route was strewn with abandoned carts, dead and dying soldiers and horses. The haste of their retreat reached the point that, in addition to those left by the French suffering in the wagons, the Cossacks found many enemy soldiers lying on the snow without blankets or clothing. After ascertaining Napoleon's retreat, Bennigsen followed him, on 7 [19] February, with the army refreshed from Königsberg, joined by 6th Division from Gonionds, entrusted to the command of Duty General Count Tolstoy. On the second day's march, in Landsberg, a sudden thaw stopped Bennigsen for a week, in completely devastated country. Eylau, Landsberg and the surrounding villages had been looted and burned out by the French during Napoleon's nine-day pause in Eylau. Napoleon had given orders to bury his fallen soldiers but frozen ground and snow made it difficult to carry out the command. The same obstacle was encountered by the peasants, who were subsequently sent by Bennigsen from Königsberg to bury the corpses. Several weeks passed before the dead were removed from the land surface. Even our generals were forced to stay in the bivouacs, because of the impossibility of spending the night in homes: occasionally finding a surviving room, only to find it home to rotting corpses.

Having crossed the Passarge, Napoleon arranged his corps as follows: Bernadotte formed the left wing, at Braunsberg [Braniewo]; Soult in the centre, at Liebstadt; Davout on the right wing, at Hohenstein; behind him the *Réserve de cavalerie*; the grenadiers and *Garde* at Osterode, where Napoleon established his headquarters. Ney remained on the right bank of the Passarge, at Guttstadt. An independent corps of Poles and French, under the command of Zajanczek [Józef Zajączek], was posted to the right of Davout, in the area of Willenberg, having orders to maintain communications between the main army and the independent corps formerly around

Ostrolenka. Securing the location of the army, Napoleon ordered the construction of bridge-head fortifications on the banks of the Passarge and established a route for his communications through Thorn to Poznan, abandoning the old route to Warsaw. Thorn was designated the main location for depots and stores of all kinds, parks and hospitals. In Warsaw, Napoleon left only Talleyrand [Charles Maurice de Talleyrand-Perigord], the Minister of Foreign Affairs, and the diplomats who came to him from various Courts. Removing all the signs of war from Warsaw, Napoleon turned this city into the centre of political affairs and leisure. At lavish dinners and daily evening gatherings, Talleyrand demonstrated the brilliant state of the French army, embedding trust in Napoleon's might in foreigners and Poles.

On 17 February [1 March], once the frost had hardened the ground, Bennigsen set out from Landsberg for Launau, and on the 20 [4 March], making Bartenstein [Bartoszyce] his headquarters, set up the army around Heilsberg in cantonments and issued the following order of battle: Tuchkov on the right wing with 5th Division and 8th Division; Sacken in the centre with 3rd Division; Prince Gorchakov on the left wing with 2nd Division and 14th Division; first reserve under Dokhturov with 4th Division and 7th Division and second reserve under Count Tolstoy with 6th Division and three regiments from 9th Division, detached from Essen 1st's independent corps to the main army. The cavalry were split into two detachments; Uvarov's [Fëdor Petrovich Uvarov] on the right flank and Prince Golitsyn's on the left. The vanguard was posted in Launau, where Prince Bagration soon returned from St Petersburg. L'Estocq was on the extreme right wing opposite Braunsberg. Platov had the Pavlograd Hussars and ten Cossack regiments; the *Ataman's*, Ilovaysky 5th's [Nikolay Vasilievich Ilovaysky], Ilovaysky 8th's [Stepan Dmitrievich Ilovaysky] and Ilovaysky 10th's [Osip Vasilievich Ilovaysky], Karpov's, Andronov's (soon to become Isaev 2nd's on his death), Sysoev's, Grekov 18th's [Timofey Dmitrievich Grekov], Yefremov's and Selivanov's and a company of Don Artillery, was positioned between Ortelsburg [Szczytno] and Willenberg, tasked to maintain communications between the main army and Essen's corps. Setting out on his mission on 2 [14] March, Platov reported that from the Battle of Eylau to 1 [13] March, in barely a month, the men of the Don had taken 37 officers and 2,254 lower ranks as prisoners of war during the army's rest at Königsberg, during the French retreat to the Passarge and on daily patrols. Harassing the enemy day and night, Napoleon was fed up with the Cossacks to such an extent that in one of the bulletins of the time he called them: 'The shame of the human species.'[1]

At the request of the King of Prussia, Bennigsen sent Prince Shcherbatov to Danzig via Pillau and the Nehrung spit [Mierzeja Wiślana], with three [Kronstadt] garrison battalions, which had just arrived in Königsberg from Russia, ordering him to take three Don regiments under his command, which had also been detached to Danzig on the will of the King of Prussia during the stay of our army at Königsberg. While sending Prince Shcherbatov on this mission, the King ordered the overall Commandant of Danzig, Graf Kalckreuth, to consider Prince Shcherbatov as his second and Military Governor of the fortress and to conclude no negotiations nor

---

1   *La honte de l'espèce humaine.*

conditions with the French without his consent. By sending a small Russian detachment to Danzig, the King of Prussia hoped to raise the fallen morale of the garrison and inhabitants.

This was the situation of the main armies in their cantonments, from the end of February until May. The reason for such prolonged inaction was primarily the exhaustion of the troops after the winter campaign and the need to reorganise them, which is why the consideration arose not to allow the campaign to reopen: on Napoleon's side, he was waiting on the fall of Danzig, while on the part of the Russians, there were food shortages and political circumstances, which will be explained below. Only a guerrilla war was waged on our left wing, where Napoleon tried to draw Bennigsen's attention, distracting him from the siege of Danzig. For this purpose, he ordered Zajanczek, located near Willenberg, to demonstrate Napoleon's intention to disrupt communications between the main Russian army and Essen's independent corps with various manoeuvres Platov was already occupying the ground designated for Zajanczek's operations and there were frequent contacts between both. The Pavlograd Hussars and Cossacks were a storm to the French and especially to Zajanczek's newly formed Poles. Napoleon reinforced him with cavalry. Bennigsen also supported Platov with 1st Jägers, the Grodno Hussars and Denisov 7th's [Vasily Timofeevich Denisov] Cossacks. Platov's operations delivered continuous success, having split his force into many detachments sent in various directions. Those especially distinguished in their search for the enemy were the Colonel-in-Chief of the Pavlograd Hussars, Chaplitz, Colonel Count O'Rourke of the same regiment and the Grodno Hussars Lieutenant-Colonel Kulnev [Yakov Petrovich Kulnev], the first of the Russian generals to lay down their lives for the Fatherland in 1812. In this partisan war, the actions of the Russians were greatly helped by the inhabitants of the surrounding areas, informing our detachments of the location and movements of the enemy. The Prussians' friendly feelings towards us was passed from parents to children. Setting out from any village on patrol, our troops were accompanied by the prayers of both old and young and, when they returned, they were met with glee and songs composed by the children in honour of the Russians. While operating against Zajanczek, Platov did not lose sight of the most important objective of his mission – to maintain communications between the army and Essen's independent corps. Through patrols, he was in continuous liaison with this corps, whose operations are described in the next chapter: hitherto we have not touched upon them, not wanting to interrupt the continuity of the passage of events in the main armies.

# 16

# Operations by Essen's Independent Corps

The objective of Essen's operations. – Napoleon's orders. – The action at Ostrów. – The decision to attack the French. – Actions at the Pissek, Szkwa and Osowiecka. – The action at Ostrolenka. – Count Wittgenstein's operations. – The inaction of the warring forces.

In early [mid] December 1806, Lieutenant-General Essen set off from the banks of the Dniester for Brest with his corps, consisting of 37,249 men and 132 guns, whereupon he was kept inactive by the contradictory orders from Field Marshal Kamensky, Count Buxhoeveden and Bennigsen, until January. Then, when the appointment of Bennigsen as Commander-in-Chief was approved giving unity of command, Essen received Bennigsen's orders: 'to advance from Brest and deploy between the Bug and the Narew, having also taken Sedmoratsky's 6th Division under command, which was stationed in Gonionds and having the operational objective of defending the Russian border between Grodno and Brest.' At the beginning of January, Essen left Brest for Brańsk, where he concentrated the corps.[1] Major-General Löwis [Fëdor Fëdorovich Löwis] commanded his vanguard, consisting of the Yaroslavl Musketeers, 8th Jägers, Akhtyrka Hussars and one Cossack regiment. His patrols extended from the banks of the Bug to the Narew and had minor clashes with enemy patrols and foragers. Löwis often harassed the French at night. They requested through a *parlementaire* that he stop the raids, citing their futility. The enemy complaint was disregarded and Löwis continued his nightly attacks, taking quite a few prisoners of war.

Essen faced Lannes' corps. Due to the Marshal falling ill at the end of December, General Savary was in command of the corps. His left wing was in occupation of Ostrolenka, while the right was in Brok, on the Bug. Napoleon ordered Savary to adopt a defensive posture, to guard the right wing of the main French army, to prevent Essen from joining Bennigsen and to hold him at all costs if he moved on Warsaw. Seeing that Savary was not moving, on 15 [27] January, Essen moved his corps from Brańsk to Wysokie Mazowieckie and reinforced Sedmoratsky's detachment in Gonionds, entrusting all the troops gathered there to the commander of 9th Division, Prince Volkonsky – [Dmitry Mikhailovich Volkonsky] who later died as a Senator. Soon after, learning about the occupation of the town of Ostrów by a

---

1   Essen's reports to the Tsar, dated 5 and 6 [17 and 18] January 1807.

strong French detachment, Essen set out to attack them. The attack took place on 22 January [3 February]. Major-General Prince Urusov [Nikolay Yuryevich Urusov] moved first towards Ostrów, while Löwis outflanked the town on the right. The French bravely resisted the attack from the front but, as Löwis outflanked them, they began to retreat. Before they could even evacuate Ostrów completely, with courage worthy of his great name, Prince Suvorov [Arkady Alexandrovich Suvorov] burst in with the Ryazhsk Musketeers and forced the enemy to flee. Our casualties from this whole action were insignificant. Five days later, the Battle of Eylau took place, after which, wanting to cause Napoleon concerns for his rear, Bennigsen ordered Essen to attack the French. Savary found this out when he captured an officer with the report from Essen, informing Bennigsen that orders concerning the attack had been received. While the French took measures for defence, Essen gave orders to operate on both banks of the Narew. He wanted to go from Wysokie-Mazowieckie directly to Ostrolenka with the main body of the corps and send Prince Volkonsky's detachment at the same time along the right bank of the Narew, from Gonionds, via Kolno. His detachment consisted of two formations; Sedmoratsky's 6th Division and three regiments from 9th Division. As Prince Volkonsky set off for Ostrolenka, Sedmoratsky was ordered by Bennigsen to lead 6th Division to join the Main Army in Königsberg and set off there, even though Prince Volkonsky begged him to delay his journey for several days, in order to carry out the attack on Ostrolenka first and then carry out the will of the Commander-in-Chief. Thus, the attack planned by Essen for the right bank of the Narew would not be carried out with great strength. Following the detachment of 6th Division to the army, all Prince Volkonsky had left were the Ukraine Musketeers, Crimea Musketeers, 10th Jägers with Ilovaysky 10th's Cossacks and three squadrons of Mitau Dragoons. He set off with them from Gonionds on 2 [14] February, crossed the Pissek river at Dobry Las and encountered a weak French vanguard at Stanisławowo the next day. The enemy conducted a slow, fighting withdrawal, which was facilitated by swamps and forests. Essen was supposed to attack that day from the left bank of the Narew, but he was late arriving – a common event with divided attacks. Knowing about the Russian attack from Dobry Las, Savary left one division for the defence of Ostrolenka, and went with the other to Stanisławowo, linked up with his vanguard here and advanced. Prince Volkonsky fell back in front of the superior enemy to the river Szkwa, positioned his force on its left bank and brought the French under crossfire as they approached the bank. Our fire and the evening darkness stopped the enemy.

The next day, 4 [16] February, Savary discovered a ford on the Szkwa and went across it to outflank us. The Russians courageously repelled the French, while Prince Volkonsky's two main assistants, the Colonel-in-Chief of the Ukraine Musketeers, Budberg [Vasily Vasilievich Budberg], was badly wounded and the Colonel-in-Chief of the 10th Jägers, Brezgun [Mikhael Petrovich Brezgun], was killed. The next in seniority after him, Colonel Zvarykin – [Fëdor Vasilievich Zvarykin] whose name is associated with the glory of the Shirvan Infantry in Emperor Alexander's foreign wars – and Lieutenant Romashkov, with the colours in his hands, led the jägers in a bayonet charge. The determined defence did not stop the French and they moved around our flanks. Prince Volkonsky hastily, but in good order, retreated to a position at Osowiecka, which he had identified the previous day but had to abandon a damaged gun, its crew and horses having all been wounded or killed. In this new position, he greeted the enemy with round shot and canister. The French advanced around the flanks again and the bitter combat continued, moreover, Lieutenant Mikhailov of 10th Jägers captured a gun with his skirmishers. He then seized a French cartridge caisson with ammunition and horses. Portepée-Ensign Nelidov and *Feldwebel* Semin, seeing that the flagpoles were broken, tore off their colours, wrapped them around themselves and continued to fight. Fending off the enemy, our men moved to a new position but even here they had to give way to superior numbers and moved into the woods located behind the positions. The guns, set at the edge of the woods by Majors Gine [Yakov Yegorovich Gine] and Nikitin [Alexey Petrovich Nikitin], stopped the French.

Savary was preparing to attack the woods when he received a report of Essen's approach to Ostrolenka. Taking most of the troops with him, Savary hastened there, ordering General Gazan to hold Prince Volkonsky. Upon arriving at Ostrolenka, Essen discovered the situation with Prince Volkonsky's detachment and sent him orders to retreat, while he, wishing to facilitate this withdrawal, launched a diversionary attack on Ostrolenka himself and then returned to Wysokie Mazowieckie.[2] Savary pursued him vigorously and took two guns complete with carriages. Lost on the ice, they slid into the water and, under enemy canister fire, no effort could save them. Being satisfied with his trophies and the repulse of the Russians, Savary, having pushed on a few *versts*, returned to Ostrolenka. Prince Volkonsky's and Essen's casualties amounted to some 1,000 men killed or wounded.[3] Essen suggested that the main reason for the failure of his operation was the detachment of Sedmoratsky's 6th Division to Königsberg and complained to the Tsar that Sedmoratsky should have remained with Prince Volkonsky for two or three days so that they could have carried out a combined attack. Emperor Alexander found Sedmoratsky blameless, in that he was obliged to obey Bennigsen's orders immediately.

Returning from the Ostrolenka, Essen, as before, was located in Wysokie-Mazowieckie and formed two cavalry detachments assigned to Major-General Lvov [Pëtr Nikolaevich Lvov] and Knorring [Karl Bogdanovich Knorring], ordering them to clear the French from the area between the Bug and the Narew. On the second day of his march, Lvov liberated 2,600 Russian and Prussian prisoners of war.[4] Soon afterwards, Napoleon reassigned Savary's corps to Marshal Masséna [André Masséna], who had arrived from Italy, ordering him to leave Ostrolenka and take up positions around Pultusk. Essen sent Major-General Count Wittgenstein [Peter Khristianovich Wittgenstein] onto the right bank of the Narew via Ostrolenka in order to monitor the French with four squadrons of Mariupol Hussars, four more from the Akhtyrka Hussars and 300 Cossacks from Chernozubov 4th's [Ilya

---

2 Essen reported to Bennigsen on 13 [25] February (No 745): 'I was forced to conduct an attack on Ostrolenka solely as a diversion for the movement of Prince Volkonsky's detachment and to release them from being completely at the mercy of the enemy on the right bank of the Narew and which, for lack of a bridge, I could not support.'
3 Prince Volkonsky's report to Essen, dated 11 [23] February, No 247 and Essen's to the Tsar, dated 8 [20] February, No 665.
4 Essen's report to Bennigsen, dated 13 [25] February, No 745.

Fëdorovich Chernozubov] Regiment. On the march, Count Wittgenstein was delayed for a long time by the reconstruction of the bridge at Ostrolenka, destroyed by the French, who had also destroyed the ferries and boats on the Narew. On 27 February [11 March], Count Wittgenstein made a crossing, took Ostrolenka and sent patrols to the left to Pultusk to monitor the French and to the right to maintain communications with Platov. Due to the small size of his detachment, Count Wittgenstein could not carry out a strong reconnaissance against the French, so Essen strengthened it with the 8th Jägers, 10th Jägers, Novorossia Dragoons and two Cossack regiments. Having received reinforcements, Count Wittgenstein closely linked his right wing with Platov and, together with the Ataman's detachment, greatly harassed the enemy. Colonel Chernozubov 4th particularly distinguished himself in these operations. Strengthening his left wing at the same time, Count Wittgenstein had clashes with Masséna's outposts but this Marshal, following Napoleon's orders to operate on the defensive, did not move from Pultusk and merely reinforced his vanguards.

As for Essen, he was inactive, like Masséna and, as before, remained in Wysokie-Mazowieckie, needing food. All the surrounding villages had been ravaged; our troops ate only potatoes, finding hardly any in the pits where the inhabitants hid them and were leaving in droves for Galicia. Contagious diseases raged in most villages. Trapped by hunger and fever, Essen believed that until the onset of spring it would be impossible for him to conduct military operations in the area between the Bug and the Narew and, without warning Bennigsen, he asked Emperor Alexander for permission to send his heavy artillery and most of the cavalry to the borders of Russia for easier provisioning.[5] Responding to Essen, Emperor Alexander strictly forbade him from considering returning troops to Russia from the theatre of war, and to make representations through Bennigsen.[6] Taking the most severe measures for provisioning, Essen spent February and March inactive and in April, due to illness, was dismissed from command of the corps, after which he soon joined the Main Army and was appointed Duty General. His corps was handed over to Tuchkov 1st – mortally wounded at Borodino.

---

5  Essen's report to the Tsar, dated 14 [26] February, No 768.
6  Supreme rescript to Essen, dated 1 [13] March.

# 17

# Emperor Alexander's Visit to The Army

---

Emperor Alexander's departure from St Petersburg for the army. – His time at Memel. – A view of the Russian Guard. – The Guard joins the army. – The Emperor's arrival at headquarters. – The Bartenstein Treaty. – Instructions to the Russian ambassador in Vienna. – The operational plan presented to the Austrians by Emperor Alexander. – Austrian mediation. – Austria's refusal to proceed with the Bartenstein Treaty. – Emperor Alexander's anger at the Viennese Court. – The Emperor's correspondence with Britain. – Relations with Sweden. – Measures to lift the siege of Danzig. – Napoleon's operations. – The decision to attack Marshal Ney. – Emperor Alexander's departure from the army.

Wanting to personally verify the situation in the theatre of war, to review his brave army and to revive the weakened morale of the Prussian Court, Emperor Alexander set off from St Petersburg on 16 [28] March for the army, via Riga and Mitau. He was accompanied by *Ober-Hoffmarshal* Count Tolstoy [Nikolai Aleksandrovich Tolstoy], Minister of Foreign Affairs Baron Budberg and Adjutants-General Count Lieven and Prince Volkonsky. At Polangen [Palanga], on 24 March [5 April], the Emperor was met by the Prussian King and spent two hours together with him. The next day, he went to Memel and stayed at the residence occupied by the Prussian Monarchs, where the King introduced him to military and civilian officials. The Tsar especially liked the former Minister of Foreign Affairs, Baron Hardenberg, gripped his hand for a long time, then led him to another room and talked to him in private. But with the then Minister of Foreign Affairs, General Zastrow, a peace advocate, the Emperor treated him coolly. After the King's dinner, His Majesty accompanied our Monarch to the residence assigned for him, where the Prussian Lieutenant-General Köhler [Georg Ludwig Egidius von Köhler], Colonels Krusemarck [Friedrich Wilhelm Ludwig von Krusemarck] and Belzig and Major Schöller were expected to be with him during his stay in Memel. Some time later, accompanied by Count Lieven and Colonel Krusemarck, the Tsar mounted a horse and visited the Prussian Princess Wilhelm and Princess Radzivil and in the evening went on foot to Baron Hardenberg and spent two hours with him. The next morning, after a long meeting between the Emperor and the King, Hardenberg was ordered to go to Jurburg, where the Monarchs intended to go. The King announced the same decree to General Zastrow but he, on various pretexts, refused to execute the order, which was due to the coldness shown to him by the Emperor and his preference for Hardenberg, who was later appointed Minister of Foreign Affairs. This was the first consequence of the meeting of Emperor Alexander with the King of Prussia.

On 27 March [8 April], at three o'clock in the morning, the King and Queen set off with the Emperor to Jurburg, to inspect the Lifeguard which had arrived there from St Petersburg. Before leaving, the Emperor gave General Köhler a snuff box with his portrait, Krusemarck a ring with a monogram, Belzig a snuff box with a monogram, and diamond rings to Schöller and the former servants of the Tsar. Near Jurburg, Emperor Alexander presented his Lifeguard to the Prussian Monarchs. These troops, having set off from the capital half way through February, marched through crackling frosts at a most forced pace; rest days occurred only after five or six days of marching. The Lifeguard Artillery set off after the infantry and cavalry and were granted only one rest day from St Petersburg to Jurburg, in Pskov. The general desire of all ranks of the guard to test themselves against the French and the bodily strength of men and horses overcame the difficulties of the march. Following the regiments came a large number of peasant carts, carrying haversacks, muskets, packs and exhausted infantrymen in shifts. There were 596 horses with the Chevalierguard Regiment, 1,192 with His Highness the Tsarevich's Ulan Regiment and 784 draught horses with each Lifeguard infantry regiment. After being reviewed by the Monarchs, the Lifeguard marched from Jurburg to join the army and the number of carts were reduced. In cavalry regiments the officers were only allowed pack horses and each infantry battalion was allowed only two carts for officers' baggage, while artillery companies were allowed only one each. On the basis of an agreement with Prussia, daily rations for each Lifeguard soldier abroad were 2½ pounds of bread, ½ pound of meat boiled in a stew with potatoes or other greens, a glass of beer or a glass of wine. In addition to straw, 4 *garnets* [13 litres or 23 pints] of oats and 10 *funt* [4.1kg or 9lb] of hay were issued to each riding and draught horse per day. For all deliveries, receipts were given, according to which our Government was obliged to pay. Despite this, the regiments constantly complained about the lack of provisions and fodder, and could hardly obtain them at a high price.[1] The roads from Jurburg were barely passable and the guard abandoned many wagons on the way, including those carrying hard-tack. On 10 [22] April the Lifeguard arrived in Schippenbeil [Sępopol] and went into cantonments; subordination into columns was discontinued; the cavalry was assigned to General Kologrivov [Andrei Semënovich Kologrivov] and the infantry to Malyutin [Pëtr Fëdorovich Malyutin]. Bennigsen gave orders for the Lifeguard to practice volley fire.

On 28 March [9 April], having despatched the Lifeguard, Emperor Alexander remained in Jurburg for four days with the Prussian Monarchs and set off for Bartenstein on 2 [14] April, where he was most graciously received by Bennigsen. Having lost confidence in himself after the Austerlitz calamity, he left Bennigsen to act at his discretion and decreed that the following orders be issued to the army:

> The victories at Pultusk and Preußisch-Eylau, won by General Bennigsen over the enemy have justified and increased the authority founded upon his

---

1  From the war diary of the Lifeguard Corps.

skill. The visit of His Imperial Majesty to His brave army does not in any way introduce the slightest change in the chain of command under which the common good of Europe is already beginning so noticeably to emerge. All orders still come from one Commander-in-Chief, General Bennigsen, in addition, reports will be delivered directly to him.

Alexander didn't do this later, in the great wars of 1813, 1814 and 1815, once experience had convinced him of the great military virtues granted to him by God. The following day, he set off for the army assembly area and found it in excellent condition. He ordered several cavalry regiments, in which the horses were weak from lack of feed, to go to the army rear areas for replenishment.

Returning to Bartenstein, the Emperor found the King of Prussia there and entered into a treaty with him on 14 [26] April, named for Bartenstein and aimed at 'consolidating a general and solid peace in Europe, secured by the guarantee of all Powers.' Russia and Prussia declared that they were strangers to self-interested views, they were not waging war to humiliate France, they did not want to interfere in matters of its internal administration, however, they cannot view the unimpeded expansion of France at the expense of other lands with indifference, by which it threatens their existence, destroying the balance of power between the Powers. Desiring one thing – peace and security for all the states, the Monarchs of Russia and Prussia wanted, having invited Austria, Britain and Sweden to join with them, to spare no expense in order to force the French Government to return to the proper borders and does not emerge from them in the future, will guarantee the independence of other Powers, reward those who suffered losses, in short, the Monarchs wanted:

> to raise an edifice that cannot be shaken or run the risk of collapsing at the first attempt to shake it.[2]

As a consequence of these principles set forth in the introduction to the treaty, firstly, Emperor Alexander undertook to use all his strength to return to the King of Prussia his territories occupied by the French and those which the King had lost since 1805. Secondly, to assert the independence of Germany, Emperor Alexander and the King of Prussia recognised the need to disband the Confederation of the Rhine, to force Napoleon to remove French troops behind the Rhine and establish a new alliance on German soil under the auspices of Austria and Prussia, and guaranteed by Russia, Britain and Sweden. Thirdly, With the consent of Austria, Britain and Sweden to start a treaty, restoring Austria to its former power by returning Tyrol to it, and in Italy the borders along the Mincio and to strengthen the influence of Britain and Sweden on matters in Germany. Fourth, return the Prince of Orange to his territories. Fifth, restore the Kings of Sardinia and Naples. Seventh [sic], ensure the integrity of Turkey. To enforce all these statutes, the Monarchs of Russia and Prussia pledged to wage an active war, not spare any efforts and not

---

2   ... d'elever un édifice qui ne puisse être ébranlé et courrir risque de crouler à la première tentative qu'on feroit pour l'ébranler.

otherwise lay down their arms, as with general conditions, acting mutually with complete openness.

The Bartenstein Treaty encompasses a repetition of Emperor Alexander's abiding principles in his ten-year struggle with Napoleon. Exactly the same principles were used by him as the foundation of the treaty with Britain of 24 March [5 April], 1805, as he was preparing for the first war and he was equally minded in the last struggle with Napoleon in the year 1814. The terms of the Bartenstein Treaty were the same, shunning conquest, by which he was guided after his triumph over Napoleon, signing the peace in Paris. But we find a remarkable difference in the fact that in 1805 and 1807 Alexander left Napoleon as the ruler of France, only setting limits on his plundering. He did not think so when experience confirmed for him the impossibility of peace while Napoleon remained on the throne. At that point, Alexander laid the first condition – the demise of Napoleon.

Inviting Austria into the alliance with Russia and Prussia, Emperor Alexander wrote to his Ambassador in Vienna:

> Announce to Austria that, in recognition of the great importance in helping us, I find that now there is nothing more harmful than the continued uncertainty about the decision of the Viennese Court, which is why I hope to receive an early and positive response. The Austrian reply will show me whether they intend to share the honour and benefits of my great protective work and will they choose the only means that is consistent with dignity and its true benefits? Will they really rely upon a corrupt system of neutrality, the consequences of which – of which in recent times there are many examples – will certainly involve them in disaster? Are they really going to give up all the auspicious events ahead of them, even from the glory of saving Europe, restoring its calm and establishing peace on just terms?

In conclusion, Emperor Alexander declared his readiness when, with the help of Austria, we could end the war with good fortune, to warn Austria of his wishes if they wanted any acquisitions.[3]

At that time, Emperor Alexander sent Major Theil van Seraskerken [Fëdor Vasilievich (Diderik Jacob) Theil van Seraskerken] to Vienna, later the Russian Envoy to the North American States, with a letter to Kaiser Franz and with an operational plan for our joint operations with the Austrians. The essence of the plan was as follows: Send the Austrian army to the area between the Warthe and the Pilica, or between the Vistula and Pilica. This movement is likely to prompt Napoleon to retreat beyond the Vistula and move against the Austrians. Should they come under attack, the Austrian army will retreat to Sandomierz or Kraków. In any case, the Russian army, mindful of the actions of the Austrians, will move quickly behind enemy lines, leaving all the Prussian troops for defensive operations on the Vistula.

---

3   Instructions to Count Razumovsky, dated 3 [15] May: *Si l'Autriche avoit quelque désir particulier à former pour l'avenir heureux, qu'assureroit son accession au traité de Bartenstein, S. M. l'Empereur de toutes les Russies se feroit un plaisir d'aller audevant des voeux de son auguste ami, l'Empereur et Roi.*

Having thus transferred the war to Galicia, it is hoped that enough food may be found there. Fortresses in Bohemia, Moravia and Silesia were to serve as manoeuvre points for the allied armies. Moreover, send strong Austrian detachments into Lusatia, Saxony and Bavaria, to operate in Napoleon's rear areas and persuade his allies to our side. Agents will go to Franconia and Swabia, prompting the inhabitants to revolt. The Austrians will wage a defensive war in Italy and occupy Tyrol, disrupting Napoleon's communication with his troops in Italy. Should Napoleon retreat to the Oder, the Allies will quickly follow him and then agree on further operations.[4] Major Theil also had the authority to negotiate with the Viennese Court concerning rations, hospitals and ammunition for the Russian troops.

While our Monarch's invitation to enter into an alliance with us was brought to Kaiser Franz in Vienna, the Austrian General Saint-Vincent, who had been at Napoleon's headquarters since the opening of the war, often repeated the offer of mediation by Austria for his reconciliation with Emperor Alexander to him. Trying to keep relations with Austria friendly with all his might, Napoleon reassured Saint-Vincent by all possible means – it is known that not many of his contemporaries could resist Napoleon's charming treatment towards them, when he wanted to entice one of them to his side. He spoke to the Austrian envoy about his sincere desire to deliver various rewards to Austria and, avoiding acting contrary to the policies of this Power, he did not apparently reject their mediation, but touched on this subject with generally vague expressions. Having detained Saint-Vincent for quite some time in his headquarters, Napoleon sent him to Warsaw to negotiate with the Minister for Foreign Affairs, Talleyrand. Honourably and hospitably hosted in Warsaw, he could not quickly carry out the assignment entrusted to him. According to Napoleon's will, Talleyrand drew the negotiations out and finally told Saint-Vincent that without asking for Napoleon's orders, who was with the army, he could not give a definitive answer to the Viennese Court. The reason for Napoleon's and Talleyrand's evasive comments was their expectation of victory over the Russians. Since 1796, in continuous relations with Austria for eleven years, Napoleon knew their policy and had no doubt that victory would be his best response and that until then the main thing was to keep them inactive. Meanwhile, prompted by the often repeated instructions of his Court, Saint-Vincent insisted on receiving a definitive answer. Having exhausted all kinds of pretexts for evasion, excuses and deferrals, on 7 [19] April, Napoleon accepted the mediation of Austria.

The Austrian Ambassador in St Petersburg, Graf von Merveldt [Maximilian Friedrich Graf von Merveldt], at the behest of his Monarch, equally offered our Court mediation by Austria in the reconciliation of Russia with Napoleon. Emperor Alexander agreed to the mediation provided Napoleon positively declared his conditions and presented the pledges of his wish for peace, for example, to return the Prussian Silesian fortresses. Alexander stated;

> In the offer of its mediation and its good offices, Austria obviously only aims to prolong the state of inactivity and impassibility which seems so

---

4   Operational plan, approved in Bartenstein 5 [17] May.

well suited to its timid and irresolute policy. As it is important for the court of Vienna to save time, in the hope of being able to then take the side that the development of circumstances will present to them as the most advantageous, at least we should not let them ignore that this motive could not escape any of the powers concerned, and that from then on it could well happen that such circumstances which would give them very lively regrets for not having seized the current moment, when their adhesion to the common cause would be a decisive weight in the balance.[5]

The news of Napoleon's acceptance of Austria's mediation came to Vienna at almost the same time as the invitation from Emperor Alexander to proceed with the Bartenstein Treaty. The Viennese Court found the terms of the treaty so extreme that they considered it impossible, even following a most brilliant war, to achieve the objectives proposed by the monarchs of Russia and Prussia.[6] Refusing to assist Emperor Alexander, Austria excused itself with the general desire for peace found in the Hungarian Diet at that time and their unpreparedness for war,[7] saying that they could not place the army on a war footing for two more years, by 1809, especially as their finances were in disorder.[8] Emperor Alexander replied that if Austria did not sign up to the Bartenstein Treaty, then they should consider the consequences themselves of what might happen to them, should our Monarch, who prefers the common good over everything, be forced to think solely of his own interests, for want of being rescued by those whose dignity and independence he is so nobly able to support.[9] Seeing from Emperor Alexander's comment that, in any possible

---

5   Instructions to Count Razumovsky in Vienna, dated 26 April [8 May]: *Dans l'offre de sa médiation et de ses bons offices, l'Autriche ne vise évidemment qu'à prolonger l'état d'inactivité et d'impassibilité qui paroit si fort convenir à sa politique timide et irrésolue. Comme il importe à la cour de Vienne de gagner du tems, dans l'espoir de pouvoir prendre ensuite le parti que le développment des circonstances lui présentera comme le plus avantageux, il ne faut pas du moins lui laisser ignorer que ce motif ne sauroit échapper à aucune des puissances intéressées, et que dèslors il pourrait bien advenir telle circonstance qui lui donneroit des regrets bien vifs de ne pas avoir saisi le moment actuel, où son adhésion à la cause commune mettroit un poids décisif dans la balance.*
6   Count Razumovsky's report, dated 24 May [5 June]: *La cour de Vienne trouve les bases du traité de Bartenstein tellement hors d'atteinte, qu'on ne sauroit y parvenir même par une continuité de succès les plus brillans, et il met en doute les moyens qui pourroient nous les procurer.*
7   Count Razumovsky's report, dated 22 May [3 June]: *La circonspection de la cour de Vienne et le désir d'éloigner de plus en plus le moment de se décider, ont été fortifiés par la disposition de la diète d'Hongrie, dont les débats ont toujours été fondés sur la nécessité de la paix et le danger d'une guerre nouvelle. Ce cri tumultueux de paix a fait impression sur l'Empereur François, et je sais que ce Prince a répété dans les épanchemens de sa confiance: 'Point de guerre!'*
8   Count Razumovsky's report, dated 22 May [3 June]: *L'armée s'est remontée d'une manière étonnante. Son apparence est plus belle que jamais, mais elle est vien loin d'avoir la consistance, qu'on regarde ici comme essentielle pour entrer en campagne, c'est à dire, qu'elle manque de tous les objets de rechange indispensables en cas de revers, comme armes de toute espèce, habillements et même de munitions suffisantes. L'archiduc Charles estime que pour les compléter entièrement on ne sauroit parvenir avant l'année 1809. Il allégue de plus le mauvais état des finances et l'impossibilité qu'elles puissent fournir aux dépenses nécessaires.*
9   Instructions for the Russian Ambassador in Vienna, Count Razumovsky, dated 23 April [5 May]: *Si l'Autriche n'adhère pas au traité de Bartenstein, ce sera à elle à calculer les suites que cela pourra avoir pour elle, si l'Empereur, qui veut avant tout le bien général, est réduit à ne*

negotiations with Napoleon, the Tsar would not pay any attention to his personal advantage, surrendering to the chances of fate and alarmed by this threat, Austria, appointing Graf Stutterheim under the command of Erzherzog Karl, to confer with Major Theil about the operational plan he had brought from Bartenstein. Suspecting that the number of Russian troops set out in the plan was exaggerated, the Viennese Court sent Graf Stutterheim to Emperor Alexander, ordering him to learn in detail about the state of our army and determine the basis for its future operations with the Austrians.

Let us turn to Britain. Equipping his Ambassador in London with complete authority to conclude an alliance with Britain in the event of their accession to the Bartenstein Treaty, Emperor Alexander wrote to the Ambassador:

> The history of our times unfortunately offers only a few examples of such transactions, the purpose of which is only the general good without any ulterior motives on the part of the contracting powers and consequently without secret articles.[10]

The Emperor also sent Colonel Engelmann to London, supplying him with a letter for King George III.[11]43. To gain the consent of the British to act with us in unison, Engelmann had to offer them the operational plan given to him by Emperor Alexander, the main features of which were as follows: the British were to land on German soil between the Elbe and the Weser and march on Hanover and Hesse-Kassel and parts of Westphalia and Franconia. It was believed that when the British appeared, uprisings would break out in these areas against Napoleon and Hanovarian and Kassel troops, disbanded by Napoleon, would join the British, as would Prussian soldiers straggling across northern Germany in many places, after the battles at Jena and Auerstedt. It was hoped that during these operations Austria would have already declared war on Napoleon and the Austrian corps which, according to Emperor Alexander, was to enter Saxony, would enter into communications with the British. The significant forces thus gathered in the rear of Napoleon were supposed to be formed into contingents from Hanover, Kassel, Prussia, Westphalia and Franconia, similar to what was done by Emperor Alexander at the

---

*penser qu'à ses propres intérêts, faute d'avoir été secouru par ceux dont il est prêt à soutenir si noblement la dignité et l'indépendance.*

10   Supreme instructions to the Russian Ambassador in London, dated 19 April [1 May]: *L'histoire de nos jours n'offre malheureusement que peu d'exemples de pareilles transactions, dont le but n'est uniquement que le bien général sans aucune arrière pensée de la part des puissances contractantes, et parconséquent sans articles secrets.*

11   *Monsieur mon frère. La conviction que j'ai que V. M. ne refusera par d'accéder à la convention que je viens de signer avec le Roi de Prusse et qui ne tend qu'à assurer les succès d'une cause pour laquelle V. M. fait depuis tant d'année de si nobles efforts, me porte, Sire, à expédier sans perte de temps l'officier que j'ai désigné pour concerter avec les militaires nommés à cet effet par V. M. tout ce qui sera relatif au plan d'opération contre l'ennemi commun. C'est le Sr. Engelmann, Colonel de mon état-major, que j'ai chargé de cette tâche; il aura l'honneur de remettre la présente à V. M. et je reclame Vos bontés et Votre confiance en sa faveur. Veuillez Sire agréer à cette occasion l'assurance des sentiments d'amitié et d'attachement avec lesquels je suis.*
*Monsieur mon frère de Votre Majesté le bon frère, ami et allié Alexandre.*

end of 1813, after the expulsion of the French from German soil. All these troops would come under the command of the British Government, on condition that they were only used against Napoleon on continental Europe, but not in the colonies and not in other parts of the world.[12]

As early as the month of February, the British had promised to land 30,000 men on German soil.[13] The British Ambassador in St Petersburg, the Marquis of Douglas [Alexander Hamilton, 10th Duke of Hamilton], repeated several times to Emperor Alexander about Britain's readiness to support Russia with all its might. On his visit to the army, the Tsar was assured of the same by the British Plenipotentiary to Prussia, Lord Hutchinson [John Hely-Hutchinson, 2nd Earl of Donoughmore]. The promises of the British were not yet fulfilled when the London Court received an invitation from Emperor Alexander to proceed with the Bartenstein Treaty. During the negotiations conducted by the Russian Ambassador in London, a sudden change occurred in the British Cabinet. The new Ministers would not agree to send more than 12,000 men to Germany, refused to assist Emperor Alexander with a loan of six million pounds Sterling, which he wanted to arrange in England through the mediation of their Government and haggled over the subsidies, which our Court sought in London for Prussia, Austria and Sweden.

The change in British politics, which was harmful to us, also had an adverse effect in Sweden. Failure to receive from the British the amount of support required by him irritated Gustav Adolf IV. When the Chamberlain Ribopierre visited him, with an invitation from Emperor Alexander to participate in the Bartenstein Treaty and with a decision to make a landing in Pomerania, he found that the Swedish King, contrary to his former relations with Russia and his hatred for Napoleon, a week before, on 6 [18] April, had concluded an armistice with him. Such were the acts by Austria, Britain and Sweden when he called them to battle for a holy cause, Powers supposedly friendly to Alexander!

After sending the Bartenstein Treaty to Vienna, London and Stockholm in mid April, Emperor Alexander would not know the decisions of the Courts there, but was sure that, driven by the disasters of Europe and their own interests, they would turn against Napoleon. In anticipation of their responses, he agreed with the King of Prussia not to start operations,[14] only to lift the siege of Danzig in the meantime. The impor-

---

12  Operational plan of 5 [17] May.
13  Report from the Russian Ambassador in London, dated 1 [13] March: *Lord Howick m'a communiqué qu'on étoit intentionné de faire passer sur le continent un corps d'armée de 30,000 hommes.*
14  Supreme instructions to the Russian Ambassador in London, dated 28 June [10 July]: *La stagnation qui a eu lieu dans notre armée, a été principalement motivée par l'espoir fondé que nous avions de voir l'Autriche et l'Angleterre prendre des mesures énergiques que paroissoient leur indiquer leur propre intérêt, non moins que le bien général. Après la communication de la convention de Bartenstein aux cours de Vienne, de Londres et de Stockholm, et les instances pressantes, qui furent réitérativement faites à cette occasion, après les assurances verbales et réitérées que M. l'ambassadeur Marquis Douglas a tant de fois données à l'Empereur sur les dispositions de sa cour à soutenir la Russie de tous ses moyens, assurances qui avoient été confirmées par Mylord Hutchinson dans les entretiens qu'il a eus avec Sa Majesté l'Empereur à l'armée, nous étions sans doute en droit de nous attendre à voir enfin réaliser les promesses, qui sous ce rapport nous avoient été si souvent faites.*

tance of this fortress was that, having captured it, Napoleon could release Marshal Lefebvre's 27,000 man siege corps and Marshal Lannes' 15,000 man reserve waiting behind it at Marienburg [Malbork] and open an offensive against us with superior forces. Holding more than 40,000 Frenchmen near Danzig, the monarchs of Russia and Prussia hoped to equal their forces in the main theatre of war until the Austrians, British and Swedes took action and, moreover, had a harbour convenient for landing troops behind Napoleon. Consideration of these circumstances prompted Emperor Alexander and the King of Prussia to send Count Kamensky to Danzig with a detachment. The day after the signing of the Bartenstein Treaty, on 15 [27] April, the Emperor personally announced to Count Kamensky the mission entrusted to him, ordering him to go to Pillau, to cross the strait connecting the Baltic Sea with the Frisches Haff [Zalew Wiślany] there and follow the Nehrung spit to Danzig, as soon as possible and without the slightest publicity of his mission. According to the Tsar, secrecy and speed were the key to success, based on the calculation that if Napoleon knew in advance about the departure of Count Kamensky, then he would strengthen his siege corps and block our detachment from entering Danzig.[15] The Monarch's prediction came true.

During these actions by Emperor Alexander, in the month of April, Napoleon was living in Schloss Finckenstein, near Osterode. He ordered Lefebvre to continue the siege of Danzig, he went there to inspect the siege works, organise the army, reorganised and replenished the corps, provided the cavalry and artillery with remounts, formed regiments from natives of Prussian Poland, encouraged his allies through strong rearmament, in a word, took the most active measures for a spring campaign. Acting with extreme caution – which was not seen in him until his unfortunate wars with Emperor Alexander in Germany and in France – Napoleon armed and supplied food not only to the fortresses along the Oder and the Vistula but also those on the Rhine. He secured the coast of France against British landings, demanded General la Romana's [Don Pedro Caro y Sureda, 3rd Marquis de la Romana] 14,000 man corps from the Court of Madrid to protect the northern coast of Germany and sent a similar number of Prussian prisoners of war to Spain in exchange for these troops, to be distributed to Spanish regiments. In the event of a breach with Austria, Napoleon increased the forces in Italy and Dalmatia. Having concluded a truce with the Swedish King, he moved some of Marshal Mortier's corps from Pomerania to Danzig and Marienwerder [Kwidzyn]; encouraged the Turkish Sultan and the Persian Shah to wage a dogged war against Russia; received the ambassadors of the Porte and Shah at Finckenstein and concluded treaties of alliance with them. Promising to return the Crimea to the Turks, he ordered his ambassador in Tsaregrad [Istanbul] to obtain permission from the Divan for free passage of Marmont's 25,000 man corps through Bosnia and Macedonia to the banks of the Danube, for combined operations with the Turks against Mikhelson's weak army and proposed the introduction of five French ships of the line into the Black Sea, which were intended to threaten the shores of southern Russia together with the Turkish fleet. He sent General Gardane [Claude Mathieu de Gardane] as Ambassador to Isfahan, accompanied by artillery officers, land and naval engineers and promised to send the Persian Shah 4,000 infantry

---

15   Operational plan, issued by Emperor Alexander to the Viennese Court, dated 5 [17] May.

and 10,000 muskets. Finally, Napoleon announced the call up of 80,000 recruits in France, which were to be enlisted in 1808, divided them into five reserve corps and entrusted their command to experienced generals who were already sitting in the Senate in retirement. Demanding donations from France, Napoleon counted the trophies acquired from the opening of the Prussian war, the capture of fortresses, the taking of guns and colours and the vast expanse of land he had covered. In front of the whole world he said to the Senate:

> Looking at the triple row of our camps and fortresses, the enemy does not dare to hope for success. The sands of Prussia, the wastes of Poland, the autumn rains and the ferocity of life did not stop the ardent desire of the army to gain peace through victory and return triumphantly to the fatherland. We are ready to make peace with Russia, on the terms signed last year by its plenipotentiary but not ratified by Emperor Alexander. To the Prussian King, we are ready to return his capital and eight million of his subjects conquered by us.

Consoling France with the image of victories, the assurance of his peacefulness, Napoleon promised the marshals, generals and the whole army great rewards awaiting them in the forthcoming spring campaign, appointing estates in the Duchy of Warsaw to the brave, bringing in twenty-five million francs in annual revenue.

In addition to the forces of Austria, Napoleon controlled the forces of all the western states from the Vistula to Lisbon and Naples. But for him the importance of the sources of power were not overwhelming when considering Alexander's enormous resources. He knew that reinforcements had arrived and were in a hurry to join the undefeated Russian army, which had held him off for five months — something that had not happened before to the great commander — and did not make room for his operations, pinned him in one place, in a tight corner between the Vistula, the Passarge and the Bug. The likelihood of more, bitter battles prompted Napoleon, when he learned about the negotiations of Emperor Alexander in Vienna and London, to renew the proposal to Prussia about a separate peace with them and then to formulate a general congress of the Powers. The material resources and the military genius of Napoleon did not cause Alexander to hesitate. He advised the Prussian King and the King shared his view – to refuse Napoleon's proposals. Unchanging in the convictions that motivated him during the ten-year struggle with Napoleon that only force could persuade him, the Emperor ordered his ambassadors to foreign Courts;

> Repeat on each occasion that His Majesty will not spare any effort in the present war, even if the convocation of the congress in question should take place.[16]

---

16  *Repétez à chaque occasion que S.M. l'Empereur, entièrement persuadée, que ce n'est que la force qui puisse ramener Bonaparte à la raison, ne rallentira pas ses efforts dans la présente guerre, quand même la convocation du congrès en question devroit avoir lieu.*

Whereupon the Russian Ambassador in London was ordered to buy 100,000 muskets from Britain.

Meanwhile, April came to an end. The main army was inactive. Only the prolonged siege of Danzig and Platov's patrols continued. Considering the dispersed locations of Napoleon's army and being convinced by reports from the men of the Don and informants that Marshal Ney's corps was at Guttstadt, isolated from Napoleon's main force, Emperor Alexander thought it a good idea to attack him. To achieve this decision, most of the army was to set off from the vicinity of Heilsberg and move to Launau and further forward, while the remaining part of the force, concentrating near Bürgerswalde [Miejska Wola], was to march on Ney's lines of communication while Platov would draw Ney's attention by attacking Allenstein. The attack was scheduled to take place on 1 [13] May.

On 29 April [11 May], Emperor Alexander set off from Bartenstein for Heilsberg and observed the deployment of 1st Division, 2nd Division, 3rd Division and 14th Division there, with the cavalry of the left wing of the army. On that same day, 7th Division and 8th Division assigned to outflank Ney and the cavalry of the right wing assembled at Bürgerswalde. The next day, on the 30 [12 May], the force from Heilsberg moved to Launau. Before dawn on 1 [13] May, Emperor Alexander went to Prince Bagration, behind whom 3rd Division and 14th Division waited, having the cavalry of the left wing of the army, 1st Division and 2nd Division in reserve. At the same time, 7th Division and 8th Division and the cavalry of the right wing arrived in Arnsdorf from Bürgerswalde, while Platov approached Allenstein, where there was a detachment of Ney's corps. The darkness of the night and the forests hid the movement of our army. With the first rays of the sun, the troops stood in their designated places. It was a beautiful May morning, the glee of the troops at the thought of fighting in sight of their Monarch, our greatly superior numbers opposing Ney, who, unaware of the attack being plotted on him, stood unsuspecting at Guttstadt, in a word, a combination of all circumstances promised a real success. Finding himself attacked from various directions, Ney would certainly have retreated, but since from Arnsdorf to Wolsfdorf [Wilczkowo] was only seven *versts* [7.4 km or 4⅔ miles] and to Heiligenthal [Świątki] was fifteen [15.8 km or 10 miles], whichever of these routes Ney turned to, he would have met Russian troops, their being closer to the front than most of his force. Everyone was eagerly awaiting the order to advance. Emperor Alexander stood with the leading troops, on the edge of the forest, when Bennigsen came up to him and reported that according to intelligence received that hour, Napoleon was on the march with all his forces, was close and it was necessary to postpone the attack on Ney. The Emperor replied to Bennigsen: 'I have entrusted you with the army and I do not want to interfere with your orders. Do as you think fit.'[17] Having said these words, the Emperor returned to Bartenstein and on the same day set off for Tilsit. On the way, he examined the battlefield at Eylau and no longer returned to the army, having been with it for four weeks.

The reasons for the postponement of the attack turned out to be unfounded: the intelligence on the approach of Napoleon was not confirmed. Having lost the chance

---

17 According to Prince Chernyshev, who was Uvarov's adjutant at the time and was standing close to the Emperor.

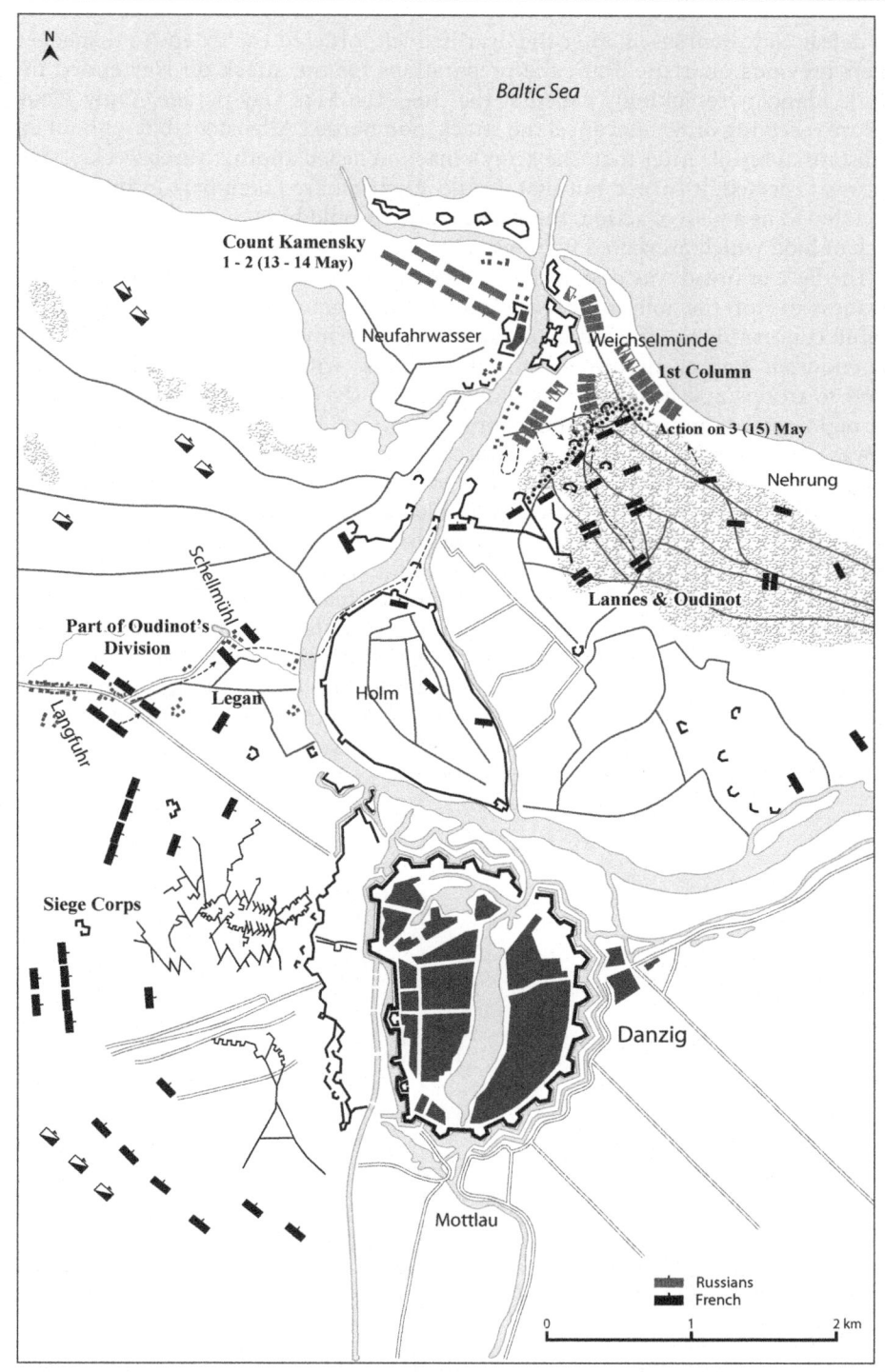

Plan of Operations at Danzig, May 1807.

to defeat Ney, Bennigsen, after the Tsar had left, ordered the troops to disperse to their previous quarters. Thus, the preparations for the attack on Ney ended in a futile manoeuvre, jokingly called at the time 'the May Day parade.' Only Platov, before receiving orders to cancel the attack, bombarded Allenstein, but without any substantial result. After that, the army's inaction lasted another three weeks. Much as was expected, it turned out that should Austria have taken part in the war and dictated to us a plan of action, the Russian army would have to consider not just the lack of food which prevented Bennigsen from undertaking an offensive.[18]

The lack of bread was due to the negligence of the authorities and their powerlessness to stop the abuses creeping into the management of provisioning. At one point, concerning the suggestion of famine in the army, Bennigsen replied: 'It must be endured. And at my dinner only three dishes will be served.'[19] The supply of food to troops and hospitals was provided exclusively by Jews. Money was given to regimental commanders and commandants of hospitals to buy rations, but it was impossible to buy supplies with cash if there were no supplies. Sometimes the generals almost came to blows with each other; bread seldom reached Prince Bagration's vanguard. His soldiers were bloated and perishing from hunger. The hospitals were in a distressing state. The British General Wilson [Sir Robert Thomas Wilson], who was in our headquarters, called them the horror of humanity – not an exaggerated expression.[20] The inhabitants of the areas occupied by our army, staggered like shadows. Infants were dying on their mothers' breasts which had dried out from hunger. The horses in some cavalry regiments, for example, in the Izyum Hussars, fell from lack of fodder even on parade, not having the strength to carry riders. Having devoured the thatched roofs of the houses, they covered the route with their corpses from the vanguard to the headquarters, Bartenstein, where many ladies had moved from St Petersburg and where feast followed feast.

---

18   Bennigsen's report to the Tsar, dated 3 [15] May, from Bartenstein: *Il est triste, Sire, que jusqu'à ce moment, manque d'approvisionnement, je dois rester dans l'inactivité, tandis que Bonaparte a des forces considérables devant Danzig et que le reste de son armée, affoiblie, occuppe une distance du Frisch-haf jusqu'au Narew, et contre laquelle j'ai des forces considérables concentrées. On me promet pour jeudi prochain assez de vivres pour que je puisse commencer les opérations. Je désire que cette promesse se réalise; alors je pourrai porter un coup sensible à l'ennemi.*
19   According to a witness; Count Vorontsov.
20   Sir Robert Wilson, [Brief Remarks on the Character and Composition of the Russian Army, and a] Sketch of the Campaign in Poland in 1806 and 1807. [London: Egerton].

# 18

# The Siege And Fall of Danzig

**The numbers of besieging troops and the garrison. – The opening of the siege. – Sorties. – The difficult service of the Russians in Danzig. – Bombardment. – Capture of the island of Holm. – The siege continues. – Count Kamensky's detachment. – Reasons for his late arrival at Danzig. – Count Kamensky's operations. – Inaction of the British frigates on the Vistula. – Negotiations regarding rations. – Prince Shcherbatov's actions in the drafting of the capitulation. – His audience with Napoleon. – Emperor Alexander's rescript to Prince Shcherbatov. – Count Kamensky's voyage from Danzig.**

Two weeks after the departure of Emperor Alexander from the army, while Bennigsen was waiting for provisions before launching offensive operations, the guerilla war subsided. Napoleon and Bennigsen conserved their forces, anticipating battles soon to come in the spring, but meanwhile the fate of Danzig was being decided.

Marshal Lefebvre's siege corps, assembled over the winter in Thorn, included some 27,000 French, Poles, Saxons and Badenese, led by their Crown Prince, the brother of Empress Elizabeth Alexeevna [Princess Louise Marie Auguste von Baden]. In the garrison, under the command of Graf Kalckreuth, there were 17,000 Prussians, including natives of Prussian Poland, three Russian garrison battalions sent to Danzig with Prince Shcherbatov and three Cossack regiments. In early [mid] March, Lefebvre set off from Thorn, encountering the Prussians close to the city of Danzig, blockading the place only on the left bank of the Vistula because the ice floating down the river prevented him from sending troops to the right bank, while he waited very quietly for his siege artillery, unable to move from the Prussian fortresses because of the bad roads. On 23 March [4 April], the French established their first parallel, the second on 1 [13] April and the third on 9 [21 April]. The sluggishness of the siege works, controlled by General Chasseloup [François, marquis de Chasseloup-Laubat], was due to the rains, the skilful operations of the fortress artillery and frequent sorties. The sorties, however, were also harmful to Graf Kalckreuth, because many Poles deserted from the garrison to the enemy during the night attacks on the French, tempted away by the subversive appeals to them by Dąbrowski [Jan Henryk Dąbrowski], commander of the Polish contingent in Lefebvre's corps. Even sentries jumped over the palisades and deserted to the enemy, informing them of what was happening inside the fortress. It became necessary to change the password and response constantly. Service in the garrison, for those who remained faithful in their duty, became painful, especially for the Russians, because unreliable soldiers could not be placed in the front line posts. As the danger increased during the siege of the city, the Russians were transferred from one place to another. The Cossacks were useless on horseback inside the fortress and were used as infantry.

On 13 [25] April, the French began to bombard Danzig from 78 guns and demanded its surrender but were refused. Meanwhile Lefebvre moved some of his troops onto the right bank of the Vistula and fortified them with redoubts. Wanting to disrupt Danzig's sea communications totally, he launched a night attack on the island of Holm, where, as well as Prussians, there were several companies from Prince Shcherbatov's detachment. Neither the Russians nor our allies took due precautions, were taken by surprise and defeated. The French established themselves on Holm and greatly fortified the woods opposite Weichselmünde [Wisłoujście]. Meanwhile, the bombardment intensified, the city was burned out and at the end of April Lefebvre reached the covered way, preparing for an assault. Graf Kalckreuth and Prince Shcherbatov were exhausted from their courageous defence, while the garrison had been weakened by disease, enemy fire and desertion. Ammunition and provisions were scarce and Lannes' 15,000 man all-arms corps was approaching Danzig, sent there by Napoleon when he learned of the imminent arrival of Count Kamensky in the mouth of the Vistula.

On 29 April [11 May], a ray of hope flashed for Danzig with the appearance of Count Kamensky within sight of Neufahrwasser [Nowy Port]. In his detachment were the Navazhinsk Musketeers, Tobolsk Musketeers, Polotsk Musketeers, Mogilev Musketeers, Archangelogorod Musketeers, 21st Jägers and one Cossack regiment, 4,475 men, with 3,500 Prussians, giving a total of 7,975 men. The delay in the arrival of Count Kamensky was due to the following: having assembled the force in Königsberg, he arrived in Pillau on 19 April [1 May], from where, according to Emperor Alexander's orders, he was to move along the Nehrung spit and proceed to Danzig, driving off any French he might encounter on the way. As the troops were being loaded onto ships, Bennigsen visited Count Kamensky: 'for greater security, do not go via the Nehrung but go by sea, to the mouth of the Vistula and from there move into Danzig, leaving Colonel Bülow [Friedrich Wilhelm Freiherr von Bülow] with three Prussian battalions on the Nehrung spit to harass the French from this direction.' Not all the vessels prepared for the crossing of the narrow Pillau Strait could be sailed on the high seas. It was necessary to hire new ships and arrange for the loading of the troops. Count Kamensky requested assistance from the Swedish and British warships around Pillau. The Swedes refused, apologising for a lack of orders from their chain of command but the British provided us with the frigate [14-gun sloop] *Falcon*. Assembling shipping with difficulty, Count Kamensky left any unnecessary loads on the shore, taking with him only fourteen field cannon, grain stocks, cartridges and shells and set sail on 28 April [10 May]. This delay was the reason that Napoleon found out about the concentration of Russian troops at Pillau, guessed the purpose of their mission and hastily sent Marshal Lannes to Danzig.

On 29 and 30 April [11 and 12 May], the ships began to arrive at Neufahrwasser. Having disembarked the troops, Count Kamensky entered into communications with Graf Kalckreuth by telegraph and received his orders to attack the enemy, at his discretion, either: on the left bank of the Vistula via Langfuhr [Wrzeszcz], or on the right bank, if Colonel Bülow, who was on the Nehrung spit, could contribute to this attack. Whatever the decision, Graf Kalckreuth promised to support the attack with a sortie. Upon learning that Bülow was being held on the Nehrung by a strong French detachment, Count Kamensky ordered an attack on the left bank of the Vistula, with the objective of breaking into the rear of the siege works. During preparations for the attack, Count Kamensky was informed by telegraph from Danzig about a concentration by the French in considerable strength at Langfuhr and Schellmühl [Młyniska], which is why he was ordered to launch an attack on the right bank of the Vistula, aiming to capture Holm in particular. Count Kamensky transferred the detachment from Neufahrwasser to Weichselmünde and launched the attack in four columns. The first under Arseniev [Nikolai Mikhailovich Arseniev] with the Navazhinsk Musketeers, two battalions of the Tobolsk Musketeers, 200 Cossacks, a Prussian infantry battalion and a squadron of dragoons; the second under Laptev with 21st Jägers, a battalion of the Tobolsk Musketeers and a combined battalion of marksmen; the third under Leontiev [Alexey Alekseevich Leontiev] with the Mogilev Musketeers and Polotsk Musketeers and 200 Cossacks; the fourth under Rembow [Michael Szabszinski von Rembow] with the Archangelogorod Musketeers, a Prussian battalion and a *Sotnia* of Cossacks. The first column was to advance along the sea shore, prevent the enemy from cutting us off from Weichselmünde and to support the second with its right wing, which was to attack the French in the fortified woods. The third was to advance on the right of the second, having the mission of capturing the bridges over the Lake [Łachy Szkutniczej] and the island of Holm. The fourth, or reserve, column was to support any weak points during the battle. Behind the second column, planks were carried, lashed together with which to make rafts in case the French burned the bridges over the Lake. The garrison of Neufahrwasser, reinforced by Prussians from Count Kamensky's detachment, were ordered to carry out a diversionary attack on the left bank of the Vistula. The British, cruising off the mouth promised to bring at least one frigate into the Vistula and put it at Legan to disrupt communications between Holm and the left bank of the Vistula.

At four o'clock in the morning on 3 [15] May, the troops advanced out of Weichselmünde. Laptev sent the combined battalion of marksmen ahead of the columns, led by Lifeguard Captain Count Balmen – [Karl Antonovich de Balmen] the beautiful hope, but fated to die too soon, robbed from the Russian army.[1] Greeted by a crossfire from the batteries erected at the edge of the woods, one of three guns and the other of four, the marksmen and, behind them, the column briskly moved into the woods, expelled the French from the first two earthworks but were stopped there. Count Kamensky ordered some of Leontiev's third column to support Laptev and hit the enemy in the flank. Filisov's [Pavel Andreevich Filisov] Polotsk Musketeers and Kozlovsky's [Mikhail Timofeevich Kozlovsky?] Mogilev Musketeers attacked: their first feat was to capture two cannon with cold steel. A

---

1 During Emperor Alexander's Turkish War, Count de Balmen was promoted to Major-General on the same day as Count Vorontsov, Saint-Priest and Paskevich. The Prince of Warsaw [Paskevich] said that he rarely met an officer in whom the qualities of a Commander-in-Chief were more apparent than in de Balmen.

hand-to-hand battle ensued and our men pressed forwards; not having time to drag them away, they spiked the captured guns. Due to the bitterness of the fighting, Count Kamensky ordered Arseniev to send two battalions into the forest from his first column, which was moving along the seashore and had not yet met the enemy, and one battalion from the Arkhangelogorod Musketeers and one Prussian battalion were brought there from the reserve. The French also brought fresh troops into action, where, on one side, Marshals Lannes and Oudinot [Nicholas Charles Oudinot] and on the other, Count Kamensky, commanded in person. They fought for a long time with varying success. The British frigate was delayed by contrary winds. Nor were any sorties made from Danzig, Graf Kalckreuth was waiting for the moment when the Russians had defeated the French before he would launch a sortie.[2] Deprived of the support of his allies, fighting the superior strength of the enemy, Count Kamensky lost hope of success and ordered the retreat; two battalions of his beloved Arkhangelogorod Musketeers constituted the rearguard. The enemy pursued for a short distance. Satisfied that they had repulsed the Russians, the French soon returned to their original positions. The fighting, which began at 4 o'clock in the morning, ended at 2 o'clock in the afternoon. The Russians lost 54 field officers and subalterns and 1,348 other ranks killed or wounded; the Prussian casualties were 159, giving a total of 1,561 men; thirty Frenchmen were taken prisoner.[3]

Reporting to Bennigsen about the unsuccessful attack, Count Kamensky wrote that it was impossible to break into Danzig and only the operations of the main army could save the fortress. Sharing this opinion, Graf Kalckreuth suggested that Kamensky load his troops onto British ships and enter the Vistula, bringing with him more gunpowder, of which he was running out. Kamensky convened a meeting of Russians and Prussians, as well as the captains of the British ships. They unanimously recognized the impossibility of entering Danzig by water but decided to try sending the gunpowder up the Vistula. The British assigned this mission to the 22-gun sloop *Dauntless*, carrying 300 cwt [15.24 tonnes] of gunpowder. On 7 [19] May, with a fair wind, she immediately raced off like an arrow under full sail, accompanied by the cheers of the allies. The French opened fire on her but without doing much damage. Suddenly, at a sharp bend in the river, her speed dropped. The French began to score hits on equipment and men. Controlling the ship became impossible and she ran aground. Canister and bullets rained down on the sloop. For a long time the British fired back, trying to get afloat but, running out of time, struck her colours. Witnessing the failure here also, Kamensky decided to stay in Neufahrwasser so that he could threaten the enemy by staying there and not extinguish the diminished hopes of relief and strike the French with all his might should they launch an assault on Danzig.

Having not received the gunpowder, Graf Kalckreuth, amidst the cries of the inhabitants of the burned out city, on the collapsing fortifications, threatened by undermining by the enemy, was in a desperate situation, all the more so since some

---

2    Schütz, *Geschichte des Krieges von Preußen und Rußland gegen Frankreich*, p. 217: *Ein Ausfall aus der Festung lag zwar im Plane des Grafen Kalkreuth, konnte aber erst nach dem Gelingen des Angriffes stattfinden, und unterblieb deshalb ganz.*
3    Count Kamensky's war diary.

of Mortier's corps had joined Lefebvre on 9 [21] May from Pomerania. Preparing for an assault, Lefebvre invited Graf Kalckreuth to surrender and become prisoners of war. The proposal was rejected, with the announcement that the garrison would defend itself to the last man unless they were allowed to leave the fortress with military honours, armed and with some of their field artillery to join the Russian army. Lefebvre relayed this response to Napoleon and he agreed to the free passage of the garrison but on condition that they: 'do not serve against the French for a year and one day and that the surrender must be signed not only by the Prussian governor but also by the Russian commander in the fortress.' Napoleon's innumerable trophies lacked one thing that he now wanted to bring about — a capitulation, signed with the name of a Russian General! Graf Kalckreuth, lacking gunpowder, accepted the terms. Although they could be considered a just reward for the brilliant defence of Danzig, Prince Shcherbatov would not agree to sign them. He wrote in his notes; 'it seemed distasteful to me to see my name on a capitulation. This word was a novelty to Russians. We had taken fortresses but had never been besieged in recent times. I decided, no matter what the cost, to save at least myself from fulfilling the conditions.' While the surrender document was being drafted, Prince Shcherbatov retired to the city ramparts, hoping that, perhaps, the matter would be completed without him. He was shortly summoned by Graf Kalckreuth, shown the agreement, already approved by both sides, and his signature was demanded. He gave in to their insistence, but an hour later announced to the French General d'Erlon – [Jean-Baptiste Drouet, Comte d'Erlon] later a Marshal – sent to Danzig for the negotiations, that the force of circumstances had coerced him into signing the surrender, not having the ability or the right to exclude the small Russian detachment from it but, as for him personally, regarding the condition; 'not to serve against the French for one year,' he must obtain the permission of Emperor Alexander. In conclusion, he asked for passports for his aide de camp, whom he intended to send to His Majesty, and until then wanted to remain a prisoner of war. The Prussians and the French argued with him that his honour would not be impugned by accepting surrender, at a time when resistance was no longer possible and would lead to certain death. Prince Shcherbatov remained adamant. Lefebvre sent passports to his aide de camp, Lopukhin [Pavel Petrovich Lopukhin?], and he left with Prince Shcherbatov's report for the Tsar.

On 15 [27] May, the garrison emerged from the fortress, some 7,000 men. The French saluted them from the glacis. Prince Shcherbatov was not with his detachment and remained at home. The next day he visited Marshal Lefebvre and was received by him with particular respect. Napoleon visited Danzig for a few hours soon afterwards, congratulated Lefebvre on becoming Duke of Danzig but was angry at the permission given to Prince Shcherbatov to remain in the fortress after the allied forces had left, ordering Adjutant-General Rapp [Jean Rapp] to announce to him, that he must live in France or Dresden for the year-long term of the capitulation, Prince Shcherbatov went to Dresden. Two months later, he arrived in Tilsit from there, where Napoleon was in all the splendour of fame and fortune. Dresden was filled with Kings and Princes, hurrying to worship the invincible one. Upon learning of Prince Shcherbatov's stay in Dresden, Napoleon sent for him, received him kindly and with a cheerful look and, extolling Danzig's defence, asked:

Plan of Operations 23 to 28 May [4 to 9 June] 1807.

'Why didn't you want to take advantage of the honourable capitulation?' Prince Shcherbatov replied; 'I could not dispose of myself without the will of Emperor Alexander and remain inactive for a year and, by surrendering to be a prisoner of war, I hoped to be exchanged quickly for any of the captured Frenchmen and return to the war.' Napoleon approved of this answer in supportive terms.[4]

Encouraged by Napoleon, on the same day, Prince Shcherbatov was blessed with the following rescript from Emperor Alexander:

> Having examined from Graf Kalckreuth's reports how bravely and indefatigably you contributed to the defence of Danzig with the troops entrusted to you, it gives me particular pleasure to express to you, on this occasion, my complete favour. Having learned, however, that upon concluding the capitulation for the surrender of Danzig, you found it difficult to carry it out and decided to stay there until you received permission from me, I hasten to deliver it to you in such a sense that, having exhausted all the means dependent on you for the salvation of the indicated fortress, having increased the generation, the conditions allowed the glory of our armed forces and finally surrendering only when there was no longer any way to defend, you have observed all that one can demand from a Russian soldier, which is why I order you to draw upon yourself the decrees of the aforementioned surrender and then come here immediately, with full assurance that I will be very pleased to see you here with me.

As for Count Kamensky, after the surrender of Danzig he was in a hurry to embark his detachment onto the ships and sail to Pillau, from where he went to Königsberg. He was followed by the Prussian garrison of Neufahrwasser. The commandant of the Weichselmünde fort did not agree with Count Kamensky's recommendation, advising him also to escape by sea and wanted to defend himself. The garrison was not as committed as their commander and, the next day, for the most part, deserted to the French. Thus Napoleon took possession of the mouth of the Vistula. For a total of fifty-one days, from the opening of the trenches to the cessation of hostilities, the siege of Danzig continued, described here briefly, only to indicate the participation of the Russians.

---

4   From the autobiographical notes of Prince Shcherbatov.

# 19

# The Spring Campaign

The deployment of the armies. – Bennigsen's intention to attack Marshal Ney. – Dokhturov's battle at Lomitten. – Prince Bagration's action against Marshal Ney. – Ney's undisturbed withdrawal. – The action of 26 May [7 June]. – Allegations against Sacken of failing to attack. – His Court-Martial. – L'Estocq's and Count Tolstoy's operations. – The concentration of Napoleon's army. – Prince Bagration's and Raevsky's actions on the banks of the Passarge. – The Russian retreat towards Guttstadt and Heilsberg. – Count Kamensky links up with the army.

There had been beautiful spring weather for several weeks but the main armies, although reinforced with fresh troops, remained inactive. In the second half of May [early June], rations began to be delivered to Bennigsen, while the troops from around Danzig came to Napoleon. There were up to 125,000 combatant men in the Russian army, including 8,000 Cossacks. Excluding L'Estocq's and Tuchkov's independent corps, each of 20,000 men, there were 85,000 men with the main army. Napoleon had up to 170,000 men under arms, of whom 27,000 were with Bernadotte and 20,000 were with Masséna and, consequently, up to 123,000 in the main army. Ready for battle, both sides stood on the ground that they had occupied in the winter. Europe's attention was drawn to a small area of land in East Prussia, where Alexander's dispute with Napoleon was soon to be finally settled. Impatiently waiting for whichever side to begin operations.

After having received provisions, Bennigsen set out to fulfil his previous mission – to defeat Marshal Ney, who was standing at Guttstadt. On 21 May [2 June], the Russian army emerged from their cantonments and, two days later, it was located as follows: Dokhturov was at Wormditt with two divisions; Sacken was at Arnsdorf with two divisions and Uvarov's cavalry of the right wing; Prince Golitsyn was behind him with two divisions and the cavalry of the left wing; the corps assembled for the attack under Prince Gorchakov, was at Seeburg [Jeziorany]. Prince Bagration did not move the vanguard from Launau, so as not to alert Ney by his movement. For the offensive on the following day, 24 May [5 June], all these formations of the force were ordered to operate as follows: Dokhturov was to attack Marshal Soult's leading troops, who were opposite Lomitten on the right bank of the Passarge and push them back over the river, cutting off Soult's communications with Ney; Prince Gorchakov was to advance from Seeburg, cross the Alle and attack Ney's right wing; Sacken, taking the reserves with him, was to go from Arnsdorf towards Wolfsdorf in the direction of Ney's rear; Bagration was to advance from Launau keeping his front towards Guttstadt; Platov was to cross the Alle at Bergfriede and cut the enemy's line of retreat; finally, L'Estocq's independent corps was to fix Bernadotte with diversionary attacks, while Tuchkov, whose place was taken by Count Tolstoy due to illness, was to make an offensive movement towards Ostrolenka.

On 24 May [5 June], at three o'clock in the morning, advancing from Wormditt towards Lomitten, Dokhturov encountered a detachment from Soult's corps based near Liebstadt, protected by abatis in the woods. Dokhturov attacked and captured the abatis. Soult sent reinforcements to the woods from his camp at Liebstadt, upon the arrival of which the abatis was recaptured by the French and a bitter battle erupted. The French were finally pushed out of the woods. Having been forbidden from crossing the Passarge by Napoleon, Soult ordered the troops retreating from the woods to return to the left bank of this river and prepared to meet Dokhturov should he intend to cross. Dokhturov followed the French and stopped on the banks of the Passarge, interrupting direct communications between Soult and Ney. Thus, Dokhturov executed the mission entrusted to him exactly but, meanwhile, the main attack on Marshal Ney was unsuccessful.

Early in the morning, Prince Bagration set off from Launau via Gronau [Gronowo] to Altkirch [Praslity], driving the French skirmishers out of the woods and took the village of Altkirch with a swift attack, in front of Ney's camp. Not seeing the approach of Sacken's column from the right and not hearing firing form Prince Gorchakov's direction, he stopped, calculating that even with a successful attack on Ney, he could only force him to retreat but no more, meanwhile, with the arrival of Sacken and Prince Gorchakov, Ney would be in a most difficult position. Ney, for his part, believing the actions of Prince Bagration to be a reconnaissance in force, led an attack on him, wishing to eject our men from Altkirch. During the action that had flared up here, Sacken finally appeared at long cannon range from the enemy's lines of communication. Ney immediately retreated, pressed so closely by Prince Bagration that he had to abandon two guns and some of his transport, including his own baggage. With a quick retreat securing himself from being surrounded, Ney quietly left, courageously fighting back at every step and, by evening, stopped at Ankendorf [Jankowo]. At night, he transferred his heavy equipment over the Passarge at Deppen [Dąbrówka] and waited with his corps at Ankendorf for our further movements. The Russian army spent the night at Glottau [Głotowo] and Queetz [Kwiecewo].

Bennigsen did not take advantage of Ney's audacious decision to spend the night in view of the Russian army, having a river in his rear. Instead of moving some of the troops at night to the Deppen crossing, Ney's only line of retreat, and then falling upon him with all his might, Bennigsen merely ordered; 'push the enemy behind the Passarge,'[1] in order to achieve this: firstly, Prince Bagration was to attack Ney at 3 o'clock in the morning; secondly, the entire army was to march on Deppen, moreover, it was not even indicated which roads to follow while it was implied, vaguely suggested 'each division is to march in a particular column, depending on its location, whereas the cavalry are to increase their columns to reduce the march.'

---

1  Actual words of the Disposition.

At the appointed hour on 25 May [6 June], Prince Bagration attacked Ney, having taken up a strong position: his left wing rested on a marsh, while the right was on wooded hills, from where Prince Bagration drove the French. Ney began to pull back and crossed the Passarge, losing up to 1,500 prisoners of war on this day; including General Roguet [François Roguet]. Our losses are not known. Count Osterman was wounded. Thus, only Dokhturov and Prince Bagration accomplished the missions assigned to them. Sacken was late, and Prince Gorchakov and Platov crossed over the Alle after Ney had already retreated. Bennigsen blamed Sacken for the failure, having been at odds with him since the Polish War of 1794. He wrote to Emperor Alexander:

> Having the honour of commanding the army, I have the misfortune that Sacken is under my command, always spoiling my operations with motives that I refrain from revealing. Probably, if the operations of 24 and 25 May [5 and 6 June] did not have all the successes that they should have, then I attribute this only to General Sacken, in obstructing or acting contrary to my orders, to which the whole army can attest.[2]

The Emperor gave orders for Sacken to face a Court-Martial. The basis of Sacken's defence before the court was that he 'could and wanted to attack the enemy but the Commander-in-Chief did not allow him to do so, having given him contradictory orders'. The contradictory testimonies of many witnesses called by the court and Sacken's deft answers caused complete disagreement between the judges. Sacken's most ardent defender in court was Colonel Count Vorontsov [Mikhail Semënovich Vorontsov]. In the testimony he submitted, with which two other members agreed, Count Vorontsov wrote in his own hand: 'We believe that General Sacken should not be found guilty of anything in this matter and that he is completely exonerated by everything that General Bennigsen had sent to him.' Subsequently, Sacken thanked Count Vorontsov, giving him an immortal page in History – the opportunity to command against Napoleon in the Battle of Craonne. For three years, until 1810, the judges could not reach an agreement. Perplexed as to what action to take, the Audit-General asked the Emperor to order a special advisory from experienced generals on the judgment of Sacken. The Emperor ordered the establishment of the Council and, appointed to it, Count Tatishchev [Alexander Ivanovich Tatishchev], Prince Salagov [Semën Ivanovich Salagov], Meller-Zakomelsky [Fëdor-Ivanovich Meller-Zakomelsky], Obreskov [Mikhail Alekseevich Obreskov], Sukin, Verderevsky [Nikolai Ivanovoch Verderevsky] and Velyaminov [Nikolai Stepanovich Velyaminov?]. The Council concluded that:

> For omissions in the actions of 24 and 25 May [5 and 6 June], Sacken should be punished under Article 29 of the Military Charter, that is, to deprive him of honour, however, out of respect for his previous forty-four years of excellent service, it is requested, having imputed him to a three-year trial, as a punishment, to dismiss him from service.[3]

---

2   Bennigsen's report, dated 26 May [7 June].
3   The Report of the Council, dated 29 April [11 May].

In the court case filed with the Audit-General, it says: 'It is not known what confirmation followed on the report of the Council.' We only know that Sacken was not dismissed but was in disfavour with the Monarch and in poverty until 1812. The following incident proves what Emperor Alexander later thought of Sacken: at the battle of Brienne, admiring Sacken's operations against the centre of the French army, where Napoleon was in command, from the Trannes-Hills, Emperor Alexander said before all of us: 'I feel so guilty in front of Sacken! This.... Bennigsen slandered him in my view. I hope now that Sacken will be pleased with me,' and gave orders for him to be awarded the St Andrew sash. The day after the battle, having given thanks to the army to the enthusiastic cheers of the soldiers and under fire from round shot from the French rearguard, the Emperor said to Sacken: 'Yesterday you defeated not only your foreign enemies but also your internal, domestic ones.'

Bennigsen did not follow Ney onto the left bank of the Passarge, having received intelligence from prisoners captured by the Cossacks that there were movements from the French army. This was in consequence of Napoleon's orders. At the first news of the attack on Ney, he hastily concentrated the army around Saalfeld. Waiting on the development of Napoleon's operations, Bennigsen deployed his troops between Guttstadt and the Passarge; Prince Bagration was at Deppen with the vanguard.

In conclusion, I must mention that the diversionary attack delivered by L'Estocq on Bernadotte had no other consequences than the wounding of this Marshal, after which his corps came under the leadership of Victor [Claude-Victor Perrin]. As for Count Tolstoy, who was ordered to operate offensively, he did not dare to move away from the Bug, due to the low numbers of his troops and because his magazines were located on the Bug: he remained in a defensive position, trying as much as possible to harm the enemy.[4] To that end, he ordered his forward screen to harass the enemy, 'pretending to mount a general attack' and Count Wittgenstein to attack the French vanguard. These orders were executed successfully. Count Wittgenstein attacked General Claparède at Olszewo-Borki, drove him back, captured two officers and 28 privates and took the enemy camp.[5] Those were the offensive operations of the Russian army in the spring campaign, threatening Ney with destruction, or captivity. Just as lightning without thunder is just a flash, so a bright idea without skilful execution remains a dream!

The day after Ney's retreat over the Passarge, on 26 May [7 June], Napoleon visited this Marshal. Having learned that the Russians were advancing, he decided to launch offensive operations and ordered the corps to assemble between Deppen and Elditten [Ełdyty Wielkie]. Receiving reports confirming French movements from the tireless men of the Don, who had swum the Passarge, Bennigsen concluded that Napoleon would attack soon and, while he did not want to shy away from combat, he hesitated in deciding where to give battle: at Guttstadt or at Heilsberg? In anticipation of Napoleon's actions, he stationed the army near Guttstadt, and ordered the construction of field fortifications there.

During the morning of 27 May [8 June], Prince Bagration was made aware of the concentration of French on the left bank of the Passarge and the thick clouds of dust

---

4   Count Tolstoy's private letter to Bennigsen, dated 31 May [12 June].
5   Count Tolstoy's report to Bennigsen, dated 31 May [12 June], No 14.

visible there, an indicator of troop movements. The Prince rode to his forward screen and became convinced of the truth of the report, having seen from our low bank numerous enemy infantry, cavalry and artillery columns.[6] It was later confirmed that these troops were hurrying under Napoleon's gaze. Having inspected them, he called the field officers, subalterns and non-commissioned officers out from the parade, spoke about the imminent onset of the final phase of the war and demanded a final effort to gain victory and a glorious peace. Prince Bagration informed Bennigsen about what was happening. Bennigsen visited the vanguard, went to the forward screen together with Prince Bagration, saw the French columns returning from their parade and announced to Prince Bagration his intention to give battle at Guttstadt, where he went to draft preliminary orders for the battle.

An hour after Bennigsen's departure from the vanguard, one infantry brigade from Soult's Corps crossed to the right bank of the Passarge via two bridges at Elditten. Raevsky [Nikolai Nikolaevich Raevsky] pulled back the Cossacks who were guarding the crossing. Bored after three months of idleness and emboldened by Napoleon's speech, the French moved forwards quickly and, contrary to the rules adopted in war, without a vanguard, without watching their rear, entered the village of Kleinenfeld [Klony]. Here Raevsky was waiting for them, having taken steps in advance for an attack. He surrounded, defeated and put to flight the French brigade. Their commander, Guyot [Etienne Guyot], paid with his life for his negligence.[7] Having accomplished this feat, Raevsky remained in Kleinenfeld. At that moment, Prince Bagration arrived. Having seen the advance of Soult's entire corps, he ordered Raevsky not to persist in the defence of Kleinenfeld and to fall back. Soult followed Raevsky to Wolfsdorf, and deployed his corps there. Meanwhile, more French troops crossed the Passarge over the bridges at Elditten and assembled in crowds at the Deppen crossing. Prince Bagration ordered the vanguard, which was at this village, to fall back to Ankendorf and to draw level with Raevsky. The French immediately began to descend on Deppen on our bank.

Expecting an attack the next morning, Prince Bagration ordered Raevsky to fall back a little closer to him that night, 27 to 28 [8 to 9 June] and stay in communication with him. Before dawn, Bennigsen informed Prince Bagration that he had changed his mind, that he would not give battle at Guttstadt, but at Heilsberg, whose surroundings had been fortified in advance and ordered Prince Bagration to hold in front of Guttstadt for as long as possible, giving the army time to cross the steep-banked Alle. Prince Bagration ordered a reconnaissance of the area where he might hold while retreating to Guttstadt and informed Raevsky of Bennigsen's new decision. On the morning of the 28 [9 June], advancing along two roads from Elditten and Deppen, the French attacked Prince Bagration at Ankendorf and Raevsky near

---

6   There is still a witness to this reconnaissance conducted by Prince Bagration – his Chief-of-Artillery, Yermelov.
7   The French do not hide their defeat. Dumas, *Précis des évènemens militaires. Tome XVIII*, p. 256: *Le général Guyot commit l'imprudence de s'engager dans le village de Kleinenfeld avant qu'il ent été reconnu. Il y fut enveloppé, et pris à dos avec toute sa brigade, qu'il y avoit compromise. Ses régimens durent se faire jour par des charges réitérées. Dans cette melée le général Guyot, plusieurs de ses officiers et 30 soldats furent tués, 90 blessés et 116 prisonniers.*

THE SPRING CAMPAIGN 159

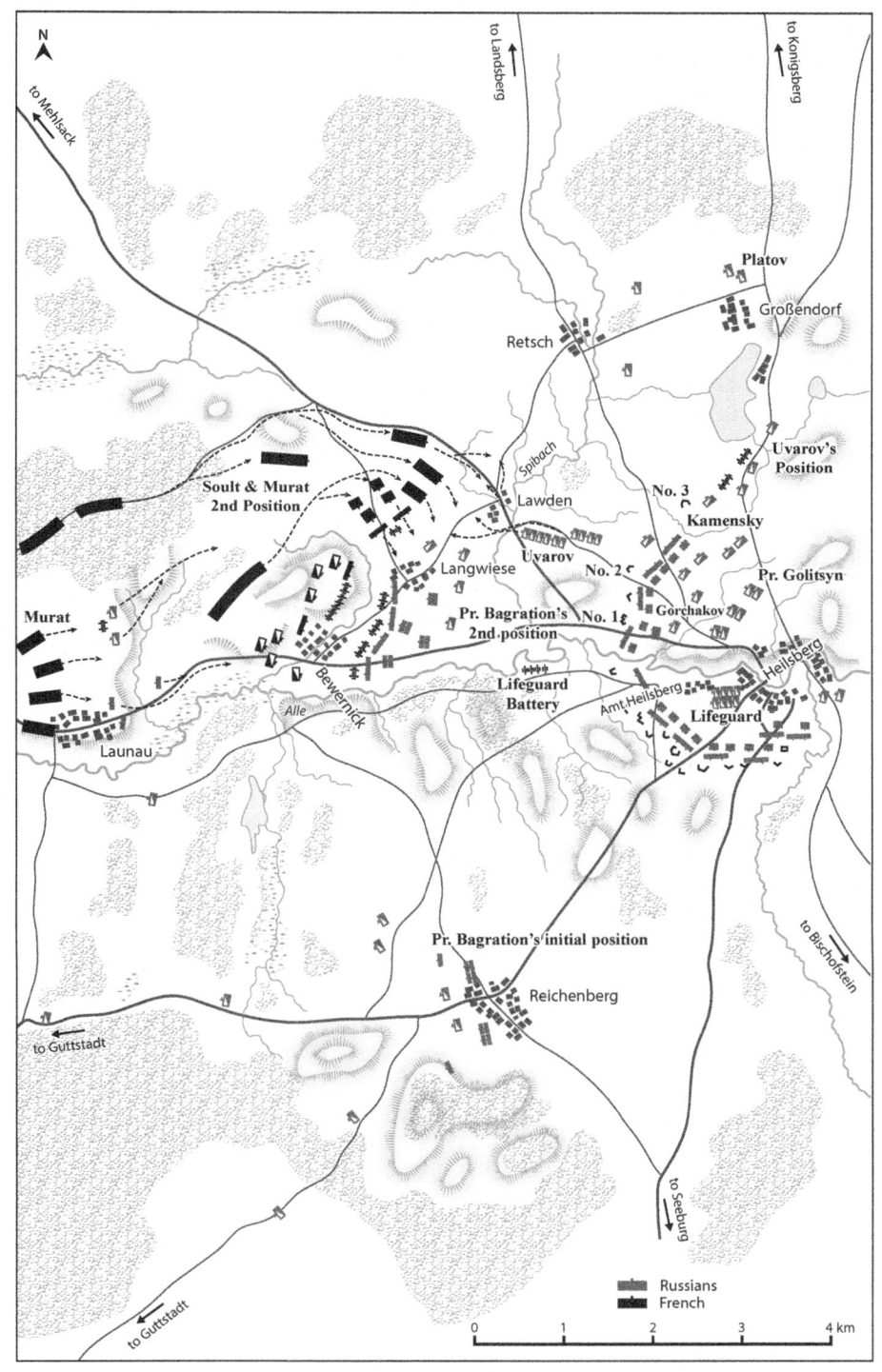

Plan of the Heilsberg Position and Vanguard Action, 29 May [10 June] 1807.

Wolfsdorf. In both places the battle was most hard fought but the record of the repulse given to the French at these villages was not preserved, since the battles that soon followed at Heilsberg and Friedland were of greater importance, so to speak, they swamped the rearguard actions that preceded them. It is only known that Prince Bagration and Raevsky fulfilled their mission, holding the French for as long as Bennigsen needed to retreat from Guttstadt. In the space of almost four hours they fought back over seven *versts* [7.4 km or 4⅔ miles]. Finally, pressed by crowds of men, they entered Guttstadt, where the French broke in after them. Giving one last rebuff here, Prince Bagration crossed the Alle. Throughout the whole action, his Chief-of-Artillery, Yermolov, covered himself in glory. The French did not follow Prince Bagration and remained in Guttstadt. Napoleon arrived there that evening. Prince Bagration settled down for the night at Reichenberg [Kraszewo], four *versts* [4.2 km or 2⅔ miles] from Heilsberg, where the army had meanwhile taken up positions. Platov had destroyed the bridges over the Alle along the stretch from Guttstadt to Heilsberg.

During the night of 28 to 29 [9 to 10 June], Count Kamensky joined the army. Following his return from Danzig, he had been part of L'Estocq's corps and did not request orders to move to the Main Army, due to the following events: A courier rode from Bennigsen to L'Estocq, who was thirty *versts* [31.5 km or 20 miles] from Kamensky. Having opened the courier's papers, Count Kamensky found Bennigsen's orders in them, which, notifying L'Estocq of the proximity of a battle, ordered him to send at least some troops to the battle supposed to take place at Guttstadt or Heilsberg. Calculating that it would take a long time for the courier to reach L'Estocq, and L'Estocq would take time to carry out the orders in such an era of warfare when each minute was precious, Count Kamensky decided to take his detachment to the army and reported this to L'Estocq. Wanting to conceal his movements from the enemy, he left Colonel Stackelberg [Otto Vladimirovich Stackelberg] with the Azov Musketeers and three squadrons of the Prussian Prittwitz's [Siegmund Moritz von Prittwitz] Hussars in his former positions. At dusk, on 27 May [8 June], Count Kamensky set off with 9,672 Russians and Prussians, covered more than seventy *versts* [73.5 km or 47 miles] in 32 hours and arrived in Heilsberg a few hours before the battle, to be greeted joyfully by Bennigsen. At the same time, Bennigsen received the following response to his report sent to Emperor Alexander about his intention to fight: 'I expect that you will fulfil that which the duty, honour and glory of Russia require of you.'

# 20

# The Battle of Heilsberg

---

> The deployment of the Russian army. – Borozdin's vanguard action. – The arrival of Prince Bagration with the vanguard. – His fight with the French. – Murat's attack on the Heilsberg position. – Napoleon's assault. – His failure. – The reasons for Bennigsen's inaction. – The continued French assaults. – Casualties. – Emperor Alexander's comments on the Battle of Heilsberg.

By early morning of 29 May [10 June], the Russian army was deployed in front of Heilsberg on both banks of the Alle, in positions fortified with redoubts. On the right bank, under Tsarevich Konstantin Pavlovich's command were three divisions; 3rd Division, 7th Division and 14th Division, with the Lifeguard in reserve, while the remainder of the army was on the left bank, with the right wing resting on Großendorf [Wielochowo]; Platov was to the right of this village with his Cossacks. The first and third battalions were arranged in line, having the second battalion behind in column. There were three reserves, each of four battalions, one for each flank and the centre and the bulk of our cavalry was also deployed on the left bank of the Alle, because the terrain here was not as hilly as on the right bank of this river. Prince Golitsyn commanded the cavalry in the centre, while Uvarov commanded the cavalry on our right wing. The vanguards were positioned in two locations; Prince Bagration's at Reichenberg and Borozdin's [Nikolai Mikhailovich Borozdin] at Launau. Knorring's detachment of scouts was at Seeburg, maintaining communications with Count Tolstoy. Three pontoon bridges had been laid across the Alle. This arrangement was adopted because Bennigsen was waiting to discover from which bank of the river Napoleon would launch his assault. The French army was then in a full blown advance from Guttstadt along the left bank of the Alle: Murat was in the lead, while Soult and Lannes followed him, having Ney and the *Garde* in reserve. Napoleon wanted these troops to attack the Russians frontally, while Davout and Mortier were to cut Bennigsen off from Königsberg, which was our main resupply depot.

Borozdin's detachment consisted of the Finland Dragoons, Nizov Musketeers, Reval Musketeers and Selivanov's Cossacks. At 10 o'clock in the morning, Murat attacked Borozdin with his leading troops and forced him to retreat from Launau to Bewernick [Bobrownik]. Bennigsen sent Major-General Lvov with the Kiev Dragoons, 2nd Jägers, Kexholm Musketeers and an *opolchenie* battalion in support. At that very moment, having received a report that the French had not been seen on the right bank of the Alle at all, Bennigsen ordered Prince Bagration, who was waiting there at Reichenberg, to march to Bewernick and placed the entire vanguard force under his command. Prince Bagration crossed the Alle at Amt-Heilsberg and, facing left, linked up with Borozdin and Lvov, who were already falling back from Bewernick. He stopped them and reformed all the troops under his command into battle formation. His right wing extended to the village of Langwiese [Długołęka], while the left rested on the river Alle. The strengthening of the Russian vanguard prompted Murat to stop the assault: he limited himself to a cannonade while waiting for Soult's corps. Bagration's Chief-of-Artillery, Yermolov, successfully replied to the French batteries. During the cannonade, Soult arrived on the battlefield and began to envelope Prince Bagration along the road between Langwiese and Lawden [Lauda]. Seeing this manoeuvre from the Heilsberg heights, Bennigsen sent Uvarov with 25 squadrons to Lawden. Meanwhile, under attack from Murat from the front and Soult from the flank, Prince Bagration began to fall back. The French quickly followed him. During this hot fight, Uvarov arrived and charged at the French. In one of these attacks the Colonel-in-Chief of His Majesty's Leib-Cuirassiers, Kozhin, the glorious cavalry general was killed. The French cavalry attacked so fiercely that they overran our guns several times but on each occasion they were repulsed by the Russian cavalry, for which, according to Yermolov, three cavalry field officers received the St George Cross; Bunyakovsky [Alexander Nikolaevich Burkhanovsky?], Rimsky-Korsakov [Yakov Yakovlevich Rimsky-Korsakov] and Vietinghoff. The courage of the Russian troops could not stop the French. They continued to advance. Prince Bagration's horse was killed under him at the crossing of the Spibach and he continued on foot until Tsarevich Konstantin Pavlovich sent him one of his horses. In the heat of the pursuit, the French rushed towards the Spibach but were stopped here by a battery which the Tsarevich had turned on their flank from the right bank of the Alle. For the skill with which the battery was handled by the Semenovsky Regiment's Lieutenant Dibich [Ivan Ivanovich Dibich or Hans Karl Friedrich Anton von Diebitsch und Narten], the Tsesarevich recommended him for the St George Cross. From this moment on the military fame of the one who showed the Russians the way through the Balkans began. Freed from the pursuit, Prince Bagration and Uvarov ascended to the position occupied by the army. Prince Bagration's detachment was then placed behind the army, weakened and exhausted by the rearguard actions.

Our description of the action so far covers the period from 10 o'clock in the morning until 4 o'clock in the afternoon. At 5 o'clock, Murat, brave but reckless, launched an attack on the strongest part of our line, having failed to examine it carefully. Assault columns, blasted by the cross-fire of Russian batteries, wavered and fell back. At the time of this action, Bennigsen directed 7th Division from the right bank of the Alle to the left, then, having realised that there was still no enemy on the right bank of the Alle, he also ordered 3rd Division and 14th Division to cross to the left bank, after which, the only force on the right bank of the river was the Lifeguard. During the period when these divisions were crossing the Alle, Napoleon arrived on the battlefield with some of Lannes' corps and the *fusiliers-grenadiers de la Garde* and began to deploy for an assault, despite the numerical superiority of the Russian army. Arranging the troops, he opened up an artillery bombardment all along the

# THE BATTLE OF HEILSBERG 163

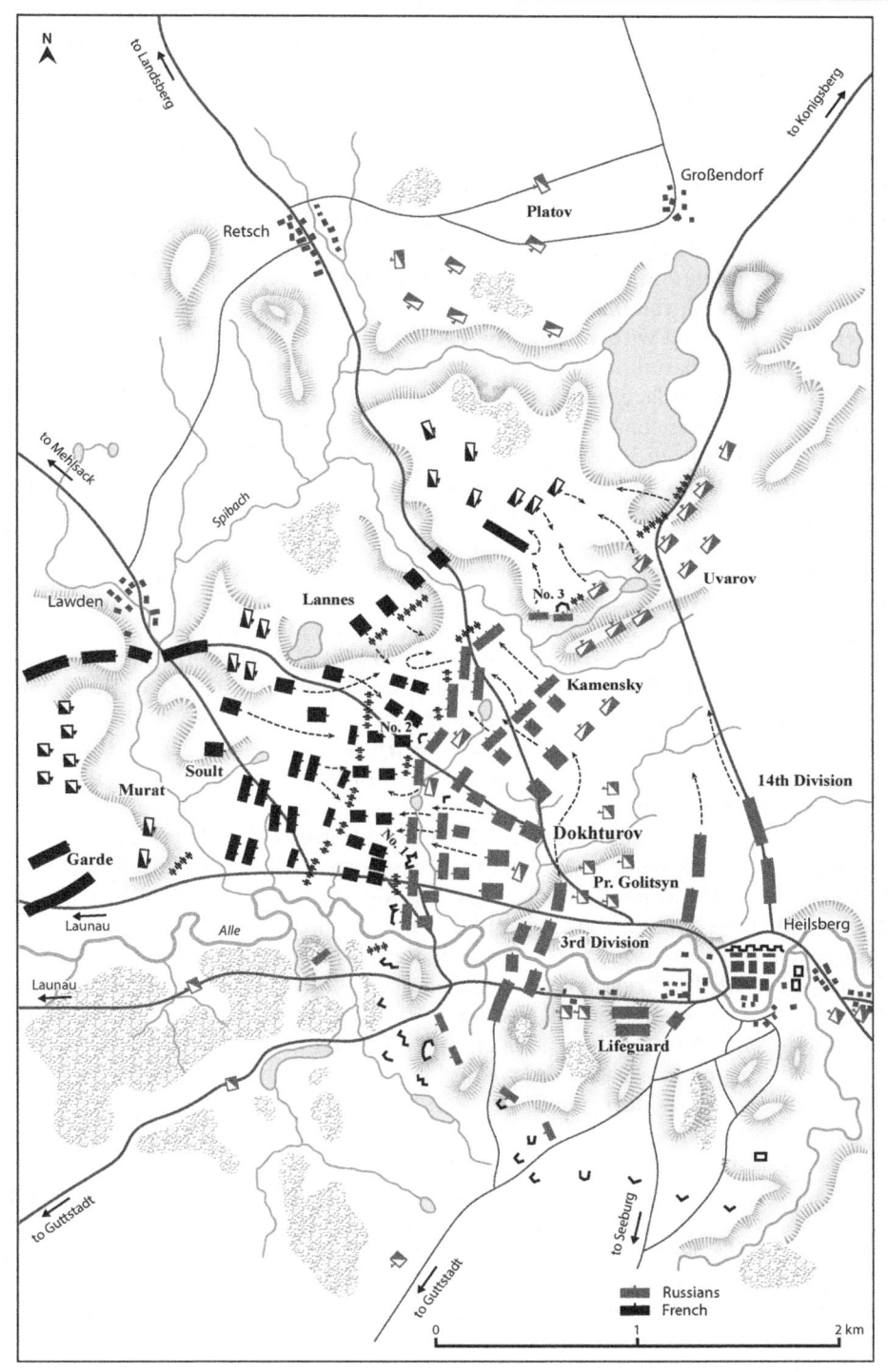

Plan of the Battle of Heilsberg, 29 May [10 June] 1807.

line and then gave orders to capture redoubt No 2 by assault, with the intention of breaking through our centre. Having calmly endured the hail of round shot and canister, the French approached the redoubt. Prince Gorchakov sent Rakhmanov's [Vasily Sergeevich Rakhmanov] Nizov Musketeers, Tuchkov 4th's [Alexander Alekseevich Tuchkov] Reval Musketeers, and Alexeev's [Ilya Ivanovich Alexeev] Mitau Dragoons to meet them. Six battalions followed in support. Rakhmanov and Tuchkov forbade firing, drove off the leading French column with the bayonet and then, after a short time, stopped the enemy advance. Desiring a decisive blow to realise his intention, Napoleon ordered Adjutant-General Savary to go straight at the redoubt with the *fusiliers-grenadiers de la Garde* leading the attackers. The orders were executed with valour. The French columns moved forwards, ignoring our fire, and one battalion of *fusiliers-grenadiers* broke into the redoubt, where a great slaughter took place, and in the meantime the area around the redoubt became blanketed by the French. A future hero of the Finnish war appeared at that moment. Without requesting orders from anyone, Kamensky led the Kaluga Musketeers, Sevsk Musketeers and Pernov Musketeers at the double and hit the French in the left flank. A most fierce hand-to-hand fight took place and the French fled back, being attacked at the same time from the front by Prince Gorchakov and Dokhturov and driven out of the redoubt, where almost an entire battalion of Napoleon's *Garde* lay stretched out. Not content with repelling the enemy, Kamensky pursued them, but without receiving support and, having met fresh French troops, he was pushed back to the redoubt, where he remained until nightfall. During the hand-to-hand fighting, the recently formed Pernov Musketeers captured the Eagle of the French *55e régiment d'infanterie de ligne* but our painful loss was the death of Major-General Warnek [Lavrenty Lavrentievich Warnek], who was killed in this close-quarter combat. Warnek was respected as a courageous, commanding warrior but was loved for his mildness.

This failure did not stop Napoleon, even though it was already getting dark. He strengthened his left wing as the last of Lannes' corps arrived on the battlefield and attacked our right, which Bennigsen had reinforced with 14th Division as soon as the French started moving in that direction. Several cavalry attacks were carried out under Uvarov's command, successfully for the most part. Platov enveloped the French left wing. The Prussian Major-General Zieten [Hans Ernst Karl von Zieten], with his Dragoon Regiment and the Black Hussars, twice crashed into the French infantry. Napoleon stopped the advance and limited himself to a cannonade.

The question remains: why did Bennigsen not take advantage of his successes and attack, having concentrated the army and surpassing Napoleon's strength? The cause was a seizure of stone disease [probably kidney stones] that tormented Bennigsen. On several occasions he had to dismount from his horse and lay on the ground. During the height of the battle, he fell into a prolonged faint leaning against a tree. The Tsarevich who was standing next to him invited the senior Army General, Kologrivov, to take over command. Kologrivov graciously refused, recognising that the duty of commander was beyond his ability. Then, at the insistence of the Tsarevich, Prince Gorchakov took on the main command of the action. Having come to his senses, Bennigsen could not ride his horse and gave orders in an exhausted voice.

THE BATTLE OF HEILSBERG 165

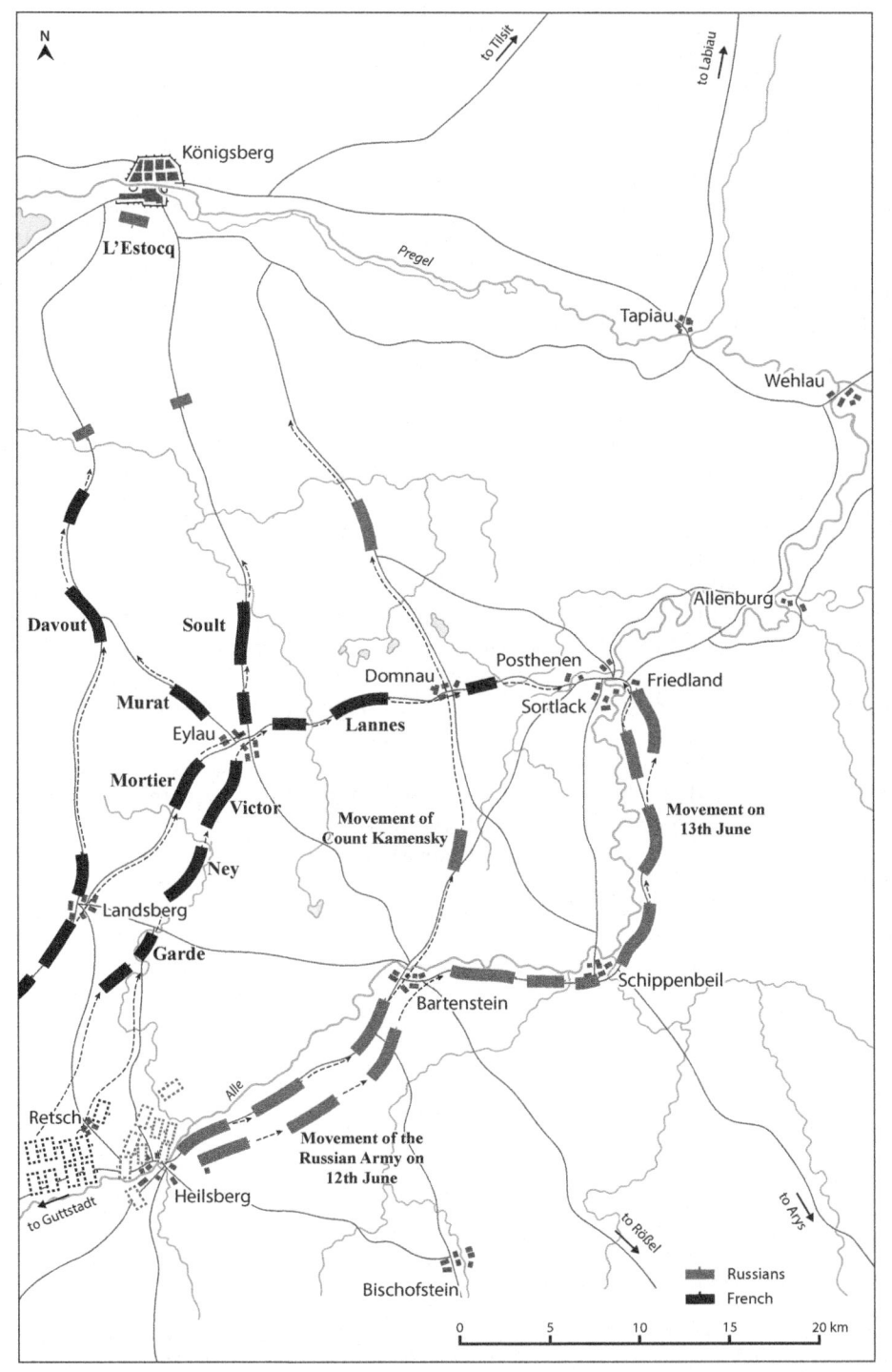

Map of Operations Between Heilsberg and Friedland.

Night fell. It was 10 o'clock in the evening and the fighting seemed to be over, when a crowd of Frenchmen appeared near Bennigsen and indicated that a new attack would soon be upon us. Indeed, at that time, after the arrival of Ney's corps on the battlefield, Napoleon resumed the attack on our centre, persisting with the idea of breaking through. A cross-fire lashed the French, the field was dotted with their corpses but the enemy were desperate to make headway. All their efforts were in vain. At the end of the eleventh hour, Napoleon gave orders to beat the retreat and withdrew to the Spibach. The Russians from redoubts No. 1 and No. 2 pushed and stabbed at the French. The bravest even crossed the stream but Bennigsen ordered everyone to return to their positions.[1]

French historians explain the repetition of Napoleon's attacks at a time when his army was not united, as his habit for victory and confidence in the extraordinary courage of the French. He so firmly hoped to drive the Russians away from the Heilsberg position, that during the morning of that day he ordered his headquarters to be set up in Heilsberg and we learned this from French surgeons captured by Cossacks on the right bank of the Alle. The surgeons had been calmly on their way to Heilsberg to set up hospitals there. The killed and wounded on our side at Heilsberg were some 6,000 men.[2] The following generals were wounded: Prince Karl of Mecklenburg [Karl August Christian zu Mecklenburg-Schwerin], Verderevsky, Foch, Passek [Pëtr Petrovich Passek], Olsufiev [Zakhar Dmitrievich Olsufiev], Duka and Laptev. Dokhturov suffered severe contusions. The French casualties, according to French authors were some 8,000 but, as we see from Bennigsen's notes, at the end of the war, Marshal Berthier told him that the killed and wounded in Napoleon's army at Heilsberg were some 13,000 men. We took 864 French prisoners of war. In Napoleon's bulletins the Battle of Heilsberg was described as a hard-fought vanguard action, although the French now recognise their total repulse.[3] For the Russians, Heilsberg was a defensive victory. Bennigsen sent his son [Adam Leontyevich Bennigsen] to Emperor Alexander with the report of the Battle of Heilsberg and the capture of a French colour by the Pernov Musketeers. The Emperor received the report and trophy while dining with the King of Prussia, and remarked: 'Only the future can show us the significance of the battle of Heilsberg and whether we will be able to exploit it.'

---

1   Bennigsen's letter to Count Tolstoy, dated 1 [13] June: *Le carnage a été terrible, et l'ennemi de nouveau battu et repoussé fut poursuivi jusqu'à Bévernik, où l'obscurité de la nuit ne nous permit pas de poursuivre nos avantages.*
2   Bennigsen's correspondence with Count Tolstoy, dated 1 [13] June.
3   Dumas, *Précis des évènemens militaires, Tome XVIII*, p. 279: *Le général Bennigsen s'étoit maintenu dans sa position et avoir repoussé sur tous les points les attaques impétueuses des françois avec beaucoup de vigueur et d'activité.*

# 21

# The Road to Friedland

**Napoleon's actions. – Bennigsen's dispositions. – The Russian withdrawal from Heilsberg. – Bennigsen's hesitancy. – The cavalry action at Friedland. – The partial crossing of the Alle by the Russian army. – French movements.**

During the rainy night following the battle of Heilsberg, the Guard and the remaining division of Ney's corps joined Napoleon. Despite this reinforcement, he abandoned his previous intention of driving the Russians from the Heilsberg position and decided to manoeuvre Bennigsen out of his fortifications. He ordered Marshals Davout and Mortier to march up the Königsberg road towards Landsberg, where he intended to follow them with all his other corps. Not knowing of Napoleon's decision, Bennigsen expected that Napoleon would renew his assault on him and, during the night of 29 to 30 May [10 to 11 June], redeployed to repel the enemy; our fighting line was reinforced with the reserves, while the Lifeguard took their place, crossing to the left bank of the Alle that night. At 6 o'clock in the morning of 30 [11 June], the Russian army stood to arms. The misty air did not allow us to see what was happening amongst the enemy troops. By 10 o'clock, it became apparent that the French had extended to their left, towards the village of Retsch [Redu]. Watching Napoleon's movements, Bennigsen strengthened his right wing. Here, in front of Großendorf, our skirmishers and the French went into action, while the Cossacks circled but nothing significant happened all day. In the evening, Napoleon marched with his army towards Landsberg.[1] The generals who were with him said that by taking this march, which gave Bennigsen the opportunity to strike the French, Napoleon was sure that Bennigsen would not take this chance and would be more concerned about maintaining his own axis of operations. Such was Napoleon's moral power on the battlefield: he could not even imagine the possibility that an opponent would dare to attack him from behind.

Confirming that the French were moving to Landsberg, Bennigsen ordered Count Kamensky to hurry through Bartenstein to join L'Estocq to protect Königsberg, while he wondered what to do. It was impossible to linger and it was necessary to

---

1   Bennigsen's report to Emperor Alexander, dated 30 May [11 June].

decide immediately.[2] He turned to Tsarevich Konstantin Pavlovich for advice and told him:

> I must choose one of three courses of action: firstly, to follow Napoleon and attack him, however, here our defeat is almost certain: Napoleon is much stronger than us; secondly, move parallel to him, preventing him from reaching Königsberg, which would be equally dangerous because we may be forced to give battle on ground disadvantageous to us; finally, the third option, leave the Heilsberg positions, march via Wehlau to the Pregel [Pregolya] and wait there for Napoleon's next move, getting closer to our reinforcements, which are not far away and then launch an offensive. I am minded to choose the third option as the safest for us. If we keep in mind only the interests of Russia, it would be best to immediately march on Bischofstein, Rößel [Reszel] and Arys, take a position between the lakes there and wait for reinforcements, or go to the Narew and link up with Count Tolstoy and the divisions of Princes Gorchakov and Lobanov, who are already close to us, after which we could move into the rear of the enemy with all our strength. But in both of these cases, we would leave Prussia to the enemy, the King of Prussia might believe that the Russians were abandoning him and we would open the entire coast of the Baltic Sea as far as St Petersburg to the enemy, therefore: the first indication of a march to Arys or to the Narew would cause great alarm. On the other hand, going beyond the Pregel to Wehlau, we could begin to observe the enemy closely and save Königsberg at the same time. On one thing I have firmly decided – not to leave anything to chance.

The Tsarevich agreed with Bennigsen's thoughts and, at his request, he went to Tilsit to report to Emperor Alexander about the situation.[3] During the night of 30 to 31 May [11 to 12 June], Bennigsen crossed the Alle with the army and, leaving three Cossack regiments on the left bank of the river to reconnoitre, marched to Bartenstein where he spent the day, hoping to get news of Napoleon's direction of travel from the Cossacks. Platov and Prince Bagration formed the rearguard. Having learned of Bennigsen's withdrawal, Napoleon sent La Tour-Maubourg [Marie-Victor-Nicolas de Faÿ de La Tour-Maubourg] across to the right bank of the Alle at Heilsberg with his dragoon division and two light cavalry brigades, ordering them to monitor the Russian army.

---

2   From Bennigsen's notes: *Assuré des intentions de Napoléon, je dois avouer qu'antant ma sécurite avoit été grande la veille, pendant l'action, autant mon embarras fut extrême sur le parti que j'avois à prendre dans ces circonstances, qui cependant demandoient une prompte détermination, mais bien refléchie, pour ne pas exposer l'armée et compromètre le salut de l'état par de fausses conjectures et de fausses mesures.*
3   From Bennigsen's notes: *Dans cette situation incertaine, je crus de mon devoir de faire un rapport à l'Empereur sur la position de l'armée et les véritables circonstances où elle se trouvoit, et sur ce qui m'engageoit à faire un meuvement retrograde derrière le Prégel par la droite de l'Alle.*

Due to the commander's struggle with exhausted physical strength, combined with the heavy responsibility lying upon him, Bennigsen's indecision began in Bartenstein – the first of a series of errors that ended the campaign in a week. Having arrived in Bartenstein, he wanted to change the decision he had made the day before, to go to Wehlau, and decided to attack Napoleon from behind if it turned out that he was really marching on Königsberg.[4] But while Bennigsen was making his mind up on an offensive, he was informed of the appearance of the French at Domnau. He hastily decided to go from Bartenstein via Schippenbeil towards Friedland, in order to prevent the French from taking possession of the crossings over the Alle in this town. Trying to forestall the enemy in Friedland, he sent Prince Golitsyn there with the Tsarevich's Ulan Regiment, Military Order Cuirassiers and four horse artillery pieces, having ordered him to occupy Friedland and to then send patrols along the left bank of the Alle to collect information about the enemy. Two hours later, Kologrivov was detached, with all the Lifeguard cavalry and 16 horse artillery pieces, to reinforce Prince Golitsyn. Having thus deployed, Bennigsen gave the army a brief rest in Schippenbeil and then continued his march on Friedland. Sent by Napoleon to observe the Russian army, La Tour-Maubourg followed them to Schippenbeil and here, crossing to the left bank of the Alle, linked up with Lannes' corps.

As he was approaching Friedland, Prince Golitsyn encountered refugee market traders, cart drivers and other logistics personnel who had fled from there. They informed him that the French had occupied Friedland: this was a cavalry detachment directed from Marshal Lannes' vanguard to conduct a reconnaissance of the right bank of the Alle. The French patrols, having seen the approach of Prince Golitsyn, returned to Friedland, where they quickly began to dismantle the bridge over the Alle. Prince Golitsyn sent the Tsarevich's Ulans to eject the French from the town. Having arrived at the river, the squadron commanders of the ulan regiment each asked their commander, Chalikov [Anton Stepanovich Chalikov], for permission to be the first to dash into the town. *Rotmistr* Volodimirov [Semën Alekseevich Volodimirov?] was granted this honour. As soon as Lieutenant Starzhinsky's first platoon rode up onto the bridge, bullets fell around them from the other side and he saw that the middle of the bridge had been dismantled. While the bridge was being repaired under fire, Starzhinsky, laying a plank over the gap, ran across to the other side of the bridge. His trumpeter and several lancers followed his example and immediately lay planks which the French had discarded at the sides of the bridge. Volodimirov's squadron and, soon after, the entire regiment broke into the town and after a bloody street-fight, ejected the French, capturing four officers and 56 lower ranks.[5] Prince Golitsyn deployed his force forwards of Friedland. Kologrivov soon arrived with the Lifedguard cavalry and as senior officer, took command of the entire detachment.

---

4   Bennigsen's report to the Tsar, dated 1 [13] June.
5   There are still witnesses to this brilliant act, who were serving at the time in the Tsarevich's Ulan Regiment: the future Commandant of Shlisselburg, Lieutenant-General Zaborinsky [Alexander Nikiforovich Zaborinsky] and the famous writer, Bulgarin [Jan Tadeusz Krzysztof Bulgarin].

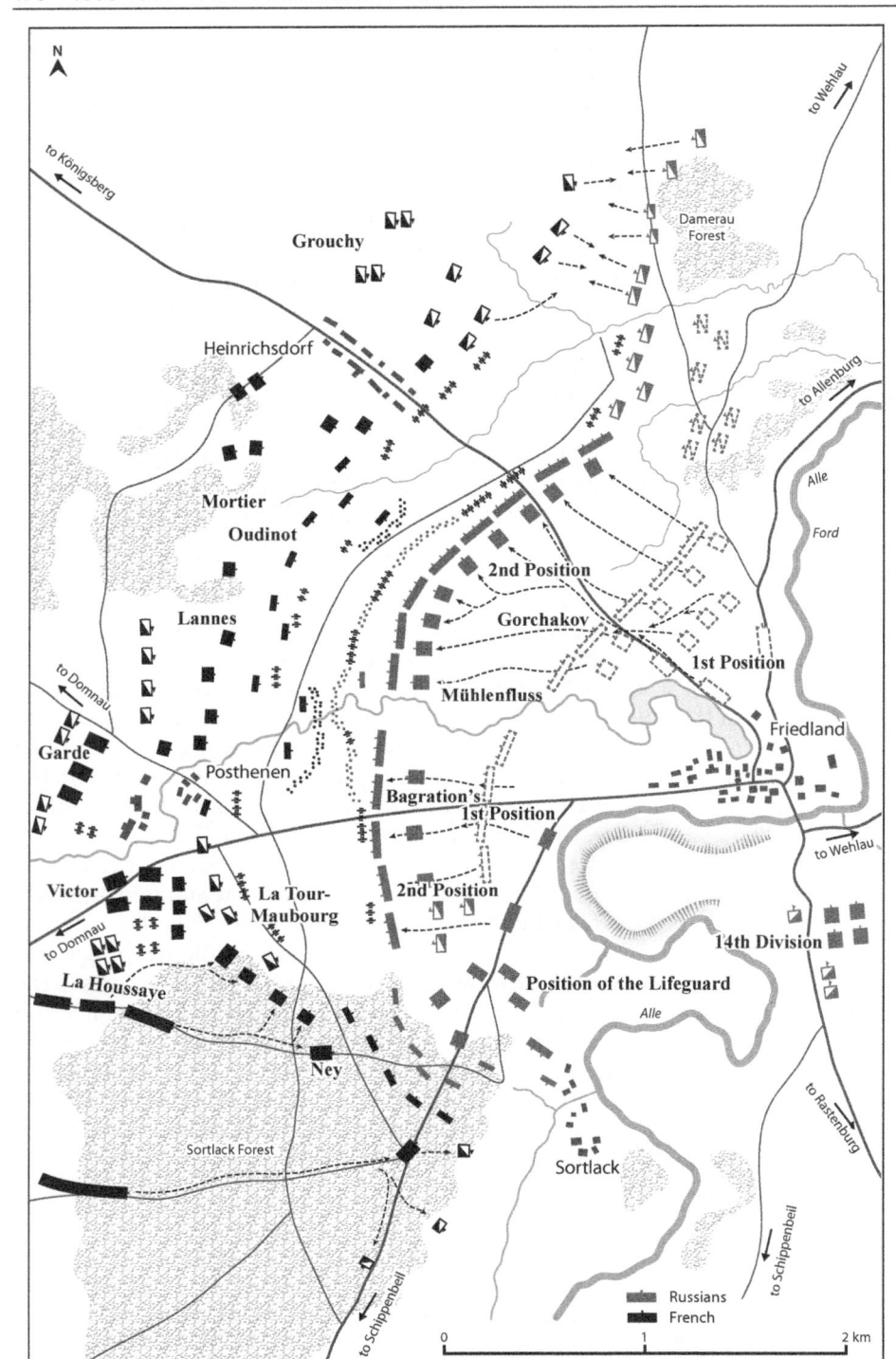

170   1806-1807 – TSAR ALEXANDER'S SECOND WAR WITH NAPOLEON

First Plan of the Battle of Friedland, 2 [14] June, dawn to five p.m.

It was eight o'clock in the evening of 1 [13] June, when Bennigsen set off from Schippenbeil towards Friedland, ahead of the army, having already ordered them to march as quickly as possible. The prisoners taken by the Tsarevich's Ulans revealed to him that Oudinot was leading Lannnes' vanguard and was stationed three *versts* [3.2 km or 2 miles] from Friedland at Posthenen [Peredovoye], the destination of Lannes' entire corps. Bennigsen ordered Dokhturov, who was marching at the head of the army, to cross to the left bank of the Alle with 7th Division and 8th Division, in support of Kologrivov and to repulse any possible night attacks. All other troops, as they arrived at the high ground near Friedland, were positioned on the right bank of the Alle, from where they were to continue the march to the river Pregel the next day. Bennigsen, on the advice of doctors, went to spend the night in Friedland himself, not finding suitable accommodation for himself on the right bank of the river. Eyewitnesses, including General Count Pahlen [Pëtr Petrovich Pahlen],[6] agree that Bennigsen, obsessed with his illness, would not have crossed the Alle if he had found a dwelling suitable for his temporary rest on the right bank and, in that case, the Battle of Friedland would not have happened.

At 11 o'clock that night, Frenchmen seized by his patrols informed Bennigsen that Lannes and Oudinot had united. Bennigsen ordered the Lifeguard infantry, with the exception of the Lifeguard Preobrazhensky Regiment, and two divisions to cross the Alle. The Lifeguard stood in the Sortlack [Temkino] forest. Two pontoon bridges were then laid over the Alle and Platov was sent downstream of the Alle with most of the Cossacks from the army, the Lifeguard Preobrazhensky Regiment, Chevalier Guard, Finland Dragoons and Olviopol Hussars, in order to seize the crossings on the Alle and the river Pregel, for which Bennigsen wanted to set off on the following day, according to the report sent to the Emperor with the Tsarevich, in order 'to attack Napoleon from Wehlau in the flank and the rear if he heads for Königsberg.'[7] Lannes, for his part, having found out from Oudinot about the situation had also reported to Napoleon, that a significant part of the Russian army was located on the left bank of the Alle at Friedland and he was holding all the routes leading from Friedland to Königsberg. Napoleon directed Victor towards Lannes' corps and, considering himself able to hold Bennigsen should he launch an offensive from Friedland, did not stop Murat, Soult and Davout from marching on Königsberg and continued the march with the remaining forces from Eylau to Domnau. Thus passed the eve of the day that decided the war!

---

6   Later a member of the State and Military Council.
7   Bennigsen's own words from his correspondence with Count Tolstoy, dated 1 [13] June, from Schippenbeil.

# 22

# The Battle of Friedland

Marshal Lannes' operations. – The deployment of the Russian army. – The battle begins. – Napoleon's arrival on the battlefield. – Napoleon's orders. – Bennigsen's orders to retreat. – Napoleon's assault. – Marshal Ney's failure. – The decisive operations of the French General Sénarmont. – The defeat of Prince Bagration. – Prince Gorchakov's operations. – Street fighting in Friedland. – The rout of the Russian army. – The damage to the combatant armies. – Comments by foreigners about the Russian army at Friedland.

At dawn on 2 [14] June, a firefight broke out between the forward screens. Due to the half light, the numbers and deployment of the opposing forces could not be calculated, neither from our side nor on the enemy's. At sunrise, once he had seen the Russians in front of him in greater numbers than he had the day before, Lannes informed Napoleon about this, not awaiting his orders but limiting his actions to skilful manoeuvres he exploited the wooded and hilly terrain, trying to hide his small numbers from us. La Tour-Maubourg's detachment soon joined him, followed by Victor's corps and Nansouty's [Étienne Marie Antoine Champion de Nansouty] Dragoon Division and Grouchy's Cuirassiers sent by Napoleon. A cannonade was begun by both sides. Bennigsen ordered the troops on the right bank of the Alle, with the exception of 14th Division, to cross to the left and to form up in front of Friedland with their backs to the Alle on ground that was bisected by the deep ravine of the Mühlen Fluss [Pravda], over which four bridges were hastily laid. 3rd Division, 4th Division, 6th Division and 7th Division and some of the cavalry deployed to the right of the ravine under Prince Gorchakov's command, resting their right wing on the Domerau woods, while the remainder of the force were on the left of the ravine under the direction of Prince Bagration. Once the deployment of our army was complete, it formed an arc with each extremity resting on the river Alle. Bennigsen justified the choice of such an unfavourable position, saying: 'I did not intend to give battle and only thought to grant a rest day to the troops, who had been on the march constantly since 21 May [2 June].'

The fighting spread little by little. It was especially fierce in the Sortlack woods on our left wing. At 9 o'clock in the morning, as the French were pushed into the depths of the forest, Bennigsen pushed the army forward a thousand paces. On our right wing, near Heinrichsdorf [Rovnoye], there were several cavalry attacks but, conducted without a specific objective, they were of no consequence. The skirmishers scattered in front of the army alternately advanced and withdrew. At times the artillery bombardment intensified and then subsided. Unwilling to attack the enemy, Bennigsen also did not want to retreat. He considered a retreat to be contrary to the dignity of the Russian army, facing, as he believed, an inferior number of enemy. Bennigsen stated;

> This action began early in the morning and developed imperceptibly against Oudinot's and Lannes' corps, without great bloodshed and against whom the honour of our armed forces would not allow us to yield the battlefield, in ignorance, I must add, of the approach of the entire French army.[1]

This acknowledgement by the commander is the key to understanding the Battle of Friedland.

Napoleon arrived on the battlefield at noon and surveyed the area, having ordered the troops which he had passed on the way to hurry to Friedland. Peering at the unfavourable position of the Russian army, he was unsure of Bennigsen's true intentions and finally said: 'Of course, other Russian troops must be hidden in some other location.' Sending officers on reconnaissance in various directions, at 3 o'clock in the afternoon he wrote to Murat, who had been detached to Königsberg. 'The cannonade began at 3 o'clock in the morning. A general battle appears to be developing. It may continue for a second day. Leave Soult opposite Königsberg and come to Friedland with the *Réserve de cavalerie* and Davout's corps. If I find the Russian army too numerous, I will restrict myself, perhaps, to a cannonade whilst I wait for your arrival.' Napoleon was bewildered, as he had been at the beginning of this campaign by Field Marshal Count Kamensky and now, at the end of the war, by Bennigsen, through their mistaken orders!

Officers placed in the Friedland bell tower informed Bennigsen about the approach of enemy columns: these were Ney's and Mortier's corps, the *Garde* and the *Réserve de cavalerie*. As they arrived, Napoleon directed them to assembly areas: Ney was on the right wing between Posthenen and the Sortlack woods; Lannes and Nansouty's Dragoon Division in the centre adjacent to the right wing and occupying the village of Posthenen; Mortier with Grouchy's Cuirassier Division and one of dragoons were on the left wing at Heinrichsdorf; Victor, the *Garde* and La Houssaye's [Armand Lebrun de La Houssaye] Dragoon Division were in reserve. Having once more inspected the dispositions of our army, Napoleon decided to go into action and ordered: firstly, as all our bridges [over the Alle] were in Friedland and there were no crossings behind Prince Gorchakov, Ney was to attack our left wing, followed by Victor, the *Garde* and La Houssaye's and La Tour-Maubourg's dragoons, pushing us back into Friedland and then take possession of the town, cutting our left wing off from the Russian troops on the other side of the Mühlen Fluss. Secondly, Lannes and Mortier were to open an artillery bombardment of our

---

1   From Bennigsen's notes: *Cette affaire commença de grand matin et s'engagea insensiblement contre les corps d'Oudinot et de Lannes, sans une grande effusion de sang, et contre lesquels l'honneur de nos armes ne permettait pas de céder le champ de bataille, j'y ajouterai dans l'ignorance de l'approche de toute l'armée française.*

right wing until Ney had driven off Prince Bagration and once our left flank had been defeated, to attack the right with all strength. During Napoleon's deployment, Bennigsen remained inactive, in spite of the reports he received about the build-up of large forces against us. Prince Bagration predicted the attack against him. This discerning commander said that the assault would be carried out on him and asked for reinforcements. Bennigsen did not leave Friedland. Finally becoming aware of the danger of his situation, he gave orders for a withdrawal to the right bank of the Alle. He wrote;

> The Russian army, already much inferior in numbers, was surprised by the arrival of Napoleon with most of his army. From that moment the French had an easy time, because prudence demanded that we not dispute the battlefield; also the army was already busy in re-crossing the Alle when the first enemy corps emerged from the woods which had concealed their approach.[2]

It was already 5 o'clock when Bennigsen's orders for the retreat were issued. Prince Gorchakov replied to Bennigsen that it would be easier for him to hold the superior enemy until dusk than to withdraw in full view. Prince Bagration, on the other hand, agreed with Bennigsen's will and ordered his rearmost troops to fall back. This had just begun, at five o'clock in the afternoon, when there was a triple salvo from twenty French guns – the signal for Ney's assault. Thus, the incoherent fighting of that morning became the prelude to the real battle. Now it began!

After the cannon signal, Ney moved forwards. A fierce firefight broke out in the Sortlack woods and the French captured them. Prince Bagration changed front, drawing back his left wing. Within an hour, Ney's columns began to emerge from the woods. Marchand's [Jean Gabriel Marchand] Division formed his right wing with Bisson's [Baptiste-Pierre-François Bisson] to his left. A Russian battery positioned on the right bank of the Alle struck Marchand's Division with canister. The French wavered and became disordered. General Sénarmont [Alexandre-Antoine Hureau de Sénarmont] wrote; 'A Russian battery deployed on the far bank of the Alle fired upon us in the flank; some of them were very close to us and one, standing on a low promontory that overlooked us, beyond a bend in the river, inflicted lethal damage on us. A general wavering in our ranks showed that our men were beginning to lose their enthusiasm under this deadly barrage.'[3]

Napoleon detached Dupont's Division to support Ney but it was too late. Russian cavalry had already managed to hack into Marchand's disordered regiments, overran them and seized an Eagle. Overcome with courage, they then charged a horse artillery battery from Dupont's Division. This was the limit of the success of our cavalry.

---

2 From Bennigsen's notes: *L'armée russe, déja beaucoup inférieure en nombre, fut surprise par l'arrivée de Napoléon avec la plus grande partie de son armée. Dès ce moment les françois eurent beau jeu, car la prudence exigea de ne pas leur disputer le champ de bataille; aussi l'armée se trouvoit déja occuppée à repasser l'Alle, quand les premiers corps ennemis sortirent du bois, qui en avoit couvert la marche.*

3 *Mémoires biographiques du Général Sénarmont.*

## THE BATTLE OF FRIEDLAND 175

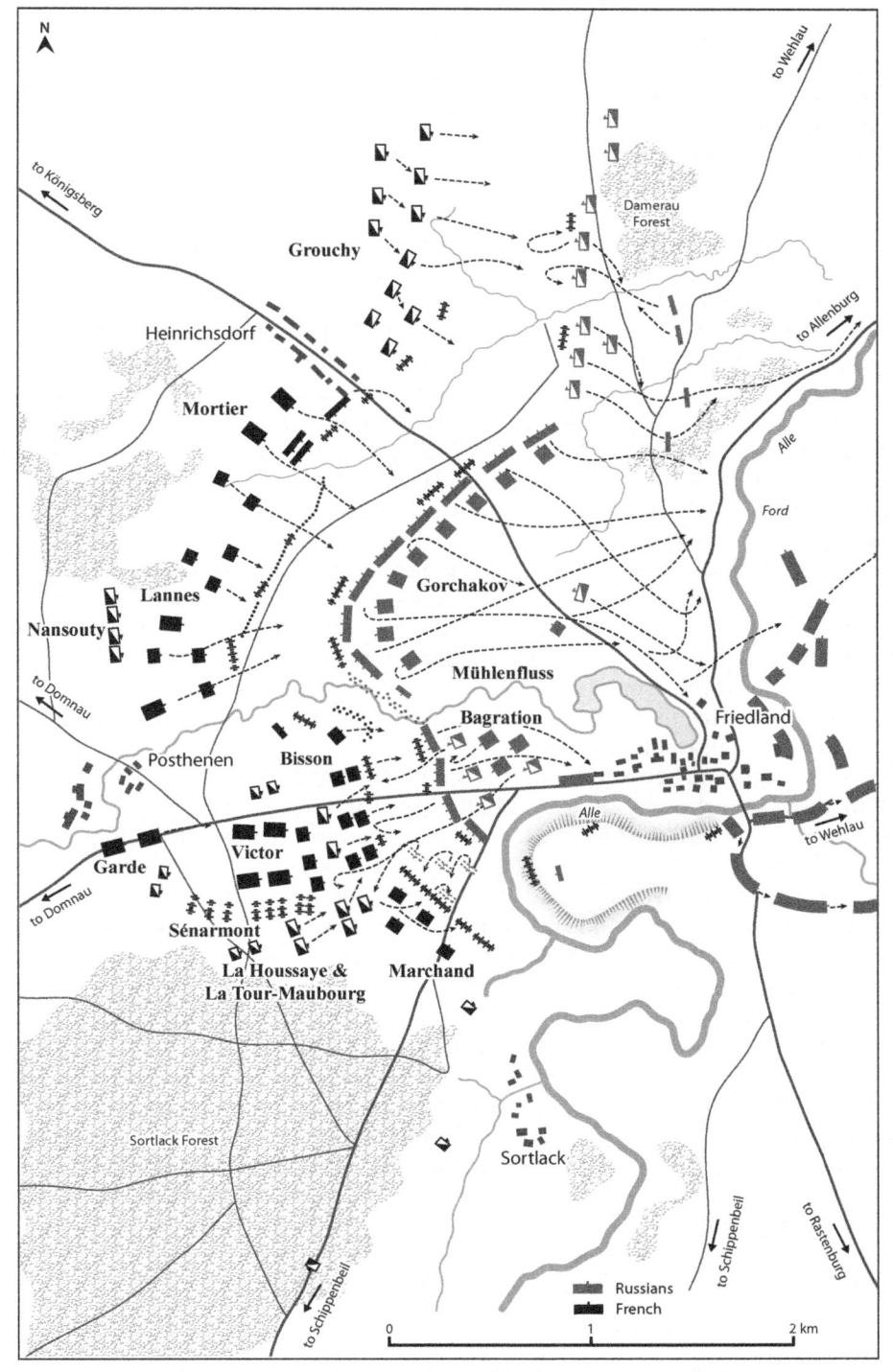

Second Plan of the Battle of Friedland, 2 [14] June, from six p.m.

Greeted with canister fire from this battery and La Tour-Maubourg's Dragoon Division, they were driven off. Victor and Napoleon's *Garde* rushed to Ney. Taking advantage of this fleeting success, Prince Bagration moved forward but the situation suddenly changed. The renowned French general, Sénarmont, with the approval of Marshal Victor, concentrated all of the corps' artillery, consisting of 36 guns, rushed off with them as fast as the horses could get up to the high ground on which Ney was forming his corps and took station at their front at a range of 180 *sazhens* [378m or 420 yds] from Prince Bagration. Firing five or six rounds from each gun, Sénarmont advanced his artillery to 90 *sazhens* [189m or 210 yds] from our line and unleashed a brutal bombardment. Surprised by the unexpected appearance of the French 36-gun battery, ours tried in vain to fire back from their individual batteries, scattered along our battle line. Only a few minutes were needed for the French to shower a concentrated hail of canister fire on each of the individual Russian batteries. Having prevailed over Prince Bagration's artillery, Sénarmont turned all his fire against the columns. The Russian front line wavered. Several regiments from our second line pressed forwards, including the Lifeguard Jägers, Lifeguard Izmailov and Lifeguard Horse. They were disordered by enemy fire, suffering heavy losses; for example, of the 520 men of Third Battalion, Lifeguard Izmailov Regiment, 400 were killed or wounded in the space of 15 minutes.[4] Napoleon, who was closely following all the developments in this bloody battle, was afraid that Sénarmont would get himself into too much trouble and sent his aide de camp Mouton [Georges Mouton?] to find out why he had gone so far forwards. The general replied; 'Do not bother me and my gunners, inform the Emperor that I guarantee success.' When Mouton returned, Napoleon, watching this famous artillery action, said with a smile; 'Artillerymen are stubborn – we'll leave them alone.'

Prince Bagration retreated onto the ground between the Alle and the ravine. With every step the space narrowed and gave the French artillery the chance to operate ever more lethally against our deep columns. Sénarmont boldly moved to a range of 46 *sazhens* [97m or 322'] from our front, firing canister at the dense mass. The Russian cavalry sent to attack him could not reach the enemy battery, being raked by their fire and turned back, increasing the confusion amongst our troops. The example of the commanders could not hold back the disorderly retreat. Prince Bagration, Raevsky, Yermolov, Baggovut, Markov and others tried to rally the troops. The canister was ripping through our ranks and, meanwhile, the French columns came forward one after another, exclaiming: '*Vive l'Empereur!*' Baggovut and Markov both fell wounded. Prince Bagration drew his sword, something he very rarely did. The Moscow Grenadier Regiment crowded around the hero, wanting to shield him from death. Bagration was oblivious to his personal safety. He reminded the grenadiers of Italy and Suvorov. Hearing his voice declaiming the great name of Suvorov, the Muscow Grenadiers rushed forward but without unity of purpose and perished. Their strength was failing. Self-sacrifice only added to the number of victims. Finally, at 8 o'clock, trapped between the town and the river, Prince Bagration set up a rearguard, entered Friedland, set fire to the suburbs and began

---

4   According to Khrapovitsky, the commander of this battalion – now Military Governor-General of St Petersburg.

to pass troops across the Alle, over bridges that had already been set alight, through a mistaken order brought by an aide de camp to the bridge commander, who was ordered to burn them.[5] The destructive extent of the enemy fire directed at Prince Bagration's troops can be seen from French returns: they wrote officially that 2,516 rounds were fired by General Sénarmont at Friedland, 362 of which were round shot, all of the remainder were canister.[6]

We now turn to Prince Gorchakov. Lannes and Mortier directed an attack on him shortly after Ney's assault on Bagration. Prince Gorchakov held courageously until on the left round shot enfiladed his line from a battery set up by the French in the area from which they had driven out Prince Bagration. At the same time, he learned about the defeat of our left flank and began to retreat. Mortier and Lannes followed him. While Prince Gorchakov's rearguard fought off the fierce French cavalry attacks, our columns hurried towards Friedland, which was already occupied by the enemy. They fiercely drove into the burning suburbs and the town surrounded by flames, under a hail of bullets and after the most bloody slaughter, drove the French from Friedland. Our thirst for vengeance was such that some of them rushed to pursue the enemy.[7] While they were clearing the French from the town, others rushed to the river. The bridges had already gone: they were burned to ashes. Discipline collapsed. Men jumped into the river, trying to swim to the other side.[8] Officers were sent in all directions to look for fords. The first ford was found by Uvarov's aide de camp, *Stabs-Rotmistr* Chernyshev of the Chevalier Guard Regiment – now Minister of War. Chernyshev's reward for this feat was the St George Cross. Subsequently, other fords were found. The troops rushed into the river, to the roar of the French batteries and ours, set on the right bank of the Alle. The extent to which the guns were moved diligently across the river is evidenced by the remarkably small losses of artillery in the general turmoil that befell the army. Bennigsen reported that we had lost four or five guns, where the carriages were shot up or the horses were killed.[9] From the records of the Artillery Department it is clear that we lost ten guns at Friedland. It was simply impossible to bring across the 29 Battery guns brought to the ford, the slope down to which had been completely ruined by the troops crossing there earlier. Count Lambert collected these guns, and, under escort from the Alexandria Hussar Regiment, took them along the left bank of the Alle to Allenburg, where he rejoined the army.

---

5   According to a witness, General Yermolov.
6   *Précis des opérations du 1err corps (Maréchal Victor).*
7   Plotho, a witness to this event, wrote the following in his *Tagebuch während des Krieges Rußland's und Preußen's gegen Frankreich, p. 167:*
    *Wer vermag zu schildernd die Verzweiflung und die Muth der tapfern Russen, ihren fürchterlichen Angriff – nicht fürchterlicher konnte er damals sein – ihr Vorrücken durch die brennende Stadt, sich entgegenstürzend der Kugelsaat, die der Feind über sie schüttelte, und die den meisten das Leben nahm. Aber fort mußte der Feind aus der Vorstadt hinaus ins Freie, und wie von Rache aufgeboten, verfolgten ihn auch dahin die gereizten Rußen.*
8   Bennigsen's report to the Tsar from Allenburg the day after the battle of Friedland: *Les troupes ne tinrent plus, et se débandèrent.*
9   Bennigsen's report to the Tsar from Allenburg the day after the battle of Friedland: *Toute l'artillerie a été sauvée, à l'exception de quatre à cinq pièces, dont les affuts avoient été brisés ou les chevaux tués.*

Our killed and wounded at Friedland were some 10,000,[10] while the French, according to the statements of their historians, lost up to 4,500 men. Major-General Mazovsky was one of those killed; Major-General Sukin had his leg torn off. At the start of Napoleon's attack, Quartermaster-General Steinheil and Duty General Essen, riding alongside each other, suffered severe contusions from a round shot that passed between them. The removal from the battlefield of these two main assistants to Bennigsen, together with his own ill health, finally destroyed the unity of command of the troops who had fought to the limits of exhaustion. One foreign witness to the battle wrote: 'Did fate once decree that Napoleon should triumph at Friedland, is this why the Russian army had to succumb so completely through no fault of their own?'[11] Another impartial eyewitness to the battle, located in Bennigsen's headquarters, the British Envoy, Lord Hutchinson, reported to his Government: 'I lack terms sufficiently strong to describe the valour of the Russians, and which would have rendered their success undoubted, if courage alone could ensure victory, but, whatever may be the end, the officers and men of the Russian army have done their duty in the noblest manner, and are justly entitled to the praise and admiration of every person, who was witness of their conduct.'[12]

---

10   Bennigsen's report to the Tsar, dated 4 [16] June.
11   Plotho, *Tagebuch de Krieges 1806 und 1807*, p. 169: *Wenn es das Schiksal einmal bestimmt hatte, daß Napoleon bei Friedland triumphieren sollte, warum mußte die Russische Armee so ganz ohne Schuld unterliegen?*
12   Sir Robert Wilson, Sketch of the campaigns in Poland, in the years 1806 and 1807, page 16.

# 23

# The Conclusion of Hostilities

The retreat of the Russian army from Friedland. – Napoleon's dispositions. – Count Kamensky's and L'Estocq's operations. – The crossing of the Neman by the Russian army. – The operations of Count Tolstoy's independent corps. – Bennigsen's thoughts on the Battle of Friedland.

That evening, at the end of the Battle of Friedland, the Russian army crossed over the Alle and marched ruefully towards Wehlau. The beautiful night was illuminated by the burning surrounding villages. Bennigsen's intention was to get over the Pregel, to link up with reinforcements and join the route to link up with L'Estocq and Count Kamensky, to whom he had sent orders to leave Königsberg. In order to secure their march, Major-General Ilovaisky 2nd, with three Cossack regiments, was ordered to burn the bridge over the Pregel at Tapiau [Gvardeysk] and to destroy all the boats and ferries on this river. After a short rest in Allenburg, where attempts were made to regroup the regiments, the army continued its march towards Wehlau and crossed the Pregel there, weakly pursued by the French. Having sent only cavalry to follow Bennigsen along the right bank of the Alle, Napoleon gave orders for: the main body to move to the Pregel along the left bank of the Alle; Masséna was to attack Count Tolstoy frontally, while Dąbrowski's joint Polish corps would proceed behind him; Murat and Davout, who had been on the march from Königsberg to Friedland at the time of the battle, but had taken no part in it, were to turn left towards Tapiau and attempt to cut Bennigsen off from the Königsberg based detachments under L'Estocq and Count Kamensky. Having issued these orders, Napoleon regarded Königsberg as easy prey, according to his calculations that L'Estocq and Count Kamensky, separated from the Russian army, of course, would not venture to defend this weakly fortified city.

After spending several hours in Wehlau and entrusting the rearguard to Prince Bagration and Platov, Bennigsen set off on a forced march to Schillupönen, where he hoped to link up with L'Estocq and Count Kamensky, whose operations were as follows: setting off from Heilsberg towards Königsberg, Count Kamensky, staying skilfully ahead of the leading enemy columns, linked up with L'Estocq near Königsberg on 1 [13] June. The following day [14 June], Murat's detachment came into view. The French opened fire with their artillery, probing our positions and preparing to attack. The attack did not take place, because Murat received orders from the Battlefield of Friedland that day to join Napoleon, leaving Soult near Königsberg. Not being able to attack the troops stationed here, Soult wanted to try his hand at negotiations and invited the Governor-General of Königsberg, Rüchel for a meeting. Rüchel asked Count Kamensky to go to the negotiations in his stead. Count Kamensky went to the forward screen and let Soult know of his readiness to see him. Soult sent General Belliard [Augustin Daniel Belliard] to Count Kamensky with a demand for the surrender of Königsberg, as Belliard recounted 'on the most favourable of terms.' Kamensky furiously replied; 'You can see that I wear the uniform of Russia and you dare to demand surrender?' Having said this, he turned his horse around and rode away. That ended the negotiations. The following day, on 3 [15] June, L'Estocq and Count Kamensky received the news of the lost battle from Bennigsen and the order to hurry towards Schillupönen or towards Tilsit. The order was executed precisely, and both generals, marching swiftly, joined Bennigsen in Schillupönen having slipped away from Murat and Davout, who had been sent by Napoleon to cut across their route. Upon learning of the departure of the allied forces from Königsberg, Soult occupied the city, where he found a huge amount of booty and blockaded the fortress of Pillau with a detachment.

Linking up with L'Estocq and Count Kamensky on 5 [17] June, Bennigsen continued his march towards Tilsit and began to cross the Neman on the 6 [18 June], where the army deployed between the villages of Pogegen [Pagėgiai] and Mikiten [Mikytai], within 4 *versts* [4.2km or 2⅔ miles] of the Neman. Depreradovich's [Nikolai Ivanovich Depreradovich] detachment held the village of Ragnit [Neman]. Prince Bagration and Platov crossed the next day, burning the bridge and stood along the Neman, whose banks had begun to be fortified. During their retreat from Friedland, each going in a separate column, they were sometimes caught by the French. Twice Murat prepared to assault Prince Bagration in strong positions. Not shy of a fight, Prince Bagration formed his cavalry, under the command of Count Lambert and Count Pahlen and waited for the attack. Murat, however, would not attack. There were several clashes with Platov's column that had no effect. One of them is remarkable for the participation of two 500 man Bashkiri commandos and a regiment of Stavropol Kalmyks that had just joined the army. In response to their enthusiastic pleas, they were put into action and fired several hundred arrows at the enemy. Astounded by the novelty of these weapons used against them, the French cavalry retreated. On 7 [19] June, Murat occupied Tilsit. As for Count Tolstoy's independent corps, after the Battle of Friedland Bennigsen ordered him to have the sole objective of protecting our borders.[1] Count Tolstoy fell back towards Białystok, leaving Count Wittgenstein and Löwis to monitor Masséna. These generals exchanged fire with the enemy when they approached but withdrew without harm to Białystok.

These were the consequences of the Battle of Friedland. With the exception of Kolberg, Pillau and Graudenz, since the Silesian fortresses had fallen in the meantime, the entire Prussian Monarchy, from the Neman to the Weser, obeyed Napoleon. Bennigsen commented in his notes; 'Of course, I would have done better not to give battle at Friedland and contented myself with fending them off with the rearguard, if the French had interfered with my movement to Wehlau, but I was misled by reports.

---

1   Bennigsen's instructions to Count Tolstoy, dated 3 [15] June, from Wehlau.

Every general can be deceived by them, as I was. All the intelligence and statements from the prisoners captured in various places were agreed that I was faced only by Oudinot, Lannes, Dąbrowski and several German regiments, while Napoleon was heading for Königsberg with the main army. My defeat should not have had any influence on the outcome of the war and should not have led to peace, because there were still many troops within our borders to defend Russia. The Battle of Friedland did not even prevent me from continuing the march to the Pregel, my intention since Heilsberg, and therefore did not change the course of hostilities. Even without it, I could not have prevented Napoleon from taking possession of Königsberg, since he was much superior to me in numbers. In any case, I had to retreat to the borders of Russia in order to link up with the reinforcements coming to me and then fight with Napoleon.' This is what Bennigsen claimed, but he argues vainly that the Battle of Friedland did not change the course of events. On the contrary: the conclusion of the armistice was its direct result.

# 24

# The Armistice

Bennigsen's thoughts on the need for an armistice. – Ziesmer's letter on this subject. – Privy Councillor Popov. – Emperor Alexander's rescript to him. – The rescript to Bennigsen. – The authority of Prince Lobanov-Rostovsky. – The beginning of negotiations for a truce. – The departure of Prince Lobanov-Rostovsky for the French army. – His conversation with Marshal Berthier. Duroc's visit to Bennigsen. – The armistice. – Prince Lobanov's report of his meeting with Napoleon. – The reasons for the truce. – Prussian correspondence with Napoleon.

Emperor Alexander was near Jurburg, inspecting Prince Lobanov-Rostovsky's 17th Division recently arrived from Moscow, when he received Bennigsen's report about the battle of Friedland. Briefly describing the course of the battle, Bennigsen reported that he was retreating behind the Pregel, where he would remain on the defensive until the arrival of the expected reinforcements. He concluded his report with the suggestion that it was necessary to enter into negotiations with the enemy in order to gain the time needed to make good the losses incurred by the army.[1] Thereafter the Foreign Minister, Baron Budberg, presented a letter to Emperor Alexander which he had received from a senior diplomatic official with the army, Ziesmer. The letter read as follows: 'With a soul torn to shreds by the distressing sights to which I have had the misfortune of being a witness, I report on the disaster that has befallen us, for General Bennigsen, not wanting to upset the Emperor, does not reveal all to Him.' After a brief outline of the battle, Ziesmer continued: 'In an instant, the army was scattered. If a subordinate might dare to speak frankly to the commander, then I'll report that we have only one option left: propose a truce as soon as possible, or enter into peace negotiations, while the army and the reinforcements coming to it arrive behind the Pregel and it might be possible to obtain more favourable conditions for peace. Our losses in men and artillery are overwhelming. Bennigsen portrayed the Battle of Friedland to the Emperor in an infinitely less gloomy way than was actually the case. I assure you that I have not exaggerated.'

---

[1] Bennigsen's report to the Tsar, written on the day after the battle of Friedland: *Je prends une position derrière le Prégel, où je me tiendrai sur la défensive, jusqu'à ce que les renforts qe j'attends seront arrivés. Néanmoins je croirois indispensable et conforme à la prudence d'entamer quelques négociations de paix, ne fut ce que pour gagner du tems pour reparer nos pertes, dont Votre Majesté décidera.*

After reading the reports of Bennigsen and Ziesmer and agreeing on the inevitably of starting negotiations, Emperor Alexander summoned Privy Councillor Popov to resolve the question: was the army really so disordered that it was necessary to end hostilities? To explain such high powers granted to Popov, it is necessary to understand the following circumstances: At a time when the provisioning and commissariat departments in the army were completely inefficient, Emperor Alexander, wanting to reduce corruption, summoned Popov from the village where he had lived during the reign of Emperor Paul. Popov's fame began when he was the head of the chancellery and a confidant under Prince Potemkin, who kept the troops he led in good health, well supplied and full of heroic spirit until his death. A fresh recollection of the brilliant state of Potemkin's army rekindled in Emperor Alexander the hope that, perhaps, Popov could eradicate the abuses that had crept into the commissariat and provisioning departments and accepted him into service at the beginning of 1807, in his personal suite and sent him to the army, ordering him to take the logistics units under his main directorate and also inform the Tsar about military events. Popov's initial actions satisfied the Emperor's expectations to such an extent that he personally wrote to Popov: 'The longer I am in communications with you, the more My pleasure is increased. Continue as you have started, be firmly assured of My gratitude to you. I am very pleased that I have found a man who puts himself above the affection that attracts corrupt indulgence and condescension to himself and prefers the interests of the service to personal rivalry.'[2]

Such was Popov's position in the army when the Emperor received the above-mentioned reports from Bennigsen and Ziesmer. Immediately, on 4 [16] June, he wrote the following to Popov in his own hand:

> I received the attached report by courier from General Bennigsen. You may easily imagine the feelings which accompanied its reading. Not having a single line from you yet and fearing to lose precious time, I decided to send a special courier to you with this letter. I have no choice but to rely on your impartial judgment. If you find that the circumstances are such as General Bennigsen describes them, that it is necessary to enter into negotiations with Bonaparte, then hand him the letter enclosed herewith addressed to him, which I allow him to interpret on my behalf concerning an armistice with Bonaparte.[3] My letter is under open seal, and I wish you also to read it. After that, Lieutenant-General Prince Lobanov, whom I have chosen to send from the Commander-in-Chief to Bonaparte, will arrive later. He will discuss everything with you personally. I look forward to hearing from you. I enclose herewith equally a copy of the letter to Budberg from an official of his department, who is with Bennigsen. This is more detailed than the general's report.[4]

---

2   The Emperor's letter, dated 19 [31] May, from Tilsit, kept by Popov's son.
3   The word 'armistice' was underlined in the original.
4   The original handwritten letter by the Tsar was kept by Popov's son.

The rescript sent to Popov addressed to Bennigsen read as follows:

> Having entrusted you with a wonderful army, which has demonstrated so many examples of courage, I was very far removed from expecting that you have not told me the news. If you have no other way to get out of this predicament, besides a truce, then I authorise you to do this, but on condition that you negotiate on your behalf. I am sending Prince Lobanov-Rostovsky to you, finding him capable in every way in these slippery negotiations. He will brief you verbally on the orders I have given him. After discussing with him and Popov, send him to Bonaparte. You can judge how hard it is for me to decide on such an act.

Furnished with these letters, Prince Lobanov came to Bennigsen's headquarters, having these Supreme Orders should he be sent to the French headquarters:

> try to conclude a ceasefire for a month, during which the forces of both sides will remain in their current locations; do not offer peace negotiations, but if the French have expressed the first inclination to end the war, answer that Emperor Alexander equally desires a reconciliation and, if the French ask whether you have been given authority to negotiate, present this authority signed by the Emperor.[5]

In the meantime, Popov had also informed the Tsar of the need to cease hostilities for a while, and handed Bennigsen a copy of the Monarch's rescript. Immediately thereafter, on 7 [19] June, they sent Major Sheping to Marshal Berthier, with a letter in which Bennigsen expressed his desire to enter into negotiations for a ceasefire on his behalf. Murat greeted Sheping affably at the outpost screen and promised to deliver Bennigsen's letter to Napoleon's headquarters. A few hours later, the French Captain Perigord [Alexandre Edmond de Talleyrand-Périgord], Talleyrand's nephew, came to us, with Napoleon's verbal reply that, wanting to end the bloodshed, Napoleon had appointed Marshal Berthier for negotiations. When executing the instructions given to him, Perigord behaved arrogantly. During lunch with Bennigsen he didn't even take his bearskin cap off his head. His arrogance lay heavily on the minds of our officers. They burned with impatience for vengeance on the victors of Friedland. It was a pleasure for the party to defer the bloody retribution for five years, until 1812.

After lunch, Prince Lobanov escorted Perigord to Tilsit, where he was received by Marshal Berthier, reporting that he; 'expressed with visible pleasure, great politeness and reciprocity, the desire to put an end to hostilities.' Starting to speak of a

---

5  Le Prince Lobanoff, lieutenant général de mes armées, est autorisé à entrer en pourparlers pour la conclusion d'une paix avec celui qui sera nommé par le gouvernement françois. Il s'en acquittera avec toute la loyauté et la franchise d'un brave militaire, en foi de quoi je le munis de cette autorisation.
Schawl, Le 6 juin.
Signé: Alexandre.

truce on behalf of Bennigsen, Prince Lobanov warned Berthier that, with all the will in the world, Emperor Alexander would not accept conditions considered beneath his dignity and, nevertheless, would not tolerate even the slightest change in Russia's borders. Berthier replied that on the part of the French, he was offended by any suggestion about the possibility of touching our borders. After this explanation, a ceasefire was agreed, setting the limits of both armies as the banks of the Neman, and from Brest along the Bug, while stopping hostilities for one month, so that in the event of a breach, one month's notice would be given to each other.

Berthier added a requirement to these conditions: to yield the Prussian occupied fortresses of Pillau, Kolberg and Graudenz to the French until the final peace, saying that they could not be defended for such a long period. Prince Lobanov objected that the issue was a ceasefire, while the taking and return of fortresses was the subject of peace negotiations, which is why he could not agree to this condition, but Bennigsen must be told in advance, Prince Lobanov added; 'and indeed, it would be necessary for such an important matter to seek the instructions of Emperor Alexander, and that it would take several days to receive a response from His Majesty.' Berthier thought this period too long, but seeing Prince Lobanov's readiness to part from him, he said: 'I must report your comment to Emperor Napoleon. He is a Meile and a half from Tilsit and I will go to him this hour. Would you care to wait here for his response?' Finding it inappropriate to stay indefinitely in Berthier's house, all the more so as night was falling, Prince Lobanov left, leaving his aide de camp with Berthier, waiting for Napoleon's reply. That ended the first meeting of the commissioners.[6] During the night of 7 to 8 [19 to 20] June, Prince Lobanov's aide de camp returned to Bennigsen and Napoleon's *Grand Maréchal du Palais*, Duroc [Géraud Christophe Michel Duroc], arrived. He offered to conclude a truce immediately if we surrendered Kolberg, Graudenz and Pillau to the French and if we refused this condition, to begin peace negotiations immediately. Bennigsen resolutely refused to surrender the fortresses, saying that it would be better to begin peace negotiations without concluding a truce but, in the meantime, either resume hostilities or, without fighting, hold the ground currently occupied by the armies. Several times Duroc asked: would Emperor Alexander agree to a separate peace without Britain participating and asked to know his opinion on this subject, as well as the will of our Monarch on how to begin negotiations, whilst assuring him of Napoleon's sincere desire to make peace.[7] Bennigsen's and Prince Lobanov's reports to the Emperor concerning their negotiations with the French were conveyed to His Highness the Tsarevich, Konstantin Pavlovich. The Tsar was with the King of Prussia in Schawl [Šiauliai] at that time. Having read the reports, he replied to Bennigsen:

> Graudenz, Kolberg and Pillau do not belong to me and my troops are not there; therefore, it is not my business to agree to their concession. The demand must be rejected. Send Prince Lobanov to Marshal Berthier with this answer and tell him that I also share their desire to make peace, that Prince Lobanov has been authorized by me to negotiate once an armistice

---

6  Prince Lobanov's report to the Tsar, dated 7 [19] June.
7  Bennigsen's report, dated 8 [20] June.

has been approved for one month, on condition that the respective armies continue to hold their positions.

Carrying out the Monarch's will, Prince Lobanov went to Tilsit. Marshal Berthier, while negotiating with him, reported the Tsar's response to Napoleon and received orders not to insist on the cession of the Prussian fortresses, but to conclude a truce. It was signed that same day with the following conditions: firstly, to cease hostilities for a month, in order to allow peace negotiations to take place during this period. Secondly, should either of the contracting parties intend to break the truce, they were obliged to give one month's notice. Thirdly, this truce did not concern the Prussian army, with whom Napoleon would conclude a separate truce. Fourth, to appoint plenipotentiaries for peace negotiations and commissioners for exchanging prisoners of war as soon as possible. Fifth, to draw the line of demarcation between the warring armies from the Kurisches-Haff along the Neman, to the confluence of the Bobr and the Narew, and from there, past Tykocin, along the left bank of the Narew.

The truce was signed in Napoleon's house, with whom Prince Lobanov had his first meeting that day and then, at seven o'clock in the afternoon, he was invited to dine with him. Prince Lobanov reported to the Tsar;

> Proceeding to the table, Napoleon, asking for Champagne and, pouring for himself and me, clinked the glasses together and drank to the health of Your Imperial Majesty. At the end of the meal, at almost 9 o'clock in the evening, I was alone with Napoleon. He was cheerful and unendingly talkative, he repeated to me more than once that he had always been faithful (*devoué*) and respected Your Imperial Majesty, that the mutual interest of both Powers always demanded an alliance and that, with Russia, he actually would not want it any other way. He concluded that the true and natural border of Russia should be the river Vistula.[8]

Unfortunately, Prince Lobanov did not describe his lengthy conversation with Napoleon in detail. His report was very brief, consisting only of the words we have quoted above.

These were the circumstances preceding the conclusion of the truce, while the real and hitherto unknown, reasons were as follows: we have seen that the day after the Battle of Friedland, Bennigsen asked Emperor Alexander for permission to cease hostilities in order to restore order in the army. Bennigsen's report was written under the influence of his illness, exacerbated by the depression of a lost battle. Everyone knows that in war, immediately after a defeat, a defeated army is usually more or less disordered. But if subordination is sacredly maintained in a broken army and the courage of commanders and soldiers has not faded, the frustration will soon disappear and all units of the force will quickly return to their previous order. So it happened with the Russian army. To Bennigsen, exhausted by physical affliction

---

8   Prince Lobanov's report to the Tsar, dated 9 [21] June.

and defeated, as well as to a frightened diplomatic official, it seemed that our troops, immediately after the Battle of Friedland, would be unable to withstand a further battle against Napoleon and so Bennigsen recommended a halt to hostilities. As we saw above, the Supreme Will followed his recommendation. But as soon as negotiations for a ceasefire began, Bennigsen examined the army and saw that, firm in their faith in God and love for Alexander, strong in composition, they were not discouraged, all their units rallied again and they longed for one thing – a bloody encounter with the French. Having seen later that his first report was exaggerated, Bennigsen wrote to Emperor Alexander:

> [T]he failure at Friedland did not diminish the courage of the troops. If circumstances demand, the army will fight just as they always have. They have already forgotten the battle of Friedland. I have the duty to assure your Majesty that in the negotiations that have arisen they would not agree to any of Bonaparte's excessive demands.

Consequently, Emperor Alexander was not inclined to continue negotiations on a truce through military necessity or lack of combat resources, because the state of the army made it possible to halt negotiations and struggle with Napoleon once more, especially since Prince Lobanov's 17th Division had arrived on the Neman from Moscow, while Prince Gorchakov's 18th Division, having set off from Kaluga, was two days march from the army. But at this time other aspects appeared, having moved Emperor Alexander to the idea of peace, namely: the inaction of the Allied Powers in a war waged by him for the benefit of Europe. The true depiction of the state of affairs at this time may be the following Supreme Command issued from Tilsit to the Russian Ambassador in Vienna:

> Your last reports, brought by Count Nesselrode, were the main reason for the conclusion of a truce. The Viennese Court assessed a period of two years were required for its preparation, a period that did not offer us a favourable outcome. Assurances of Britain's help were more positive, but they were slow in their execution. The landings long promised and prepared by the British have not arrived on land. The cash subsidies delivered by Britain to the Allied Powers, including Austria, are insufficient to cover the costs of even one Power. Thus, Russia has been abandoned by the Powers, the interests of which should have encouraged them to participate in a war undertaken for the independence of Europe. Russia fought alone, unsupported by our allies, because the resources of Prussia cannot be taken into account, being almost completely destroyed at the very beginning of the war. Russia fought not against France alone, but against all of southern Europe ruled by Bonaparte, who were involved in a war completely contrary to their interests. The huge resources of southern Europe were joined by sources from most of Germany and even the Prussian Monarchy, skilfully turned to his benefit by the head of the French Government. With such a great disproportion of forces, the constant courage of the Russian troops destroyed

the plans of the enemy four times.[9] For several months our troops bore the burden of the unequal struggle alone and, of course, they would have repulsed the latest enemy attempts if Bennigsen's mistakes had not led to a catastrophe, which, with Napoleon's numerical superiority, should have been foreseen sooner or later. The unwillingness of the Allied Powers to participate in the war has prompted the Emperor to confine himself to the interests and honour of Russia and enter into negotiations for reconciliation with the French Government. If the aims of the war have not been achieved, if the limits of French domination have not been set, then we are not to blame. The consequences will fall upon those who, contrary to the most robust politics and the very fortunate chances of war, persisted in maintaining the opinion, incited by them in ignorance of their own interests and committed a lack of resolve.

These were the reasons for the ceasefire, which had the Treaty of Tilsit as a direct consequence.

In conclusion, it remains to state the actions of Emperor Alexander's ally, the King of Prussia. This ill-fated Monarch was in Memel when he received the news of the Battle of Friedland. Pending a decision from Emperor Alexander, the King ordered the departure of his wife and children to Riga and ordered that postal horses be prepared for them from Memel to Riga. The treasury and valuable objects began to be loaded onto ships for transit to Russia. Soon thereafter, the King received an invitation from our Tsar to go to visit him in Schawl. From here, the Monarchs travelled together through Jurburg to the village of Puktutzenen, four *versts* [4.2km or 2⅔ miles] from Bennigsen's headquarters. Deprived of almost all his forces and his state and compelled by force of circumstances to coordinate his posts with the operations of Emperor Alexander, the Prussian King sent Graf Kalckreuth to conclude a cessation of hostilities with Napoleon, at the same time as Prince Lobanov was signing the truce. Greeted affably by Napoleon, Graf Kalckreuth informed him of the King's desire to allow Hardenberg to participate in the negotiations. Stamping his feet, Napoleon answered angrily:

> I have no wish to meet Hardenberg, I have no faith in his authority and I would prefer to wage war for another forty years just to prevent him from negotiating.

Fulfilling Napoleon's demands, Graf Kalckreuth signed a truce on behalf of Prussia with him, on the same terms as our truce with Napoleon. Events were weighing heavily on the mind of the Prussian King. He wrote to the King of Sweden:

> Circumstances prompted Emperor Alexander to conclude a truce. In my terrible situation, I could not part ways from Russia: I regret to obey the necessity.

---

9 'Four times', was written in these instructions in Emperor Alexander's own handwriting. Of course, he meant by these words the battles of Pultusk, Golymin, Eylau and Heilsberg.

25

# Treaty of Tilsit

> Napoleon's proposal to Emperor Alexander about meeting. – Preparations on the Neman. – Emperor Alexander's arrival on the Neman. – Meeting with Napoleon. – Preparations for Emperor Alexander's visit to Tilsit. – His reception from Napoleon. – The King of Prussia's visit to Tilsit. – Life in Tilsit. – Negotiations. – Emperor Alexander's correspondence with Napoleon. – Contents of the Treaty of Tilsit. – Features of the original Treaty of Tilsit. – Awarding of honours. – The entertaining of the Lifeguard Preobrazhensky Battalion. – The impossibility of entertaining the French Guard. – Napoleon's peace with Prussia. – Prussian thanks to Emperor Alexander.

On 12 [24] June the armistice was ratified, Napoleon ordered *Grand Maréchal du Palais* Duroc to congratulate Emperor Alexander on the cessation of hostilities and offer a meeting.[1] The Emperor accepted the invitation, after which they agreed to meet the next day, the 13 [25 June], on the Neman. Here, just out from the left bank of the river, Napoleon ordered the construction of two quadrangular pavilions on a raft, covered with white canvas. One, assigned for Emperor Alexander and Napoleon, was vast and prettier, the other, for their retinue, was smaller. On our side on the gables, a huge letter A was painted in green, while on the other, facing Tilsit, was a similar sized N. Thousands of curious inhabitants from Tilsit and French military covered the left bank of the Neman. Napoleon's *Garde* also stood there, facing the river. Two squadrons of Chevalier Guards and a squadron of Prussian Guards were deployed on our bank, near a ruined inn, the Übermemelschen Krug, where the Tsar wanted to wait after arriving from Amt-Baublain from his headquarters, before boarding a boat to go to the meeting no earlier and no later than Napoleon.

At around 11 o'clock in the morning, wearing the uniform of the Lifeguard Preobrazhensky Regiment, sash and ribbon of the Order of St Andrew, Emperor Alexander arrived at the Übermemelschen Krug with the King of Prussia accompanied by a large retinue, he entered the tavern, sat by the window, and put his hat and gloves on the table. The room was full of generals. All was quiet. Half an hour later, the *Flügel-Adjutant* stationed on the bank hastily opened the front door of the inn and said: 'It is time to go, Your Majesty.' The Emperor took his hat and gloves from

---

1   Count Lieven's letter to Count Tolstoy, dated 12 [24] June: *Duroc a été aujourd hui chez l'Empereur, pour demander une entrevue avec Bonaparte.*

the table, and calmly left the room, talking with the King of Prussia. All eyes were on the Neman. Napoleon, with a magnificent retinue, wearing the ribbon of the *Légion d'honneur*, galloped on his horse between two rows of the *Garde*. The cheers of acclaim from his select warriors reached our shore.

Alexander and Napoleon got into boats at the same time. The Tsar was accompanied by: Tsarevich Konstantin Pavlovich, Bennigsen, the Foreign Minister Baron Budberg and generals; Count Lieven, Uvarov and Prince Lobanov-Rostovsky. Murat, Berthier, Bessières, Duroc and Caulaincourt [Armand-Augustin-Louis de Caulaincourt] were with Napoleon. As both boats pushed off, the grandness of the spectacle, the expectation of world events prevailed over all emotions. During the river crossing, Alexander and Napoleon were silent. Napoleon stood in the boat with his arms folded across his chest. Having arrived at the raft a few seconds before Emperor Alexander, he quickly climbed aboard and hurried to meet the Tsar. When our Monarch stepped onto the raft, the powerful rivals shook hands with one another and, without uttering a word, entered the pavilion. At that moment, a large vessel with armed soldiers pushed off from the left bank of the Neman — there were twenty of them — and positioned themselves between the raft and our shore. The meeting between Alexander and Napoleon lasted an hour and 50 minutes,[2] after which they summoned to themselves the individuals of their retinue and mutually introduced them to one another. Napoleon showed particular kindness to Bennigsen and, amongst other things, said to him: 'I have always marvelled at your prudence; you were most vicious at Eylau.'[3] During the whole meeting, the King of Prussia stood on the banks of the Neman with Prince Volkonsky – [Pëtr Mikhailovich Volkonsky] now the Minister of the Imperial Court – speaking a few words with him but was mostly silent. During that fateful hour, as the future of his Monarchy was being decided, he constantly turned his eyes and ears to the raft, as if wishing to listen to the conversations of both Emperors. At one point he rode down the bank into the river and stopped when the water was up to the belly of his horse.[4] Returning from the meeting, the Emperor went to his headquarters with the King. The details of his conversation with Napoleon and then with the Prussian King are unknown. We only know that at first Napoleon did not intend to see the King, deciding to destroy Prussia as a political entity. Softened by the intercession of Emperor Alexander, he agreed to accept the ill-fated Monarch and not demand the surrender of Kolberg, Pillau and Graudenz from him. The next day, the Emperor went to Napoleon with the King. The meeting, as before, took place on the Neman. Accepting his fate, the King appeared before the victor, not forgetting his high status. Incidentally, Napoleon repeated his determination to exclude Hardenberg from the peace negotiations, decrying the Prussian troops and civilian direction. Upon returning from the meeting, the King was in a most melancholy mood. Emperor Alexander commented that Napoleon's conversation

---

2   According to Prince Mikhail Semënovich Vorontsov, standing on the bank of the Neman with his watch.
3   From Bennigsen's autobiographical notes: *J'ai toujours admiré votre prudence; vous avez été bien méchant à Eylau.*
4   According to Prince Pëtr Mikhailovich Volkonsky.

was very unpleasant for the King.[5] The famous raft on the Neman, where Alexander and Napoleon had their amicable meetings was immortalised in stone, paint and poetry. Rather, others portrayed them from the beautiful picture by Horace Vernet [Antoine Charles Horace Vernet].

Napoleon invited Emperor Alexander to declare Tilsit neutral ground and move there for negotiations. The offer was accepted. The monarchs agreed to divide Tilsit into two parts, one for the Russians and the other for the French, to each have a battalion of Russian and French Guards and several dozen cavalry for escort duty in the town. As commandant of our part of Tilsit, the Emperor appointed the commander of the Lifeguard Preobrazhensky Regiment, Colonel Kozlovsky – [Mikhail Timofeevich Kozlovsky] now a Privy Councillor – and ordered him to liaise with Duroc concerning the division of Tilsit and the posting of sentries. Arriving in Tilsit, Kozlovsky received written conditions already approved by Napoleon from Duroc, which were consistent with those that he and the Tsar had agreed verbally, with the addition that challenges, responses and watchwords would be common to the Russian and French troops.[6] Napoleon appointed Bailly de Monthion [François Gédéon Bailly de Monthion] as the commandant of his part of the town, who held a position in the French army similar to our Duty General. After reading the conditions, the Emperor ordered Kozlovsky to move the First Battalion of the Lifeguard Preobrazhensky Regiment, several Chevalier Guards and Lifeguard Cossacks into Tilsit and to confirm this with the French as politely as possible. It was strictly forbidden to call Napoleon 'Bonaparte' and until then we had not used any other name.

On the following day, 15 [27] June, the Emperor travelled to Tilsit. Napoleon met him on the banks of the Neman and both went to the house assigned to the Tsar. His Majesty was followed into Tilsit by: Tsarevich Konstantin Pavlovich, Baron Budberg, *Ober-Hoffmarschal* Count Tolstoy [Nikolai Alexandrovich Tolstoy], Privy Councillor Popov, Adjutants-General Count Lieven, Prince Volkonsky and Prince Trubetskoy [Vasily Sergeevich Trubetskoy], Lieutenant-General Prince Lobanov and Major-General Phull. Soon afterwards, the following were summoned to Tilsit: Prince Kurakin – [Alexander Borisovich Kurakin] later Ambassador to Paris – Attorney-General Bekleshov [Alexander Andreevich Bekleshov], generals Sukhtelen and Uvarov, Privy Councillor Lashkarev – [Sergey Lazarevich Lashkarev] who

---

5   From the statements of an eyewitness, Baron Schladen [Friedrich Heinrich Leopold von Schladen]: *Preußen in den Jahren 1806 und 1807*, p. 245.
6   The original conditions, written by Duroc and kept by Privy Councillor Kozlovsky, were as follows:
    *La ville de Tilsit sera neutralisée et partagée en deux parties pour les logements de L. L. M. M. l'Empereur Alexandre et l'Empereur Napoléon, et ceux des personnes de leur suite. La partie, où sera situé le palais de S. M. l'Empereur Alexandre, sera occupée par un bataillon de la garde impériale russe, et commandée par un officier supérieur. La partie, où sera situé le palais de S. M. l'Empereur Napoléon, sera occupée par un bataillon de la garde impériale française, et commandée par un officier supérieur. Les troupes de part et d'autre prendront poste demain à huit heures du matin. Le grand maréchal de la cour de S. M. l'Empereur de Russie fera dans la partie, qui lui est affectée, les logements des personnes de la suite de Sa Majesté. Le mot d'ordre sera le même pour les deux partis.*

signed the Treaty of Jassy together with Prince Bezborodko [Alexander Andreevich Bezborodko] – Chamberlain Ribopierre and Count Nesselrode. On the day of the Emperor's arrival in Tilsit, Napoleon was given the challenge, response and watchword: 'Alexander, Russia, Splendour' (*Alexandre, Russie, Grandeur*), while on the following day those given to the Tsar were: 'Napoleon, France, Courage' (*Napoléon, France, Bravoure*). On the third day, it was agreed that Napoleon alone would issue passwords, after which they were sent daily to our commandant in sealed envelopes.[7]

Napoleon did not want the King of Prussia to live in Tilsit. The King visited Emperor Alexander every day in this town. There were French sentries assigned to the house allotted for him. Five days later, at the request of Emperor Alexander, Napoleon agreed to the King's residence in Tilsit, but on condition not to bring Prussian troops in and to continue the posting of French sentries for him. Even here Napoleon ceded to the Tsar, who tried his best to ease the fate of his friend and permitted the minimum number of Prussian troops necessary to be allowed into Tilsit in order to guard the King; they were selected from the Prince Heinrich Infantry Regiment. None of the Russians were allowed to visit Tilsit, except for the adjutants sent there on the occasion of the army's correspondence with Imperial headquarters. Overcome with curiosity to see Napoleon, despite the prohibition: generals and officers took to going to Tilsit in frock-coats.

The Emperors lived about 500 paces from each other. The mornings began in fact with the High Chamberlains Tolstoy and Duroc visiting to inquire, the former about the health of Napoleon and the latter about the health of Alexander. At about five o'clock the Emperors, sometimes with the King of Prussia, went for a walk, or watched the exercises of the French troops located near Tilsit in magnificent camps. Napoleon usually rode a horse at full gallop, by the shortest route, not by road, but across fields and ravines. Therefore, the Tsar assigned Lifeguard Hussars as his escort instead of the Chevalierguard, because of the weight of their horses. After inspecting, exercising or walking, Emperor Alexander always dined with Napoleon. Sometimes the Prussian King, Tsarevich Konstantin and the *Grand Duc de Berg*, Murat, were invited to dinner. They sat down at the table at 8 o'clock. Then the Monarchs would part for a short time. About 10 o'clock in the evening, Napoleon would visit the Tsar on foot, alone, without retinue or aides de camp, in his famous hat and gray frock coat, at the sight of which western Europe was trembling. Napoleon remained alone with the Tsar until well after midnight.

Meanwhile, peace negotiations were held, from our side, Princes Kurakin and Lobanov and Talleyrand for the French. But these dignitaries were only executors

---

7   The following challenges, responses and watchwords issued by Napoleon were kept in the original by Privy Councilor Kozlovsky.
    *Socrate: Sion: Silence.*
    *Pompée: Plaisance: Patience.*
    *Némours: Nion: Nation.*
    *Titus: Tarbes: Terreur.*
    *Rodrigue: Rochefort: Richesse.*
    *Marius: Mons: Magnanimité.*
    *Luxembourg: Lion: Lumière.*
    *Vandome: Vitry: Vigueur.*

of decisions determined by Alexander and Napoleon in their evening conversations, covered forever with impenetrable secrecy. Only a few views on matters, exchanges of ideas so to speak, from both great men are known to us from letters they wrote to each other in Tilsit in the mornings, in addition to those that took place prior to the evening meetings, or in order to resolve misunderstandings that arose between the commissioners. Although these letters are precious for History, they are, however brief, a necessary explanation of the time when Alexander and Napoleon decided the fate of the civilised world.

Five letters written by Napoleon to Emperor Alexander in Tilsit have been preserved in our state archives. In the first letter, dated 21 June (3 July),[8] in which Napoleon writes of his efforts to reconcile his policies and the interests of his peoples with an extreme desire to please Emperor Alexander, he forwards to the Tsar, as an explanation of the draft prior to his conversation with our Monarch, the draft treaties of peace and alliance and two notes dictated by him.[9] In the first he sets out his thoughts about the Ionian Islands, and seeks to prove that it is harmful to Russia to occupy them due to their remoteness from these islands and that they should be under the protection of France, because this Power, neighbouring it in the Ionian Islands, has all the resources to prevent the Turks from going there and especially the British, trying to dominate the keys to all the seas. Napoleon wrote;

> It would be much more beneficial for Russia to take care of its areas lying on the shores of the Black Sea than to maintain military forces on the shores of the Adriatic, where a clash between the Russians and the French could occur.

In the second appendix to the first letter, Napoleon covered the benefits of natural borders in general terms and invited Emperor Alexander to set the Russian border along the Neman, before it flows into the Baltic Sea.[10]

In the second letter, dated 22 June (4 July), Napoleon assures of his desire to maintain friendship and alliance with Russia and to eliminate all the reasons that could cause a clash between these Powers.[11] In the annex to the letter, he wrote:

---

8 *Monsieur mon Frère, j'envoie à Votre Majesté Impériale deux petites notes sur Corfou et la rive gauche de l'Elbe, afin de bien tirer au clair un mésentendu, qui paroit avoir eu lieu dans notre conversation. Je lui envoie également un projet de traité patent, et un traité d'alliance, qui restera secret pendant tout le tems que Votre Majesté et moi le jugeront convenable. Le traité d'alliance explique de quelle manière doivent être entendues la médiation de Votre Majesté que j'accepte pour l'Angleterre, et ma médiation que Votre Majesté accepte pour la Porte. Tout cela forme l'ensemble des dispositions que nous avons arrêtées. J'ai cherché à concilier la politique et l'intérêt de mes peuples avec l'extrême désir que j'ai d'être agréable à Votre Majesté. Je passerai chez Elle à cinq heures, avant d'aller à la promenade, pour causer sur ces différens sujets. Sur ce, je prie Dieu, etc. Signé: Napoléon.*
9 The header of each note states: *Note dictée par S. M. l'Empereur et Roi.*
10 *Il est d'une politique éclairée dans les circonstances actuelles de fixer les limites de la Russie d'une manière définie et précise. Des territoires mal clos et mal déterminés donnent lieu à une foule de discussions, qui souvent dégénèrent en guerre ouverte.*
11 *Monsieur mon Frère, j'envoie à Votre Majesté une note sur la discussion qui nous occupe. Votre Majesté y verra mon désir de me tenir constamment dans une position d'amitié et d'alliance*

The geographic relationship between Russia and France in the current situation are just as favourable as their trade relations, so much so that even in a state of war the two powers would not know where to meet to fight. Border disputes, small customs wars, disputes over water, disputes over subsistence and a thousand and one small subjects of quarrels which cool and usually precede open breaches and are the preludes of the wars which nations make, are completely foreign to us, so that to seek reasons for animosity and cooling between us, it would be necessary to have recourse to the most abstract and imaginary wrongs. The boundless friendship and confidence that the Emperor Alexander's high qualities inspired in the Emperor Napoleon made the heart seal that which reason had already established and approved. In this situation, beware of doing anything that changes the general relationships of trade and geography that nature has established between the two states. To elevate Prince Jérôme [Jérôme Bonaparte] to the throne of Saxony and Warsaw would mean almost instantly undermining our relationship. There would not be a customs quarrel over the Neman, an altercation over commerce, a police dispute, which did not go immediately and directly to the heart of Emperor Napoleon and by this political fault alone we would have torn apart our treaty of alliance and friendship and prepared more real subjects of misunderstanding than those which have hitherto existed. The policy of Emperor Napoleon is that his influence should not go beyond the Elbe and he adopted this policy because it is the only one which could be reconciled with the system of sincere and constant friendship which he has contracted with the great empire of the North. Also, the countries, located between the Neman and the Elbe, will be the buffer which will separate the great empires, will absorb the pin pricks which precede the blast of cannon between nations. In such a great era, that which matters above all is to fix relationships and boundaries. We must remember what evils intertwined states produce, witness the transit through Ansbach.[12]

---

*avec la Russie, et d'écarter tout ce qui pourroit s'opposer directement ou indirectement à cette belle et grande pensée. Sur ce, je prie Dieu, etc. Signé: Napoléon.*

12  *Les rélations géographiques de la Russie et de la France dans la situation actuelle des choses sont tout aussi favorables que leurs rélations de commerce, tellement que même en état de guerre les deux puissances ne sauront où se rencontrer pour se battre. Discussions de limites, petite guerre de douanes, discussions pour les eaux, discussions pour les subsistances, et un mille et un petits sujets de querelles qui refroidissent, et précedent ordinanirement les brouilleries ouvertes et sont les préludes des guerres que se font les nations, nous sont totalement etrangères, de sorte que pour chercher des raisons d'animosité et de refroidissement entre nous, il faut avoir recours aux choses les plus abstraites et les plus imaginaires. L'amitié et cette confiance sans bornes qu'ont inspiré à l'Empereur Napoléon les hautes qualités de l'Empereur Alexandre ont fait sceller par le coeur ce qu'avait déjà établi et approuvé la raison. Dans cette situation des choses, gardons nous de rien faire qui change les rapports généraux de commerce et de géographic que la nature a établis entre les deux états. Appeler le Prince Iérome au trone de Saxe et de Varsovie, c'est presque dans un seul instant bouleverser tous nos rapports. Il n'y aura pas une querelle de douane sur le Niemen, une altercation de commerce, une discussion de police, qui n'aille sur le champ et directement au coeur de l'Empereur Napoléon, et par sette seule faute*

In conclusion, Napoleon repeated to Emperor Alexander his proposal to extend the territory of Russia to the mouth of the Neman, taking Memel, in exchange for which Saxony was to cede an area on the right bank of the Elbe to Prussia equivalent to that surrendered to Russia by Prussia.

The third letter, dated 24 June (6 July), contains Napoleon's opinions regarding the disagreement between the commissioners over compensation for Prussia and the resolution of Russia's land borders. Ours wanted to draw the border to Serock. Napoleon was of the opinion:

> The Russian eagle could be seen from the walls of Warsaw. This would really be too clear an indication that Warsaw was destined to pass under Russian domination.[13]

And, for the third time, offered the river Neman as the border of Russia.

In the fourth letter, also dated 24 June (6 July), referring to the possibility of a war between Russia and Britain, Napoleon wrote to the Tsar:

> If it is necessary for Your Majesty to declare it, the month of December seems the most advantageous time, because it gives five months, during which the first heat will be absorbed in Britain and during which this Power will have time to understand the immense consequences that will result for them from such a reckless struggle. Moreover, the squadron under Admiral Senyavin [Dmitry Nikolaevich Senyavin], located in Corfu, will have time to return to Russia by December.[14]

In the fifth letter, Napoleon drew the Emperor's attention to an annex, which contained his thoughts on matters with Britain, Turkey and Dalmatia.[15] Unfortunately, the annex is not in our archives.

---

*politique nous aurons déchiré notre traité d'alliance et d'amitié, et préparé des sujets plus réels de mésintelligence que ceux aui ont existés jusqu'ici. La politique de l'Empereur Napoléon est que son influence ne dépasse l'Elbe, et cette politique il l'a adoptée, parceque c'est la seule qui puisse se concilier avec le système d'amitié sincère et constante qu'il a contracté avec le grand empire du Nord. Aussi, les pays, situés entre le Niémen et l'Elbe, seront la barrière qui séparera les grands empires, amortira les coups d'épingles, qui entre les nations précèdent les coups de canon. Dans une époque aussi grande, ce qu'il importe surtout, c'est de bien fixer les rapports et les limites. Il faut se rappeler ce que produisent de maux les états entremelés, temoin le passage d'Anspach.*

13 *L'aigle russe eroit vue des murs de Varsovie. Ce seroit véritablement une indication trop claire, que Varsovie est destinée à passer sous la domination russe.*

14 *S'il est nécessaire que Votre Majesté la déclare, le mois de Décembre paroit l'époque la plus avantageuse, parceque c'est celle qui donne cinq mois, pendant lesquels la première chaleur s'amortira en Angleterre, et pendant lesquels cette puissance aura le temps de comprendre les immenses conséquences qui résulteront pour elle d'une lutte aussi imprudente.*

15 *MonsieurMonsieur mon Frère, j'envoie à Votre Majesté une idée sur la manière dont je conçois que doivent être commencées nos affaires actuelles avec l'Angleterre. Je lui envoie également un petit résumé de ce qu'il paroitroit convenable de faire relativement à nos affaires de la Porte et de la Dalmatie. Sur ce, je prie Dieu, etc. Signé: Napoléon.*

Of Emperor Alexander's letters to Napoleon in Tilsit, three have survived. All of them are hand-written. In the first letter, dated 22 June [4 July], returning the draft peace and alliance treaties to Napoleon with his comments, the Emperor wrote:

> My requests are moderate; they are disinterested, since I only plead the cause of an unfortunate ally. Your Majesty's power will not be affected by it. On the contrary, you will acquire a new glory, that of pacifying Europe in a sound manner, satisfying the desires of the parties concerned and binding them to the preservation of the order of things that is going to be established by it.[16]

A handwritten note by Emperor Alexander, attached to his second letter, dated 24 June [6 July],[17] sets out the opinion of our Monarch regarding misunderstandings that occurred between the commissioners in deciding our western borders. Furthermore, the Emperor repeated to Napoleon his petition for the Prussian King. The Tsar wrote, amongst other things:

> I testified to Emperor Napoleon, that I was ready to acquiesce to his plans to cede Jever and the Septinsular [Republic], but he will remember at the same time how my wishes were pronounced to improve the fate of an unfortunate ally. It is with confidence that I appeal to his justice, to this friendship which he shows me, and which made me conceive a hope so heartening for the future. It only depends on Emperor Napoleon to prove this friendship to me, to change my hope into certainty and to cement forever this alliance between Russia and France which must create the happiness of the whole globe. As for Memel and its territory, I am prepared to give it up.[18]

The Emperor's third letter, dated 25 June [7 July], under cover of which he sent to Napoleon a draft alliance treaty that would apply equally to Russia's ally, the King of Naples. Since his fate had not been clearly stated in the draft treaty, the Tsar wrote to Napoleon:

---

16  *Mes demandes sont modérées; elles sont désentéressées, puisque je ne plaide que la cause d'un allié malheureux. La puissance de Votre Majesté n'en souffrira pas la moindre atteinte. Vous acquererez au contraire une gloire nouvelle, celle de pacifier l'Europe d'une manière solide, contentant les désirs des partis intéressés, et les liant par la à la conservation de l'ordre des choses qui va s'établir.*

17  *Monsieur mon Frère, la conférance que nos plénipotentiaires ont eue hier, motive de ma part la Note que je joins à cette lettre. C'est mon désir sincère de former notre union sur des bases solides et inébraulables, qui me guide uniquement dans ma démarche. Elle est trop juste pour ne pas entrer dans mes raisons. Sur ce, je prie Dieu, etc. Signé: Alexandre.*

18  *J'ai témoigné à l'EmpereurNapoléon, que j'étais prêt pour acquiescer à ses plans de céder Jéver et les Sept-Iles, mais il se rappelera en même temps combien mes voeux étaient prononcés pour améliorer par ces cessions le sort d'un allié malheureux. C'est avec confiance que j'en appèle à sa justice, à cette amitié qu'il me témoigne, et qui m'a fait concevoir un espoir si riant pour l'avenir. Il ne dépend que de l'Empereur Napoléon de me prouver cette amitié, de changer mon espoir en certitude et de cimenter à jamais cette union entre la Russie et la France qui doit faire le bonheur du globe entier. Quant à Mémel et à son territoire, je suit prêt à y renoncer.*

Being ready to conclude the treaty of alliance that Your Majesty sent me, may I remind him of the article that he was ready to add to it concerning my recognition of King Joseph [Joseph Bonaparte] as King of Sicily, as soon as the conquest of this island might be carried out. In reciprocity Your Majesty wanted to assign the Balearic Islands to King Ferdinand, or those of Rhodes and Candia [Crete].[19]

The Treaty of Tilsit was signed on 25 June [7 July] and ratified on 27 [9]. The main articles of the treaty were as follows:

1. The Duchy of Warsaw was created from the Polish regions belonging to Prussia and was transferred to the full possession of the Saxon King.
2. To establish as many natural borders as possible between Russia and the Duchy of Warsaw, the Białystok *Oblast* was annexed to Russia.
3. Danzig was declared a free city, under the auspices of the Kings of Prussia and Saxony.
4. The Dukes of Coburg, Oldenburg and Mecklenburg-Schwerin had their territories returned but the harbours of the last two Dukes would be occupied by French garrisons until the reconciliation of Britain with France.
5. Emperor Alexander agreed to mediate in the reconciliation of Britain with Napoleon, on the condition that it would be accepted by Britain within one month, counting the period from the date of exchange of ratifications of the Tilsit Treaty.
6. Emperor Alexander recognised Napoleon's brothers as Kings: Joseph of Naples, Louis of Holland and Jérôme of Westphalia; he equally recognized the Confederation of the Rhine, the titles of its members and the status of new members who might join the Confederation.
7. Emperor Alexander ceded to the King of Holland the full title and possession of *Herrschaft* Jever in Ost Friesland.
8. Napoleon assumed mediation in the reconciliation of Russia with the Porte; Russian troops were to withdraw from Moldavia and Wallachia and the Turks were not to occupy these areas until a final peace between Russia and the Porte.
9. Emperor Alexander and Napoleon mutually guaranteed the integrity of their territories.
10. The protocols of the Courts of St Petersburg and the Tuileries, both between them and in the discussions of the ambassadors, ministers and envoys whom they accredit from each another, are established on the rules of perfect equality.

The following secret conditions were added to the ten articles published in the public domain:

---

19 *Prêt à conclure le traité d'alliance que Votre Majesté m'a envoyé, je lui rappèle l'article qu'elle étoit disposée à y ajouter sur ma reconnoissance du roi Joseph comme roi Sicile, aussitôt que la conquête de cette ile sera faite. En réciprocité Votre Majesté vouloit assigner au roi Ferdinand les iles Baléares, ou celles de Rhodes et Candie.*

1. Russian troops would be evacuated from the Bocca di Cattaro [Bay of Kotor].
2. The Septinsular Republic would come under full possession of Napoleon.
3. Napoleon undertook not to touch those subjects of the Porte, particularly the Montenegrins, who had collaborated with the Russians in military operations against the French such that they continue to remain at peace.
4. Emperor Alexander promised to recognize King Joseph of Naples as King of Sicily once King Ferdinand was compensated with the Balearic Islands, Candia, or other possessions of a similar prestige.
5. If, in reconciliation with England, Hanover should be annexed to the Kingdom of Westphalia, then Prussia should be compensated with an area on the left bank of the Elbe, with a population of three to four hundred thousand souls.
6. The following Princes, from whom Napoleon had deprived of territories, to be issued annual pensions for life, as well as to their spouses, if they outlive their husbands, in Dutch Guilders, namely: Kurfürst Hesse-Kassel, 200,000, Herzog Braunschweig, 100,000 and Prince of Orange, 60,000 and they would receive this money, the first two from the King of Westphalia, Jérôme, and the latter from the *Grand Duc de Berg*, Murat.
7. The Dowager Duchess of Anhalt-Zerbst, who, by the will of our Court, is to receive an income from *Herrschaft* Jever, ceded by Emperor Alexander to Napoleon, 60,000 Dutch guilders to be paid annually by King of Holland, Louis.

Then, in Tilsit, Emperors Alexander and Napoleon concluded a secret treaty of alliance with the following content:

1. Both Emperors pledged to fight as one at sea and on land, in all wars that Russia or France might wage against any European Power.
2. In the event of such a war, they would conclude a special condition on the number of troops mobilised by them and on the places for operations and, if necessary, would use all their strength.
3. To conduct hostilities by mutual agreement and not conclude peace separately.
4. If Britain did not accept the mediation of Russia, or, having accepted it, did not sign a treaty by 1 [13] November, on condition that all Powers recognize the equality of Flags at sea and return the colonies that it conquered from France and its allies since 1805, then Emperor Alexander would give orders for a note to be submitted to the British Cabinet, with an unequivocal announcement that if in one month, by 1 [13] December, Britain did not accept the above conditions, then Russia would ally with France against them.
5. Following such a refusal by Britain, Russia and France would simultaneously invite Denmark, Sweden and Portugal to close their harbours to the British and to withdraw their envoys from London and if any of the three Powers did not agree to this proposal, Russia and France would declare war on them and in the event of a breach with Sweden, they would force Denmark to fight them.
6. France and Russia would urgently invite Austria to accede to the 4th article of this treaty, so that in the indicated events they would declare war on Britain.

7. If Britain, at a specified time and on the terms announced to them, made peace, then Hanover would be returned to them, in return for the French, Spanish and Dutch colonies that they ceded.
8. If the Porte did not accept the mediation of France for reconciliation with Russia or, having accepted it, did not conclude a treaty within three months, then Emperor Alexander and Napoleon would take all of European Turkey, leaving the Sultan only Tsaregrad [Istanbul] and Rumelia [Greece].

The original acts of the Tilsit Treaty are all the more curious because there were three personal amendments made by Emperors Alexander and Napoleon, which are not visible in the treaties – since the Monarchs never negotiated personally – and each was signed by both. Looking at the signatures of the great names placed one beside the other, we are involuntarily transported by our imagination into the cramped room of the house in Tilsit where Alexander lived and resurrects before us the time spent by him and Napoleon. But Providence did not wish to grant many years to the political structure that they built in Tilsit. Five years later and the same Neman River, on the banks of which in 1807 had been friendly, they defined, in the expression of Alexander, 'the fate of the globe,' saw the beginning of their life-and-death struggle.

On the day of ratification of the peace, secret and alliance treaties, Emperor Alexander and Napoleon exchanged Orders. The Tsar awarded the St Andrew ribbon to Murat, Talleyrand and Marshal Berthier, while Napoleon presented the *Légion d'honneur* to Tsarevich Konstantin Pavlovich, Prince Kurakin, Prince Lobanov and Baron Budberg. Then Emperor Alexander, wearing the ribbon of the *Légion d'honneur*, and Napoleon that of St Andrew, rode one after the other and met half way across the street, along whose sides were battalions of their Guards, face to face. After mutual congratulations on the ratification of the treaties, Napoleon rode up to the Lifeguard Preobrazhensky battalion and said to the Tsar: 'Your Majesty, would you allow me to place the Order of the *Légion d'honneur* on the bravest of your soldiers, on the one who performed better than the others in the current war?' Alexander replied: 'I beg your Majesty's permission to consult with the regimental commander' and asked Kozlovsky: 'To whom do we give it?' – 'To whomever you command' – 'Well, you have to tell him', said the Emperor. Kozlovsky summoned the front rank soldier, Lazarev [Alexey Yevdokimovich Lazarev]. Napoleon produced the *Légion d'honneur* and put it on Lazarev, giving orders for him to receive 1,200 francs annually. Returning home, the Emperor sent Napoleon the insignia of the Military Order for the bravest of the French soldiers. Later, as the Ambassador in St Petersburg, Caulaincourt invited Lazarev to his balls and dinners and presented him with the ribbon of the Order of the *Légion d'honneur*.[20]

On the same day, by order of Napoleon, his *Garde* battalion hosted an out-door lunch for the battalion of the Lifeguard Preobrazhensky Regiment. Each of our Guardsmen sat next to a French soldier. The treat was on silver service for everyone and the most fun. The Lifeguard Preobrazhensky tried on French uniforms and

---

20   According to Privy Councillor Kozlovsky.

bearskin caps and the French tried Russian uniforms and shakos and then some fell under the table. Emperor Alexander wanted to host Napoleon's battalion but we did not have a dinner service. Showing his displeasure, he said to Count Tolstoy: 'Draw at least twenty-five *Chervonets* per man, but try to have a lunch' – 'So, are you commanding putting *Chervonets* in front of each soldier?' Count Tolstoy answered with his usual frankness, 'We have only a twelve-setting dinner service; you did not give orders to bring more than this on campaign.'[21] During their stay in Tilsit, the Russians were generally guests of the French. Our army was fed from their provisions. Every day, at one o'clock in the afternoon, Berthier had lunch for our generals and officers who often invited them to dinner as did Caulaincourt and Duroc.

Napoleon's treaty with the Prussian King took place two days after the ratification of the treaties with Russia. The circumstances that preceded this peace were as follows: The authorities for Prussia were Graf Kalckreuth and Graf Goltz [August Friedrich Ferdinand von der Goltz] and Talleyrand for France. The original proposal by the Prussians was to divide Turkey between Emperor Alexander and Napoleon and, by rewarding Russia and France with areas torn away from the Turkish Sultan, keep Prussia in the status in which it was before the war of 1806. This proposal was not successful. Then the Prussian commissioners presented Talleyrand with various conditions, of course, most favourable for their fatherland. Talleyrand answered them every time that Napoleon's main priority was to make peace with Emperor Alexander, after which business with Prussia would be easy. Finally, on 22 June [4 July], Napoleon summoned Graf Dönhoff [August Friedrich Philipp von Dönhoff], who was serving the Prussian King and announced to him that the preliminary and indispensable conditions for peace between him and Prussia would be the removal of Hardenberg from service and ordering him to choose a place of residence 140 *versts* [147 km or 93 miles] from the capital of Prussia. Napoleon's demand was fulfilled, and Graf Goltz was appointed Minister of Foreign Affairs in the place of Hardenberg.

Wanting to soften Napoleon for the forthcoming negotiations, the Prussian Ministry persuaded the King to invite his wife from Memel, where she was staying, to the village of Puktocenen, near which the Russian army was located. On 23 June [5 July], the Queen arrived at this village. On the following day, Napoleon sent Caulaincourt to her to request the honour of dining with him in Tilsit, adding that upon her arrival in this town, he would rush to be the first to visit her. The Queen went to Tilsit, accepted a visit from Napoleon, dined with him and returned to Puktocenen, filled, in the words of Napoleon, with joyful hopes of the possibility of concluding a peace that was not too painful. Those were the first happy moments for the Prussian Monarchy since the defeat of the Prussians at Jena and Auerstedt. Their joy was short-lived. A few hours later, upon the return of the King and his wife from Tilsit to Puktocenen, Graf Goltz visited Their Majesties with earth shattering news. He informed them that shortly after their departure from Tilsit, Napoleon invited him to his house and met him with the following speech delivered in a stern voice:

---

21  For the current generation, it must be said that Count Tolstoy was with Emperor Alexander for many years, accompanied him on all his wars and travels to the Vienna Congress and enjoyed a special position with the Monarch.

All that I said to the Queen were polite words; they don't commit me to anything. I have firmly decided to put the border of Prussia on the banks of the Elbe. Having finished matters with Emperor Alexander, I do not even intend to enter into negotiations with Prussia. Your King owes everything to Emperor Alexander's chivalrous affection for him: without him, the King's dynasty would lose the throne and I would give Prussia to my brother Jérôme. Under such circumstances, your Monarch should consider it a favour on my part that I leave anything in his power.

Then, after using the most offensive and abusive language towards Prussia, Napoleon sent Count Goltz to Talleyrand. A new humiliation awaited the Prussian Minister there. Without entering into any discussion with him, Talleyrand pulled out several sheets of paper from his writing desk that contained all the articles of the treaty dictated by Napoleon for Prussia, read the terms to Count Goltz, not even letting him look at them and, at the end of the reading, said:

> There will be no concessions on the part of Emperor Napoleon. His Majesty wishes to return to Paris as soon as possible and the treaty must be signed the day after tomorrow.[22]

At the time appointed by Napoleon, the treaty was agreed by the Prussian King. The main articles of the treaty were as follows: Prussia lost more than four million subjects, paid Napoleon almost five hundred million francs of indemnity, as well as the maintenance and provisioning of the French garrisons in occupation of Küstrin, Stettin and Glogau and pledged not to keep more than 40,000 troops. Comforting the King of Prussia, Napoleon told him that such was the changeable nature of the fortunes of war. The King responded: 'You cannot know how painful it is to lose hereditary land!' Faith was the greatest comfort for the King of Prussia. He was resigned to the calamity that befell his monarchy, as an act of the will of God, humbly submitted to it and for six years courageously bore the burden that weighed on him.

This harsh treaty was, however, a boon for Prussia, preserving its existence granted by Napoleon only at the insistence of Emperor Alexander. The fourth article of the Tilsit Treaty states:

> Emperor Napoleon, out of respect for the Emperor of All the Russias and expressing his sincere desire to unite both nations with the bonds of trust and unshakable friendship, agrees to return to the King of Prussia, an ally of His Majesty the Emperor of All the Russias, all those conquered territories, towns and lands, which are indicated below.

Thereafter it was calculated that Prussia was left with five million subjects in the areas granted by Napoleon under the peace treaty. Consequently, Napoleon returned

---

22  Freiherr von Schladen, *Preußen in den Jahren 1806 und 1807*, p. 260.

these lands not to his defeated enemy, the Prussian King, but to the ally of Emperor Alexander; the King did not receive some of his conquered Monarchy through the generosity and political calculations of Napoleon but from the intercession of Alexander. Thus, Providence guided the Blessed Monarch not to allow the destruction of Prussia at Tilsit and after six years then to return to it the prestige lost in 1807. But one of the sad phenomena of the moral world would be Alexander's fate – the ingratitude of nations. Not even a quarter of a century has passed since he saved Prussia twice and the grateful memory of their saviour and his army has already disappeared from the hearts of the Prussians!

# 26

# Activities After The Treaty of Tilsit

> Emperor Alexander's manifesto. – Charity for widows and orphans of the dead. – Welfare for the wounded. – Bennigsen's dismissal from the appointment of Commander-in-Chief. – The appointment of Count Buxhoeveden in his place. – Orders for the army. – The opolchenie affair. – Gratitude for the Don Army. – The punishment of Provisioning and Commissariat officials.

In publishing a Manifesto concerning the ending of the war and the conclusion of the Tilsit Treaty, Emperor Alexander expressed his gratitude to the State and the army. He stated:

> Everywhere, where the voice of honour called upon the troops, all the dangers of battle facing them disappeared. Their famous deeds will be unforgettable in the annals of national glory and the grateful Fatherland, as an example to posterity, will always remember them. The nobility, following in the footsteps of their ancestors, marked themselves not merely through the sacrifice of property but also by their complete willingness to lay down their lives for the glory of the Fatherland. The merchants and all other classes, sparing neither labour nor goods, carried the burden of war with a joyful feeling and were ready to sacrifice everything for the security of the State.

Emperor Alexander gave orders that the widows of generals, field officers, and subalterns killed in action, or died from wounds, were to receive their husbands' full salaries as a pension until their deaths. Upon the spouses' death, a pension would be paid to their children, males up to sixteen years of age, if they hadn't entered service before that time, whilst it would be paid to females before marriage, or joining one of the state educational institutions. Field officers and subalterns, who were discharged for having received serious wounds or injuries during battle were paid their entire salary until their death and they were given a gratuity to travel to wherever they wished to live. Lower ranks, with wounds prohibiting their continued service, were placed in invalid homes established in St Petersburg, Moscow, Kiev, Smolensk Kursk and Chernigov. While these homes were being built, the wounded lower ranks were placed in the institutions of the Orders of Public Charity and were given salaries and rations. Those who didn't want to enter invalid homes were given full salaries or goods in kind at their place of residence, where they were entrusted to the special protection of the governors of provinces. Those who during the war, according to Bennigsen, were mentioned in despatches for Supreme grace for their courage, reduced the time limit for receipt of the Military Order: field officers to two years and subalterns a year.

The day after the conclusion of peace, Bennigsen was sent the following Supreme Rescript – evidence of the Emperor's displeasure with him.

> Having received your repeated requests to release you from service, signing the treaty has now given me cause to agree to your wishes, which has been issued today in an order to the army.

Count Buxhoeveden was appointed Commander-in-Chief in Bennigsen's place and was summoned from Riga to Tilsit. The Emperor ordered him to send 1st Division to St Petersburg and direct all other troops to three camps arranged at Disna [Dzisna], Vitebsk and Orsha, giving the troops a daily meat ration and wine twice a week during their march to the camps and during their stay there. The Emperor granted the army a one-off payment of 96,462 roubles to repair damaged equipment and to replace carts lost during the fighting, as well as to buy draught horses, harness and tools, in accordance with the returns submitted by regiments. The Bialystok Musketeer Regiment was formed from the three garrison battalions that had been under the command of Prince Shcherbatov during the defence of Danzig, named in memory of the accession of the Białystok *Oblast* to Russia.

Under the chairmanship of Privy Councillor Popov, a commission was established in Memel, whose duty it was to repay the Prussian Government for the bread, fodder, wine, hospital supplies and other consumables received from them for our troops, settle accounts with regiments and commands with the money allotted to them and requisitioned from the inhabitants by them for supplies, to credit the commissariat and provision commissions, suppliers and expenses of all sums allotted to the army. All persons who had received cash and supplies in their department were required to report to this commission. Their activities lasted for many years due to the extreme complexity of army accounts and were so slow that the very name of the Memel Commission turned into a saying, meaning an occupation, or exercise, whose conclusion could not be envisaged.

The residents of the newly acquired Białystok Oblast were sworn into Russian citizenship. An announcement from the Synod banned events from the war with France from being read in churches, ordering priests not to borrow ideas from them for their sermons in the future. Retired servicemen called up during the war were sent to their former dwellings, were awarded, upon settlement of their pay, travel and fodder expenses, not exceeding a the third of their salary, according to the distance to their chosen destination.

In accordance with a verbal agreement between Emperor Alexander and Napoleon, Russian prisoners of war in France received clothes and equipment from the French Government. The commander of the Tsarevich's Ulan Regiment, Baron Meller-Zakomelsky [Yegor Ivanovich Meller-Zakomelsky], captured by the enemy at Austerlitz, was appointed commander of our prisoners of war. He was ordered to lead them to Russia, formed into battalions and was to assign battalion and company commanders at his discretion. Meller-Zakomelsky's senior generals were ordered to return to Russia.[1] The situation of the Russians captured by the French in the wars between 1805 and 1807 had been difficult. Napoleon put them under pressure to enter French service with coercion and deprivation of all kinds, which plunged our men into squalor. Those unfortunates who agreed to change their oath of allegiance and to serve with Napoleon's colours, were found in La Tour d'Auvergne's and Fürst von Isenburg's [Karl Friedrich Ludwig Moritz von Isenburg-Birstein] regiments,[2] of which the former was sent to Naples and the latter to Spain, where almost all perished.

The *opolchenie* were disbanded and, to ease the lot of his subjects, Emperor Alexander ordered:

1. Soldiers killed in action or who had died from wounds, were mutilated or diseased, would be off-set against conscripts required from communities and landlords;
2. Soldiers were exempt from poll taxes and quit-rent for 1807;
3. Communities and landowners would be allowed to nominate soldiers in place of conscripts, or accept them back into their former homes. Soldiers entering service under this article were distributed according to their ability to the Lifeguard, field regiments, navy, garrisons, provincial companies, standing and fire brigades or the construction and maintenance of fortresses, without denying any from getting married. Men for the Lifeguard were chosen from soldiers over 35 years old and not shorter than 2 *arshins* and 7 *vershoks* [1.73m or 5' 8¼"].

Former *opolchenie* weapons were withdrawn for storage in the arsenals. One *opolchenie* battalion assembled from specific estates, known as 'Imperial', in respect of its courage, was granted the rights and privileges conferred upon Lifeguard regiments and joined the Lifeguard; later it served as the basis for the Lifeguard Finland Regiment. Emperor Alexander granted an honorary standard to the Don Army, consisting of 139 field officers and subalterns, and 4,196 lower ranks, for their service during the war of 1806 to 1807. In general, the great European glory of the Don Army and its famous *Ataman*, Platov, began with this war. Finally, in his righteous anger, the Emperor deprived the officials of the Provisioning and Commissariat Departments of the right to wear army uniform, finding them at fault in that most of them, having the motive of enrichment from the money entrusted to them, fixed prices for all supplies with greedy suppliers and inflated costs, meanwhile, the troops suffered from shortages of all necessities and important operations were halted to the detriment of the State.

---

1   Instructions from Adjutant-General Count Lieven to Meller-Zakomelsky, personally amended by Emperor Alexander, in Tauroggen, dated 28 June [10 July].
2   Report to Kutuzov by *Flügel-Adjutant* Lanskoy [Pavel Sergeevich Lanskoy], sent to Napoleon for the exchange of prisoners, dated 15 [27] March, 1806.

# 27

# Conclusions

After a three-week stay in Tilsit, Emperor Alexander parted on the most friendly terms with Napoleon, promised to visit him in Paris and, on 28 June [10 July], departed for St Petersburg via Tauroggen [Tauragė] and Riga.[1] Just as our Monarch was departing from Tilsit, the Austrian General Graf Stutterheim arrived there, sent by the Viennese Court to learn in detail about the state of the Russian army and agree with us concerning mutual military operations. The emissary was too late. Dissatisfied with Austrian actions, Emperor Alexander would not receive Graf Stutterheim. In this instance, having been sent to the Russian Monarch, Stutterheim suddenly found himself in Napoleon's headquarters. Napoleon granted him an audience, was extremely kind to him and he received from him [Napoleon] an expression of gratitude for the neutrality observed by the Austrian Government during the recent war. The report by Graf Stutterheim from Tilsit, that Alexander would not do him the honour not only of a conversation but also not even a visual acknowledgement, scandalised the Austrians.[2] They saw themselves deprived of Emperor Alexander's intercession and abandoned to the whims of Napoleon. Their fears for the future soon came true. Two years had not passed between the time when, in 1807, they did not heed Alexander's arguments and Napoleon again triumphed over them, conquered Vienna and Austria had to pay for peace through the cession of vast territories. The day after Emperor Alexander left Tilsit, Napoleon went from there to Paris, greeted ceremonially all the way by Courts and peoples.

Emperor Alexander arrived back in St Petersburg on 10 [22] July. The outcome of Alexander's second war with Napoleon did not meet the objectives for which he had mobilised. He started this second war, wanting, together with Prussia, to curb Napoleon and considered the shift in the balance of power of the greater part of Western Europe to him and the confirmation of the idea of his invincibility, since it was believed that Fate had determination not to allow Alexander to defeat Napoleon following the campaigns ending with Austerlitz and Friedland. The advantages

---

1 Five months after the Tilsit Treaty, Napoleon wrote to Emperor Alexander, from Venice, dated 25 November (7 December): *Je suis vraiment heureux de voir se consolider l'ouvrage de Tilsit. Je le serai davantage lorsque Votre Majesté tiendra sa promesse de venir à Paris. Ce sera un moment vien doux pour moi et pour mes peuples. Nous viendrons à bout de l'Angleterre; nous pacifierons le monde, et la paix de Tilsit sera, je l'espère, une nouvelle époque dans les fastes du monde.*
2 Count Razumovsky's report, dated 9 [21] July.

of the Tilsit Treaty, apparently, were on the side of Napoleon. The benefits for Emperor Alexander seemed insignificant. What did the Białistok *Oblast* mean to enormous Russia, compared with the increase in power obtained by Napoleon at Tilsit? Everyone knew Emperor Alexander's indignation against Napoleon from the time of the assassination of the *duc* d'Enghien, saw his resolve in defending an oppressed Europe and everyone knew the constant aim of his foreign policy – to curb Napoleon's hunger for power by force of arms. The Treaty of Tilsit completely changed the policy of the Russian Monarch and created his closest rapprochement with Napoleon. Such a quick and unexpected transition from hostility to friendship was regarded in Russia as an act of coercion, incompatible with the dignity of the great Russian Empire, which had recently been announced through solemn curses against Napoleon at the altar of God. The Treaty of Tilsit was considered not only offensive, but even harmful to Russia, since the breach between Russia and Britain followed shortly afterwards and stopped our trade, causing difficulty with the circulation of cash and a decline in the value of paper money. Therefore, the news of this peace was received in Russia with a sense of offence to the dignity of the state. The orders in the capital and in the cities for the illumination of houses during the celebration of peace was barely observed by the low glimmer of a few lamps. The signatories of the Tilsit Treaty, Prince Kurakin and Prince Lobanov, were nicknamed the Princes of Peace – a title then in use by the reviled Spanish Minister Godoy [Manuel Godoy y Álvarez de Faria].

The Treaty of Tilsit was a consequence of the need for Emperors Alexander and Napoleon to end the war but not the subsequent coercion. Both were prompted to seek peace by important circumstances. Napoleon, absent from France for nine months, could no longer delay his return to Paris, where his presence was necessary. Napoleon's power, not being based on the sanctity of a legitimate succession, was only supported by the thunder of victories. For Napoleon, each failure shook his power, threatening a shock to the political structure erected by him. His most zealous apologists confess to the truth of this.[3] With such a relationship, could he dare to begin a further offensive operation in crossing the Neman? Immeasurable Russia was spread in front of Napoleon, with its own, inexhaustible resources, without means for the enemy, Russia, where six hundred thousand territorial troops had already taken up arms. To cross the Neman with those forces that Napoleon

---

3   Bignon, a more reliable historian of Napoleon than most, in his *Histoire de France sous Napoléon, Tome VIII*, p 344, wrote: *La situation de Paris auroit dû faire comprendre à Napoléon, qu'une absence qui le tenoit à trois on quatre cents lieues de sa capitale n'étoit jamais sans quelque danger pour lui. Dès 1807 il semble que cette réflexion eut dû le frapper, lorsqu'après la bataille d'Eylau il eut la corageuse patience de prendre ses quartiers d'hiver dans un village entre Koenigsberg et Varsovie. En ces divers circonstances, le général en chef faisoit son devoir, l'Empereur en avoit d'autres. Il n'état pas bon pour le chef d'un état, dans une position comme la sienne, de laisser un champ trop libre à des passions ennemies. C'est dans les jours douteux, où un combat incertain interrompoit une série de victoires, que se réveilloient les souvenirs de l'ancienne dynastie et de la république, ou du moins les ambitions qui croyoient avoir quelque avantage à recueillir du retour de l'une ou de l'autre. Les partisans des Bourbons, comme les républicains, ne levoient la tête qu'autant qu'ils croyoient l'Empereur dans l'embarras, et quelques serviteurs du gouvernement les caressoient plus on moins, selon qu'ils jugeoient pouvoir le faire avec plus on moins de certitude d'impunité.*

had at the time meant to chase after the experienced and courageous who had no care for their existence. Even a victory won by Napoleon in the Lithuanian swamps and forests placed him in great difficulty faced with the impossibility of replenishing the army with men and ammunition beyond the range of the source of his supply. Behind Napoleon, from the Neman to the Rhine, Germany was burning with a thirst for vengeance. Conscious of the relations between Austria and Emperor Alexander at the time, we consider it probable that the Austrians would have put an end to their inaction upon the news of Napoleon's invasion of Russia. The British finally began to fulfil their promises, landing 6,000 men in Pomerania during the Tilsit negotiations. The truce concluded by the Swedish King with the French had expired and Gustav Adolf, agreeing subsidies with the British, was ready to resume hostilities. There was no doubt about the complicity of the Hanoverians and the men of Hesse-Kassel. It was also hoped that Prussian officers and soldiers straggling around in large numbers in northern Germany would join with them. True, there were French troops on German soil but could it be imagined that Napoleon would decide to fight in Russia when his marshals would have to wage a separate war in Germany, in his rear? With considerations of the indescribable entanglement of affairs that would have occurred after Napoleon's passage over the Neman, with no hope of his success within Russia, the conclusion of peace was made necessary for Napoleon, while we saw from the very beginning of the armistice negotiations how hasty he was to end hostilities.

Emperor Alexander also had no more reason to fight. It was not for his own defence that he had started the second war with Napoleon but for the protection of other states and they were indifferent spectators of the bloody battles that raged between the Vistula and the Neman from December to June. Fervently wanting to overthrow Napoleon's dominance over them, but fearing him, they expected decisive victories from Alexander and only then, once Napoleon had been defeated by the Russians, did they intend to join Russia to complete his downfall. Such timid and self-serving scheming drained Alexander's patience. He no longer wanted to sacrifice the blood of his army to support a cause, in which those for whom he had mobilised refused to participate, and when, in order to continue the struggle with Napoleon, our Monarch would have to transfer the theatre of war to Russia and condemn his own regions to devastation.

Emperor Alexander later stated:

> During these events, I was guided by the eternally unchanging rules of justice, selflessness and constant care for my allies. I have not neglected anything to support and protect them. Notwithstanding the diplomatic relations conducted at my command, I twice fought against Napoleon and, of course, they will not blame me for any personal views. Seeing the gradual destruction of the order which for several centuries had constituted the foundation of the peace and prosperity of Europe, I felt that the duty and dignity of the Russian Emperor compelled me not to remain an idle spectator of such destruction. I did everything that was humanly possible. But, in that situation, to which, due to the indiscretions of others, things were brought when I alone had to fight against France, supported by the huge

forces of Germany, Italy, Holland, even Spain, when I was completely abandoned by my allies, finally, when I saw the borders of my State at risk from errors and circumstances that I couldn't immediately avert, I had every right to take advantage of the offers made to me several times during the war by Napoleon. Then I, in turn, decided to offer him a truce, after which peace soon followed.[4]

State affairs should be considered not as single separate elements and not at the time when they are enacted: one must be aware of their consequences. From this point of view, the Tilsit Treaty is one of the most advantageous that Russia has ever concluded: it served as a direct reason for a breach with Sweden and gave Emperor Alexander the opportunity to use greater forces in the ongoing war against Turkey. His war with Sweden and the war with the Porte gained Finland and Bessarabia for Russia, secured St Petersburg and the central frontiers of our country. These acquisitions came from a close relationship forged in Tilsit between Emperor Alexander and Napoleon. Under no other circumstances would Napoleon view the loss of territory from Turkey and Sweden disinterestedly, these ancient allies of France, always supported by them. Emperor Alexander would have the benefits of the Tilsit Treaty confirmed two years later, on signing the Fredrikshamn [Hamina] Treaty, and five years later, by concluding the Treaty of Bucharest. Contemporaries did not realize the great importance of the conquest of Finland and Bessarabia, dazzled at the time by the gigantic power of Napoleon. But his predominance over all countries from the Neman to Lisbon and from Hamburg to Calabria raised his hubris to such a degree that after the Tilsit Treaty he already considered himself permitted to exploit every opportunity. Since then, his avarice and arbitrariness knew no limits, annexing foreign territory to France not only by force of arms but also by decree, destroying the existence of states, splitting Europe, drawing borders on a whim, not respecting the relations of policy and trade, violating the rights of states. The immense power acquired by Napoleon in the Tilsit Treaty was the cause of his downfall. Consequently, the benefits he acquired in Tilsit, which seemed unprecedented by contemporaries, were transient benefits, fleeting, when the achievements of Alexander, gained as a result of the same treaty, were consolidated in perpetuity by Russia.

Emperor Alexander gained an invaluable benefit from his second war with Napoleon by the fact that the talents of many generals, until then little known, had developed here. In addition to the name long adored in Russia of Prince Bagration, and those famous from the war of 1805, Dokhturov and Count Wittgenstein, there were men in this second war whose names were still barely recognised in our country and some were completely unknown: Barclay de Tolly, Sacken, Raevsky, Tuchkov, Baggovut, Count Pahlen, Count Osterman, Markov, Count Kutaisov, Prince Shcherbatov, Laptev, Dorokhov, Prince Eugen von Württemberg, Prince Iashvili, Gogel, Bistrom, Yermolov, Count Lambert, Count Kamensky, Kulnev,

---

4   Instructions, dated 14 [26] September 1807, to Count Tolstoy on his appointment as Ambassador to Paris.

Count Orlov-Denisov and others. Having discovered the abilities of such generals and colonels, Alexander saw on whom he could rely during times of anxiety in the state.

Generally, the second war between Emperor Alexander and Napoleon covered the Russian army with brilliant military glory. Wherever Napoleon directed his blows, everywhere he found an irresistible rebuff. The great commander had exhausted his genius, his troops had exhausted their gusts of high courage, but for six months they could not crush the Russian army anywhere – as is testified: Pultusk, Golymin, Eylau, Heilsberg. Alexander's commander facing Napoleon, was one of the most skilful generals of his time, however, although he was far inferior in talents to his rival, he was defeated by him only once, at Friedland, when he was exhausted under the burden of a serious illness. Throughout the campaign, the Russians constantly maintained their superiority over the French in military matters. Exhausted by hunger, withstanding the attacks of a superior enemy led by Napoleon, before whom the Austrian and Prussian armies had disappeared within a few days, could one, otherwise, dispute the stubborn battles that marked the war of 1806 and 1807?

The Tilsit Treaty concluded the first phase of Emperor Alexander's political activity. After a two-part contest with Napoleon, he saw the impracticality of relying on his allies and the need to rely purely on himself. From that point on, he focussed his prime attention on foreign policy matters and the consolidation of the might of his Russia, vigilantly following Napoleon's every move. Having never lost faith in the good intentions of humanity, Alexander thought to find in Napoleon a worthy colleague in regal concerns regarding the fortunes of the people, but he was ready for a third time to call him to the judgment of God, should Napoleon betray his faith in him and to break the vows of unity given at Tilsit for the common good. And when the hour chosen by Providence struck, Alexander broke out in a thunderstorm at the violator of oaths, declaring war on him – without peace.

# CONCLUSIONS 211

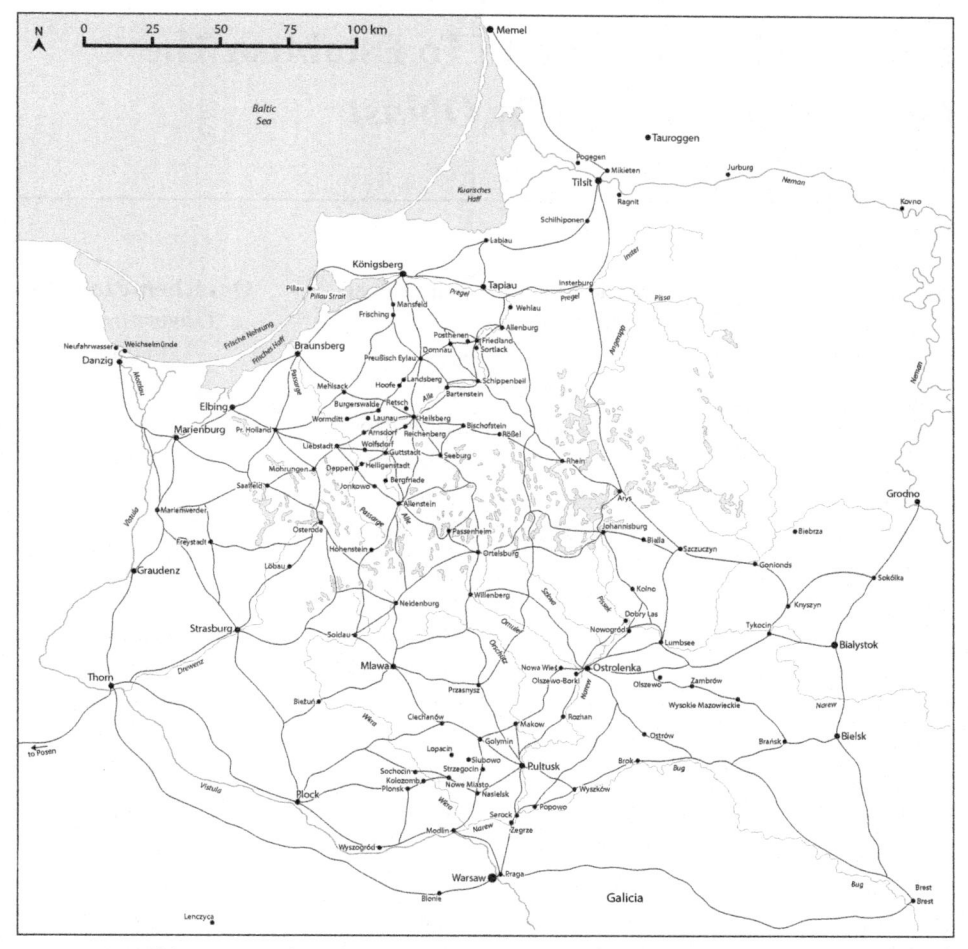

Map of the History of the Second War Between Emperor Alexander and Napoleon, in 1806 and 1807.

# Appendix 1

# Schedule Of The Number Of Men Needed From Each Governorate To Establish The *Opolchenie*, Divided By *Oblast*

| 1st Oblast | Opolchenie in each Governorate | 5th Oblast | Opolchenie in each Governorate |
|---|---|---|---|
| St Petersburg | 11,000 | Orël | 19,000 |
| Novgorod | 19,000 | Kursk | 23,000 |
| Tver | 30,000 | Voronezh | 18,000 |
| Olonets | 6,000 | Kharkov | 15,000 |
| Yaroslavl | 24,000 | Total: | 75,000 |
| Total: | 90,000 | **6th Oblast** | |
| **2nd Oblast** | | Kiev | 21,000 |
| Estonia | 8,000 | Poltava | 26,000 |
| Livonia | 20,000 | Kherson | 4,000 |
| Courland | 12,000 | Yekaterinoslav | 8,000 |
| Pskov | 20,000 | Total: | 59,000 |
| Total: | 60,000 | **7th Oblast** | |
| **3rd Oblast** | | Kostroma | 15,500 |
| Vitebsk | 23,000 | Vologda | 11,000 |
| Mogilev | 25,000 | Nizhegorod | 16,500 |
| Smolensk | 30,000 | Kazan | 16,000 |
| Chernigov | 33,000 | Vyatka | 18,000 |
| Total: | 111,000 | Total: | 77,000 |
| **4th Oblast** | | | |
| Moscow | 29,000 | | |
| Tula | 29,000 | | |
| Kaluga | 24,000 | Grand Total: | 612,000 |
| Vladimir | 29,000 | | |
| Ryazan | 29,000 | | |
| Total: | 140,000 | | |

# Appendix 2

# Order of Battle of Bennigsen's Corps

**2nd Division, Count Osterman's**
His Majesty's Leib-Cuirassiers
Kargopol Dragoons
Izyum Hussars
Ilovaisky 9th's Cossacks
Yefremov 3rd's Cossacks
Pavlov Grenadiers
St Petersburg Grenadiers
Rostov Musketeers
Yelets Musketeers
1st Jägers
20th Jägers
2 × battery artillery companies
2 × light artillery companies
1 × horse artillery companies
1 × pioneer company
**4th Division, Prince Golitsyn's**
Military Order Cuirassiers
Pskov Dragoons
Poland Horse
Grekov 9th's Cossacks
Grekov 18th's Cossacks
Tula Musketeers
Tenginsk Musketeers
Navazhinsk Musketeers
Tobolsk Musketeers
Polotsk Musketeers
Kostroma Musketeers
3rd Jägers
2 × battery artillery companies
3 × light artillery companies
1 horse artillery companies
1 × pontoon company
1 × pioneer company

**3rd Division, Sacken's**
Malorussia Cuirasssiers
Courland Dragoons
Sumy Hussars
Ilovaisky 10th's Cossacks
Papuzina's Cossacks
Taurida Grenadiers
Lithuania Musketeers
Koporsk Musketeers
Murom Musketeers
Chernigov Musketeers
Dnieper Musketeers
21st Jägers
2 × battery artillery companies
3 × light artillery companies
1 × horse artillery company
1 × pontoon company
1 × pioneer company
**6th Division, Sedmoratsky's**
Yekaterinoslav Cuirassiers
Kiev Dragoons
Alexandria Hussars
Tatar Horse
Popov 5th's Cossacks
Vilna Musketeers
Nizov Musketeers
Volhynia Musketeers
Reval Musketeers
Staroskol Musketeers
4th Jägers
2 × battery artillery companies
3 × light artillery companies
1 × horse artillery company
1 × pioneer company

# Appendix 3

# Order of Battle of Buxhoeveden's Corps

**5th Division, Tuchkov's**
Riga Dragoons
Kazan Dragoons
Yelisavetgrad Hussars
Lithuania Horse
Gordeev 1st's Cossacks
Perm Musketeers
Mogilev Musketeers
Kaluga Musketeers
Sevsk Musketeers
24th Jägers
25th Jägers
2 × battery artillery companies
2 × light artillery companies
1 × horse artillery company
**8th Division, Essen 3rd's**
St Petersburg Dragoons
Livland Dragoons
Olviopol Hussars
Sysoev 1st's Cossacks
Kiselev's Cossacks
Moscow Grenadiers
Vyborg Musketeers
Schlüsselburg Musketeers
Staro-Ingermanland Musketeers
Archangelogorod Musketeers
Podolsk Musketeers
7th Jägers
4 × battery artillery companies
1 × horse artillery companies
1 × pioneer company

**7th Division, Dokhturov's**
Moscow Dragoons
Ingermanland Dragoons
Pavlograd Hussars
Malakhov's Cossacks
Andronov's Cossacks
Yekaterinoslav Grenadiers
Vladimir Musketeers
Pskov Musketeers
Azov Musketeers
Voronezh Musketeers
Moscow Musketeers
5th Jägers
2 × battery artillery companies
3 × light artillery companies
1 × horse artillery company
1 × pontoon company
1 × pioneer company
**14th Division, Anrep's**
Finland Dragoons
Mittau Dragoons
Grodno Hussars
Belozersk Musketeers
Ryazan Musketeers
Uglits Musketeers
Sofia Musketeers
23rd Jägers
26th Jägers
1 × battery artillery company
2 × light artillery companies
1 × pontoon company

# Appendix 4

# Order of Battle of Essen 1st's Corps

**9th Division, Volkonsky's**
Glukhov Cuirassiers
Novorossia Dragoons
Mariupol Hussars
Chernozubov 4th's Cossacks
Andreyanov 2nd's Cossacks
Astrakhan Grenadiers
Orël Musketeers
Ukraine Musketeers
Crimea Musketeers
Galits Musketeers
10th Jägers
2 × battery artillery companies
3 × light artillery companies
1 × horse artillery company
1 × pioneer company

**10th Division, Meller-Zakomelsky's**
Kharkov Dragoons
Chernigov Dragoons
Akhtyrka Hussars
Karasev's Cossacks
Kirsanov's Cossacks
Kiev Grenadiers
Ryazhsk Musketeers
Yaroslavl Musketeers
Bryansk Musketeers
Kursk Musketeers
Vyatka Musketeers
8th Jägers
4 × battery artillery companies
1 × horse artillery company
1 × pontoon company
1 × pioneer company

# Index

Alexander I, Tsar of Russia 11-17, 28-31, 34, 36-40, 42-45, 52, 55, 56, 66, 68, 72-75, 77, 79-81, 83, 84, 86, 90, 98, 106, 114, 117-118, 120-126, 132-133, 134-144, 147-149, 151, 153-154, 156-157, 160, 166-168, 182-202, 203-205, 206-210
Alexeev, Ilya Ivanovich 164
Alle river [Łyna] 92-93, 120, 154-156, 158, 160, 161-162, 166, 167-169, 171-174, 176-177, 179
Allenburg [Druzhba] 120, 177, 179
Allenstein [Olsztyn] 83, 88-89, 92, 144, 146
Althof [Orekhovo] 109, 114, 116
Altkirch [Praslity] 155
Andreev, Yakov Andreevich 93
Andreyanov 2nd [Cossack regimental commander] 98, 215
Andronov [Cossack regimental commander] 128, 214
Anhalt-Zerbst, Friederike Auguste Sophie, Fürstin von 198
Ankendorf [Jankowo] 155, 158
Anrep, Roman Karlovich 44, 48, 57-58, 60, 63, 76-77, 84, 86, 214
Ansbach 15, 43, 194
Apolda 24, 26
Arnim, Alexander Wilhelm von 25
Arnoldi, Ivan Karlovich 114
Arnsdorf [Lubomino] 98, 144, 154
Arseniev, Nikolai Mikhailovich 149-150
Arys [Orzysz] 82, 168
Auerstedt 24-26, 28, 52, 55, 140, 200
Augereau, Charles Pierre François 20, 22, 24, 28, 42-43, 47-48, 57, 71-72, 79, 89, 92-93, 96, 103, 105, 109-112, 117
Auklappen [Maloje Osjornoje] 106, 112, 114
Austerlitz [Slavkov u Brna] 11, 13-15, 33, 34, 41, 44-45, 73, 86, 135, 204, 206
Baggovut, Karl Fedorovich 43, 47, 58, 64, 66, 96-99, 105, 107, 112, 115, 176, 209

Bagration, Peter Ivanovich, Prince 87-88, 90, 92, 95, 96-100, 103, 105-107, 119, 125, 127-128, 144, 146, 154-158, 160, 161-162, 168, 172, 174, 176-177, 179-180, 209
Balearic Islands 197-198
Balmen, Karl Antonovich comte de 149
Bamberg 17, 20, 22
Barclay de Tolly, Mikhail Bogdanovich 42-43, 47-48, 50, 57, 63-66, 73, 82, 92, 96-100, 102-103, 105-106, 209
Bartenstein [Bartoszyce] 128, 135-142, 144, 146, 167-169
Bashkirs 180
Bauska 36
Bavarian Army 20, 22, 32
Bayreuth 20, 22, 43
Beker, Nicolas Léonard 64
Bekleshov, Alexander Andreevich 191
Belliard, Augustin Daniel 180
Benkendorff, Alexander Khristoforovich 125
Bennigsen, Adam Leontyevich 166
Bennigsen, Leonty Leontievich 13-17, 36-37, 41-45, 47-48, 53, 55, 57-58, 60, 63-66, 68, 69-71, 73, 75, 76-81, 82-83, 87-88, 89-90, 92-93, 96-100, 103, 105-106, 107, 109-112, 114-118, 119-122, 124-126, 127-129, 130-133, 135-136, 144, 146, 147-148, 150, 154-158, 160, 161-162, 164, 166, 167-169, 171, 172-174, 177-178, 179-181, 182-188, 190, 204, 213
Berg, Burkhard Maksimovich 55
Bergfriede [Barkweda] 92-93, 155
Berlin 14-17, 22, 28, 30-32, 52-53
Bernadotte, Jean-Baptiste 20-22, 24, 26, 28-30, 42-43, 47, 57, 79, 71, 83-84, 86-90, 92, 96, 103, 109, 115-116, 119, 127, 154-155, 157
Berthier, Louis-Alexandre 83, 90, 92, 115, 166, 184-186, 190, 199-200
Bertrand, Henri-Gatien 121-122
Bessarabia 37, 209
Bessières, Jean-Baptiste 20, 42-43, 47, 57, 81, 111, 190
Bewernick [Bobrownik] 161-162

Białystok 82, 180, 197, 204
Biała 80, 82, 88
Bieżuń 81
Bignon, Louis Pierre Édouard, Baron 66, 118, 207
Birsen [Biržai] 36
Bischofstein [Bisztynek] 83, 168
Bisson, Pierre François Jean Gaspard 174
Bistrom, Karl Ivanovich 52, 99, 209
Black Sea 142, 193
Blonie [Błonie] 42
Blücher, Gebhard Lebrecht von 25, 29-30
Bocca di Cattaro [Bay of Kotor] 198
Bogdanov, Nikolai Ivanovich 114
Borozdin, Nikolai Mikhailovich 161-162
Bossmanslake [Łachy Szkutniczej] 149
Brańsk 82, 130
Braunsberg [Braniewo] 127-128
Braunschweig 32
Braunschweig-Wolfenbüttel, Karl Wilhelm Ferdinand, Graf von 14, 20-22, 25, 198
Bremen 13
Breslau [Wrocław] 21, 32
Brest 36-37, 44-45, 47-48, 78, 80-82, 130, 185
Brezgun, Mikhail Petrovich 131
Brieg [Brzeg] 32
Britain [United Kingdom of Great Britain and Ireland] 11, 14-16, 39, 121-122, 124, 126, 136-137, 140-141, 144, 185, 187, 195, 197-199, 207
Brok 89, 130
Budberg, Andrey Yakovlevich, Baron 17, 38, 43, 45, 78, 122, 134, 182-183, 190-191, 199
Budberg, Vasily Vasilievich 131
Bug river 48, 79-80, 90, 130, 132-133, 143, 157, 185
Bülow, Friedrich Wilhelm, Freiherr von 148-149
Bürgerswalde [Miejska Wola] 144
Buttelstedt 26
Buxhoeveden, Fëdor Fëdorovich, Count 16, 36-37, 43-45, 48, 57-58, 60, 62, 66, 69-70, 72-73, 76-81, 130, 204, 214
Calabria 124, 209

Candia [Crete] 197-198
Catherine II, 'the Great' Tsarina of Russia 45, 66, 86
Caulaincourt, Armand-Augustin-Louis de 190, 199-200
Chalikov, Anton Stepanovich 169

Chaplitz, Yefim Ignatievich 72, 129
Chasseloup-Laubat, François, marquis de 89, 147
Chernigov 36, 203, 212
Chernozubov 4th, Ilya Fëdorovich 132-133, 215
Chernyshev, Alexander Ivanovich 118, 144, 177
Chichagov, Pavel Vasilievich 34
Ciechanów 72
Claparède, Michel Marie 65, 157
Coburg 22
Coburg, Dukes of 197
Colbert-Chabanais, Auguste François-Marie de 83
Compans, Jean Dominique 112
Confederation of the Rhine 13, 20, 28, 32, 79, 123, 136, 197
Corbineau, Claude Louis Constant Juvenal Spirit Gabriel 111
Cossacks (Don Army) 35-36, 42, 48, 52, 58, 63-64, 83-84, 86-87, 90, 96-100, 102, 107, 111, 114-115, 119, 127-130, 132-133, 147-149, 154, 157-158, 161, 166- 168, 171, 191, 205, 213-215
Courland 212
Crimea 142
Cross of the Military Order of St George [for non-commissioned ranks] 39, 199
Czarnowo 43, 47-48, 52-53, 55, 58, 73
Dąbrowski, Jan Henryk 147, 179, 181

Dahlmann, Nicolas 111
Dalmatia 142, 195
Danzig [Gdańsk] 30, 42, 79, 82, 89, 128-129, 141-142, 144, 146, 147-151, 153-154, 160, 197, 204
Darmstadt 13
Darmstadt Army 88
Davout, Louis Nicolas 20, 22, 24-26, 28, 32, 42-43, 47, 52, 57-58, 64, 66, 71-72, 79, 89, 92, 96, 103, 109-112, 114-115, 117, 127, 161, 167, 171, 173, 179-180
Davydovsky, Yakov Yakovlevich 48, 50, 66
Dekhterev, Nikolay Vasilyevich 105, 118
Denisov 7th, Vasily Timofeevich 129
Denmark 198
Depkin, Gustav Karlovich 55
Deppen [Dąbrówka] 155, 157-158
Depreradovich, Nikolai Ivanovich 180
Desjardin, Jacques 109-110
Dessau 28-29
Dibich, Ivan Ivanovich 162

Disna [Dzisna] 204
Dniester river 35, 44, 130
Dobry Las 131
Dokhturov, Dmitry Sergeevich 44, 48, 57-58, 69-73, 76, 78, 107, 111-112, 128, 154-156, 166, 171, 209, 214
Dolgorukov 3rd, Mikhail Petrovich, Prince 87-88, 92, 98, 118
Dolgorukov 5th, Vasily Yurievich, Prince 65, 102-103
Domerau woods 172
Domnau [Domnovo] 107, 169, 171
Dönhoff, August Friedrich Philipp, Graf von 200
Dornburg 24, 26
Dorokhov, Ivan Semënovich 64, 100, 102, 209
Douglas, Marquis of – see Hamilton
Dresden 28, 37, 151
Duka, Ilya Mikhailovich 118, 166
Dumas, Guillaume-Mathieu 55, 66, 84, 115, 158, 166
Dupont, Pierre Antoine 84, 86, 174
Duroc, Géraud Christophe Michel 185, 189-192, 200
Dutch Army 28, 32
Eisenach 20, 22

Elbe river 22, 25, 29-30, 37, 140, 193-195, 198, 201
Elbing [Elbląg] 79, 83-84, 86
Elditten [Ełdyty Wielkie] 157-158
Erfurt 20, 22, 26, 28, 31
d'Erlon, Jean-Baptiste Drouet, comte 151
Essen 1st, Ivan Nikolaevich 14, 37, 44-45, 47-48, 69, 75, 78-82, 89, 128-129, 130-133, 215
Essen 3rd, Peter Kirillovich 44, 48, 57-58, 60, 70, 76-77, 118, 178, 214
Estonia 212
Eylau – see Preußisch Eylau
Federov, Alexander Ilyich 69

Ferdinand IV of Naples and I of Sicily 11, 136, 196
Filisov, Pavel Andreevich 149
Finland 35, 78, 82, 106, 209
Foch, Alexander Borisovich 110, 118, 166
Frankfurt am Main 13, 20
Franz I, Kaiser von Österreich 13, 39, 73-74, 124, 137-138
Frauendorf [Babiak] 98, 100
Frederici, Yermolai Karlovich 68

French Army Units and Formations: *14e régiment d'infanterie de ligne* 111. *51e régiment d'infanterie de ligne* 115. *55e régiment d'infanterie de ligne* 111, 164. *108e régiment d'infanterie de ligne* 115. *Cavalerie de la Garde* 111. *Chasseurs à Cheval* 64, 102, 119-120. *Chasseurs à Cheval de la Garde* 111. Fürst von Isenberg's Regiment 205. *Fusiliers-grenadiers de la Garde* 162, 164. *Garde impériale* 20, 22, 24, 28, 42-43, 47, 52, 57, 59, 79, 89-90, 92, 96, 103, 109-110, 127, 161, 164, 167, 173, 176, 189-191, 199. La Tour d'Auvergne Regiment 205. *Réserve de cavalerie* 20, 24, 42, 47, 52, 57, 59, 89, 96, 103, 110-112, 127, 173. *Vieille Garde* 111
Friedland [Pravdinsk] 169, 171, 172-174, 176-178, 179-181, 182, 184, 186-188, 206, 210
Freyburg 24-25
Freystadt [Kisielice] 88, 93
Friant, Louis 25, 52, 112, 115
Friedrich August III, Kurfürst von Sachsen 13, 28
Friedrich Wilhelm III, King of Prussia 13-16, 22, 25-26, 30-31, 36-37, 42, 53, 83, 120-123, 125, 128-129, 135-136, 141-142, 166, 168, 185, 188, 189-190, 192, 201
Frisching river [Prokhladnaya] 120
Frolov, Grigory Nikolaevich 52, 66, 97
Fulda 20, 28

Galicia 43, 81, 122, 133

Gardane, Claude Mathieu de 142
Gazan, Honoré Théodore Maxime 64, 132
George III, King of England 140
Georgenthal [Jurki] 84, 86
Gine, Yakov Yegorovich 132
Glatz [Kłodzko] 32
Glogau [Głogów] 30-31, 201
Glottau [Głotowo] 155
Gluskov, Lieutenant 48, 50
Gogel, Fëdor Grigoriev 84, 86, 97, 209
Golenishchev-Kutuzov, Mikhail Illarionovich 34, 45, 59, 106, 205
Golitsyn, Dmitry Vladimirovich, Prince 41, 70-73, 78, 87-88, 92, 128, 154, 161, 169, 213
Goltz, August Friedrich Ferdinand, Graf von der 200-201
Golymin [Gołymin] 48, 57-59, 66, 69-73, 76, 79, 210
Gonionds [Goniądz] 82, 127, 130-131

Gora 52
Gorchakov 2nd, Andrei Ivanovich, Prince 35, 126, 128, 154-156, 164, 168, 172-174, 177, 187
Gordeev 1st [Cossack regimental commander] 214
Gordeev, Athanasius Demidovich 96-97
Götzen der Jüngere, Friedrich Wilhelm von 125
Graudenz [Grudziądz] 29-30, 42-43, 79, 88, 180, 185, 190
Grekov 9th [Cossack regimental commander] 213
Grekov 18th, Timofey Dmitrievich 128, 213
Grodno 14, 36-37, 41, 59, 62, 66, 79, 81, 82, 130
Gronau [Gronowo] 155
Großendorf [Wielochowo] 161, 167
Grouchy, Emmanuel de 111, 172-173
Grünhöfchen [Grądzik] 105
Gudin, César Charles Étienne 25, 52, 64-65, 112
Gustav Adolph IV, King of Sweden 141, 208
Guttstadt [Dobre Miasto] 83, 96, 127, 144, 154-155, 157-158, 160-161
Guyot, Étienne 158
Halle 21, 24, 29

Hamburg 13, 75, 209
Hameln 30-31
Hamilton, Alexander, Duke of 141
Hanover 11, 14-15, 32, 41, 121, 140, 198-199
Hanseatic cities 13, 32
Hardenberg, Karl August von 15, 134-135, 188, 190, 200
Hassenhausen 25
Haugwitz, Christian August Heinrich Kurt Graf 15, 122
d'Hautpoul, Jean Joseph Ange 111
Heiligenthal [Świątki] 144
Heilsberg [Lidzbark Warmiński] 83, 96, 128, 144, 157-158, 160, 161-162, 166, 167-168, 179, 181, 188, 210
Heinrichsdorf [Rovnoye] 172-173
Hely-Hutchinson, John, Earl of Donoughmore 141, 178
Heudelet de Bierre, Étienne 109-110
HMS Dauntless 150
HMS Falcon 148
Hof 22
Hohenlohe-Ingelfingen, Friedrich Ludwig, Fürst zu 20-22, 24-26, 28-30
Hohenstein [Olsztynek] 83, 127

Holland [Bataafse Republiek and Koninkrijk Holland] 11, 16, 123, 197-199, 209
Holm 148-149
Hoofe [Dwórzno] 100, 102-103, 105
Iashvili, Levan Mikhailovich, Prince 48, 92, 99, 114

Ilmenau 22
Ilovaisky 2nd [Cossack regimental commander] 179
Ilovaisky 5th, Nikolai Vasilievich 128
Ilovaisky 8th, Stepan Dmitrievich 128
Ilovaisky 9th, Grigory Dmitrievich 99-100, 213
Ilovaisky 10th, Osip Vasilievich 128, 131, 213
Ionian Islands (Septinsular Republic) 35, 193, 196, 198, Corfu 195
Isaev 2nd [Cossack regimental commander] 128
Istanbul – see Tsaregrad
Italy 11, 13, 32, 95, 132, 136, 138, 142, 176, 209
Jena 21-22, 24, 26, 28, 39, 41-42, 57, 140, 200

Jever [Herrschaft Jever] 196-198
Jérôme Bonaparte, King of Westphalia 32, 194, 197-198, 201
Johannisburg [Pisz] 78-79
Jomini, Antoine Henri, Baron de 66, 115
Jonkowo 92-93, 96, 106, 109
Joseph Bonaparte, King of Naples 13, 197
Jurburg [Jurbarkas] 36, 120, 126, 134-135, 182, 188
Kakhovsky, Mikhail Vasilievich 45

Kakhovsky, Pëtr Demyanovich 111, 118
Kalckreuth Friedrich Adolf Graf von 26, 128, 147-151, 153, 188, 200
Kaluga 35, 126, 187, 212
Kamensky, Mikhail Fedotov, Count 34, 39, 44-46, 47, 52, 55, 57-60, 62-63, 66, 69-70, 73, 76-81, 130, 173
Kamensky, Nikolai Mikhailovich, Count 82, 92-93, 107, 112, 115, 118, 142, 148-150, 153, 160, 164, 167, 179-180, 209
Kapellendorf 24
Karasev [Cossack regimental commander] 215
Karl August, Herzog von Weimar 13, 16, 22, 24-25, 28-29
Karl, Erzherzog von Österreich-Teschen [Archduke Charles] 39-40, 73, 124, 140
Karpov [Cossack regimental commander] 128

Kaschaunen [Kaszuny] 98
Kassel 20, 28, 32, 123-124, 140, 208
Kazan 212
Kellermann, François Étienne Christophe 32
Kherson 212
Kiev 36, 45, 203, 212
Kirsanov [Cossack regimental commander] 215
Kiselev [Cossack regimental commander] 111, 214
Kharkov 36, 212
Klein, Dominique Louis Antoine 111-112
Kleinenfeld [Klony] 158
Klüx, Joseph Friedrich Karl von 81, 121
Kniper, Willim Karlovich 66
Knobelsdorff, Friedrich Wilhelm Ernst Baron von 15
Knorring, Bogdan Fëdorovich 78, 116, 125
Knorring, Karl Bogdanovich 65-66, 132, 161
Knyszyn 78
Köhler, Georg Ludwig Egidius von 134-135
Kolozomb [Kołozą b] 43, 47-48
Königsberg [Kaliningrad] 42, 81-83, 89, 93, 103, 107, 109-110, 116-117, 119-120, 127-128, 131, 148, 153, 161, 167-169, 171, 173, 179-181
Kobryn 36
Kochubey, Victor Pavlovich, Count 38
Kolberg [Kołobrzeg] 30, 180, 185, 190
Kolno 131
Kologrivov, Andrei Semënovich 135, 164, 169, 171
Konstantin Pavlovich, Tsarevich 125, 161-162, 164, 168, 171, 185, 190-192, 199
Korff, Fëdor Karlovich 112, 118
Kösen 24-25
Kostroma 212
Kovno [Kaunas] 120
Kozhin, Sergei Alekseevich 64, 66, 162
Kozlovsky, Mikhail Timofeevich 191-192, 199
Kozlovsky, Platon Timofeevich 149
Kraków 137
Kreutz, Kipriyan Antonovich, Baron 87
Kronach 22
Krusemarck, Friedrich Wilhelm Ludwig von 134-135
Kudryavtsev, Vasily Filippovich 55
Kulm 53, 58
Kulnev, Yakov Petrovich 129, 209
Kunheim, Johann Ernst von 25
Kurakin, Alexander Borisovich, Prince 191-192, 199, 207

Kurisches Haff 186
Kursk 203, 212
Küstrin [Kostrzyn] 28-31, 201
Kutaisov, Alexander Ivanovich 107, 111, 114, 118, 209
Kutchitten [Znamenskoye] 112, 114-116
Kutuzov – see Golenishchev-Kutuzov
Lacy, Boris Petrovich 34

La Houssaye, Armand Lebrun de 173
Lambert, Karl Osipovich, comte de 52-53, 55, 65-66, 96-98, 177, 180, 209
Landsberg [Górowo Iławeckie] 97-98, 100, 103, 105, 127-128, 167
Langfuhr [Wrzeszcz] 149
Langwiese [Długołęka] 162
Lannes, Jean 20, 22, 24, 28, 30, 42-43, 47, 52, 57-59, 64-66, 79, 89, 130, 142, 148, 150, 161-162, 164, 169, 171, 172-173, 177, 181
Laptev, Vasily Danilovich 72, 115, 149, 166, 209
Lasalle, Antoine-Charles-Louis, comte de 109
Lashkarev, Alexander Sergeevich 48
Lashkarev, Pavel Sergeevich 84, 86
Lashkarev, Sergey Lazarevich 191
La Tour-Maubourg, Marie-Victor-Nicolas de Faÿ de 168-169, 172-173, 176
Launau [Łaniewo] 100, 128, 144, 154-155, 161
Lawden [Lauda] 162
Lazarev, Alexey Yevdokimovich 199
Lbov, N.N. Captain 50
Lefebvre, François Joseph 20, 89, 142, 147-148, 151
Legan Środkowy 149
Légion d'honneur 190, 199
Legrand, Claude Juste Alexandre Louis 106, 109-110
Leipzig 22, 25
Lenczyca [Łęczyca] 33
Leontiev, Alexey Alekseevich 149
Leopold III, Herzog von Dessau 13
Lesseps, Barthélemy 12
L'Estocq, Anton Wilhelm von 41-43, 47, 57, 80-81, 83, 87-88, 92-93, 96, 103, 107, 109, 112, 114-116, 118, 120, 128, 154-155, 157, 160, 167, 179-180
Leval, Jean François 109-110
Liebstadt [Miłakowo] 83-84, 87, 96, 127, 155
Lieven, Ivan Andreevich, Count 11, 118, 121, 134, 189-191

## INDEX

Lieven, Khristofor Andreevich, Count 34
Lisbon 75, 143, 209
Lithuania 208
Livonia 212
Lobanov-Rostovsky, Dmitry Ivanovich, Prince 35, 126, 168, 182-188, 190-192, 199, 207
Löbau [Lubawa] 88-90
Lomitten 154-155
London 11, 37, 39, 45, 121-124, 126, 140-141, 143-144, 146, 198
Lopacin [Łopacin] 70-72
Louis XVIII, King of France 120
Louis Bonaparte, King of Holland 13, 197-198
Louis-Ferdinand von Preußen, Prince 22
Löwenstern, Karl Fedorovich 109
Löwis, Fëdor Fëdorovich 130-131, 180
Lübeck 13, 30
Lucchesini, Girolamo 28, 30
Lukyanovich, Andrey Fëdorovich 97
Lumbsee [Łomża] 62, 77
Lutsk 42
Lvov, Pëtr Nikolaevich 132, 161-162
Magdeburg 21, 26, 28-29, 31

Mahnsfeld [Polevoye] 119
Mainz 28, 32
Makow [Maków] 48, 57, 60, 69-71, 73, 76, 79, 81
Malakhov [Cossack regimental commander] 97, 214
Malyutin, Pëtr Fëdorovich 135
Marburg. 123
Marchand, Jean Gabriel 174
Marienburg [Malbork] 142
Marienwerder [Kwidzyn] 142
Markov, Yevgeny Ivanovich 82-84, 86-87, 96-99, 105, 107, 118, 176, 209
Masséna, André 132-133, 154, 179-180
Massenbach, Christian Karl August Ludwig von 21, 24, 26
Mazovsky, Nikolai Nikolaevich 55, 178
Mecklenburg-Schwerin [Herzogtum Mecklenburg-Schwerin] 197
Mecklenburg-Schwerin, Friedrich Franz, Herzog zu 32
Mecklenburg-Schwerin, Karl August Christian, Herzog zu 166
Mecklenburg-Strelitz, Queen Luise Auguste Wilhelmine Amalie Herzogin zu 21, 135, 200-201
Mehlsack [Pieniężno] 127

Meller-Zakomelsky, Fëdor Ivanovich 156
Meller-Zakomelsky, Peter Ivanovich 44, 215
Meller-Zakomelsky, Yegor Ivanovich 204-205
Memel [Klaipėda] 80-81, 120-122, 124, 134, 188, 195-196, 200, 204
Merlin, Pavel Ivanovich 55
Merveldt, Maximilian Friedrich, Graf von 138
Mikhelson, Ivan Ivanovich 36-37, 142
Mikiten [Mikytai] 180
Milhaud, Édouard Jean-Baptiste 112
Minsk 36
Mitau [Jelgava] 120, 134
Mitsky, Ivan Grigorievich 53
Mlawa [Mława] 57, 79, 81, 89
Modlin [Nowy Dwór Mazowiecki] 43, 52
Mogilev 212
Mohrungen [Morąg] 84, 86-87
Moldavia 37, 197
Möllendorff, Wichard Joachim Heinrich von 21, 26, 28
Mollwitten [Molwity] 109, 112
Mondtken [Mątki] 92
Montbrun, Louis Pierre de 64
Montesquiou-Fezensac, Raymond Aymeric Philippe Joseph de 26
Monthion, François Gédéon Bailly de 191
Morand, Charles Antoine Louis Alexis 25-26, 52, 112
Mortier, Adolphe Édouard Casimir Joseph 20, 28, 32, 142, 151, 161, 167, 173, 177
Moscow 12, 35, 38, 45, 126, 182, 187, 203, 212
Moshinsky, Denis Denisovich 53, 55
Moszyn 65
Müffling, Philipp Friedrich Carl Ferdinand von, genannt Weiß 21
Mühlenfluss stream, Friedland [Pravda] 172-173
Murat, Joachim, Grand Duke of Berg 13, 20-22, 24, 28-30, 42-43, 47, 52, 89, 92, 96-98, 103, 105, 109-111, 120, 161-162, 171, 173, 179-180, 184, 190, 192, 198-199
Nansouty, Étienne Marie Antoine Champion de 172-173

Naples 11, 16, 75, 143, 205
Napoleon I, Emperor of the French 11-17, 20-22, 24-26, 28-33, 34, 36-40, 41-43, 45-46, 47-48, 50, 52-53, 55, 57-59, 65-66, 71-75, 77-79, 81-84, 88, 89-90, 92-93, 96, 100, 102-103, 105-106, 107, 109-112, 115-118, 119-126, 127-129, 130-133,

136-144, 146-148, 151, 153, 154-158, 160, 161-162, 164, 166, 167-169, 171, 172-174, 176, 178, 179-181, 183-188, 189-202, 204-205, 206-210
Narew river 43, 48, 52-53, 55, 57-58, 70, 76-81, 90, 124, 130-133, 146, 168, 186
Narie lake 87
Nasielsk 53, 55, 57-59
Naumburg 22, 24-25
Nehrung spit [Mierzeja Wiślana] 128, 142, 148-149
Neidenburg [Nidzica] 81, 89
Neipperg, Adam Albert, Graf von 43
Neisse [Nysa] 32
Neman river 42, 59, 180, 185, 187, 189-191, 193-195, 199, 207-209
Nesselrode, Karl Vasilevich, Count 17, 46, 187, 192
Netherlands – see Holland
Neufahrwasser [Nowy Port] 148-150, 153
Ney, Michel 20, 22, 24, 28-29, 42-43, 47, 57, 79, 81, 83-84, 89, 92-93, 96, 103, 109-110, 114-117, 127, 144, 146, 154-157, 161, 166, 167, 173-174, 176-177
Nezvizh 36
Nicholas I, Tsar of Russia 72
Nienburg 30-31
Nikitin, Alexey Petrovich 132
Nizhegorod 212
Nordhausen 26
Novgorod 212
Novosiltsev, Nikolai Nikolaevich 38, 125
Nowa Wieś 76
Nowe Miasto 50, 64-65, 70
Nowogród 77-79
Nuremburg [Nürnberg] 13, 75
Obreskov, Mikhail Alekseevich 156

Oder river 28-30, 32, 75, 138
Okunin 52
Oldenburg [Herzogtum Oldenburg] 197
Oldenburg, Peter Friedrich Ludwig von 32, 197
Olonets 212
Olsufiev, Zakhar Dmitrievich 166
Olszewo-Borki 157
Open [Opin] 98
Orange, Willem Frederik, Prince of 13, 16, 25-26, 28, 136, 198
Orël 212
Order of St Andrew the First-Called 118, 157, 189, 199
Order of St George 50, 55, 66, 72-73, 95, 118, 162, 177, 204

Order of St Vladimir 118
Orlov-Denisov, Vasily Vasilyevich, Count 210
O'Rourke, Joseph Kornilovich 111, 129
Orsha 204
Ortelsburg [Szczytno] 128
Osipov, Stepan Leontyevich 55
Osowiecka 131
Osten-Sacken, Fabian Wilhelmovich 41, 63-65, 70, 87-88, 107, 112, 114, 128, 154-157, 209, 213
Osterman-Tolstoy, Alexander Ivanovich 41, 43, 47, 52-53, 55-56, 57-58, 60, 62, 63-66, 73, 82, 107, 111-112, 114-115, 156, 209, 213
Osterode [Ostróda] 87-88, 127, 142
Ostrolenka [Ostrołęka] 41, 43, 47-48, 57, 60, 62, 63, 66, 69, 76-77, 80, 89, 128, 130-133, 155
Ostrów Mazowiecka 130-131
Ottoman Porte 14, 40, 45-46, 74, 86, 136, 142, 149, 193, 195, 197-200, 209
Oudinot, Nicholas Charles 150, 171, 173, 181
Pacthod, Michel-Marie 84
Pahlen, Pëtr Petrovich, Baron 69, 72-73, 77, 87, 112, 114, 118, 171, 180, 209
Palibin, Ivan Nikiforovich 55
Palm, Johann Philipp 75
Papuzina [Cossack regimental commander] 213
Paris 12, 15, 17-18, 33, 90, 118, 121, 137, 191, 201, 206-207, 209
Passarge river [Pasłęka] 127-128, 143, 154-158
Passek, Pëtr Petrovich 166
Passenheim [Pasym] 88, 92
Pavlovsk 68
Peace of Pressburg 16
Perrin, Claude-Victor 157, 171-173, 176-177
Perm 38
Pershin, Peter Ivanovich 50
Persia 40, 142
Phull, Karl Ludwig August Friedrich von 21, 29, 191
Pilica river 137
Pillar, Yegor Maksimovich 114
Pillau [Baltiysk] 42, 128, 142, 148, 153, 180, 185
Pinsk 36
Pirogov, Ippolit Ivanovich 72
Pissek river 131
Platov, Matvey Ivanovich, *Ataman* 107, 114-115, 127-129, 133, 144, 146, 155-156, 160-161, 164, 168, 171, 179-180, 205
Plauen 22

## INDEX

Plonsk [Płońsk] 47
Plotsk [Płock] 42-43, 47
Pogegen [Pagėgiai] 180
Polangen [Polanga] 134
Poltava 36, 212
Pomerania 32, 141-142, 151, 208
Pomiechowo 52-53
Ponevezha [Panevėžys] 36
Popov, Vasily Stepanovich 45, 183-184, 191, 204
Popov 5th [Cossack regimental commander] 213
Popowo 48, 57-58, 63, 76
Portugal 198
Posthenen [Peredovoye] 171, 173
Potemkin, Grigory Alexandrovich, Prince 45, 86, 183
Potapov, Alexey Nikolaevich 72
Potapov, Peter Ivanovich 48
Poznań 31-33, 128
Pozzo di Borgo, Karl Osipovich 40, 74
Praga 42-43, 89
Pregel river [Pregolya] 168, 171, 179, 181, 182
Prenzlau 30
Preußisch Eylau 103, 105-106, 109-110, 114, 116-118, 119-120, 124-125, 127-128, 131, 135, 144, 171, 188, 190, 207, 210
Prussian Army Units & Formations: Black Hussars 164. *Infanterie-regiment* Prinz Heinrich 192. '*Kameraden*' 115. *Leibgarde* 15, 189. Prittwitz's Hussars 160. Zieten's Dragoons 164
Pskov 135, 212
Pultusk [Pułtusk] 41-43, 46, 47, 53, 55, 57-60, 63, 65-66, 68, 69-74, 76-77, 79-81, 89, 132-133, 135, 188, 210
Queetz [Kwiecewo] 155

Raden, Fëdor Fëdorovich 73

Raevsky, Nikolai Nikolaevich 158, 160, 176, 209
Ragnit [Neman] 180
Rakhmanov, Vasily Sergeevich 164
Rapp, Jean 151
Razumovsky, Andrei Kirillovich, Count 11, 73-75, 121-122, 124, 137, 139, 206
Reichenberg [Kraszewo] 160, 161-162
Rembow, Michael Szabszinski von 149
Retsch [Redy] 167
Rezvy, Dmitry Petrovich 107
Rhine river 11, 13, 15-17, 20, 30, 32, 37, 136, 142, 208

Rhine [Ryn] 82
Rhodes 197
Ribopierre, Alexander Ivanovich 46, 141, 192
Riga 79-80, 134, 188, 204, 206
Rimsky-Korsakov, Alexander Mikhailovich 36, 41, 79, 126
Rimsky-Korsakov, Yakov Yakovlevich 162
Roguet, François 93, 156
Romana, Don Pedro Caro y Sureda de la 142
Rößel [Reszel] 168
Rozhan [Różan] 57, 66, 76-77
Rtishchev, Nikolai Fedorovich 35
Rüchel, Ernst von 20-22, 24-26, 83, 114-115, 120, 180
Rumelia Eyalet 199
Russian Army Units and Formations: I Corps 87. II Corps 87. III Corps 87. IV Corps 87. 1st Division (Lifeguard) 126, 144, 204. 1st Jägers 48, 50, 63-64, 66, 99, 102, 129, 213. 2nd Division 41, 107, 128, 144, 213. 2nd Jägers 161. 3rd Division 41, 70, 107, 128, 144, 161-162, 172, 213. 3rd Jägers 48, 50, 63-64, 66, 92, 99, 102-103, 213. 4th Division 41, 70, 106-107, 109, 128, 172, 213. 4th Jägers 52, 63-64, 96-97, 213. 5th Division 44, 48, 76, 107, 128, 214. 5th Jägers 84, 86, 97, 214. 6th Division 41-42, 82, 127-128, 130-132, 172, 213. 7th Division 44, 48, 76, 107, 128, 144, 161-162, 171-172, 214. 7th Jägers 86, 97, 214. 8th Division 44, 76, 79, 105, 107, 128, 144, 171, 214. 8th Jägers 130, 133, 215. 9th Division 44, 128, 130-131, 215. 10th Division 44, 215. 10th Jägers 131-133, 215. 14th Division 35, 44, 48, 76, 107, 112, 128, 144, 161-162, 164, 172, 214. 15th Division 35. 16th Division 35. 17th Division 35, 126, 182, 187. 18th Division 35, 126, 187. 20th Jägers 52, 55, 63, 92, 99-100, 102-103, 213. 21st Jägers 58, 72, 148-149, 213. 23rd Jägers 214. 24th Jägers 35, 105, 214. 25th Jägers 35, 77, 84, 97-98, 214. 26th Jägers 35, 214. 27th Jägers 35. 28th Jägers 35. 29th Jägers 35. 30th Jägers 35. 31st Jägers 35. 32nd Jägers 35. Akhtyrka Hussars 130, 132, 215. Alexandria Hussars 42, 52-53, 64, 96-98, 177, 213. Arkhangelogorod Musketeers 92, 148-150, 214. Army Abroad 45, 78-79. Arzamas Dragoons 35. Astrakhan Grenadiers 215. Azov Musketeers 160, 214. Belozersk Musketeers 96-97, 214. Brest Musketeers 35. Bryansk Musketeers

215. Chernigov Dragoons 215. Chernigov Musketeers 63-65, 213. Chevalier Guard 118, 135, 171, 177, 189, 191-192. Courland Dragoons 87, 98, 111, 213. Crimea Musketeers 131, 215. Dnieper Musketeers 58, 71-72, 213. Dniester Army 35-36. Dorpat Dragoons 35. Finland Dragoons 35, 77, 161, 171, 214. Galits Musketeers 215. Glukhov Cuirassiers 215. Grodno Hussars 35, 129, 214. His Majesty's Leib Cuirassiers 64, 97, 103, 105, 162, 213. Ingermanland Dragoons 105, 214. Izyum Hussars 48, 50, 52-53, 64, 92, 99-100, 102, 105, 111, 146, 213. Kaluga Musketeers 164, 214. Kargopol Dragoons 64, 68, 105, 213. Kamchatka Musketeers 35. Kazan Dragoons 214. Kexholm Musketeers 161. Kharkov Dragoons 215. Kiev Dragoons 63-64, 161, 213. Kiev Grenadiers 215. Koporsk Musketeers 63, 213. Kostroma Musketeers 58, 70-72, 99, 102, 213. Kremenchug Musketeers 35. Kronstadt Garrison Regiment [later Bialystok Musketeers] 128, 204. Kursk Musketeers 215. Libau Musketeers 35. Lifeguard 35, 39, 99, 126, 135, 149, 161-162, 167, 169, 171, 205. Lifeguard Artillery 35, 135. Lifeguard Cossacks 191. Lifeguard Finland Regiment 205. Lifeguard Horse 176. Lifeguard Hussars 192. Lifeguard Izmailov Regiment 176. Lifeguard Jägers 35, 176. Lifeguard Preobrazhensky Regiment 66, 171, 189, 191, 199. Lithuania Horse 214. Lithuania Musketeers 63-64, 213. Livland Dragoons 110, 214. Lubny Hussars 35. Malorussia Cuirassiers 58, 71-72, 97, 111, 213. Mariupol Hussars 132, 215. Military Order Cuirassiers 58, 70-73, 97, 103, 111, 169, 213. Mingrela Musketeers 35. Minsk Musketeers 35. Mittau Dragoons 35, 131, 164, 214. Mogilev Musketeers 148-149, 214. Moscow Dragoons 71-72, 115, 214. Moscow Grenadiers 105, 110, 176, 214. Moscow Musketeers 71-72, 214. Murom Musketeers 63-64, 213. Navazhinsk Musketeers 63, 148-149, 213. Neva Musketeers 36. Neyshlot Musketeers 35. Nezhin Dragoons 35. Nizov Musketeers 63, 161, 164, 213. Noble Regiment 35. Novorossia Dragoons 133, 215. Okhotsk Musketeers 35. Olviopol Hussars 99-100, 102, 171, 214. *Opolchenie* 37-39, 126, 161, 205, 212. Orël Musketeers 215. Pavlograd Hussars 58, 72, 111, 115, 128-129, 214. Pavlov Grenadiers 52-53, 55, 63-64, 213. Perm Musketeers 214. Pernov Musketeers 35, 164, 166. Podolsk Musketeers 214. Poland Horse/Ulans 63, 65-66, 99, 111, 213. Polotsk Musketeers 63, 148-149, 213. Pskov Dragoons 58, 70-72, 97 213. Pskov Musketeers 84, 86, 98, 105, 214. Reval Musketeers 63, 65, 161, 164, 213. Riga Dragoons 110, 214. Rostov Musketeers 52, 55, 63, 213. Ryazan Musketeers 112, 214. Ryazhsk Musketeers 131, 215. Schlüsselburg Musketeers 110, 214. Serpukhov Dragoons 35. Sevsk Musketeers 164, 214. Sofia Musketeers 96, 105, 214. Staro-Ingermanland Musketeers 214. Staroskol Musketeers 63-64, 96-97, 213. St Petersburg Dragoons 105-106, 214. St Petersburg Grenadiers 52-53, 55, 63, 213. Sumy Hussars 58, 71-72, 87, 213. Tatar Horse/Ulans 63, 65-66, 82, 213. Taurida Grenadiers 58, 71-72, 116, 213. Tenginsk Musketeers 48, 50, 63-64, 92, 213. Tiraspol Dragoons 35. Tobolsk Musketeers 63, 148-149, 213. Tsarevich's Ulans 135, 169, 171, 204. Tula Musketeers 63, 65, 213. Uglits Musketeers 92-93, 214. Ukraine Musketeers 131, 215. Vilna Musketeers 63, 213. Vladimir Musketeers 110, 214. Volhynia Musketeers 63, 213. Voronezh Musketeers 116, 214. Vyatka Musketeers 215. Vyborg Musketeers 87, 114-115, 214. Wilmanstrand Musketeers 35. Yakutsk Musketeers 35. Yamburg Dragoons 35. Yaroslavl Musketeers 130, 215. Yekaterinoslav Cuirassiers 64, 213. Yekaterinoslav Grenadiers 84, 86, 98, 214. Yelets Musketeers 63, 213. Yelisavetgrad Hussars 69, 84, 86, 90, 97-98, 105, 111, 214

Ryazan 212

Saalburg 22
Saale river 21, 22, 24, 36
Saalfeld 22
Saalfeld in Ostpreußen [Zalewo] 93, 157
Saint-Hilaire, Louis-Vincent-Joseph Le Blond, comte de 109-112
Saint Petersburg 12, 14, 29, 34-35, 46, 70, 75, 79-81, 87, 106, 117-118, 122, 125, 127-128, 134-135, 138, 141, 146, 168, 176, 197, 199, 203-204, 206, 209, 212

INDEX 225

Saint Petersburg Gazette 75
Salagov, Semën Ivanovich, Prince 156
Saltykov, Nikolai Ivanovich 34, 38
Sama river 36
Sandomierz 137
Sausgarten [Bolshoye Ozornoye] 107, 109, 112, 115-116
Savary, Anne Jean Marie René 89, 119, 130-132, 164
Saxon Army 20, 24, 28-29, 147
Saxony [Kurfürstentum Sachsen] 16, 24, 138, 140, 194-195, 197
Sedmoratsky, Alexander Karlovich 41-43, 62, 82, 130-132, 213
Scharnhorst, Gerhard Johann David von 21
Schawl [Šiauliai] 184-185, 188
Schellmühl [Młyniska] 149
Schillupönen [Pokrovskoye] 179-180
Schippenbeil [Sępopol] 135, 169, 171
Schleiz 20, 22
Schloditten [Zagorodnoe] 107
Schmettau, Friedrich Wilhelm Karl, Graf von 25
Schmoditten [Ryabinovka] 109, 116
Schoeler, Reinhold Otto Friedrich August von 81
Schöning, Ernst Emanuel Sigismund von 114
Schweidnitz [Świdnica] 32
Schweinfurt 20, 22
Seeburg [Jeziorany] 154, 161
Selivanov [Cossack regimental commander] 128, 161
Sénarmont, Alexandre-Antoine Hureau de 174, 176-177
Sensburg [Mrągowo] 88
Senyavin, Dmitry Nikolaevich 195
Serock 89, 195
Serpallen [Kashtanovka] 107, 109-112
Shakhovskoy, Ivan Leontievich, Prince 53, 55
Shcherbatov, Alexey Grigorievich, Prince 71-73, 102, 128, 147-148, 151, 153, 204, 209
Sicily 11, 124, 197-198
Sienken [Żołędnik] 100
Silesia 14, 16, 32, 36, 41, 75, 124, 138, 180
Simbirsk 38, 97
Slubowo [Ślubowo] 70-71
Smolensk 35, 203, 212
Sochocin 43, 47-48, 57, 66
Sokółka 78
Soldau [Działdowo] 81
Sömmerda 26
Somov, Andrey Andreevich 65, 82, 106, 118
Sortlack [Temkino] 171-174
Soult, Jean-de-Dieu 20, 22, 24-25, 28-30, 42-43, 47-48, 57, 71, 73, 79, 89, 92-93, 96, 103, 105, 109-110, 127, 154-155, 158, 161-162, 171, 173, 179-180
Spain 142, 199, 205, 209
Spandau 30-31
Spibach stream 162, 166
Stackelberg, Gustav Ottonovich, Count 15-16
Stackelberg, Otto Vladimirovich 160
Stadion, Johann Philipp Karl Joseph, Graf von 73, 125
Stal, Karl Gustavovich 64, 68
Stanisławowo 131
Stavitsky, Maxim Fëdorovich 65, 68, 117
Stavropol Kalmyks 180
Steinheil, Thaddeus Fedorovich 46, 78, 116, 118, 125, 178
Stettin [Szczecin] 29-31, 201
Strasburg [Brodnica] 43, 47, 81
Strzegocin 55-56, 57-58, 70-71
Stutterheim, Graf von 140, 206
Suchet, Louis-Gabriel 64-65
Sukhozanet, Ivan Onofrievich 100
Sukhtelen, Pëtr Kornilovich 34, 191
Sukin, Alexander Yakovlevich 96, 156, 178
Suvorov, Alexander Vasilievich 21, 46, 86, 95, 176
Suvorov, Arkady Alexandrovich, Prince 131
Sweden 11, 16, 136, 141, 198, 209
Sysoev 1st, Vasily Alekseevich 97, 128, 214
Systerbäck [Sestroretsk] 36
Szkwa river 131
Talleyrand-Perigord, Alexandre Edmond de 184

Talleyrand-Perigord, Charles Maurice de 128, 138, 192, 199-201
Tapiau [Gvardeysk] 179
Tatishchev, Alexander Ivanovich, Count 156
Tauentzien von Wittenberg, Friedrich Heinrich Bogislav, Graf 20, 22
Tenknitten [Shirokoye] 105
Theil van Seraskerken, Diderik Jacob [van Tuyll van Serooskerken] 137-138, 140
Thorn [Toruń] 30, 37, 42-43, 47, 57, 79, 87-90, 92, 128, 147
Thüringer Wald 21-22, 24-25, 28
Tilsit [Sovetsk] 144, 151, 168, 180, 183-188, 189, 191-193, 195-202, 203-205, 206-210
Titov, Vasily Petrovich 118

Tolstoy, Count Pëtr Aleksandrovich 14, 17, 34, 44-46, 60, 70, 78, 80, 116, 127-128, 155, 157, 161, 166, 168, 179-180
Tolstoy, Count Nikolai Aleksandrovich 134, 191-192, 200, 209
Treaty of Bucharest 209
Treaty of Fredrikshamn 209
Treaty of Potsdam 15
Trubetskoy, Vasily Sergeevich 191
Tsaregrad [Istanbul] 142, 199
Tsarskoye Selo 45
Tschenstochau [Częstochowa] 32
Tuchkov 1st, Nikolay Alekseevich 44, 57-58, 69, 76, 78, 82, 87-88, 107, 110, 115, 128, 133, 154-155, 209
Tuchkov 4th, Alexander Alekseevich 164
Tula 36, 212
Turkey – see Ottoman Porte
Tver 212
Tykocin 78-79, 82, 186
Tyrol 16, 136, 138
Übermemelschen Krug 189

Ubri, Pëtr Yakovlevich 12
Ulm 11, 22, 42-43, 57
Unstrut river 24-25
Urusov, Nikolay Yuryevich, Prince 131
Uvarov, Fëdor Petrovich 128, 144, 154, 161-162, 164, 177, 190-191
Vandamme, Dominique Joseph René 32

Vasiliev, Alexander Mikhailovich 68
Vedel, Dominique Honoré Antoine Marie, comte de 65
Verderevsky, Nikolai Ivanovich 156, 166
Vernet, Antoine Charles Horace 191
Victor – see Perrin, Claude-Victor
Vienna 11, 16, 30, 37, 40, 73-75, 121-122, 124-126, 137-139, 141, 143, 187, 200, 206
Viennese Court 16-17, 40, 73, 124, 137-140, 142, 187, 206
Vilna [Vilnius] 32, 36, 46, 59, 79
Vincent, Karl, Freiherr von 74, 138
Vistula river 30, 32, 37, 40, 41-43, 47, 75, 79, 89-90, 92, 116, 120-121, 124, 137, 142-143, 147-150, 153, 186, 208
Vitebsk 204, 212
Vladimir 212
Volkonsky, Dmitry Mikhailovich, Prince 44, 130-132, 134, 215
Volkonsky, Pëtr Mikhailovich, Prince 190-191
Vologda 212

Voronezh 212
Vorontsov, Mikhail Semënovich 66, 116, 156, 190
Vorontsov, Semën Romanovich 11, 45, 122-124, 146, 149
Vuich, Nikolai Vasilievich 97-98
Vyatka 38, 212
Vyazmitinov, Sergey Kuzmich 34, 38
Wallachia 37, 197

Waltersmühl [Konradowo] 96-97
Warlack [Worławki] 97
Warnek, Lavrenty Lavrentievich 164
Warsaw 36-37, 41-43, 47, 66, 79, 84, 89-90, 128, 130, 138, 143, 149, 194-195, 197
Warthe river [Warta] 137
Warschkeiten [Warszkajty] 105
Wartensleben, Leopold Alexander von 25
Wehlau [Znamensk] 107, 168-169, 171, 179-180
Weichselmünde [Wisłoujście] 148-149, 153
Weimar 20, 22, 24-26, 28
Weser river 11, 120, 140, 180
Westphalia [Fürstentum Oberhessen and Königreich Westphalen] 140, 197-198
Wilhelm I, Landgrave of Hesse-Kassel 16, 28, 198
Willenberg [Wielbark] 89-90, 128-129
Wilson, Sir Robert Thomas 146, 178
Winning, Christian Ludwig von 28, 30
Wittenberg 24, 28-30
Wittgenstein, Peter Khristianovich, Count 132-133, 157, 180, 209
Wkra river 43, 47-48, 52, 57-58, 66, 70, 73, 81
Wolfsdorf [Wilczkowo] 93, 97, 154, 158, 160
Wormditt [Orneta] 83-84, 93, 127, 154-155
Württemberg Army 32
Württemberg, Eugen Friedrich Heinrich, Herzog von 21, 24, 29
Württemberg, Friedrich Eugen Karl Paul Ludwig von 68, 209
Wysokie Mazowieckie 78, 80, 130-133
Wyszogród 79
Yaroslavl 212

Yefremov 3rd, Ivan Yefremovich 48, 128, 213
Yekaterinoslav [Dnipro] 36, 212
Yermolov, Alexey Petrovich 72, 86, 98, 105-106, 114, 160, 162, 176-177, 209
Yershov, Pëtr Ivanovich 48, 64
Yurkovsky, Anastasiy Antonovich 42, 90, 97, 111, 118

Zajączek, Józef 127, 129

Zambrów 78
Zapolsky, Andrey Vasilievich 118
Zastrow, Friedrich Wilhelm Christian von 30, 120, 122, 134
Zegrze 43, 47, 53, 58

Ziegenhain 123
Ziesmer 182-183
Zieten, Hans Ernst Karl von 164
Zhigulin, Nikolai Semënovich 65-66, 99
Zhivkovich, Ilya Petrovich 55
Zvrykin, Fëdor Vasilievich 131.

# From Reason to Revolution – Warfare 1721-1815

http://www.helion.co.uk/series/from-reason-to-revolution-1721-1815.php

The 'From Reason to Revolution' series covers the period of military history 1721–1815, an era in which fortress-based strategy and linear battles gave way to the nation-in-arms and the beginnings of total war.

This era saw the evolution and growth of light troops of all arms, and of increasingly flexible command systems to cope with the growing armies fielded by nations able to mobilise far greater proportions of their manpower than ever before. Many of these developments were fired by the great political upheavals of the era, with revolutions in America and France bringing about social change which in turn fed back into the military sphere as whole nations readied themselves for war. Only in the closing years of the period, as the reactionary powers began to regain the upper hand, did a military synthesis of the best of the old and the new become possible.

The series will examine the military and naval history of the period in a greater degree of detail than has hitherto been attempted, and has a very wide brief, with the intention of covering all aspects from the battles, campaigns, logistics, and tactics, to the personalities, armies, uniforms, and equipment.

## Submissions

The publishers would be pleased to receive submissions for this series. Please contact series editor Andrew Bamford via email (andrewbamford@helion.co.uk), or in writing to Helion & Company Limited, Unit 8 Amherst Business Centre, Budbrooke Road, Warwick, CV34 5WE

## Titles

No 1  *Lobositz to Leuthen: Horace St Paul and the Campaigns of the Austrian Army in the Seven Years War 1756-57* (Neil Cogswell)

No 2  *Glories to Useless Heroism: The Seven Years War in North America from the French journals of Comte Maurés de Malartic, 1755-1760* (William Raffle (ed.))

No 3  *Reminiscences 1808-1815 Under Wellington: The Peninsular and Waterloo Memoirs of William Hay* (Andrew Bamford (ed.))

No 4  *Far Distant Ships: The Royal Navy and the Blockade of Brest 1793-1815* (Quintin Barry)

No 5  *Godoy's Army: Spanish Regiments and Uniforms from the Estado Militar of 1800* (Charles Esdaile and Alan Perry)

No 6  *On Gladsmuir Shall the Battle Be! The Battle of Prestonpans 1745* (Arran Johnston)

No 7  *The French Army of the Orient 1798-1801: Napoleon's Beloved 'Egyptians'* (Yves Martin)

No 8  *The Autobiography, or Narrative of a Soldier: The Peninsular War Memoirs of William Brown of the 45th Foot* (Steve Brown (ed.))

No 9  *Recollections from the Ranks: Three Russian Soldiers' Autobiographies from the Napoleonic Wars* (Darrin Boland)

No 10  *By Fire and Bayonet: Grey's West Indies Campaign of 1794* (Steve Brown)

# INDEX

No 11 *Olmütz to Torgau: Horace St Paul and the Campaigns of the Austrian Army in the Seven Years War 1758-60* (Neil Cogswell)

No 12 *Murat's Army: The Army of the Kingdom of Naples 1806-1815* (Digby Smith)

No 13 *The Veteran or 40 Years' Service in the British Army: The Scurrilous Recollections of Paymaster John Harley 47th Foot – 1798-1838* (Gareth Glover (ed.))

No 14 *Narrative of the Eventful Life of Thomas Jackson: Militiaman and Coldstream Sergeant, 1803-15* (Eamonn O'Keeffe (ed.))

No.15 *For Orange and the States: The Army of the Dutch Republic 1713-1772 Part I: Infantry* (Marc Geerdinck-Schaftenaar)

No 16 *Men Who Are Determined to be Free: The American Assault on Stony Point, 15 July 1779* (David C. Bonk)

No 17 *Next to Wellington: General Sir George Murray: The Story of a Scottish Soldier and Statesman, Wellington's Quartermaster General* (John Harding-Edgar)

No 18 *Between Scylla and Charybdis: The Army of Elector Friedrich August of Saxony 1733-1763 Part I: Staff and Cavalry* (Marco Pagan)

No 19 *The Secret Expedition: The Anglo-Russian Invasion of Holland 1799* (Geert van Uythoven)

No 20 *'We Are Accustomed to do our Duty': German Auxiliaries with the British Army 1793-95* (Paul Demet)

No 21 *With the Guards in Flanders: The Diary of Captain Roger Morris 1793-95* (Peter Harington (ed.))

No 22 *The British Army in Egypt 1801: An Underrated Army Comes of Age* (Carole Divall)

No 23 *Better is the Proud Plaid: The Clothing, Weapons, and Accoutrements of the Jacobites in the '45* (Jenn Scott)

No 24 *The Lilies and the Thistle: French Troops in the Jacobite '45* (Andrew Bamford)

No 25 *A Light Infantryman With Wellington: The Letters of Captain George Ulrich Barlow 52nd and 69th Foot 1808-15* (Gareth Glover (ed.))

No 26 *Swiss Regiments in the Service of France 1798-1815: Uniforms, Organisation, Campaigns* (Stephen Ede-Borrett)

No 27 *For Orange and the States! The Army of the Dutch Republic 1713-1772: Part II: Cavalry and Specialist Troops* (Marc Geerdinck-Schaftenaar)

No 28 *Fashioning Regulation, Regulating Fashion: Uniforms and Dress of the British Army 1800-1815 Volume I* (Ben Townsend)

No 29 *Riflemen: The History of the 5th Battalion 60th (Royal American) Regiment, 1797-1818* (Robert Griffith)

No 30 *The Key to Lisbon: The Third French Invasion of Portugal, 1810-11* (Kenton White)

No 31 *Command and Leadership: Proceedings of the 2018 Helion & Company 'From Reason to Revolution' Conference* (Andrew Bamford (ed.))

No 32 *Waterloo After the Glory: Hospital Sketches and Reports on the Wounded After the Battle* (Michael Crumplin and Gareth Glover)

No 33 *Fluxes, Fevers, and Fighting Men: War and Disease in Ancien Regime Europe 1648-1789* (Pádraig Lenihan)

No 34 *'They Were Good Soldiers': African-Americans Serving in the Continental Army, 1775-1783* (John U. Rees)

No 35 *A Redcoat in America: The Diaries of Lieutenant William Bamford, 1757-1765 and 1776* (John B. Hattendorf (ed.))

No 36  *Between Scylla and Charybdis: The Army of Friedrich August II of Saxony, 1733-1763: Part II: Infantry and Artillery* (Marco Pagan)

No 37  *Québec Under Siege: French Eye-Witness Accounts from the Campaign of 1759* (Charles A. Mayhood (ed.))

No 38  *King George's Hangman: Henry Hawley and the Battle of Falkirk 1746* (Jonathan D. Oates)

No 39  *Zweybrücken in Command: The Reichsarmee in the Campaign of 1758* (Neil Cogswell)

No 40  *So Bloody a Day: The 16th Light Dragoons in the Waterloo Campaign* (David J. Blackmore)

No 41  *Northern Tars in Southern Waters: The Russian Fleet in the Mediterranean 1806-1810* (Vladimir Bogdanovich Bronevskiy / Darrin Boland)

No 42  *Royal Navy Officers of the Seven Years War: A Biographical Dictionary of Commissioned Officers 1748-1763* (Cy Harrison)

No 43  *All at Sea: Naval Support for the British Army During the American Revolutionary War* (John Dillon)

No 44  *Glory is Fleeting: New Scholarship on the Napoleonic Wars* (Andrew Bamford (ed.))

No 45  *Fashioning Regulation, Regulating Fashion: Uniforms and Dress of the British Army 1800-1815 Vol. II* (Ben Townsend)

No 46  *Revenge in the Name of Honour: The Royal Navy's Quest for Vengeance in the Single Ship Actions of the War of 1812* (Nicholas James Kaizer)

No 47  *They Fought With Extraordinary Bravery: The III German (Saxon) Army Corps in the Southern Netherlands 1814* (Geert van Uythoven)

No 48  *The Danish Army of the Napoleonic Wars 1801-1814, Organisation, Uniforms & Equipment: Volume 1: High Command, Line and Light Infantry* (David Wilson)

No 49  *Neither Up Nor Down: The British Army and the Flanders Campaign 1793-1895* (Phillip Ball)

No 50  *Guerra Fantástica: The Portuguese Army and the Seven Years War* (António Barrento)

No 51  *From Across the Sea: North Americans in Nelson's Navy* (Sean M. Heuvel and John A. Rodgaard)

No 52  *Rebellious Scots to Crush: The Military Response to the Jacobite '45* (Andrew Bamford (ed.))

No 53  *The Army of George II 1727-1760: The Soldiers who Forged an Empire* (Peter Brown)

No 54  *Wellington at Bay: The Battle of Villamuriel, 25 October 1812* (Garry David Wills)

No 55  *Life in the Red Coat: The British Soldier 1721-1815* (Andrew Bamford (ed.))

No 56  *Wellington's Favourite Engineer. John Burgoyne: Operations, Engineering, and the Making of a Field Marshal* (Mark S. Thompson)

No 57  *Scharnhorst: The Formative Years, 1755-1801* (Charles Edward White)

No 58  *At the Point of the Bayonet: The Peninsular War Battles of Arroyomolinos and Almaraz 1811-1812* (Robert Griffith)

No 59  *Sieges of the '45: Siege Warfare during the Jacobite Rebellion of 1745-1746* (Jonathan D. Oates)

No 60  *Austrian Cavalry of the Revolutionary and Napoleonic Wars, 1792–1815* (Enrico Acerbi, András K. Molnár)

No 61  *The Danish Army of the Napoleonic Wars 1801-1814, Organisation, Uniforms & Equipment: Volume 2: Cavalry and Artillery* (David Wilson)

# INDEX 231

No 62 *Napoleon's Stolen Army: How the Royal Navy Rescued a Spanish Army in the Baltic* (John Marsden)

No 63 *Crisis at the Chesapeake: The Royal Navy and the Struggle for America 1775-1783* (Quintin Barry)

No 64 *Bullocks, Grain, and Good Madeira: The Maratha and Jat Campaigns 1803-1806 and the emergence of the Indian Army* (Joshua Provan)

No 65 *Sir James McGrigor: The Adventurous Life of Wellington's Chief Medical Officer* (Tom Scotland)

No 66 *Fashioning Regulation, Regulating Fashion: Uniforms and Dress of the British Army 1800-1815 Volume I* (Ben Townsend) (paperback edition)

No 67 *Fashioning Regulation, Regulating Fashion: Uniforms and Dress of the British Army 1800-1815 Volume II* (Ben Townsend) (paperback edition)

No 68 *The Secret Expedition: The Anglo-Russian Invasion of Holland 1799* (Geert van Uythoven) (paperback edition)

No 69 *The Sea is My Element: The Eventful Life of Admiral Sir Pulteney Malcolm 1768-1838* (Paul Martinovich)

No 70 *The Sword and the Spirit: Proceedings of the first 'War & Peace in the Age of Napoleon' Conference* (Zack White (ed.))

No 71 *Lobositz to Leuthen: Horace St Paul and the Campaigns of the Austrian Army in the Seven Years War 1756-57* (Neil Cogswell) (paperback edition)

No 72 *For God and King. A History of the Damas Legion 1793-1798: A Case Study of the Military Emigration during the French Revolution* (Hughes de Bazouges and Alistair Nichols)

No 73 *'Their Infantry and Guns Will Astonish You': The Army of Hindustan and European Mercenaries in Maratha service 1780-1803* (Andy Copestake)

No 74 *Like A Brazen Wall: The Battle of Minden, 1759, and its Place in the Seven Years War* (Ewan Carmichael)

No 75 *Wellington and the Lines of Torres Vedras: The Defence of Lisbon during the Peninsular War* (Mark Thompson)

No 76 *French Light Infantry 1784-1815: From the Chasseurs of Louis XVI to Napoleon's Grande Armée* (Terry Crowdy)

No 77 *Riflemen: The History of the 5th Battalion 60th (Royal American) Regiment, 1797-1818* (Robert Griffith) (paperback edition)

No 78 *Hastenbeck 1757: The French Army and the Opening Campaign of the Seven Years War* (Olivier Lapray)

No 79 *Napoleonic French Military Uniforms: As Depicted by Horace and Carle Vernet and Eugène Lami* (Guy Dempsey (trans. and ed.))

No 80 *These Distinguished Corps: British Grenadier and Light Infantry Battalions in the American Revolution* (Don N. Hagist)

No 81 *Rebellion, Invasion, and Occupation: The British Army in Ireland, 1793-1815* (Wayne Stack)

No 82 *You Have to Die in Piedmont! The Battle of Assietta, 19 July 1747. The War of the Austrian Succession in the Alps* (Giovanni Cerino Badone)

No 83 *A Very Fine Regiment: the 47th Foot in the American War of Independence, 1773–1783* (Paul Knight)

No 84 *By Fire and Bayonet: Grey's West Indies Campaign of 1794* (Steve Brown) (paperback edition)

No 85 *No Want of Courage: The British Army in Flanders, 1793-1795* (R.N.W. Thomas)

No 86 *Far Distant Ships: The Royal Navy and the Blockade of Brest 1793-1815* (Quintin Barry) (paperback edition)

No 87  Armies and Enemies of Napoleon 1789-1815: Proceedings of the 2021 Helion and Company 'From Reason to Revolution' Conference (Robert Griffith (ed.))

No 88  The Battle of Rossbach 1757: New Perspectives on the Battle and Campaign (Alexander Querengässer (ed.))

No 89  Waterloo After the Glory: Hospital Sketches and Reports on the Wounded After the Battle (Michael Crumplin and Gareth Glover) (paperback edition)

No 90  From Ushant to Gibraltar: The Channel Fleet 1778-1783 (Quintin Barry)

No 91  'The Soldiers are Dressed in Red': The Quiberon Expedition of 1795 and the Counter-Revolution in Brittany (Alistair Nichols)

No 92  The Army of the Kingdom of Italy 1805-1814: Uniforms, Organisation, Campaigns (Stephen Ede-Borrett)

No 93  The Ottoman Army of the Napoleonic Wars 1798-1815: A Struggle for Survival from Egypt to the Balkans (Bruno Mugnai)

No 94  The Changing Face of Old Regime Warfare: Essays in Honour of Christopher Duffy (Alexander S. Burns (ed.))

No 94  The Changing Face of Old Regime Warfare: Essays in Honour of Christopher Duffy (Alexander S. Burns (ed.))

No 95  The Danish Army of the Napoleonic Wars 1801-1814, Organisation, Uniforms & Equipment: Volume 3: Norwegian Troops and Militia (David Wilson)

No 96  1805 – Tsar Alexander's First War with Napoleon (Alexander Ivanovich Mikhailovsky-Danilevsky, trans. Peter G.A. Phillips)

No 97  'More Furies then Men': The Irish Brigade in the service of France 1690-1792 (Pierre-Louis Coudray)

No 98  'We Are Accustomed to do our Duty': German Auxiliaries with the British Army 1793-95 (Paul Demet) (paperback edition)

No 99  Ladies, Wives and Women: British Army Wives in the Revolutionary and Napoleonic Wars 1793-1815 (David Clammer)

No 100  The Garde Nationale 1789-1815: France's Forgotten Armed Forces (Pierre-Baptiste Guillemot)

No 101  Confronting Napoleon: Levin von Bennigsen's Memoir of the Campaign in Poland, 1806-1807, Volume I Pultusk to Eylau (Alexander Mikaberidze and Paul Strietelmeier (trans. and ed.))

No 102  Olmütz to Torgau: Horace St Paul and the Campaigns of the Austrian Army in the Seven Years War 1758-60 (Neil Cogswell) (paperback edition)

No 103  Fit to Command: British Regimental Leadership in the Revolutionary & Napoleonic Wars (Steve Brown)

No 104  Wellington's Unsung Heroes: The Fifth Division in the Peninsular War, 1810-1814 (Carole Divall)

No 105  1806-1807 – Tsar Alexander's Second War with Napoleon (Alexander Ivanovich Mikhailovsky-Danilevsky, trans. Peter G.A. Phillips)